German Legal System and Legal Language

Cavendish
Publishing
Limited

German Legal System and Legal Language

A General Survey
Together with Notes and a German Vocabulary

Howard D Fisher, LLB (Lond) (Hons)
Rechtsanwalt and Solicitor

Cavendish
Publishing
Limited

First published in Great Britain 1996 by Cavendish Publishing Limited,
The Glass House, Wharton Street, London WC1X 9PX
Telephone: 0171-278 8000   Facsimile: 0171-278 8080

British Library Cataloguing-in-Publication Data.

Fisher, Howard
German Legal System and Legal Language
1 Law – Germany   I Title
344.3

ISBN 1-85941-229-7

Printed and bound in Great Britain

In Memory of my Parents

FOREWORD

Germany has one of the most scientific legal systems anywhere in the world. For a person with English as his or her mother tongue to seek to understand that system is not easy, even with a legal education. Why is this so? The principal reason lies in the fact that, for historical reasons, the methods and sources of German and English law have developed differently. Another reason is the German language and its seemingly endless supply of formal terminology. Certainly, legal and everyday language are not the same anywhere, but where can this be more so than in Germany?

If the linguistic complexities were not enough, the enormous codification of practically every area of law in Germany will remain a formidable obstacle to comprehension of the German system for a foreigner, even after the dawn of the 'new' Europe after 1993.

This book contains a general survey in the English language of the structure and concepts of some of the main areas of German law. My aim has thereby been to provide a basic insight into the German legal system and technical language. The book is based on my understanding and study of German laws and texts and constitutes a summary and introduction only. A more detailed account, for example, of the *Grundgesetz* and the BGB, would have involved lengthy exposition, which I wanted to avoid. Understanding the layout of the various laws is, in my view, the main task for the newcomer (see Chapter X, note 63).

In particular, the book does not deal with German company law outside the BGB and HGB, tax or building law nor with many of the numerous statutes in the fields of private and public law to be found in the handbook collections *Schönfelder* and *Sartorius*. These areas can be considered at another time.

It should also be mentioned that police and private international law are merely touched upon and that a description of certain provisions in the law of civil and criminal procedure still needs to be added (Chapter XII, p 90 and Chapter XVI, p 111).

To well-versed German lawyers and experts the book will, I am sure, provide opportunity for criticism of misunderstanding, errors and incompleteness. Readers are, therefore, advised to consult German laws, authorities and guides in their original versions for the necessary detail or in cases of doubt.

Readers with a love for plenty of case-law should always remember that it is a fact that the German legal system is almost entirely based on codifications. This book only contains references to a handful of cases, most of which stem from the *Sourcebook on German Law* by Raymond Youngs. They concern the *Grundgesetz*, the first two Books of the BGB and the StGB (Chapters II, VII, VIII, X and XV).

I do not hold the book out as a work on comparative law. If that is what is sought, I would draw the reader's attention to the scholarly study in the field of private law by Zweigert and Kötz, who make the interesting prediction that 'the day may not be too far distant when the project of a European Civil Code will be undertaken' (Chapter 14 II).

Whatever the chances of such a Code ever being enacted, I would venture to wager that the long-established and highly-developed concepts contained in the various codifications of German law will remain in use for so long as German is spoken. The vital role of language and the question of popular acceptance should not be underestimated.

I hope that, despite such imperfections as it may have, this book will prove useful to those native English speakers who deal with legal matters in Germany, to those who wish to try to 'grasp the nettle' of the German legal system and legal language for the first time and to those who aim to qualify as German lawyers. Comments and suggestions regarding the book are welcome.

I have endeavoured to maintain correct and consistent translation and to cross-reference the text, Notes and Appendices.

Howard D Fisher
Frankfurt am Main
January 1996

MATERIALS

In order to be able to derive use from and follow the explanations in this book, it is essential to have the texts of German (federal) laws (*Gesetzestexte*) to hand. They are available in various forms, of which very well-known are the regularly updated paperback editions published by DTV/Beck and the handbook collections entitled *Schönfelder: Deutsche Gesetze* and *Sartorius I: Verfassungs- und Verwaltungsgesetze der Bundesrepublik Deutschland* and *Sartorius II: Internationale Verträge/Europarecht*. I would also particularly recommend *Creifelds: Rechtswörterbuch*, which is a concise German legal dictionary, and Raymond Youngs' *Sourcebook on German Law*, which contains a selection of many instructive German texts with English translations and commentary.

Additionally, reference can be made to the numerous textbooks (*Lehrbücher*) and commentaries (*Kommentare*) on the various areas of German law, if more detailed advice is required. Included in my bibliography are many standard books for German law students.

BIBLIOGRAPHY

Battis/Gusy: *Einführung in das Staatsrecht*; (C F Müller, 1991, 3rd edn)

Baur/Grunsky: *Zivilprozeßrecht*; (Alfred Metzner/Luchterhand, 1994, 8th edn)

Bergerfurth: *Der Zivilprozeß*; (Rudolf Haufe, 1991, 6th edn)

Baumann: *Einführung in die Rechtswissenschaft*; (C H Beck, 1989, 8th edn); referred to in the Notes as Baumann (ER)

Baumann: *Grundbegriffe und System des Strafrechts*; (Kohlhammer, 1979, 5th edn); referred to in the Notes as Baumann (GBS)

Beitzke/Lüderitz: *Familienrecht*; (C H Beck, 1996, 27th edn)

Brox: *Allgemeiner Teil des Bürgerlichen Gesetzbuchs*; (Carl Heymanns, 1994, 18th edn); referred to in the Notes as Brox (AT)'

Brox: *Allgemeines Schuldrecht*; (C H Beck, 1995, 22nd edn); referred to in the Notes as Brox (AS)

Brox: *Besonderes Schuldrecht*; (C H Beck, 1995, 20th edn); referred to in the Notes as Brox (BS)

Brox: *Grundbegriffe des Arbeitsrechts*; (Kohlhammer, 1993, 11th edn); referred to in the Notes as Brox (GBA)

Brox: *Erbrecht*; (Carl Heymanns, 1994, 15th edn); referred to in the Notes as Brox (ER)

Bull: *Allgemeines Verwaltungsrecht*; (C F Müller, 1993, 4th edn)

Capelle/Canaris: *Handelsrecht*; (C H Beck, 1995, 22nd edn)

Creifelds: *Rechtswörterbuch*; (C H Beck, 1995, 13th edn)

Drews/Wacke/Vogel/Martens: *Gefahrenabwehr: Allgemeines Polizeirecht (Ordnungsrecht) des Bundes und der Länder*; (Carl Heymanns, 1986, 9th edn)

Dulckeit/Schwarz/Waldstein: *Römische Rechtsgeschichte*; (C H Beck, 1995, 9th edn)

Eisenhardt: *Gesellschaftsrecht*; (C H Beck, 1994, 6th edn)

Engisch: *Einführung in das juristische Denken*, (Kohlhammer, 1983, 8th edn)

Erichsen: *Allgemeines Verwaltungsrecht*; (Walter de Gruyter, 1995, 10th edn)

Fikentscher: *Schuldrecht*; (Walter de Gruyter, 1992, 8th edn)

Flume: *Allgemeiner Teil des Bürgerlichen Rechts*, Volume 2: *Das Rechtsgeschäft*; (Springer-Verlag, 1992, 4th edn)

Gallwas: *Grundrechte*; (Alfred Metzner, 1985, 1st edn)

Gesetzestexte: see Materials

Giemulla/Jaworsky/Müller-Uri: *Verwaltungsrecht*; (Carl Heymanns, 1994, 5th edn)

Gierke/Sandrock: *Handels- und Wirtschaftsrecht I*; (Walter de Gruyter, 1975, 9th edn)

Grundsätze des anwaltlichen Standesrechts (BRAK Richtlinien)

Haft: *Aus der Waagschale der Justitia*; (C H Beck/DTV, 1990, 2nd edn)

Hanau/Adomeit: *Arbeitsrecht*; (Alfred Metzner/Luchterhand, 1994, 11th edn)

Hesse: *Grundzüge des Verfassungsrechts der Bundesrepublik Deutschland*; (C F Müller, 1995, 20th edn)

Hofmann: *Handelsrecht*; (Alfred Metzner/Luchterhand, 1993, 8th edn)

Hueck: *Gesellschaftsrecht*; (C H Beck, 1991, 19th edn)

Jakobs: *Strafrecht Allgemeiner Teil*; (Walter de Gruyter, 1993, 2nd edn)

Jauernig: *Zivilprozeßrecht*; (C H Beck, 1993, 24th edn); referred to in the Notes as Jauernig (ZP)

Jauernig: *Zwangsvollstreckungs- und Konkursrecht*; (C H Beck, 1990, 19th edn); referred to in the Notes as Jauernig (ZVS)

Kaiser: *Bürgerliches Recht*; (C F Müller, 1994, 5th edn)

Kallwass: *Privatrecht*; (U Thiemonds, 1992, 14th edn)

Klunzinger: *Einführung in das Bürgerliches Recht*; (Franz Vahlen, 1995, 6th edn); referred to in the Notes as Klunzinger (*Einführung*)

Klunzinger: *Grundzüge des Handelsrechts*; (Franz Vahlen, 1994, 8th edn); referred to in the Notes as Klunzinger (*Grundzüge*) (HR)

Klunzinger: *Grundzüge des Gesellschaftsrechts*; (Franz Vahlen, 1994, 8th edn); referred to in the Notes as Klunzinger (*Grundzüge*) (GR)

Köbler: *Deutsche Rechtsgeschichte*; (Franz Vahlen, 1990, 4th edn)

Köhler: *BGB Allgemeiner Teil*; (C H Beck, 1994, 22nd edn)

Kötz: *Deliktsrecht*; (Alfred Metzner/Luchterhand, 1994, 6th edn)

Kraft/Kreutz: *Gesellschaftsrecht*; (Alfred Metzner, 1992, 9th edn)

Krause/Thoma: *Strafrecht Allgemeiner Teil*; (Kohlhammer, 1985, 3rd edn)

Kriele: ESJ *Grundrechte*; (C H Beck, 1986, 1st edn)

Langenscheidt: *Taschenwörterbuch Englisch* (pocket German/English dictionary)

Laufs: *Rechtsentwicklungen in Deutschland*; (Walter de Gruyter, 1992, 4th edn)

Leipold: *Erbrecht*; (J C B Mohr, 1993, 10th edn)

Loewenheim: *Bereicherungsrecht*; (C H Beck, 1989, 1st edn)

Löwisch: *Allgemeiner Teil des BGB*; (C H Beck, 1991, 5th edn)

Maurer: *Allgemeines Verwaltungsrecht*; (C H Beck, 1995, 10th edn)

Medicus: *Bürgerliches Recht*; (Carl Heymanns, 1995, 17th edn); referred to in the Notes as Medicus (BR)

Medicus: *Schuldrecht I Allgemeiner Teil*; (C H Beck, 1995, 8th edn); referred to in the Notes as Medicus (AT)

Medicus: *Schuldrecht II Besonderer Teil*; (C H Beck, 1995, 7th edn); referred to in the Notes as Medicus (BT)

Model/Creifelds/Lichtenberger/Zierl: *Staatsbürger-Taschenbuch*; (C H Beck, 1995, 28th edn)

Naucke: *Strafrecht*; (Alfred Metzner, 1991, 6th edn)

Otto: *Grundkurs Strafrecht (Allgemeine Strafrechtslehre)*; (Walter de Gruyter, 1992, 4th edn); referred to in the Notes as Otto (AS)

Otto: *Grundkurs Strafrecht (Die einzelnen Delikte)*; (Walter de Gruyter, 1995, 4th edn); referred to in the Notes as Otto (ED)

Rehbinder: *Einführung in die Rechtswissenschaft*; (Walter de Gruyter, 1995, 8th edn)

Roxin: *Strafverfahrensrecht*; (C H Beck, 1995, 24th edn)

Rüthers: *Allgemeiner Teil des BGB*; (C H Beck, 1993, 9th edn)

Sartorius I and II: see Materials

Schellhammer: *Zivilprozeß*; (C F Müller, 1994, 6th edn); referred to in the Notes as Schellhammer (ZP)

Schellhammer: *Zivilrecht nach Anspruchsgrundlagen*; (C F Müller, 1994, 1st edn); referred to in the Notes as Schellhammer (ZR)

Schlechtriem: *Schuldrecht Allgemeiner Teil*; (J C B Mohr, 1994, 2nd edn); referred to in the Notes as Schlechtriem (AT)

Schlechtriem: *Schuldrecht Besonderer Teil*; (J C B Mohr, 1993, 3rd edn); referred to in the Notes as Schlechtriem (BT)

Schmidt-Aßmann: *Besonderes Verwaltungsrecht*; (Walter de Gruyter, 1995, 10th edn)

Schönfelder: see Materials

Schulte: *Grundkurs im BGB*; (C F Müller, 1992, 4th edn, vol 1; 1992, 3rd edn, vol 2; 1991, 2nd edn, vol 3)

Schunck/De Clerck: *Allgemeines Staatsrecht und Staatsrecht des Bundes und der Länder*; (Reckinger & Co, 1990, 13th edn)

Schwab/Prütting: *Sachenrecht*; (C H Beck, 1994, 25th edn); referred to in the Notes as Schwab/Prütting

D Schwab: *Einführung in das Zivilrecht*; (C F Müller, 1995, 12th edn); referred to in the Notes as Schwab (*Einführung*)

D Schwab: *Familienrecht*; (C H Beck, 1995, 8th edn); referred to in the Notes as Schwab (F)

Söllner: *Grundriß des Arbeitsrechts*; (Franz Vahlen, 1994, 11th edn)

Stern: *Verwaltungsprozessuale Probleme in der öffentlich-rechtlichen Arbeit*; (C H Beck, 1995, 7th edn)

Wesel: *Juristische Weltkunde*; (Suhrkamp, 1992, 6th edn); referred to in the Notes as Wesel (JW)

Wesel: *Fast alles, was Recht ist*; (Eichborn, 1994, Study edn); referred to in the Notes as Wesel (FR)

Westermann: *Grundbegriffe des BGB*; (Kohlhammer, 1994, 14th edn); referred to in the Notes as Westermann (*Grundbegriffe*)

Westermann: *Sachenrecht: Volume I Grundlagen und Recht der beweglichen Sachen* (1990) and *Volume II Immobiliarsachenrecht* (1988) (C F Müller, 1988/1990, 6th edn); referred to in the Notes as Westermann (SR)

Wolf: *Sachenrecht*; (C H Beck, 1994, 12th edn)

Wolff/Bachof/Stober: *Verwaltungsrecht I*; (C H Beck, 1994, 10th edn)

Youngs: *Sourcebook on German Law* (Cavendish, 1994); referred to in the Notes as the *Sourcebook*

Zweigert and Kötz: *Einführung in die Rechtsvergleichung auf dem Gebiet des Privatrechts*. English title: *An Introduction to Comparative Law* by Tony Wei; (Oxford University Press and J C B Mohr (Paul Siebeck), 1987, 2nd edn)

References in the notes to the books listed above are by author's surnames unless otherwise stated above and are made with grateful acknowledgment to the relevant authors and publishers.

CROSS-REFERENCES

The notes and the vocabulary (Appendix A) provide supplementary information to that in the text. They include cross-references to chapters in the text, to books listed in the bibliography (eg Creifelds: *Rechtswörterbuch* and the *Sourcebook on German Law*) and to relevant statutory provisions.

The paragraph register (Appendix C) and the table of cases (Appendix D) are also cross-referenced to the text, notes and vocabulary.

Paragraphs which can be found translated into English in the *Sourcebook on German Law* are indicated in the paragraph register by a T.

In case information sought is not located in the text or in the index, reference should be made to the notes, the vocabulary and the other appendices.

CONTENTS

Contents

CHAPTER I

HISTORICAL INTRODUCTION[1]

The present-day German legal system has its roots in Roman law.

The first compilation of Roman law was contained in the Twelve Tables, which was published during the Roman Republic in 450 BC. The Twelve Tables provided the basic legal code of Rome for almost a thousand years.

The end of the western Roman Empire in 476 AD, following the incursion of Germanic peoples from the east, led to a revival of Roman jurisprudence from the classical period (the first and second centuries AD) in the eastern part of the Empire. Between the years 528 and 534 AD the Emperor Justinian initiated a collection of imperial Roman law from the reign of Hadrian (117-138 AD) onwards in a *Codex* (code) and a collection in fifty books of the writings of numerous classical Roman jurists in the *Digesta* (digests) or *Pandectae* (pandects). Together with an introductory textbook, the *Institutiones* (institutions) – based on the writings of the jurist Gaius, the *Codex* and *Digesta* are referred to as the *Corpus iuris civilis* (body of civil law) of Justinian.[2]

A copy of the *Digesta* was discovered in north Italy in the 11th century and Roman law became the subject of renewed attention by such scholars as Irnerius and his pupils, the *Quattuor Doctores* Bulgarus, Hugo, Jacobus and Martinus in the 12th century. The University of Bologna, the oldest university in Europe, became famous for the study of Roman law and, in the 13th century, Accursius completed his *Glossa ordinaria* (ordinary gloss), which remained authoritative for centuries thereafter.[3]

In the 14th century, Roman law was further developed in the commentaries of the jurists Bartolus and Baldus.[4]

The scholastic revival of Roman law in the Middle Ages spread across continental Europe. In Germany, a multitude of regional legal sources then existed, the most well-known of which is the *Sachsenspiegel* (Saxon Mirror) of

---

1   See generally: Dulckeit/Schwarz/Waldstein; Haft; Kaiser (Section I, Chapter 1); Köbler; Laufs; Model/Creifelds/Lichtenberger, Part I B (11-25); and Wesel (JW). See also Creifelds under Code civil, *Constitutio Criminalis Carolina*, *Deutsches Reich*, Grotius, *Heiliges Römisches Reich Deutscher Nation*, *Historische Rechtsschule*, Jhering, *Naturrecht*, Pufendorf, *Reichskammergericht*, *Reichsverfassung*, *Römisches Recht*, *Rezeption*, *Sachsenspiegel* and Savigny.

2   By the time of the late classical jurists, the original republican division of law into *ius civile* (civil law), *ius gentium* (public international law) and *ius honorarium* (honorary law (of the magistrate or *praetor*)) gave way to a distinction between *ius privatum* (private law) and *ius publicum* (public law), which gradually became more important. See Chapter IX (note 1) below.

   See also: Haft, Part C, 2 and Wesel (JW), Chapter IV.

3   It was said: *Quidquid non agnoscit glossa, non agnoscit curia* (what is not acknowledged by the gloss is not acknowledged by the court).

4   It was said: *Nemo bonus iurista nisi bartolista* (no-one is a good jurist, if he does not follow Bartolus).

1221-24. However, Roman law was gradually taken up: the so-called *Rezeption des römischen Rechts* (reception of Roman law).[5]

By 1495, the date of the establishment of the highest German court (the *Reichskammergericht* (Imperial Chamber (Court)), Roman law took precedence as the general law (*das gemeine Recht* or *ius commune*) of the Holy Roman Empire (of the German Nation) (*Heiliges Römisches Reich (Deutscher Nation)*).[6]

However, the fields of criminal procedure and punishment were governed by the *Constitutio Criminalis Carolina* of 1532, which contained a mixture of German and ecclesiatical principles and remained of some influence until the reforms of the 19th century.[7]

In the 17th century, there was a change. The age of reason brought about a gradual departure from the traditional principles of Roman law and a return to the principles of natural law.[8]

In Holland, the pioneer of public international law, Grotius, wrote *De jure belli ac pacis libri tres* (Three books on the law of war and peace) in 1625. His view of law as the product of human reason and mans inborn *appetitus societatis* (social appetite), where contract forms the binding element (*pacta sunt servanda*),

---

5   In England, where a case law system has dominated since the 13th century, the influence of Roman law has been limited. The distinction between common law and equity reflects the Roman law distinction between *ius civile* and *ius honorarium*; under the latter, the magistrate was able to apply *aequitas* (fairness) when reaching his decision.

    See Haft, Part C, 3 and 5; Laufs, Chapter III; Wesel (JW), Chapter V.

6   The (first) German Empire is regarded as having been founded with the coronation of Otto I in Rome in 962 AD and was first referred to as the Holy Roman Empire (of the German Nation) towards the end of the 15th century.

    The Holy Roman Empire ended in 1806 following the establishment of the *Rheinbund* (Confederation of the Rhine) between various German principalities having allegiance to France.

    After the defeat of Napoleon at Waterloo, the *Rheinbund* was superseded by the *Deutscher Bund* (German Confederation), which was established at the Congress of Vienna in 1815.

    The *Deutscher Bund* lasted until 1866, when, following Austria's defeat by Prussia (under Bismarck) at Königgrätz, Prussia and the other north German states formed the *Norddeutscher Bund* (North German Confederation).

    Following Prussia's victory over France in the war of 1870/71 and the accession of the south German states, the (second) German Empire was proclaimed at Versailles on 18 January 1871. It lasted until the declaration of the Weimar Republic on 9 November 1918.

    See: Creifelds under *Rheinbund*, *Deutscher Bund* and *Norddeutscher Bund*; Model/Creifelds/Lichtenberger, Part I A (9), I B (12-17).

7   See note 12 in this Chapter. See also Haft, Part C, 4; Laufs, Chapter IV, 4.

8   The principles of natural law had already been considered by Plato and Aristotle in Greece in the 4th century BC in their writings regarding justice and the state. Natural law was also developed by the Stoa and Cicero. See Wesel (JW), Chapter VI.

was followed in Germany by Pufendorf, Thomasius and Wolff at the beginning of the 18th century.[9]

At the end of the 18th century, reason was criticised in the philosophy of Kant, in favour of the general freedom of the individual.[10]

Despite this, however, the ideas of natural law and the Enlightenment influenced three important codifications:[11]

- the *Allgemeines Landrecht für die preußischen Staaten* (General Law for the Prussian States (ALR)) of 1794;

- the *Code Civil des Français* (French Civil Code, also known as the *Code Napoléon* (Napoleonic Code)) of 1804; and

- the Austrian *Allgemeines Bürgerliches Gesetzbuch* (General Civil Code (ABGB)) of 1811.

In 1814, a dispute broke out between two German jurists as to the need for a codification of civil law[12] in Germany.[13]

In favour of a uniform, national statute was Professor Thibaut from Heidelberg. Against it was the famous Professor Savigny from Berlin.

---

9   It was also followed, at the end of the 18th century, in the philosophy of Hegel.

In England, on the other hand, Hobbes presented a different view in his work *Leviathan* (1651): protection by the state was necessary for man's own good, because man's natural condition was anti social, wolf like (*homo homini lupus*) and belligerent (*bellum omnium contra omnes*). The state was the supreme monster, born of human's natural fear. The positive law of the state was justified by its authority and required to be obeyed (*auctoritas non veritas facit legem*). Indeed, this can still be said to be the justification for the concept of the unrestricted sovereignty of Parliament in England, where there is no written constitution.

See: Haft, Part D, 4 to 6, 8; Wesel (FR), Chapter 2 (*Verfassungen*).

10 Kant later influenced Savigny. See Haft, Part D, 7.

11 Regarding these see Haft, Part C, 6 and 7; Laufs, Chapter VI, 1 and 2.

12 In the field of criminal law, Feuerbach laid the foundation for modern criminal legislation. He drafted the Bavarian Criminal Code of 1813 and coined the phrase *Nulla poena sine lege*: there can be no punishment without law, ie punishability depends on the strict text of criminal legislation, which, therefore, requires exact drafting.

To Feuerbach, the purpose of punishment was general prevention of crime. In contrast, von Liszt later developed the theory of the special prevention of the particular criminal, for whom the Criminal Code was the *Magna Charta*.

See: Haft, Part E, 2 and 9; Wesel (JW), Chapter X.

Regarding Savigny and the historical school see: Haft, Part E, 1; Laufs, Chapter VII, 2; Wesel (JW), Chapter VII.

13 In keeping with the status of the *Deutscher Bund* as a mere *Staatenbund* (confederation of (independent) states), there were numerous regional laws in force in Germany at the time.

The unification of German law first only really set in with the establishment of the (second) German Empire in 1871 (eg the *Strafgesetzbuch* and *Allgemeines Deutsches Handelsgesetzbuch* (ADHGB) of 1861 and the *Zivilprozeßordnung, Strafprozeßordnung, Gerichtsverfassungsgesetz* and *Konkursordnung* of 1877).

See Köbler, § 7 B I 2 and Laufs, Chapter VII, 3.

Savigny was a founder of the so-called *Historische Rechtsschule* (historical school), which regarded law as an organic product of history (*Geschichte*). According to Savigny, law was not based on *Vernunft* (reason) or *Willkür* (arbitrariness), but was *Gewohnheitsrecht* (customary law) and originated from the *Volksgeist* (spirit of the people).

Roman law already provided the best available methodic system and the basic principles; an unorganic codification was unnecessary and could be dangerous.

During the 19th century, jurists such as Puchta and Windscheid followed Savigny's views, but changed the emphasis to a scientific approach to law (the so-called *Pandektenwissenschaft* (science of the pandects)). Roman law was taught and refined on a scientific basis throughout Germany. Abstraction was the order of the day: the solution to every legal problem lay in the application of formal, abstract legal concepts (*Begriffsjurisprudenz* (conceptual jurisprudence)).

Begriffsjurisprudenz dominated at the time the German Civil Code (BGB) was finally enacted in 1896, but the theory's positivist dogma was criticised by Jhering (who regarded law as motivated by the protection of human aims (*Zwecke*) and interests (*Interessen*): (*Interessenjurisprudenz*)) and, subsequently, by the so-called free (sociological) legal school at the start of the 20th century.)[14]

With the coming into force of the BGB on 1 January 1900 a long period of development of Roman law ended, but its principles live on.

---

14 Another critic of *Begriffsjurisprudenz* and positivism was Otto von Gierke (1841-1921), whose *Genossenschaftstheorie* stressed the importance to German law of the social (co-operative) component.

   To the members of the free school (Ehrlich, Weber), law depends not on words, but on social acceptance and social facts.

   In contrast, it was the positivist pure theory of law of Kelsen that the legal system is based on norms (and ultimately on a *Grundnorm*) and that these are open to judicial interpretation. That such interpretation can be unlimited was demonstrated by Rüthers in his book *Die Unbegrenzte Auslegung* (1968) following the perversion of positivism during the Nazi tyranny.

   Regarding Jhering, von Gierke, Weber and Kelsen, see Engisch, Chapter VIII; Haft, Part E, respectively 3, 5, 7 and 8. See also Creifelds under Gierke, Otto von and Weber, Max, Köbler, § 7 B I 3 and Laufs, Chapter IX, 2.

   Regarding *Rechtspositivismus* see: Creifelds; Haft, Part F, 6. Regarding *Begriffsjurisprudenz* see: Creifelds; Haft, Part F, 8. Regarding *Interessenjurisprudenz* see Haft, Part F, 9. Regarding the free school see Haft, Part F, 10. Regarding the perversion of law under the Nazis see Laufs, Chapter XI.

CHAPTER II

THE FEDERAL STATE

THE DIVISION OF POWER

In Germany, state power (*Staatsgewalt*) is not centralised. Germany is divided into the Federal Republic (*Bundesrepublik* or *Bund*) as the main state (*Zentralstaat*) and its constituent states (*Länder*).[1]

Each state (*Land*) is a member of the whole, but at the same time maintains its own state power; it is not fully independent, as otherwise the Federal Republic would be a confederation of states (*Staatenbund*). The *Bund* is a federal state (*Bundesstaat*), a new state created by the joining together of its members.

THE PASSING OF LAWS

The *Bund* and the *Länder* are each entitled to pass laws (*Gesetze*) and their respective competence to do so (*Gesetzgebungskompetenz*) is laid down in the (federal) constitution (*Grundgesetz*/GG/Basic Law).[2]

Article 70 GG lays down a presumption in favour of the competence of the *Länder*, but the constitution allocates to the *Bund* the right to pass laws in the most important fields; this right is either exclusive (*ausschließlich*: Article 71 GG) or concurrent (*konkurrierend*: Article 72 GG) or permits the *Bund* to lay down a general framework (*Rahmen*) for legislation by the *Länder* (Article 75 GG). The

---

1   The *Bund* and its member states (*Gliedstaaten*) together form the *Gesamtstaat* (whole state). See: Baumann (ER), Part IV, § 13 II 2 (a); Creifelds under *Bundesstaat*.

Only the *Bund* enjoys full sovereign authority in external relations. See Battis/Gusy, Part A, § 4 I and Article 32 GG.

Regarding the current international position of the *Bund* see also Articles 23-27 GG and the comments under Article 23 GG in the *Sourcebook*, Chapter 2.

2   The immediate precursors of the Grundgesetz were the constitution of the (unified) German Empire of 16 April 1871 and the constitution of the Weimar Republic (the *Weimare (Reichs) Verfassung*) of 11 August 1919. The latter lasted until the *Ermächtigungsgesetz* (Enablement Law) of 24 March 1933 empowered Hitler to override it.

The constitution of the Weimar Republic had, for the first time, enacted (in its second part) a catalogue of *Grundrechte* (Basic Rights), which were later suspended by Hitler.

At a meeting of the National Assembly in the Paulskirche in Frankfurt am Main in 1848 a catalogue of *Grundrechte* had been formulated and a national constitution agreed upon, but they never came into force.

Regarding the Paulskirche assembly see Creifelds under *Nationalversammlung* and Laufs, Chapter VIII, 2.

law of the *Bund* takes precedence over that of the *Länder* (Article 31 GG: *Bundesrecht bricht Landesrecht*).[3]

THE EXECUTIVE

The administration (*Verwaltung*) of Germany is divided between the *Bund* and the *Länder* as carriers (*Träger*) thereof. The key to an understanding of the term *Verwaltungsträger* (carrier of administration) and, thus, of the construction of the executive in Germany, is the recognition that *Verwaltungsträger* have specific *Organe* (organs) and (as a subsidiary term) *Behörden* (authorities).[4]

Executive power (*vollziehende Gewalt*) is exercised in the following forms:

- administration by the *Bund* (*bundeseigene Verwaltung*)
- administration by the *Länder* (*landeseigene-* or *Länderverwaltung*)
- administration by the *Länder* on instruction by the *Bund* (*Auftragsverwaltung*).[5]

The *Bund* and the *Länder* can administer either directly (*unmittelbar*) or indirectly (*mittelbar*) by delegation to other carriers. Such carriers of indirect state administration (*Staatsverwaltung*) are the public (*öffentliche*) corporations (*Körperschaften*), institutions (*Anstalten*) and foundations (*Stiftungen*).[6]

---

3   For a review of the relationship between the Bund and the *Länder* see Wesel (FR), Chapter 2 (*Der Bund und die Länder*). Wesel points out that in the field of legislation, the *Länder* are merely left with residual areas (*Restbestände*; for example, police and building law) and that decisions of the (federal) courts of the *Bund* have a significant influence on the judicature in the courts of the *Länder*.

     Only in the area of administration do the *Länder* remain predominant. See: Chapter II p 7 below; Model/Creifelds/Lichtenberger, Part I D II (54-57); and the comments under Article 31 GG and Articles 70-78 GG in the *Sourcebook*, Chapter 2.

4   A part of a *Behörde* (or, indeed, a *Behörde* itself) is frequently described as an *Amt* (office). See: Bull, Section I, § 3 and § 4; Erichsen, Part VII, § 56; Maurer, Part 6, § 21.

     Regarding the term *Verwaltung*, its forms and functions see: Bull, Section I, § 1 and § 2 7; Erichsen, Part I, §§ 1-2; Maurer, Part 1, § 1.

5   Administration by the *Länder* is the norm: see Creifelds under *Verwaltungskompetenz*, Chapter V and Chapter XIII.

6   See: Creifelds under *Mittelbare Staatsverwaltung*; Erichsen, Part VII, § 57; Maurer, Part 6, §§ 22-23.

     Public *Körperschaften*, *Anstalten* and *Stiftungen* are all *juristische Personen des öffentlichen Rechts* (juristic persons of public law). Rehbinder (Chapter II, § 17 III) defines them as follows:

     Körperschaften des öffentlichen Rechts are *Verbände mit Rechtspersönlichkeit* (Associations with legal personality);

     Anstalten are organisationally independent *Verwaltungseinheiten* (administrative units);

     Stiftungen are *mit Rechtspersönlichkeit ausgestattete Vermögensmassen* (accumulations of assets endowed with legal personality). They are dedicated to a particular purpose (*Zweck*).

     Körperschaften des öffentlichen Rechts have members (*Mitglieder*). According to the criteria governing membership, they can be *Gebietskörperschaften* (territorial corporations; eg the *Gemeinden* (local communities)) or *Personalkörperschaften* (personal corporations; eg the various professional and commercial chambers (*Kammern*) and high schools (*Hochschulen*). See Creifelds under *Körperschaften des öffentlichen Rechts* and *Selbstverwaltung*. ...

The activity of the executive (*Verwaltungstätigkeit*) is usually official (*hoheitlich*). By contrast, however, it can also perform its administrative functions (*Verwaltungsaufgaben*) fiscally (*fiskalisch*) in the forms available under private law: so called *Verwaltungsprivatrecht* or *Verwaltung in Privatrechtsform*.[7]

Thus, *Anstalten* are part of the wider term *öffentliche Einrichtungen* (public facilities). In each *Land*, the statute governing local authorities (the *Gemeindeordnung*) lays down a (public legal) right of admission (*Zulassung*) for its residents (*Einwohner*). The use of the relevant facility itself can, however, be governed by private law. Although the executive has freedom of choice (*Wahlfreiheit*), it remains bound to observe the restrictions of public law (*öffentlich-rechtliche Bindungen*) generally (eg the basic rights).

This so-called two-tier theory (*Zweistufentheorie*) has the important procedural consequence that, depending on the party involved on the side of the executive, a dispute may fall within the jurisdiction of the administrative courts (§ 40 VwGO) or within that of the ordinary courts (§ 13 GVG).[8]

THE ADMINISTRATION OF JUSTICE

The administration of justice in Germany is divided into five branches (*Zweige*):

- the ordinary jurisdiction (*ordentliche Gerichtsbarkeit*);
- the employment jurisdiction (*Arbeitsgerichtsbarkeit*);

---

6 ... *The Bundesbank* (Federal Bank (in Frankfurt am Main)) is a *bundesunmittelbare juristische Person des öffentlichen Rechts* (a public corporation under the direct control of the Bund). See Creifelds under *Bundesbank*.

Anstalten have users (*Benutzer*). Depending on their degree of independence, *Anstalten* can have full, partial or no legal capacity, ie they can be *(voll)rechtsfähig* (eg the radio and television stations (*Rundfunk- und Fernsehanstalten*); the *Bundesanstalt für Arbeit* (Federal Office of Employment)), *teilrechtsfähig* or *nichtrechtsfähig* (eg schools, hospitals, museums). See Creifelds under *Anstalten des öffentlichen Rechts*.

Regarding juristic persons of private law see Chapter XI, p 81. In private law, apart from the Stiftung (foundation; §§ 80-88 BGB), the main types of juristic person are all corporately organised and have members.

7 A related distinction is that between *Eingriffsverwaltung* (intervention administration) and *Leistungsverwaltung* (service administration).

Eingriffsverwaltung is a type of *hoheitliche Verwaltungstätigkeit*, the prime example being the activity of the police.

Leistungsverwaltung today covers wide areas of state supply and support, for example in the field of social security, health, education and transport. Its common purpose is the provision of services for the welfare of members of the public (*Daseinsvorsorge*). Leistungsverwaltung can be exercised both *hoheitlich* (eg the grant of a state benefit) and *fiskalisch* (eg the grant of a loan).

See: Chapter VIII, Note 4; Chapter X, Note 16 and Chapter XVI, Note 19. See also: Creifelds under *Eingriffsverwaltung, Fiskus, Hoheitsaufgaben, Leistungsverwaltung* and *Verwaltungsprivatrecht*; Erichsen, Part I, § 2 and Part III, Section 4 (§§ 31-32); Giemulla/Jaworsky/Müller-Uri, Book I, Chapter 3 A.

8 See: Chapters VI, IX and XII, Note 17; Bull, Section II, § 6 7; Maurer, Part 1, § 1 II 4, § 3 II 3, § 3 III 4(d); Part 4, § 17 I, Part 6, § 23 II 2(e) and Part 7, § 25 VI 2; Erichsen, Part III, §§ 31-32 and Part V, § 44; Schmidt-Aßmann, Part II, VI 1.

- the (general) administrative jurisdiction (*allgemeine Verwaltungsgerichtsbarkeit*);
- the social jurisdiction (*Sozialgerichtsbarkeit*);
- the finance jurisdiction (*Finanzgerichtsbarkeit*).[9]

The administration of justice is carried by the state, ie the *Bund* is responsible for the federal courts specified in the Basic Law and the *Länder* for the others (Article 92 GG).

THE *RECHTSSTAAT* PRINCIPLE

It is a founding and unalterable principle of the Basic Law that the *Bund* and the *Länder* are democratic and social republican states in which the rule of law prevails (*Rechtsstaaten*) (Articles 20(i), 28(i) and 79(iii) GG).[10]

THE ORIGIN, SEPARATION AND BINDING OF STATE POWER

Article 20(ii) GG sets out other fundamental principles.

Firstly, all state power (*Staatsgewalt*) in the *Bund* and the *Länder* springs from the people (*Volk*): the principle of the sovereignty (or right of self-determination) of the people (*Volkssouveränität*).

Secondly, state power is exercised by the people in elections and plebiscites: the principle of representative democracy.[11]

Thirdly, state power is exercised by separate special organs of the legislature (*gesetzgebende Gewalt/Gesetzgebung*), executive (*vollziehende Gewalt/Verwaltung*) and judicature (*rechtsprechende Gewalt/Rechtsprechung*): the principle of the separation of powers (*Gewaltenteilung*).

---

9 See the appendix to Creifelds and Chapter XIX.

10 Article 20 GG describes the principal elements of a *Rechtsstaat*. However, the term itself (which dates from the 19th century) is not defined in the Basic Law and, indeed, is only mentioned in Article 28(i) GG.

See Wesel (JW), Chapter IX and Wesel (FR), Chapter 2 (*Die Staatsfundamentalnorm des Artikels 20*) and Chapter 5 (*Das Privatrecht als Modell*). Wesel points out that the opposite of a *Rechtsstaat* is a *Polizeistaat* (police state) and that the primary function of administrative law is the protection of the (assets of the) individual against the state (*Individual(güter)schutz*).

Regarding Articles 20, 28 and 79(iii) GG see the comments under those Articles in the *Sourcebook*, Chapter 2.

See also: Battis/Gusy, Part A, §§ 2-7; Creifelds under *Verfassungsänderung*; Erichsen, Part I, § 3 I; Hesse, Part II (§§ 4-8).

11 The Basic Law only provides for plebiscites (*Abstimmungen/Volksentscheide*) in the case of a new division of the federal territory (*Neugliederung des Bundesgebietes* (Article 29 GG)). See Wesel (FR), Chapter 2 (*Volksabstimmungen*).

By Article 20(iii) GG the legislature is bound to the constitutional order (*verfassungsmäßige Ordnung*) and the executive and judicature to statute and law (*Gesetz und Recht*).[12]

The binding (*Bindung*) of the executive to statute is referred to as the *Gesetzmäßigkeit der Verwaltung* (*Vorbehalt des Gesetzes*) and the priority of statute as the *Vorrang des Gesetzes*.[13]

THE *FREIHEITLICHE DEMOKRATISCHE GRUNDORDNUNG*

The *freiheitliche demokratische Grundordnung* is the basic order of freedom and democracy upon which, by common consent, Germany is constructed. It includes:

- the *Rechtsstaat* principle;
- the people's right of self-determination (*Selbstbestimmungsrecht*);
- the separation of powers;[14]
- the binding of the legislature to the constitutional order and of the executive and judiciary to statute and law;
- the multi-party system (*Mehrparteiensystem*);[15]
- the independence of the judges (*Unabhängigkeit der Richter*);[16]
- the basic rights;[17]
- the *Rechtsschutzgarantie*.[18]

The concept of the *freiheitliche demokratische Grundordnung* is occasionally used in German statutes eg in Article 18 GG (*Verwirkung von Grundrechten* (forfeiture of basic rights)), in Article 21(ii) GG (*Verfassungswichrigkeit von Parteien* (unconstitutionality of political parties)) and in criminal provisions concerning treason (*Verrat*) and similar offences (§§ 86(ii) and 93(ii) StGB).[19]

---

12 Law includes the Basic Law (see generally Battis/Gusy, Chapter 6 and Chapters VII and XIII).

13 Regarding the principle of the *Gesetzmäßigkeit der Verwaltung* see: Bull, Section II, § 6 1-3; Erichsen, Part I, § 3 II 1; Giemulla/Jaworsky/Müller-Uri, Book I, Chapter 3 B; Maurer, Part 2, § 6.

14 See: Model/Creifelds/Lichtenberger, Part I D IV (63); Hesse, Part III, Section 2 (§§ 13-14).

15 Certain fundamental principles regarding the political parties are set out in Article 21 GG. For further information see: Creifelds under Parteien; Hesse, Part II, § 5 II 6; and the comments under Article 21 GG in the *Sourcebook*, Chapter 2.

   Regarding the German electoral system, see also: *The All Germany Election Case* (*Sourcebook*, Chapter 2) and Creifelds under *Wahlrecht (öffentliches)*.

16 See Creifelds under *Unabhängigkeit des Richters* and Chapter XIX.

17 See Chapter VIII.

18 See Chapter VIII.

19 See Hesse, Part III, Section 4 (§ 22) and the comments under Article 21 GG in the *Sourcebook*, Chapter 2.

CHAPTER III

THE SUPREME FEDERAL ORGANS[1]

The main supreme organs of the *Bund* (*oberste Bundesorgane*) are:

- the Federal Parliament (*Bundestag*);
- the Federal Council (*Bundesrat*);
- the Federal President (*Bundespräsident*);
- the Federal Government (*Bundesregierung*).[2]

The *Bundestag* is an organ of the legislature, while the *Bundesrat* is an organ through which the *Länder* assist (*mitwirken*) in the passing of federal laws and in the administration of the *Bund* (Article 50 GG).

The *Bundespräsident* (the head of state of the Bund) and the *Bundesregierung* are organs of the executive.

The *Bundesregierung* consists of the Federal Chancellor (*Bundeskanzler*) and the federal ministers (*Bundesminister*) (Article 62 GG). The ministries themselves are supreme federal authorities (*oberste Bundesbehörden*).

Further supreme federal organs are:

- the (emergency) Joint Council (*gemeinsamer Ausschuß*);
- the Federal Assembly (*Bundesversammlung*);
- the Federal Constitutional Court (*Bundesverfassungsgericht*).[3]

The supreme federal organs are laid down in Articles 38-69 of the Basic Law and in § 1(i) of the Law relating to the Federal Constitutional Court (*Bundesverfassungsgerichtsgesetz* (BVerfGG)).

---

1   See: Baumann (ER), Part IV, § 13 II 2; Creifelds under *Organe der BRep, Verfassungsorgane* and *Zweikammersystem*; Wesel (FR), Chapter 2 (*Die Obersten Staatsorgane*); Model/Creifelds/ Lichtenberger, Part I D III (58-62); Hesse, Part III, Section 3 (§§ 15-19).

2   In Germany, the Federal Government is appointed by the Federal Parliament (parliamentary democracy). *Cf* USA (presidential democracy). See Wesel (FR), Chapter 2 (*Parlamentarische Demokratie*). See also Creifelds under *Gesetzgebende Gewalt, Präsidialdemokratie* and *Staatsoberhaupt*.

3   See Wesel (FR), Chapter 2 (*Der Hüter der Verfassung*) and the comments above Article 93 GG in the *Sourcebook*, Chapter 2.

CHAPTER IV

THE SUPREME AND OTHER FEDERAL AUTHORITIES

The highest executive organs of the *Bund* are the *Bundespräsident* and the *Bundesregierung*. Beneath them, the administration (*Verwaltung*) of the *Bund* is built up on the following levels:

- the supreme federal authorities (*oberste Bundesbehörden*);
- the upper federal authorities (*Bundesoberbehörden*);
- the (middle) federal authorities (*Bundesbehörden*);
- the lower federal authorities (*Bundesunterbehörden*).

The supreme federal authorities are:

- the Federal Ministries (*Bundesministerien*);
- the Federal Presidential Office (*Bundespräsidialamt*);
- the Federal Chancellor's Office or Chancellery (*Bundeskanzleramt*);
- the Press and Information Office of the Federal Government (*Presse- und Informationsamt der Bundesregierung*);
- the Federal Accounts Court (*Bundesrechnungshof*).

The upper federal authorities are usually entitled *Bundesamt für...* (federal office for/of ...).

Examples of (middle) federal authorities are the various *Direktionen* (directorates) eg the *Bundesbahndirektion* (Federal Railway Directorate) and the *Oberpostdirektion* (Upper Post Directorate).

The best example of a lower federal authority is the local *Postamt* (post office). The *Finanzämter* (tax offices) are, however, lower authorities of the *Länder*; the *Oberfinanzdirektion* (Upper Finance Directorate) is hybrid (ie it is both a federal authority and one of a *Land*).

Unlike the middle and lower federal authorities, the competence of the upper federal authorities extends to the whole federal territory (*Bundesgebiet*).[1]

---

1   For examples, see Creifelds under *Bundesoberbehörden*. For the structure of federal authorities see Creifelds under *Verwaltungsbehörden 1: Bundesbehörden*. See also Model/Creifelds/ Lichtenberger, Part I E (91-110).

CHAPTER V

THE *LÄNDER*

INTRODUCTION

Before the reunification (*Wiedervereinigung*) of Germany on 3 October 1990, the following eleven *Länder* were constituent member states of the *Bund*:

- Baden-Württemberg;
- Bayern (Bavaria);
- Berlin;
- Bremen;
- Hamburg;
- Hessen;
- Niedersachsen (Lower Saxony);
- Nordrhein-Westfalen (North Rhine-Westphalia);
- Rheinland-Pfalz (Rhineland-Palatinate);
- Saarland;
- Schleswig-Holstein.

Berlin, Bremen and Hamburg are city states (*Stadtstaaten*).

Since reunification, the following five states in the former East Germany (the *neue Bundesländer* (new federal states)) now also form part of the *Bund*:

- Brandenburg;
- Mecklenburg-Vorpommern;
- Sachsen (Saxony);
- Sachsen-Anhalt;
- Thüringen (Thuringia).[1]

Each *Land* has its own constitution (*Landesverfassung*).

The Basic Law requires that the constitutional order in the *Länder* must accord with the principles of a republican, democratic and social *Rechtsstaat* (Article 28(i), first sentence GG; homogeneity clause) and that the people must have a representative body (*Vertretung*) following general, direct, free, equal and secret elections (Article 28(i), second sentence GG).

Each *Land* has as its organs: a parliament (usually known as the *Landtag*), a government (usually known as the *Landesregierung* and usually headed by a *Ministerpräsident* (prime minister)), an accounts court (*Rechnungshof*) and (except in Berlin and Schleswig-Holstein) a constitutional court (usually known as the *Verfassungsgerichtshof*).[2]

---

1   See Creifelds under *Einigungsvertrag*.
2   See Chapter VII.

STATE ADMINISTRATION IN THE *LÄNDER*

In the absence of other provisions in or allowed by the Basic Law, there is a presumption (*Vermutung*) that state administration in the *Länder* is within their competence (*Zuständigkeit*; Article 30 GG). The *Länder*, therefore, usually carry out the administration of federal laws (*Bundesgesetze*) as their own matter (*als eigene Angelegenheit*; Article 83 GG) through their authorities (*Landesbehörden*; Article 84 GG).[3]

State administration in the *Länder* is direct and indirect and is usually constructed on the following levels:

- upper level (*Oberstufe*);
- middle level (*Mittelstufe*);
- lower level (*Unterstufe*).

In the *Stadtstaaten*, Saarland and Schleswig-Holstein, there is no middle level.

The upper level is composed of the ministries and state chancelleries (*Staatskanzleien*) acting as *oberste Landesbehörden*, to which the *Landesämter* (*Landesoberbehörden*) directly report.

Each *Land* is (usually) divided into governmental areas or districts (*Regierungsbezirke*) headed by a president (*Regierungspräsident*). The governments (*Regierungen*) of these areas make up the middle level.

The lower level is composed of lower administrative authorities or lower authorities of the *Länder* (*untere Verwaltungsbehörden* or *untere Landesbehörden* = direct state administration) and local authorities (usually known as (*Land*)*Kreise* and *Gemeinde*), which can function both as such (= indirect state administration) or as lower authorities of the *Länder* (ie they have a *Doppelfunktion* (double function)).

The *Länder* are represented at the *Bund* through the *Bundesrat* and by ministers (of the *Länder*) responsible for federal matters (*Bevollmächtigte beim Bund*).[4]

---

3   See Chapter XIII.

4   For further information regarding the *Länder*, their respective organs and authorities, see Model/Creifelds/Lichtenberger, Part I, Sections F and G (114–140); Creifelds under *Länder* and under *Verwaltungsbehörden 2: Landesbehörden*.

CHAPTER VI

LOCAL GOVERNMENT

Beneath the *Bund* and the *Länder*, the communal bodies on the third (lower) level are the territorial corporations/local authorities (*Gebietskörperschaften/Kommunen*), usually known as the (*Land-)Kreise* (circles) and the *Gemeinden* (communes – ie the most local communal bodies).[1]

Gemeinden can either belong to a *Kreis* (*kreisangehörig*) or be independent thereof (*kreisfrei*). The same applies to a city (*Stadt*), which term is used to describe a municipal *Gemeinde*. Once a city reaches a certain size or importance, it can become a *kreisfreie Stadt*.

The relevant local government laws in the *Länder* are the (*Land-)Kreis-* and *Gemeinde- Ordnungen*.[2]

The Basic Law guarantees the right of the *Gemeinden* (and the *Kreise*) to administer all local matters (*alle Angelegenheiten der örtlichen Gemeinschaft*) themselves under the auspices (*Aufsicht*) of the state (*Recht der Selbstverwaltung*; Article 28(ii) GG). The *Gemeinden* are entitled to pass by-laws (*Satzungen*).[3]

The *Gemeindeordnungen* provide for the *Gemeinden* in the various *Länder* to be composed in different forms. Usually, the organs of a *Gemeinde* are known as:

- the *Gemeindevertretung/Stadtverordnetenversammlung/Gemeinderat* (the legislative organ) and

- the *Ober-Bürgermeister/Magistrat/Gemeindeverwaltung* (the executive organ).

Local matters extending beyond the capacity of a *Gemeinde* (*überörtliche Angelegenheiten*) are dealt with by the (*Land-)Kreis*, which has the following organs:

- the *Kreis* Parliament (*Kreistag*);

- the *Kreis* Council (*Kreisausschuß*);

- the Chief Executive (*Landrat* or, in Lower Saxony and North Rhine-Westphalia, the *Oberkreisdirektor*).

The *Landrat* has a dual role: he performs the administrative matters of the *Kreis* itself (*Selbstverwaltungsangelegenheiten/eigene Aufgaben*) and, as the lower level of (indirect) administration by the state (*Land*), matters which the *Land* allocates (*überträgt*) to the *Kreis* (*Auftragsangelegenheiten/übertragene Aufgaben*).

The *Land* can also allocate matters to a *kreisfreie Stadt*.

---

1   The term *Gemeindeverband* (*Gemeinde* association) is used to describe a conglomeration of territorial corporations above *Gemeinden*, eg *Kreise* and so-called *Gesamtgemeinden*. See: Maurer, Part 6, § 23 I 5; Schmidt-Aßmann, Section I.

2   They are *Landesgesetze*: see Creifelds under *Landkreisordnungen* and *Gemeindeordnungen*.

3   See: Creifelds under *Satzung* and *Satzungsgewalt (-befugnis)*; Erichsen, Part II, § 7 VI. *Cf Gesetz*.

CHAPTER VII

THE CONSTITUTION (*GRUNDGESETZ*)

INTRODUCTION

The federal constitution of the *Bund* (*Grundgesetz*/Basic Law) dated 23 May 1949 contains 146 Articles and is divided into 11 main Sections:

I   The basic rights (*Grundrechte*): Articles 1-19.

II   The *Bund* and the *Länder*: Articles 20-37.[1]

III-VI The supreme federal organs (or constitutional organs (*Verfassungs-organe*)): Articles 38-69:

    III The *Bundestag*: Articles 38-48.

    IV The *Bundesrat*: Articles 50-53.

    IVaThe *Gemeinsamer Ausschuß* (Joint Council): Article 53a.

    V The *Bundespräsident*: Articles 54-61.

    VI The *Bundesregierung*: Articles 62-69.

VII   Legislative competence and procedure: Articles 70-82 (entitled *Die Gesetzgebung des Bundes*).[2]

VIII   Administration of federal laws: Articles 83-91 (entitled *Die Ausführung der Bundesgesetze und die Bundesverwaltung*).

IX   The judicature: Articles 92-104 (entitled *Die Rechtsprechung*).[3]

---

1   These Articles are arranged in the *Sourcebook* (Chapter 2) as follows:

- Article 20
- Political parties (Article 21)
- Flag (Article 22)
- International relations (Articles 23-27)
- The states (Articles 28-31)
- External relations (Article 32)
- Citizen's rights (Article 33)
- Officials and authorities (Articles 34-36)
- Coercion by the *Bund* (Article 37).

2   These Articles are arranged in the Sourcebook (Chapter 2) as follows:

- Legislative powers and procedure (Articles 70-78)
- Altering the constitution (Article 79)
- Regulations (Article 80)
- Special cases (Articles 80a-81)
- Coming into force (Article 82).

3   These Articles are arranged in the *Sourcebook* (Chapter 2) as follows:

- The courts (Article 92)
- The Federal Constitutional Court (Articles 93-94)
- The federal courts (Articles 95-96)
- Judges (Articles 97-98)
- Constitutional issues (Articles 99-100)
- Special courts (Article 101)
- Criminal law and the right to be heard (Articles 102-103)
- Freedom (Article 104).

X   Finances: Articles 104a-115 (entitled *Das Finanzwesen*).

XI   Transitional and final provisions: Articles 116-146.[4]

RANK OF THE BASIC LAW

The Basic Law ranks higher than other legal norms (*Rechtsnormen*), which must be interpreted so as to conform with it (*verfassungskonforme Auslegung*).

A statute (*Gesetz*) can be formally or materially unconstitutional (*verfassungswidrig*). The judiciary (which is independent: Article 97(i) GG) has the right to check whether this is so (*richterliches Prüfungsrecht*).

THE FEDERAL AND STATE CONSTITUTIONAL COURTS

The competence (*Zuständigkeit*) of the Federal Constitutional Court (*Bundesverfassungsgericht*) is set out in Article 93 GG (and in § 13 BVerfGG);[5] or, in the case of the constitutional court of a *Land*, in its constitution (and VerfGG).

The decisions of the Federal Constitutional Court bind the constitutional organs of the *Bund* and the *Länder*, as well as all courts and authorities (§ 31(i) BVerfGG).

If a court considers a *Gesetz* upon which its decision depends to be unconstitutional, it is obliged to refer the (legal) question as appropriate to the Federal Constitutional Court or the constitutional court of the *Land* (*Landesverfassungsgericht*):[6] so-called concrete norm-control (*konkrete Normkontrolle*; Article 100(i) GG).[7]

Otherwise, under its *richterliches Prüfungsrecht*, the court can decide incidentally (*inzident*) itself – the so-called incidental control (*Inzidentkontrolle*) – as it can anyway in the case of norms ranking below statutes (eg *Rechtsverordnungen* = statutory regulations).[8]

---

4   Sections VIIIa (Articles 91a-91b) and Xa (Articles 115a-115l) of the Basic Law deal with, respectively, joint matters (*Gemeinschaftsaufgaben*) in which there is co-operation (*Mitwirkung*) by the *Bund* and matters of national defence (the *Verteidigungsfall* (defence situation)).

5   Whereas access to the administrative courts is available pursuant to a general clause (§ 40(i) VwGO), the categories of case in which the constitutional courts have jurisdiction are precisely specified (*Enumerationsprinzip* (enumeration principle)); a matter not falling within a particular category is *unzulässig* (inadmissible).
    Cf Chapter XIV (note 9) and see Creifelds under *Verfassungsstreitigkeiten* (a)-(n); Model/Creifelds/Lichtenberger, Part I D IV (72-74)

6   In Baden-Württemberg, Bremen, Hessen and Niedersachsen, the constitutional court of the *Land* is called the *Staatsgerichtshof*. See also Creifelds under *Verfassungswidrigkeit von Gesetzen*.

7   Another name for the *konkrete Normkontrolle* is the *Vorlageverfahren* (reference procedure).

8   The incidental decision of a court is merely binding on the parties: cf § 121 VwGO and § 322 ZPO. ...

On application by the government of the *Bund* or a *Land* or $1/3$ of the members of the *Bundestag*, the Federal Constitutional Court can decide whether a norm (including one below a statute) is unconstitutional or whether the law of a *Land* is incompatible with federal law: so-called abstract norm-control (*abstrakte Normkontrolle*; Article 93(i) No 2 GG).

If the norm is found to be unconstitutional or the law incompatible, it is declared void (§ 78 BVerfGG).

Any person can apply to the Federal Constitutional Court by way of constitutional complaint (*Verfassungsbeschwerde*) (usually only after normal legal channels have been exhausted)[9] on the basis that one of its basic rights (or those in Articles 20(iv), 33, 38, 101, 103 and 104 GG) has been infringed by the (German) public power (*öffentliche Gewalt* ie by the legislature, executive or the judiciary; Article 93(i) No 4a GG and § 90(i) and § 90(ii) BVerfGG).[10]

In order for the complaint to be admissible (*zulässig*) the infringement must affect the complainant individually, currently and directly (*selbst, gegenwärtig und unmittelbar*).[11]

Local authorities can also apply to the Federal Constitutional Court in the event that a federal statute infringes their right of self-administration (Article 93(i) No 4b GG).

If it allows the complaint, the Federal Constitutional Court pinpoints the relevant breach of the Basic Law. In the case of a court decision, it quashes it

---

8 … A norm below a *Landesgesetz* (state statute) can also be challenged in the OVG under § 47 VwGO (the so-called norm-control procedure (*Normkontrollverfahren*): see Chapter XIV. If the OVG declares the norm void, its decision is of general effect (*allgemein verbindlich*; §47(vi), second sentence VwGO).

See Gallwas, Chapter 12 (12.1.3 and 12.1.4).

9 § 90(ii), second sentence BVerfGG contains an exception to the usual requirement of the exhaustion of normal legal channels (*Erschöpfung des Rechtswegs*): the Federal Constitutional Court can hear a constitutional complaint immediately, if it is of general importance or if a severe and unavoidable disadvantage would accrue to the complainant, if the complainant were referred in the first instance to ordinary legal proceedings. See the *Investment Aid Act Case* (*Sourcebook*, Chapter 3).

10 See the comments under Article 93 GG in the Sourcebook, Chapter 2.

11 Where a provision in a statute (*Gesetz*) requires a particular act of implementation (*Vollzugsakt*) by the executive, a complaint against the statutory provision itself can only be brought before the Federal Constitutional Court exceptionally (*ausnahmsweise*).

The complainant must usually wait for the implementing measure and then – in accordance with the subsidiarity principle (*Subsidiaritätsprinzip*) – (first) challenge it in the administrative court, since it is only at the stage of the implementing act that the complainant can allege that he is directly affected (*unmittelbar betroffen*) and that the implementing act amounts to an attack (*Eingriff*) on his legal sphere (*Rechtssphäre*).

See Kriele, Fall 19 (the *Volkszählung* (public census) decision of the Federal Constitutional Court of 15 December 1983; *Aus den Gründen*: B). See also Chapter VIII, note 10.

and refers it back to a competent court;[12] in the case of a (provision in a) statute, it declares it void (§ 95 BVerfGG).[13]

The decision of the Federal Constitutional Court regarding a norm has statutory force (*Gesetzeskraft*; § 31(ii) BVerfGG).

The Federal Constitutional Court can also decide (*inter alia*) in disputes:

- between supreme federal organs regarding the interpretation of the Basic Law (Article 93(i) No 1 GG; *Organstreit*);[14]
- between the *Bund* and *Länder* regarding their constitutional rights and obligations (Article 93(i) No 3 GG; *Bund/Länder Streit*).

---

12 As, for example, in Kriele, Fall 3 (the *Lüth/Harlan* decision of the Federal Constitutional Court of 15 January 1958; also referred to in Chapter VIII, notes 5 and 8 below).

13 As, for example, in Kriele, Fall 4 (the *Apotheken* (chemists) decision of the Federal Constitutional Court of 11 June 1958). See the comments in connection with that case under Article 12 GG in the *Sourcebook*, Chapter 3.

Alternatively, the Federal Constitutional Court can declare the (provision in the) statute compatible (*vereinbar*) or incompatible (*unvereinbar*) with the Basic Law. See: § 31(ii) BVerfGG; Battis/Gusy, § 7V (305); and the following cases:

- Kriele, Fall 18 (*Naßauskiesung* (wet gravelling)). In connection with that decision see the comments on expropriation (*Enteignung*) under Article 14(iii) GG in the *Sourcebook*, Chapter 3.
- Kriele, Fall 11 (*Numerus clausus*). A *numerus clausus* (fixed number) of university admissions may be incompatible with the Basic Law. Training (*Ausbildung*) is the first stage to the exercise of a profession (*Berufsausübung*) under Article 12(i) GG. See also Chapter VIII, note 4.
- The *Housework Day Case* (*Sourcebook*, Chapter 3).

14 An *Organstreit* can also be initiated by a parliamentary grouping (*Fraktion*) or political party. See Hesse, Part III, Section 3, § 19 II 2.

For the application to be admissible, the applicant must allege that a measure or omission of the other party injures its rights and obligations under the Basic Law or that it is directly endangered by it; § 64(i) BVerfGG.

A measure includes a Federal Government decision (*Beschluß der Bundesregierung*): see the *Bosnia Flight Exclusion Zone Case* (*Sourcebook*, Chapter 2).

CHAPTER VIII

THE BASIC RIGHTS

INTRODUCTION[1]

The basic rights (*Grundrechte*) are dealt with at the beginning of the Basic Law (Articles 1-19 GG).[2]

Certain of the basic rights only benefit Germans (Articles 8(i), 9(i), 11(i) and 12(i) GG).

Despite the precedence of federal laws over that of the *Länder* (Article 31 GG; *Bundesrecht bricht Landesrecht*), those basic rights also contained in constitutions of the *Länder* remain in force so far as they accord with Articles 1-18 GG (Article 142 GG).

The basic rights bind (*binden*) the legislature, executive and judicature as directly applicable law (*unmittelbar geltendes Recht*; Article 1(iii) GG).

The main groupings are those of freedom rights (*Freiheitsrechte*) and equality rights (*Gleichheitsrechte*).

The basic rights are principally regarded as defensive rights (*Abwehrrechte*) against attacks (*Eingriffe*) by the state. However, they also include certain institutional guarantees and are the expression of an objective value-order (*Wertordnung*).[3]

Increasingly, there is a tendency to regard certain of the basic rights as conferring the right to claim positive action from the state (*Grundrechte as Leistungsrechte*).[4]

The applicability of basic rights in the area of private relations (the so-called *Drittwirkung* of basic rights) is not generally accepted, although they can indirectly (*mittelbar*) be called in aid in the interpretation of private law.[5]

---

1   Regarding the nature of the basic rights, the entitlement to claim them and their effect see the *Sourcebook*, Chapter 3 (Introduction).

2   In the Basic Law, the structural principles of state follow the basic rights and commence in Article 20. This is a reaction to the crimes of the Nazi period and should be compared with the position under the constitution of the Weimar Republic and the so-called *Paulskirche Verfassung*. See Wesel (FR), Chapter 2 (*Menschenrechte*) and Chapter II, Note 2 above.

3   As in the *Film Director Case (Lüth/Harlan) (Sourcebook*, Chapter 6).

4   *Leistungsrechte* can be enforced by the administrative courts. See Wesel (FR), Chapter 5, which deals with the distinction between *Eingriffsverwaltung* and *Leistungsverwaltung* (*Daseinsvorsorge*), a distinction first drawn in 1938 by Ernst Forsthoff in his book *Die Verwaltung als Leistungsträger*. By way of example, Wesel draws attention to a case decided by the Federal Administrative Court in 1954 (BVerwGE 1 159; *Fürsorgeunterstützung* (welfare support)). See also Chapter II, Note 7 and Chapter X, Note 16.

    In the *Numerus clausus* case *Leistungsrechte* were referred to as *Teilhaberechte* (rights to participate (in state services)). See Chapter VII, note 13.

5   See Kriele, Fall 3 (*Lüth/Harlan; Aus den Gründen*: B II 3-4).

    For examples of the indirect (secondary) effect of basic rights in cases involving claims for tort see the *Sourcebook*, Chapter 6: …

It is customary to speak of the addressee (*Adressat*) of a *Grundrecht*, its carrier (*Träger*), its protected area (*Schutzbereich*) and its infringement (*Verletzung*).

LIMITATION OF BASIC RIGHTS[6]

It is possible for basic rights to be limited (*eingeschränkt*). In many cases, the right for this to be done through or on the basis of a statute (*durch Gesetz oder aufgrund eines Gesetzes*) is expressly reserved in the various Articles of the Basic Law (so-called *Gesetzesvorbehalt*). The limiting statute must apply generally and not only to an individual case and the Article being limited must be cited (Article 19(i) GG: the *Zitiergebot*).

It is also possible for the limits (*Schranken*) of a basic right to be implicit (*immanent*) in the relevant basic right or interpreted by means of a balancing (*Abwägung*) between conflicting rights.[7]

The limitation of basic rights is itself limited by so-called (often unwritten) *Schranken-Schranken*:

- an express limitation of a basic right must itself be interpreted in the light of the basic right (the so-called *Wechselwirkungstheorie* (theory of reciprocal effect));[8]

- in no case can the essence (*Wesensgehalt*) of a basic right be touched (*angetastet*; Article 19(ii) GG));

- the so-called *Übermaßverbot* (prohibition of excess), which flows from the principle that the executive must act in accordance with statute and law (Article 20(iii) GG: *Bindung der Verwaltung an Gesetz und Recht/Gesetzmäßigkeit und Rechtmäßigkeit der Verwaltung*). The measures undertaken by the executive must be suitable (*geeignet*), necessary (*erforderlich*) and in fair relation to the intended goal (*verhältnismäßig*);[9]

---

5 ... • The *Publication of a Letter Case*;
   • The *Newspaper Delivery Obstruction Case*; and
   • The *Film Director Case*.

   In the first case, Articles 1 and 2 GG played a part; in the second, Articles 5 and 8 GG were considered, whilst in the third, Article 5 was decisive.

6 See also the *Sourcebook*, Chapter 3 (Limitations on the Basic Rights).

7 As in Kriele, Fall 8 (the *Mephisto (Gründgens/Mann)* decision of the Federal Constitutional Court of 24 February 1971; *Aus den Gründen* C IV).

   Regarding the process of *Abwägung* (balancing), which had to be carried out by the Federal Constitutional Court in the context of an application for an *einstweilige Anordnung* (temporary order) under § 32 BVerfGG, see: the *Bosnia Flight Exclusion Zone Case* and the *East German Politicians Trial Publicity Cases* in the *Sourcebook*, Chapters 2 and 3.

8 As in the *Film Director Case* (*Sourcebook*, Chapter 6; Kriele, Fall 3 (*Lüth/Harlan; Aus den Gründen*: B II 2)).

9 The status and content of the *Verhältnismäßigkeitsgrundsatz* (principle of proportionality) are explained in the *Sourcebook*, Chapter 3. Application of the principle is also illustrated by the *Arrested Admiral Case* (rules about arrest) and the *Shootings at the Berlin Wall Case* (law of the former GDR; *Sourcebook*, Chapter 7).

- essential (political) decisions (*wesentliche Entscheidungen*) must be taken by the legislature and cannot be delegated to the executive (*Wesentlichkeitsprinzip*).[10]

An infringement (*Verletzung*) of a basic right is only legitimate (a so-called *rechtmäßiger Eingriff*), if it is covered (*gedeckt*) by a *Gesetzesvorbehalt*, which is itself not limited by a *Schranken-Schranken*.

THE ACTUAL RIGHTS[11]

Article 19(iv) GG guarantees the right of everyone to go to law (usually to the administrative courts), if his rights are infringed by the executive (*Rechtsschutzgarantie*). This right is supplemented by the right to lodge a constitutional complaint (Article 93(i) No 4a GG).[12]

The following basic rights are included in Articles 1-17 of the Basic Law:

- human dignity (Article 1(i) *Menschenwürde*);
- free development of the personality/freedom of action (Article 2(i) *freie Entfaltung der Persönlichkeit/allgemeine Handlungsfreiheit*);
- the right to life and bodily integrity (Article 2(ii), first sentence *Recht auf Leben und körperliche Unversehrtheit*);
- freedom of the person (Article 2(ii), second sentence *Freiheit der Person*);
- equality before the law (Article 3(i) *Gleichheit vor dem Gesetz*);
- equal rights of men and women (Article 3(ii) *Gleichberechtigung zwischen Mann und Frau*);[13]
- no discrimination or preference due to sex, descent, race, language, home, origin, belief, religion or political views (Article 3(iii) *Benachteiligungs-und Bevorzugungsverbot*);
- freedom of belief, conscience and confession (Article 4(i) *Freiheit des Glaubens, Gewissens und des Bekenntnisses*);
- the right to conscientious objection against military service (Article 4(iii) *Recht zur Kriegsdienstverweigerung aus Gewissensgründen*);[14]

---

10 The legislature can, by *Gesetz*, empower the executive (government or ministers) to issue a *Rechtsverordnung* (statutory instrument). However, in accordance with the *Rechtsstaat* principle (*Gesetzmäßigkeit der Verwaltung*), the *Gesetz* must specify the content, purpose and extent of the authorisation (*Inhalt, Zweck und Ausmaß der Ermächtigung*) and it must be stated in the *Rechtsverordnung* itself upon what legal basis (*Rechtsgrundlage*) it is being issued: Article 80(i) GG.

See Creifelds under *Rechtsverordnung* and *Wesentlichkeitsprinzip*. See also the comments under Article 80 GG in the *Sourcebook*, Chapter 2 and *Zustimmungsgesetz*.

11 See also the *Sourcebook*, Chapter 3 (*The Basic Rights Themselves*), where, successively, Articles 1-3, 6-14 and 15-19 GG are treated.

12 Although Article 93(i) No 4a GG refers to specific (basic) rights and is in this respect narrower than the *Rechtsschutzgarantie*, it includes acts of the legislature and the judiciary. The term *öffentliche Gewalt* in Article 93(i) No 4a GG is, therefore, wider than in Article 19(iv) GG.

13 Article 3(ii) GG was the appropriate *Prüfungsmaßstab* (standard against which the statutory provision in question was examined) In the *Housework Day Case* (*Sourcebook*, Chapter 3).

14 Conscription is dealt with in Article 12a GG.

- freedom of expression (*Meinungsfreiheit*), press freedom (*Pressefreiheit*), freedom of reporting (*Freiheit der Berichterstattung*) and freedom of information/access to public sources (*Informationsfreiheit*) (Article 5(i));

- freedom of art, science, research and teaching (Article 5(iii) *Freiheit der Kunst, Wissenschaft, Forschung und Lehre*);

- protection of marriage and the family (including illegitimate children) (Article 6 *Schutz der Ehe und der Familie*);

- state supervision of the school system (*Schulwesen*); participation in religious instruction (*Religionsunterricht*) (Article 7);

- freedom of assembly (Article 8(i) *Versammlungsfreiheit*);

- freedom of (private) association (Article 9(i) *Verein(igung)sfreiheit* or *Vereinsautonomie*) and freedom to form coalitions (*Koalitionsfreiheit*: Article 9(iii));

- secrecy of communication by letter, post and telephone (Article 10(i) *Brief-, Post-und Fernmeldegeheimnis*);

- freedom of movement (*Freizügigkeit*) and freedom of establishment (*Niederlassungsfreiheit*) (Article 11(i));

- free choice of workplace and occupation (Article 12(i) *Freiheit der Arbeitsplatz- und Berufswahl*);

- inviolability of the home (Article 13(i) *Unverletzlichkeit der Wohnung*);

- guarantee of property and succession (Article 14(i) *Garantie des Eigentums und des Erbrechts*);

- prohibition on removal of citizenship and extradition (Article 16 *Verbot der Ausbürgerung und Auslieferung*);

- right of asylum (Article 16a *Asylrecht*);

- right of petition (Article 17 *Petitionsrecht*).[15]

---

15 In addition to the basic rights listed in Articles 1-17 GG, the Basic Law also contains the following rights:
- the (ultimate) right of all Germans to resist anyone attempting to overturn the constitutional order (Article 20(iv) GG: the *Widerstandsrecht*);
- the right of persons involved in legal proceedings to a proper judge as laid down by statute (Article 101(i), second sentence GG: the *Anspruch auf einen gesetzlichen Richter*);
- the right of persons involved in legal or administrative proceedings to a proper hearing in accordance with law (Article 103(i) GG: the *Anspruch auf rechtliches Gehör*);
- the right of the perpetrator of a crime only to be punished, if punishability is fixed by statute before the act is committed (Article 103(ii) GG: *nulla poena sine lege*);
- the right of the perpetrator of a crime not to be punished more than once for the same crime (Article 103(iii) GG: *ne bis in idem*);
- the right of a person not to be deprived of his or her freedom except on the basis of and in the manner prescribed by a formal statute (Article 104(i) GG: the *formelle Freiheitsgarantie* (formal guarantee of freedom), which supplements Article 2(ii), second sentence GG). ...

15...Regarding these specific rights (apart from the *Widerstandsrecht*) see: Chapter XIX; Chapter XII; Chapter XIII (§ 28 VwVfG); Chapter XV (note 3); Chapter XII (note 5); and Chapter XVI.

For further information regarding the basic rights generally see, for example: Battis/Gusy, Part B (§§ 8-14); Baumann (ER), Part IV, § 13 II 3; Hesse, Part III, Section I (§§ 9-12); Schunck/De Clerck, Part II, Section A (Chapter 2)); Model/Creifelds/Lichtenberger, Part I, Section D I (46-53); Creifelds under *Grundrechte*; Gallwas; Kriele.

CHAPTER IX

PUBLIC AND PRIVATE LAW

INTRODUCTION

German law divides itself strictly into public law (*öffentliches Recht*) – dealing with the relationship of the individual to the state and other carriers of public power – and private law (*Privatrecht*) – dealing with the relationship of citizens amongst each other.[1]

German private law has two main branches:

- civil law (*bürgerliches Recht*), the main source of which is the *Bürgerliches Gesetzbuch* (Civil Code (BGB)); and
- commercial and company law (*Handelsrecht* and *Gesellschaftsrecht*).

It is important to note here, however, that the subject-matter of private law in Germany is dealt with in numerous secondary and special statutes (*Neben- und Sondergesetze*), apart from the BGB and the statutes relating to commercial and company law eg in the fields of property and landlord and tenant law, employment law, traffic and public liability law, insurance and intellectual property law.

The main branches of German public law are:

- state and constitutional law (*Staats- und Verfassungsrecht*);
- administrative law (*Verwaltungsrecht*);
- tax law (*Steuerrecht*);
- criminal law (*Strafrecht*);
- procedural law (*Prozeßrecht*);
- public international law (*Völkerrecht*).[2]

§ 40(i) VwGO gives access to the administrative court in all public law disputes of a non-constitutional nature, unless a federal statute expressly gives another court jurisdiction.

DISTINGUISHABILITY OF NORMS

There are various theories as to how to establish whether a particular norm falls within the area of private or public law, for example:

---

1 *Publicum ius est, quod ad statum rei Romanae spectat, privatum quod ad singulorum utilitatem* (attributed to Ulpian).

   See Baumann (ER), Part I, § 2 II 1; Rehbinder, Chapter II, § 13 I-III and Chapter IV, § 26, where codified law and case law are compared.

2 The various branches and statutes of public and private law are listed in the Appendix to Creifelds.

   See also Baumann (ER), Part I, § 2 II; Rehbinder, Chapter II, § 13 V and VI; Schwab (*Einführung*), Part I, Chapter 4.

- the interest theory, which asks if the norm serves the interests of the state or those of the individual;
- the subordination theory, which asks if the legal relationship between the parties is on equal terms (*auf der Grundlage der Gleichordnung*) or one of dominance and subordination (*Über- und Unterordnung*); and
- the modified subject or special rights theory (*Sonderrechtstheorie*), which asks if the norm necessarily only benefits or is directed at a carrier of public power (*ob eine Norm nur ein Träger öffentlicher Gewalt berechtigt oder verpflichtet*).[3]

Norms can also be distinguished according to whether they:

- are norms of material or formal law. Formal law (*formelles Recht*) deals with the application (*Anwendung*) and carrying out (*Durchsetzung*) of material law (*materielles Recht*), which contains the substantive provisions. Examples of formal law are procedural law (*Prozeßrecht/Verfahrensrecht*) and the law governing the various court jurisdictions (*Gerichtsbarkeiten*);
- are norms of federal or state law or norms with only more limited application ie those which are set by *Körperschaften* and *Anstalten*;
- are compulsory norms (*zwingende Normen*: *ius cogens*) or dispositive norms (*nachgiebige Normen/dispositives Recht*: *ius dispositivum*). Dispositive norms are largely to be found in private law, where the important principles of freedom of contract (*Vertragsfreiheit*) and private autonomy (*Privatautonomie*) prevail. Thus, the contract law of the BGB usually only applies in the absence of an agreement between free contracting parties;[4]
- emanate from statute/statutory instrument (*Gesetz*) or custom (*Gewohnheit*).

---

3 A critique of the various theories is contained in Maurer, § 3 III.

  See also: Bull, Section I, § 2 6; Creifelds under *Verwaltungsprivatrecht*; Rehbinder, Chapter II, § 13 IV; Wesel (FR), Chapter 5 (*Von der Vertikalen zur Horizontalen*); Chapter II (note 8) and Chapter XIX.

4 See Creifelds under *Vertrag* II and Chapter X, p 35 (*Privatautonomie*).

CHAPTER X

PRIVATE LAW: THE CIVIL CODE (BGB)[1]

INTRODUCTION

The Civil Code (*Bürgerliches Gesetzbuch*) of 18 August 1896 came into force on 1 January 1900.[2]

It is the most important source (*Quelle*) of Private law in Germany. It consists of 2,385 paragraphs divided into five books:[3]

Book I: *Allgemeiner Teil* (general part); §§ 1-240;

Book II: *Schuldrecht* (law of obligations); §§ 241-853;

Book III: *Sachenrecht* (law of property); §§ 854-1296;

Book IV: *Familienrecht* (family law); §§ 1297-1921; and

Book V: *Erbrecht* (law of succession); §§ 1922-2385.

Each Book (*Buch*) is divided into *Abschnitte* (sections), which are in turn subdivided into *Titel* (titles).

BOOK I: THE *ALLGEMEINER TEIL* (§§ 1-240 BGB)[4]

The key rules contained in Book I of the BGB (the *Allgemeiner Teil*); §§ 1-240) are valid for all the other books of the BGB and are of general application for the whole of German private law.

The *Allgemeiner Teil* (AT) is divided into seven sections.

Terminology to note

A knowledge of the following terminology is essential for an understanding of the BGB:

Die Rechtsfähigkeit

The capacity to be a carrier of rights and obligations (*die Fähigkeit, Träger von Rechten und Pflichten zu sein*).[5]

---

1   General summaries for initial reading can be found in Baumann, Part II (§§ 3-8) and Model/Creifelds/Lichtenberger, Part 3 F (302-362); Westermann (*Grundbegriffe*). See also Creifelds under *Bürgerliches Recht*.

2   For the historical background see: Chapter I; Laufs, Chapter IX, 2; Wesel (JW), Chapter VII. See also Köbler, § 7 B III.

3   See Baumann (ER), Part II, § 3; Kallwass, Section 1 (§§ 2-4); see also the diagram in Klunzinger (*Einführung*), Part I (§ 2, Section I; *Die im BGB geregelten Sachgebiete*).

4   See generally: Brox (AT); Creifelds; Kaiser, Part I; Kallwass, Section 1, § 8; Klunzinger (*Einführung*), Part II (§§ 4-20); Köhler; Löwisch; Model/Creifelds/Lichtenberger, Part 3 F (303-310); Rüthers; Schellhammer (ZR), Book 3 (Parts 33-43); Westermann (*Grundbegriffe*), Chapters 1-7.

5   See: Baumann (ER), Part II, § 5 I; Rüthers, Chapter 4, §§ 13-15; and the comments on the legal capacity of persons and the right to (use of) a name (§ 12 BGB) in the *Sourcebook*, Chapter 4 (following the *Injured Foetus Case*).

Die Rechtssubjekte *(legal subjects or persons)*[6]

Only *Rechtssubjekte* possess *Rechtsfähigkeit*. *Rechtssubjekte* are either natural persons (*natürliche Personen = Menschen*, ie humans) or juristic persons (*juristische Personen*). These concepts are dealt with in Section 1 of the *Allgemeiner Teil* (entitled *Personen*; §§ 1-89).

Die Rechtsobjekte *(legal objects)*[7]

A *Rechtsobjekt* is any thing/matter (*Gegenstand*) with which the law can concern itself.

If a *Gegenstand* is corporeal, it is known as a *Sache*. *Sachen* are dealt with in Section 2 of the *Allgemeiner Teil* (entitled *Sachen*; §§ 90-103).

Other *Rechtsobjekte* are *Immaterialrechtsgüter* (intellectual property) and *Rechte* (rights).

Unlike *Rechtssubjekte*, *Rechtsobjekte* have no rights and usually belong to *Rechtssubjekte*.[8]

Das subjektive Recht *(subjective (legal) right)*[9]

A *subjektives Recht* is conferred upon a person by the legal system (*Rechtsordnung*) to protect his interests.

A *subjektives Recht* is the legal power (*Rechtsmacht*) or legally protected interest (*rechtlich geschütztes Interesse*) of the individual, as opposed to the objective law (*das objektive Recht*), which is the sum total of all valid norms. It is to be distinguished from the so-called *Rechtsreflex* (legal reflex), which is the non-enforceable favouring of an individual by the legal system.

With certain exceptions, the state has a monopoly regarding the protection of a subjective legal right.[10]

6　See the diagrams in Baumann (ER), Part II (§ 5, Section V) and Klunzinger (*Einführung*), Part II, Chapter 1 (§ 4, Section I).

　　See also Köhler, Part 3, §§ 8-9; Rehbinder, Chapter II, § 14 I; Schwab (*Einführung*), Part II, Chapters 1-3.

　　A natural person can acquire rights before birth: see the *Injured Foetus Case* (*Sourcebook*, Chapter 4).

7　See Baumann (ER), Part II, § 6, Köhler, Part 4, §§ 10-11 and Rüthers, Chapter 3, §§ 10-12. See also the diagram in Kaiser, Section I, Chapter 9.

8　The *Rechtsobjekte* belonging to a *Rechtssubjekt* constitute its *Vermögen* (assets).

　　Subject to certain exceptions (§§ 850ff ZPO), the *Vermögen* is available for creditors. See Rüthers, Chapter 3, § 12, where the similarly vague (commercial) term *Unternehmen* (enterprise, business) is also explained.

9　Regarding the term *subjektives Recht*, see Rehbinder, Chapter II, § 14 II-IV; §§ 15-16; Rüthers, Chapter 2, § 4.

10　See Köhler, Part 2, § 7 and Rüthers, Chapter 2, § 8.

One speaks of the acquisition (*Erwerb*) and transfer (*Übertragung/Übergang*) of a subjective legal right and of limits (*Grenzen*) on its exercise.[11]

Subjective legal rights are divided into the following main types.[12] The first two are absolute rights (*absolute Rechte*), effective against everyone. The others are relative rights (*relative Rechte*), as they are only directed against individual persons within a particular legal relationship:

- *Herrschaftsrechte* (rights of dominance): they give power over *Gegenstände* (eg *Sachen*; they are then known as real rights (*dingliche Rechte*)). The most comprehensive *dingliches* (*Herrschafts-*)*recht* is *Eigentum* (ownership). Power over incorporeal things (eg *Ansprüche*) is known as *Inhaberschaft* (entitlement/ownership).

- *Persönlichkeitsrechte* (personality rights). A general right to one's personality is based on Article 2 of the Basic Law.

- *Ansprüche* (claims). An *Anspruch* is defined in § 194(i) BGB as *das Recht, von einem anderen ein Tun oder ein Unterlassen zu verlangen* (the right to demand an act or omission from another). A contractual *Anspruch* is known as a *Forderung* (§ 241 BGB).

An *Anspruch* must always have an *Anspruchsgrundlage* (basis), the conditions of which must all be fulfilled if the *Anspruch* is to be *begründet* (well-founded).[13]

---

11 Regarding the former two, see Rüthers, Chapter 2, § 6 and note 98 in this chapter; regarding the latter, see Rüthers, Chapter 2, § 7 and note 35 in this chapter.

12 See Baumann (ER), Part II, § 8 II; Köhler, Part 2, § 5 II; Rüthers, Chapter 2, § 5; Schwab (*Einführung*), Part III, Chapters 1-6. See also the diagram in Klunzinger (*Einführung*), Part II, Chapter 1 (§ 5, Section II; *Subjektive Rechte*).

Rehbinder (Chapter II, § 15) explains the distinction between an *Anspruch* and a subjective legal right. Whilst today the former (ie the remedy) is treated as flowing from the right, historically an *Anspruch* was the precursor of a subjective legal right. As a present day example of the *Schluß vom Anspruch auf das Recht*, Rehbinder refers to § 823(i) BGB.

13 Very many civil claims are based on *Anspruchsgrundlagen* contained in the norms (referred to as *Anspruchsnormen*) of the BGB.

However, the great majority of the norms of the BGB (indeed, all those in the *Allgemeiner Teil*) themselves do not form the basis for claims. They are merely accessory norms (*Hilfsnormen*), which supplement or modify the *Anspruchsnormen*. See Rehbinder, Chapter II, § 11.

An *Anspruchsnorm* can often be recognised by its formulation: usually, '*kann verlangen ...*' (can demand) or – as the counterpart of a right is an obligation (*Verpflichtung*) – '*ist verpflichtet ...*' (is obliged) or '*haftet für ...*' (is liable for).

An *Anspruch* can be distinguished according to whether it is:

- contractual (*schuldrechtlich*);
- real (*sachenrechtlich or dinglich*);
- based on family law (*familienrechtlich*); or
- based on the law of succession (*erbrechtlich*).

Apart from originating from an *Anspruchsnorm*, an *Anspruch* can also arise out of a *Rechtsgeschäft* (legal transaction) directly or be based on a supplementary principle developed outside the BGB (eg the principle of *culpa in contrahendo* ((cic) blame during (in the course of) (preliminary) negotiations (quasi-contract)) or *positive Vertragsverletzung* ((PVV) positive breach of contract)). ...

- *Gestaltungsrechte* (formulation rights). Their exercise enables their *Inhaber* to influence a particular legal situation (eg the right of challenge (*Anfechtung*), the right to give notice (*Kündigung*), the right of withdrawal/rescission (*Rücktritt*)).[14]
- *Gegenrechte* (counter-rights). These enable a defendant to negate an *Anspruch*. They are classified as *Einwendungen* and *Einreden*.[15]
- *Familienrechte* (family rights), eg parental rights.

Subjective rights exist both in private and public law (a public subjective right is a *subjektives öffentliches Recht*).[16]

Das Rechtsverhältnis

The legal relationship between *Rechtssubjekte* or between *Rechtssubjekte* and *Rechtsobjekte*. It gives rise to (subjective) legal rights and/or duties (*Rechte und Pflichten*).[17]

13...A lawyer, who has to check (*prüfen*) whether a person has an *Anspruch* (claim) against another person, must always ask himself: '*Wer will was, von wem, und woraus?*' (Who wants something, from whom, and based on what?).

See Brox (AT), Part III, § 30 II and III; Creifelds under *Anspruch* (and *actio*); Fikentscher, Introduction, § 1 I; Köhler, Part II, § 6 I; and Klunzinger (*Einführung*), Part I (§ 3, Section IV) where a table of important *Anspruchsgrundlagen* in the BGB is set out.

See also note 73 in this chapter below and Wesel (FR), Chapter 3 (*Allgemeine Begriffe*): Wesel explains that before *Windscheid* coined the term *Anspruch* in 1851, the prevalent thinking was in terms of particular procedural actions. He compares this with the present-day situation: today, an *Anspruch* is something which exists *außerhalb der Gerichte* (outside the courts) *von Mensch zu Mensch* (from person to person).

14 *Gestaltungsrechte* are subject to exclusion periods (*Ausschlußfristen*), ie they can only be exercised within certain statutory or contractually agreed time-limits. See Rüthers, Chapter 2, § 9 III.

15 *Einwendungen* are distinguished according to whether they are *rechtshindernd* (ie negate the very existence of an *Anspruch*) or rechtsvernichtend (ie destroy an *Anspruch*, which is acknowledged to exist). *Einreden* do not attack the *Anspruch* as such, but allege facts preventing it from being realised (*rechtshemmend*).

To make matters more complicated, the ZPO refers to both *Einwendungen* and *Einreden* as merely *Einreden*.

See Creifelds under *Einrede* and Klunzinger (*Einführung*), Part I, § 3 (Section IV), where the types (and examples) of *Einwendungen* and *Einreden* are set out. See also Köhler, Part 2, § 6.

16 See Chapter VIII, note 4 above and Maurer, Part 2, § 8 I. Maurer describes the *Fürsorgeunterstützung* case as a fundamental decision and refers to the problem of basic rights as *Leistungsrechte*.

17 Strictly speaking, *Rechte und Pflichten* (rights and duties) are the *Rechtsfolgen* (legal consequences) arising from a *Rechtssatz* (legal provision, ie one laid down in a *Gesetz* (statute)). A *Rechtsverhältnis* is, more correctly, (merely) a *Lebensbeziehung* (an actual relationship in everyday life).

The typical structure of a *Rechtssatz* is that particular *Rechtsfolgen* are attached (*geknüpft*) to and conditional on the fulfillment of a specific *Tatbestand* (substantive part/content (of a norm)). ...

Die Privatautonomie *(private autonomy (principle))*

It is a basic principle of the legal order *(Rechtsordnung)* that the individual is free to select and enter into legal relationships on such terms as he or she wishes. It incorporates the individual's freedom to conclude a legal transaction (such as a contract: *Vertragsfreiheit*).[18]

Das Rechtsgeschäft *(legal transaction)*[19]

A *Rechtsgeschäft* is composed of at least one *Willenserklärung* (declaration of will) and can be unilateral *(einseitig* eg a will) or multilateral *(mehrseitig* eg a contract). By means of a *Rechtsgeschäft*, a *Rechtssubjekt* can achieve a legal consequence *(Rechtsfolge)* and create or vary a legal relationship *(Rechtsbeziehung)* to another *Rechtssubjekt* or to a *Rechtsobjekt*.

Rechtshandlungen *(legal actions)*[20]

The term *Rechtsgeschäft* is part of the more general term *Rechtshandlung*. To be additionally distinguished are:

- a *Rechtshandlung* directed to achieving a factual consequence eg the setting of a time-limit, consent to an operation. This is an action similar to a *Rechtsgeschäft (rechtsgeschäftsähnliche Handlung)* and the provisions concerning *Geschäftsfähigkeit* and *Willenserklärungen* are applied analogously.

- a pure factual act *(Tathandlung* or *Realakt)*. Like a *Rechtsgeschäft*, it can lead to a legal consequence, not because of a *Willenserklärung*, but due to the general law eg statutory acquisition of ownership. However, it requires no *Geschäftsfähigkeit*.

---

17 ...For a proper understanding of German law, the (abstract) concepts of *Tatbestand* and *Rechtsfolge* are fundamentally important.

   For further details, see the discussion in Engisch, Chapter II. Engisch points out that a *Rechtssatz* lays down what ought to occur – it is a *Sollenssatz* and is usually expressed as an imperative (ie leads to *Pflichten*). A different type of *Rechtssatz* is one which consists of the grant *(Gewährung)* of a *subjektives Recht*. See also: Creifelds under *Rechtsverhältnis*; Chapter X (note 59) and Chapter XV (note 13).

18 *Vertragsfreiheit* is not unlimited: see Rüthers, Chapter 1, § 3; Kallwass, Section 2, Chapter 1 (§§ 9-12). See also Chapter IX above.

   For a critique of the problem of *Vertragsfreiheit*, see Wesel (FR), Chapter 3 *(Vertrag)*.

19 See generally: Brox (AT), Part II, §§ 4-27; Köhler, Part 5, §§ 12-22; Rüthers, Chapter 7; Schwab *(Einführung*, Part V. See also the diagram in Klunzinger *(Einführung)*, Part II, Chapter 2 (§ 7, Section IV; *Menschliches Handeln)* and the *Sourcebook*, Chapter 4 (Legal Transactions).

   For a discussion of the history and *Problematik* of the terms *Rechtsgeschäft* and *Willenserklärung* see Flume, Chapter I, § 2 4 and 5.

   Wesel defines the most important *Rechtsgeschäft* (the *Vertrag* (contract)) as '*die Verwandlung des Willens in Recht*' (the transformation of will into law). See Wesel (FR), Chapter 3 *(Vertrag)*.

20 As note 18 in this chapter. The concepts of *Rechtsgeschäft* and *Rechtshandlung* can also be translated as juristic act and legal act (as in Zweigert and Kötz, Part II A I (Chapter 31 I).

Die Geschäftsfähigkeit *(capacity to undertake a Rechtsgeschäft)*

Only natural persons are *geschäftsfähig* and can declare their will by means of a *Willenserklärung*. Thus, only natural persons can conclude a *Rechtsgeschäft* alone. The statutory representatives of persons not fully *geschäftsfähig* are their *gesetzliche Vertreter*.[21]

The provisions of the *Allgemeiner Teil* regarding *Rechtsgeschäfte* (§§ 104-185 BGB) (Section 3)

Geschäftsfähigkeit, *Willenserklärung* and *Rechtsfolge* form the main elements of a valid *Rechtsgeschäft*. *Rechtsgeschäfte* are dealt with in Section 3 of the *Allgemeiner Teil* (§§ 104-185).

Section 3 is divided into six titles:

Title 1: *Geschäftsfähigkeit* (capacity to undertake a *Rechtsgeschäft*); §§ 104-115.

Title 2: *Willenserklärung* (declaration of will); §§ 116-144.

Title 3: *Vertrag* (contract); §§ 145-157.

Title 4: *Bedingung* (condition). *Zeitbestimmung* (time provision); §§ 158-163.

Title 5: *Vertretung* (representation/agency). *Vollmacht* (power of attorney); §§ 164-181.[22]

Title 6: *Einwilligung* ((prior) consent). *Genehmigung* (approval); §§ 182-185.

Title 1

Although the BGB contains no specific provision to that effect, it proceeds on the basis that *Geschäftsfähigkeit* (the capacity to undertake a *Rechtsgeschäft*) commences with the age of majority (*Volljährigkeit*), which, by § 2, is 18 years.

The BGB distinguishes sharply between:

* persons who have no *Geschäftsfähigkeit* at all, referred to as *geschäftsunfähig*;
* those who enjoy limited *Geschäftsfähigkeit*, referred to as *beschränkt geschäftsfähig*; and
* those who are fully *geschäftsfähig*.[23]

§ 104 BGB defines those who are *geschäftsunfähig*, ie infants under seven and persons permanently mentally disturbed.

---

21 Examples of *gesetzliche Vertreter* are: parents of minors, guardians and members of an OHG.

    The organs of a *juristische Person* (juristic person) are not, strictly speaking, *gesetzliche Vertreter*: they act for the *juristische Person* itself and are not its representatives. However, the *Vorstand* (board of directors) of a *Verein* is treated as a *gesetzlicher Vertreter* (§ 26(ii) BGB) and the *Geschäftsführer* (director(s)) of a GmbH hold(s) a corresponding position (§ 35 GmbHG).

    See Creifelds under *Stellvertretung* (*Vertretungsmacht*); see also Chapter XI, note 24 in this chapter and Chapter XII, notes 18 and 25.

22 See Chapter XII (§§ 78-90 ZPO). The German law of representation and the position where there is an undisclosed principal is discussed by Zweigert and Kötz, Part II A I (Chapter 39 IV-VI).

23 See Zweigert and Kötz, Part II A I (Chapter 32 (entitled *Contractual Capacity*)).

The *Willenserklärung* of somebody who is *geschäftsunfähig* is void (*nichtig*), as is that declared (not received!) by a person in a state of unconsciousness or suffering from a temporary intellectual impairment (§ 105).

A child between seven and 18 years of age is a *Minderjähriger* (minor) and is *beschränkt geschäftsfähig* in accordance with §§ 107-113 (§ 106). As a result, to make a *Willenserklärung* he needs the prior consent (*Einwilligung*) of his parents, except if he receives merely a legal (not commercial!) advantage (*lediglich einen rechtlichen Vorteil*) from the transaction (§§ 107, 1629).[24]

Whilst the entry into a contract (*Vertrag*) by a minor involves him in obligations, his receipt of property (for example, by way of gift) is regarded as a legal advantage and requires no approval (*Zustimmung*).

§§ 108-110 deal with the position where a contract is concluded by a minor without prior consent. Its validity is then dependant on the subsequent consent (*Genehmigung*) of his parents, until which time it is referred to as being *schwebend unwirksam* ie its validity is in abeyance. If consent is refused, the contract is finally void. In the meantime, the other party has certain rights to demand a statement regarding the *Genehmigung* from the parents and to withdraw from the transaction (§§ 108(ii) and 109).

A contract concluded by a minor without approval is regarded as valid from the start, if the contractually required *Leistung* (performance) is (immediately) effected (*bewirkt*) with *Mitteln* (funds) given to him by his parents for that purpose or placed at his free disposal by his parents (or by a third party with their approval): so-called pocket-money, § 110. Prior consent is deemed to have been granted.

A contract with a minor can, therefore, be approved by parents before or after its conclusion. If it turns out to be void, that does not affect the property level (*sachenrechtliche Ebene*) of the transaction, which is abstract. However, the minor has been unjustly enriched: he has received something (*etwas*) without a legal basis (*ohne rechtlichen Grund*), the return of which (*Herausgabe*) the other party can claim (§ 812).

Although the fact that one is not or no longer enriched (§ 818(iii)) is usually a defence to such a claim, this does not apply in the event that there is bad faith (*Bösgläubigkeit*) on the part of the minor and he is unable to return the item due to his own fault (*Verschulden*): he is then liable for damages (§§ 818(iv), 819(i), 292, 990, 989: so-called *verschärfte Haftung*).[25]

The approval of the guardianship court is required, if parents or guardians wish to engage in certain property or other transactions for the child (§§ 1643, 1821, 1822).

---

24   See Zweigert and Kötz, Part II A I (Chapter 39 III) and Chapter XII, notes 18 and 25 below.
25   See note 96 in this chapter.

Title 2

§§ 116-144 contain a rag-bag of important provisions concerning

- the interpretation (*Auslegung*) of a *Willenserklärung* (§ 133);
- the challengeability (*Anfechtbarkeit*) and nullity (*Nichtigkeit*) of a *Willenserklärung/Rechtsgeschäft* (§§ 116-124, 125, 134, 138, 139-144);[26]
- the form of a *Rechtsgeschäft* (§§ 125-129);
- the validity of a *Willenserklärung* (ie the question of its making (*Abgabe*) and receipt (*Zugang*)) (§§ 130-132);
- the content (*Inhalt*) of a *Rechtsgeschäft* (§§ 134-138).

The term *Willenserklärung*

The BGB nowhere contains a definition of a *Willenserklärung*. Instead, it contains numerous provisions regulating the ability of a person to make a *Willenserklärung* and the validity, form, interpretation and content of a *Willenserklärung* and *Rechtsgeschäft*. Moreover, Section 3 of the *Allgemeiner Teil* (headed *Rechtsgeschäfte*) proceeds on the basis that a *Rechtsgeschäft*, also nowhere defined, consists of one or more *Willenserklärungen*; indeed, Title 2 is headed *Willenserklärung*.[27]

But what is a *Willenserklärung*?

The word itself indicates that a *Willenserklärung* has two components:[28]

1 the (internal) will (*Wille*) to bring about a legal consequence; and
2 the (external) declaration (*Erklärung*) showing what legal consequence is desired.

More exactly, one customarily says that the first component comprises the following elements:

- the *Handlungswille*, ie the will to act at all;
- the *Rechtsbindungswille*, ie the will to be legally bound by one's act; and
- the *Geschäftswille*, ie the will to engage in a particular transaction.[29]

The second component (the *Erklärung*) does not have to consist of a particular formulation.

---

26 Whilst §§ 116-124 BGB refer to the nullity and challengability of a *Willenserklärung*, §§ 125, 134, 138 and 139-144 BGB refer to the nullity of a *Rechtsgeschäft*. See also notes 37, 41 and 42 in this chapter.

A *Rechtsgeschäft*, which is *nichtig* ((null and) void), is referred to as being *absolut unwirksam* (absolutely ineffective). To be distinguished therefrom is a *Rechtsgeschäft*, which is *schwebend unwirksam* (in suspense (pending the consent (*Genehmigung*) of another person or authority), or a *Rechtsgeschäft*, which is *relativ unwirksam* (relatively ineffective). See Creifelds under *Unwirksamkeit eines Rechtsgeschäfts*.

27 References in Title 2 are sometimes to a *Willenserklärung* and sometimes to a *Rechtsgeschäft* (see the breakdown of §§ 116-144 at the beginning of Chapter X).

28 See Rüthers, Chapter 6, § 18; Creifelds under *Willenserklärung* I; Kallwass, Section 2, Chapters 2 and 3 (§§ 13-22).

29 See the comments under 'declaration of will' (the concept) in the *Sourcebook*, Chapter 4. An additional element is sometimes said to be the so-called *Erklärungsbewußtsein* (consciousness of the declaration), but the dominant school of thought does not regard this as essential.

A particular act can (and often does) constitute a *Willenserklärung* not only when it is expressed, but also when it is implied from conduct (*schlüssiges Verhalten*).[30] Silence (*Stillschweigen*) itself, however, does not, as a rule, suffice.[31]

If one of the two components is missing, there is no *Willenserklärung*. If the two components diverge, the *Willenserklärung* is either challengeable (*anfechtbar*) or void (*nichtig*).[32]

Validity of a *Willenserklärung*[33]

At what moment does a *Willenserklärung* become valid? The following rules apply:

- a *Willenserklärung* made to another person, who is absent, becomes effective from the moment of its receipt (*Zugang*; § 130(i));[34]
- a *Willenserklärung* made to a person having no or only limited *Geschäftsfähigkeit* is normally only valid if made to the persons statutory representative (§ 131).

When a *Willenserklärung* requires to be received by another person it is referred to as being *empfangsbedürftig*. A *nichtempfangsbedürftige Willenserklärung* only has to be placed into circulation (*abgegeben*), eg a will (*Testament*).

Interpretation of a *Willenserklärung*[35]

The BGB proceeds on the assumption that a *Willenserklärung* should only be challengeable (*anfechtbar*) by its maker in certain limited cases (§§ 119, 120 and 123) and that the upholding of a *Willenserklärung* (and consequent validity of the legal transaction) is desirable in the interests of legal certainty and clarity (*Sicherheit und Klarheit des Rechtsverkehrs*). (Beneficial) interpretation takes precedence over challengeability (*Auslegung geht Anfechtung vor*).

§ 133 sets out the general principle that a *Willenserklärung* should not be interpreted literally, but in accordance with the real will (*wirkliche Wille*) of the

---

30 Thus, a *Willenserklärung* exists, if a person making a declaration, acting with appropriate care and in accordance with business custom, could have perceived it as such and it was so understood by the recipient: see the *Unintended Declaration of Will Case* (*Sourcebook*, Chapter 4).

31 See note 49 below and the exceptions listed under declaration of will (the concept) in the Sourcebook, Chapter 4.

32 See Creifelds under *Willensmängel* and below under nullity and challengability of a *Willenserklärung*.

33 See Rüthers, Chapter 6, § 20; Kallwass, Section 2, Chapter 4 (§§ 23-24).

34 A preliminary requirement is that the person making the *Willenserklärung* could and did reckon with it reaching the correct recipient: see the *Misdirected Withdrawal Declaration Case* (*Sourcebook*, Chapter 4).

  Actual knowledge on the part of the recipient is not required. It suffices, if the *Willenserklärung* is in the area of control of the recipient (*Machtbereich des Empfängers*) and the recipient can fairly be expected to become aware of it.

35 See Rüthers, Chapter 6, § 19 and the comments under § 133 BGB and § 157 BGB in the *Sourcebook*, Chapter 4 and Chapter 5.

person involved. Surrounding circumstances can be taken into account, but only insofar as the interests of legal certainty and clarity allow, ie where a *Willenserklärung* is *empfangsbedürftig*, the recipient can only go by what is recognisable to her (*erkennbar*). It is her point of view that requires protection and counts if interpretation of a *Willenserklärung* becomes necessary (*Auslegung vom Empfängerhorizont*).

Always to be considered together with § 133 is § 157 BGB, which requires contracts to be interpreted in accordance with the principle of trust and good faith (*Treu und Glauben*) taking account of custom/common practice (*die Verkehrssitte*).[36]

---

36 See Zweigert and Kötz, Part II A I (Chapter 37 III).

The phrase *Treu und Glauben* is also used in § 242 BGB:

Der Schuldner ist verpflichtet, die Leistung so zu bewirken, wie Treu und Glauben mit Rücksicht auf die Verkehrssitte es erfordern. (The debtor is obliged to effect performance in such a manner as trust and good faith require, taking custom /common practice into account.)

§ 242 is one of the best known paragraphs of the BGB. See the comments under § 242 BGB in the *Sourcebook*, Chapter 5. Although, strictly, § 242 is a norm of the law of obligations and, in terms, only refers to the *Schuldner* (debtor), it is acknowledged to express a general legal principle (*allgemeiner Rechtsgrundsatz*) of *bona fides* (good faith) of application throughout the German legal system: persons must conduct themselves fairly when exercising their rights and performing their duties.

§ 242 is a general clause (*Generalklausel*), which can supplement, limit or amend the content of a claim (*Anspruch*). It does not itself constitute the basis for a claim (*Anspruchsgrundlage*). § 242 has three functions, as follows:

1   to supplement the duties (*Pflichten*) of parties to a *Schuldverhältnis* (the *Ergänzungs-funktion* (supplementary function));

2   to control and limit (*beschränken*) the exercise of rights (the *Kontrollfunktion* (control function)); and

3   exceptionally, to enable a correction and adaptation (*Anpassung*) of legal relationships and even the development of the law by the judiciary (*richterliche Rechtsfortbildung*) (the *Korrekturfunktion* (corrective function)).

Thus, under 1, parties to a contractual relationship have certain accessory or supplementary duties (*Nebenpflichten*), for example:

• a duty of consideration (*Rücksichtspflicht*) towards the other party;

• a duty of protection (*Schutzpflicht*) towards each other;

• a duty to give the other party necessary clarification (*Aufklärungspflicht*) and information (*Auskunftspflicht*);

• a duty of co-operation (*Mitwirkungspflicht*); and

• a general duty of faithful performance (*Leistungstreuepflicht*).

A breach of a *Nebenpflicht* is one of the main grounds for a claim for positive breach of contract (*positive Vertragsverletzung* (PVV)) and *culpa in contrahendo* (cic). See, respectively, in this chapter, note 73 and note 13. See also the *Allergy to Hair Tonic Case* in the *Sourcebook*, Chapter 5. …

Nullity and challengeability of a *Willenserklärung*[37]

Even if a *Willenserklärung* is clear, it can be void by operation of law (*nichtig*) or challengeable (*anfechtbar*) by its maker. One must always ask: are there any reasons for the nullity or challengeability of the *Willenserklärung*? (*Liegen Nichtigkeits- oder Anfechtungsgründe vor?*)

The consequence of the challenge (*Anfechtung*) of a *Willenserklärung* is that the *Willenserklärung* is regarded as void from the start (*von Anfang an nichtig*; § 142(i)).[38]

However, *Anfechtbarkeit* and *Nichtigkeit* are not the same: *Anfechtung* is a *Gestaltungsrecht* (formulation right), which must be exercised to be effective. Until then, the *Willenserklärung* is valid. If a *Willenserklärung* or *Rechtsgeschäft* is *nichtig*, it never had any effect.

A *Willenserklärung* is *nichtig* (void) in the following cases:

- incapacity (*Geschäftsunfähigkeit*; § 105);

- if the necessary subsequent consent (*Genehmigung*) to a contract entered into by a minor is not forthcoming (§ 108(i));

- if the person making the *Willenserklärung* is conscious of one of the following circumstances:

  - he has a mental reservation (*geheimer Vorbehalt*) about what he is declaring and the other party knows this (§ 116);[39]

---

36 ...Under 2, it constitutes a prohibited exercise of a right (*unzulässige Rechtsausübung*; also referred to as an abuse of a right (*Rechtsmißbrauch*)):

- if the exercise of the right is disproportionate (*unverhältnismäßig*), excessive (*übermäßig*) or grossly unjust (*grob unbillig*);

- if the person seeking to exercise the right would thereby benefit from his own prior dishonest conduct (*unredliches früheres Verhalten*); or

- if the person seeking to exercise the right would thereby place himself in conflict with his prior conduct (*venire contra factum proprium*). A sub-category here is the legal institute of *Verwirkung* (the forfeiture of a right (of the claimant)).

Under 3, § 242 has been used to permit a flexible reaction in abnormal situations (the German hyperinflation in 1923), in cases of the *Wegfall der Geschäftsgrundlage* (falling-away (collapse) of the basis of the transaction) and in times of legal emergency (*Rechtsnotstand*). See Klunzinger (*Einführung*), Part III, § 24 I; Brox (AS), Chapter 4, § 6; Medicus (AT), Part 3, § 16.

37 In both cases *Willensmängel* (defects of will) exist: the *Willenserklärung* is defective (*fehlerhaft*). See Rüthers, Chapter 7, § 24.

38 The wording of § 142 BGB (which refers to an *anfechtbares Rechtsgeschäft*) is incorrect, as only a *Willenserklärung* is challengeable (see: §§ 119, 120 and 123 BGB).

Because of the abstraction principle, *Anfechtung* usually only affects the validity of the obligational transaction (the *Verpflichtungsgeschäft*); the property level remains abstract. Restitution is effected via the law of unjust enrichment (§§ 812ff BGB). See, in this chapter, notes 25, 58 and 96.

39 A reservation (*Vorbehalt, protestatio*) must be declared to be effective. No account is taken of it if it does not accord with the external circumstances: *protestatio facto contraria* (*non valet*). See Creifelds under *Willenserklärung* and the *Bus Station Case* (*Sourcebook*, Chapter 5).

- he is making the *Willenserklärung* with the agreement of the other party only for the sake of appearance (*nur zum Schein*; § 117);
- the *Willenserklärung* is not meant seriously and he expects the other party to realise that (§ 118).

In order to safeguard the interests of legal certainty and clarity, the *Anfechtung* (challenge) of a *Willenserklärung* is subject to various restrictions:

- a *Willenserklärung* can only be challenged on certain statutory grounds (*Anfechtungsgründe*), which are:[40]
  - mistake (*Irrtum*); § 119, distinguished by the BGB into three types: *Inhaltsirrtum* (mistake as to content/meaning), *Erklärungsirrtum* (mistake in the declaration itself) and (in § 119(ii)) *Eigenschaftsirrtum* (mistake as to a particularly important quality of the person or thing concerned);
  - false transmission (*falsche Übermittlung*; § 120);
  - fraudulent deceit (*arglistige Täuschung*) or illegal threat (*widerrechtliche Drohung*) of or to the person making the *Willenserklärung*; § 123.
- the *Anfechtung* must be declared; § 143(i);
- the *Anfechtung* must be exercised within a particular time-limit (*Anfechtungsfrist*); §§ 121(i) and 124(i). In the case of §§ 119 and 120, this must be forthwith (*unverzüglich*), ie without blameworthy delay (*ohne schuldhaftes Zögern*) and in the case of § 123, within a year.
- the *bona fide* recipient of a *Willenserklärung* challenged under § 119 or § 120 is entitled to compensation for the damage suffered in reliance on the validity of the declaration (§ 122).

Form and nullity of a *Rechtsgeschäft*

The BGB distinguishes four forms for a *Rechtsgeschäft*:

- writing as required by statute (*gesetzliche Schriftform*; § 126);
- writing as desired by the parties to the *Rechtsgeschäft* (*gewillkürte Schriftform*; § 127);
- notarial documentation (*notarielle Beurkundung*; § 128);
- public certification (*öffentliche Beglaubigung*; § 129).[41]

  A *Rechtsgeschäft* is *nichtig* (void):

- if it lacks the necessary statutory form (§ 125, 1st sentence);[42]

---

40 See Creifelds under *Anfechtung von Willenserklärungen*. See also Zweigert and Kötz, Part II A I (Chapter 38 (entitled *Mistake, Deceit, and Duress*)) and the comments under §§ 119–123 BB in the *Sourcebook*, Chapter 4.

41 See Creifelds under *Form(erfordernisse, -vorschriften)*. The requirement of a particular form (*Formzwang*) in a statute serves various purposes: see Rüthers, Chapter 7, § 23 I–V.

42 This is the rule; exceptions are very limited. See: Rüthers, Chapter 7, § 23 VII; Zweigert and Kötz, Part II A I (Chapter 34 (entitled *Formal Requirements*)); and the comments under §§ 125–127 BGB in the *Sourcebook*, Chapter 4.

- if it is itself the object of a statutory prohibition (*gesetzliches Verbot*) and contravenes it (§ 134);

- if it is *sittenwidrig*, ie breaches good morals (*gute Sitten*); § 138(i).[43]

Title 3

The term *Einigung*

If two or more *Willenserklärungen* correspond (*übereinstimmen*), the parties are said to have reached a consensus or agreement (*Einigung*).[44]

The conclusion of a contract (*Vertrag*) usually depends on an *Einigung* (this is clear from §§ 154 and 155).[45]

An *Einigung* can be achieved by mere joint statement or, more commonly, by exchange of offer (*Angebot*) and acceptance (*Annahme*). It is this means of reaching an *Einigung* that is dealt with in §§ 145-157.[46]

§§ 145-157 only handle the question of how an *Einigung* is reached by offer and acceptance. They do not deal with the questions of the content (*Inhalt*), form or legal consequences (*Rechtsfolgen*) of an *Einigung*, ie:

- on what points must the *Willenserklärungen* of the parties correspond?

- does the *Einigung* require a particular form?

- what duties (*Pflichten*) result?

The particular provisions of each area of law (contract, property, family, succession, company) contain the replies to these questions.

Rules governing offer and acceptance

By § 145, an offeror is bound to his offer (*Angebot*)[47] unless, as is commonly done, he excludes his liability by such phrases as *freibleibend* (subject to availability) or *ohne Obligo* (without obligation).

An offer expires (*erlischt*) if it is refused (*abgelehnt*). If, however, it is desired to accept an offer, the acceptance (*Annahme*)[48] must:

- usually be declared in some form; and

- reach the offeror in time (*rechtzeitig*; § 146), ie immediately (*sofort*) where both parties are present or within such a period as the offeror can expect

---

43 See: Rüthers, Chapter 7, § 25 I and III; Zweigert and Kötz, Part II A I (Chapter 35 (entitled *Illegality and Immorality*)); and the comments under § 138 BGB in the *Sourcebook*, Chapter 4.

44 The term *Willensübereinstimmung* (correspondence of *Willenserklärungen*) is also used.

45 Exceptionally, a contract can be concluded in certain cases of so-called alternative conduct (*sonstiges Verhalten*) eg where an expired contract is merely continued (*fortgesetzt*) or where the conclusion of the contract is effected by silence. See Chapter X (Rules governing offer and acceptance).

46 See Rüthers, Chapter 8, § 27.

47 Referred to in §§ 145-153 BGB as Antrag. See Zweigert and Kötz, Part II A I (Chapter 33 (entitled *Offer and Acceptance*) IV and V). See also the comments under § 145 BGB in the *Sourcebook*, Chapter 5.

48 Like an offer, it is an *empfangsbedürftige Willenserklärung*.

under normal circumstances (*unter regelmäßigen Umständen*) or as he may specify (§§ 147 and 148).

If the acceptance is delayed (*verspätet*) or contains additions, restrictions or other amendments (*Erweiterungen, Einschränkungen oder sonstige Änderungen*), it is deemed to be a new offer (in the latter case, together with a refusal of the original offer) from the accepting party (§ 150).

Exceptionally, it is possible for a contract to be concluded without an acceptance being declared, if such a declaration is not customarily to be expected (*nach der Verkehrssitte nicht zu erwarten*, eg booking of an hotel room) or is waived by the offeror (§ 151).[49]

However, some form of acceptance is always required and silence or inaction (*Schweigen; Nichtstun*) does not suffice, unless:

- it is agreed upon between the parties as having the effect of an acceptance; or

- the person to whom the offer is made is a businessman (*Kaufmann*), in which case he must, in certain circumstances, reply forthwith (*unverzüglich*) if he is not to be bound.[50]

Failure to reach an *Einigung*

The BGB contains two difficult provisions (§§ 154 and 155) dealing with so-called *Einigungsmängel* (*Dissens*), ie the situation where the parties do not reach a fully matching consensus (*Einigung*).

When considering §§ 154 and 155, one must bear in mind that a contract (*Vertrag*) can contain both:

- *wesentliche Bestandteile* (essential components; *essentialia negotii*): if the parties fail to reach agreement on points essential to the particular contract, their relationship is one of *Total-dissens* (total disagreement) – §§ 154 and 155 do not refer to this situation; and

- *Nebenpunkte* (accessory points), ie those points on which, in accordance with the declared will of at least one party, an *Einigung* is necessary. Here, §§ 154 and 155 lay down certain rules of interpretation (*Auslegungsregel*) in the event of doubt (*im Zweifel*, ie where the situation cannot be clarified):

---

49 Thus, relationships can be construed as contracts on the basis of pure factual conduct (*tatsächliches Verhalten*) or socio-typical behaviour (*sozialtypisches Verhalten*), even in the absence of an express declaration (of acceptance): see the *Hamburg Parking Case* and the *Bus Station Case* (*Sourcebook*, Chapter 5).

However, this doctrine (established in 1943 by Haupt) is open to the criticism that it runs contrary to the principle that persons who are not *geschäftsfähig* require protection (*Schutz des Nichtgeschäftsfähigen*). See: Brox (AS), Chapter 3, § 4 III; Creifelds under *Faktischer Vertrag* and *Schuldverhättnis*; Rüthers, Chapter 8, § 27 IV.

50 This is the case in the circumstances laid down in § 362 HGB and where a *Kaufmann* receives a commercial letter of confirmation (*kaufmännisches Bestätigungsschreiben*). However, an *Auftragsbestätigung* (confirmation of order) is merely the same as an acceptance. See Creifelds under *Bestätigungsschreiben* and *Vertrag* I.

- if an *Einigungsmangel* is *offen* (open), ie both parties are aware that the outstanding point(s) still require(s) to be agreed, the contract is deemed not to have been concluded; § 154;

- if an *Einigungsmangel* is *versteckt* (hidden), ie the parties conclude a contract unaware that the outstanding point(s) is or are still outstanding, the parties are deemed to have agreed the contract as it stands, so far as can be assumed that the contract would also have been concluded without agreement on the outstanding point(s); § 155.

The situation which § 155 has in mind is that where the wording in an agreement is objectively ambiguous and each of the parties attaches a different meaning to it. It is to be distinguished from the situation where the parties merely use a false description of an item and in fact mean the same thing (*falsa demonstratio (non nocet)*).

Title 4

The term *Bedingung* (condition) as contained in §§ 158-163 is used solely in the sense of a future uncertain event (*zukünftiges ungewisses Ereignis*). It can be either *aufschiebend* (suspensive) or *auflösend* (resolutive) in effect.[51]

The conditions contained in a contract (*Vertrags-* or (*Allgemeine*) *Geschäftsbedingungen*)[52] or laid down by law (*Rechtsbedingungen*) are not *Bedingungen* in the sense of §§ 158-163.

Also to be distinguished is the term *Zeitbestimmung* (time provision; § 163), which refers to the specification of a date or time for the start or end of a *Rechtsgeschäft*.

The prime example of a suspensive condition is purchase under reservation of title (*Eigentumsvorbehalt*), where the purchaser only becomes owner on condition of full payment of the purchase price. Until then, he has a so-called *Anwartschaftsrecht* (right of expectancy)[53] and is protected against hindering acts by the other party (vendor):

- if in the meantime the other party frustrates or impairs his future right by his (the other party's) *Verschulden* (fault), he can claim damages (§ 160);

- if the other party undertakes a *Verfügung* over the item in the meantime (eg purports to transfer title again to someone else), the *Verfügung* has no effect against him (§ 161);[54]

and

- if in bad faith (*wider Treu und Glauben*) the other party prevents the condition coming into effect, it is deemed to have come into effect (§ 162).

---

51 Regarding the different types of *Bedingung* and their legal consequences see Rüthers, Chapter 8, § 28 II and IV.

52 Regarding *Allgemeine Geschäftsbedingungen* see: Klunzinger (*Einführung*), Part II, § 10 III; Schwab (*Einführung*), Part V, Chapter 5; Zweigert and Kötz, Part II A I (Chapter 31 III). See also Creifelds under *Allgemeine Geschäftsbedingungen* and the comments regarding the AGBG under § 242 BGB in the *Sourcebook*, Chapter 5.

53 See p 72 at (d).

54 *Aliter* in the event of *bona fide* acquisition.

The rest of the *Allgemeiner Teil* (§§ 186-240 BGB) (Sections 4-7)

The remaining sections of the *Allgemeiner Teil* are as follows:

Section 4. *Fristen* (time limits). *Termine* (time periods); §§ 186-193.

Section 5. *Verjährung* (limitation); §§ 194-225 (see Exposé).

Section 6. *Ausübung der Rechte* (exercise of rights). *Selbstverteidigung* (self-defence). *Selbsthilfe* (self-help); §§ 226-231.

Section 7. *Sicherheitsleistung* (provision of (suitable forms of) security: §§ 232-240.

Exposé: *Verjährung* (§§ 194-225 BGB) (Section 5)

- By § 194(i) BGB an *Anspruch* is subject to *Verjährung* (limitation). Certain claims are, however, not so subject and are *unverjährbar*, eg those relating to the land register (§§ 898, 902).

  Verjährung constitutes a *Leistungsverweigerungsrecht*, ie it gives the debtor the right to decline performance (§ 222(i)). However, if the debtor wishes to rely on it in proceedings, it must be raised by him, ie it is a so-called *Einrede* and not an *Einwendung* (which the court takes into account of its own accord).

- The actual limitation periods (*Verjährungsfristen*) are set out in §§ 195-197 BGB. By § 195 the normal *Verjährungsfrist* is 30 years.

  §§ 196-197 lay down a short limitation period (*kurze Verjährung*) for certain claims. Thus, by § 196(i) No 1, a two year limitation period applies to claims of *Kaufleute* (businessmen), *Fabrikanten* (manufacturers) and *Handwerker* (manual workers) concerning delivery of goods (*Waren*) and carrying out of work (*Arbeiten*) or other persons business (*fremde Geschäfte*), unless with regard to the business of the recipient (in which case a four year period applies; § 196(ii)).

  Other persons whose claims are subject to the two year limitation period include freight and shipping companies (§ 196(i) No 3), innkeepers (No 4), private employees (No 8), doctors, dentists and lawyers (Nos 14 and 15).

  Outstanding amounts of interest, rent, and pensions become statute-barred after four years (§ 197).

  The normal limitation period of 30 years begins when the *Anspruch* arises (§ 198, first sentence). The *kurze Verjährung* of two or four years begins with the end of the year in which the *Anspruch* arises (§ 201, first sentence).

- In certain cases, *Verjährung* is prevented from running (*gehemmt*), eg where a creditor grants a respite (*Stundung*)[55] where faulty work carried out under a

---

55 In the absence of contrary arrangement or provision regarding the time for performance (*Leistungszeit*), performance can be required by the creditor or undertaken by the debtor immediately (*sofort*): § 271(i) BGB.

If the debtor has an immediate duty to perform (*Leistungspflicht*), the *Leistung* is referred to as being *fällig* (due). By means of a *Stundung*, the *Fälligkeit* (time at which the *Leistung* is due) of the *Leistung* can be postponed. See Klunzinger (*Einführung*), Part III, Chapter 2 (§ 26 I) and Creifelds under *Leistungszeit*.

contract of service (*Werkvertrag*) needs to be rectified or during marriage in the case of claims between spouses (§§ 202-207 and 639(ii)).

Alternatively, *Verjährung* can be interrupted (*unterbrochen*), eg by the debtors acknowledgement of debt (*Anerkenntnis*), by the issue of a writ (*Klage*) or service of a default notice (*Mahnbescheid*), by a claim of set-off (*Aufrechnung*) or issue of a 3rd party notice (*Streitverkündung*) in proceedings or by acts of enforcement (*Vollstreckungshandlungen*); §§ 208-216.

The effect of such an interruption (*Unterbrechung*) is that the period up to it is not taken into account and that after it ends a (full) new *Verjährung* begins; § 217.

* A debtor who satisfies an *Anspruch*, which has become statute-barred, has no right of reclaim, even if he did not know of the *Verjährung* (§ 222(ii)). However, the *Verjährung* of an *Anspruch* does not prevent a mortgagee or chargee from enforcing his mortgage or charge (§ 223(i)).

Whilst by agreement a limitation period can be shortened, *Verjährung* cannot be excluded or rendered more difficult (§ 225).

BOOK II: THE LAW OF OBLIGATIONS
(§§ 241-853 BGB)[56]

Introduction

Book II of the BGB is entitled *Recht der Schuldverhältnisse* (law of obligations). It consists of seven Sections, which are traditionally divided into a general part (*Allgemeiner Teil* (AT): Sections 1-6, §§ 241-432) and a special part (*Besonderer Teil* (BT): Section 7, §§ 433-853).

The general part sets out, for example, the principles governing the content, disturbance and termination of contracts, damages and assignment, while the special part sets out in 25 titles provisions regarding various individual types of contract – which apply in the absence of contrary agreement - and statutory obligations.

Points to note

It is important to understand the following:

1 The main example of a *rechtsgeschäftliches Schuldverhältnis* is the *Vertrag* (agreement or contract).[57]

2 German law distinguishes rigidly between the law of obligations (*Schuldrecht*) and the law of property (*Sachenrecht*).

---

56 For further information, see generally: Creifelds; Kaiser, Parts II-IV; Klunzinger (*Einführung*), Parts III and IV (§§ 21-57); Brox (AS) and (BS); Medicus (AT) and (BT); Model/Creifelds/Lichtenberger, Part 3 F (311-332a); Fikentscher; Schellhammer (ZR), Books 1 and 2 (Parts 1-32); Schlechtriem (AT) and (BT); Westermann (*Grundbegriffe*), Chapters 8 to 13.

57 See 3 below. See also Zweigert and Kötz, Part II A I (Chapter 31 II).

By means of the abstraction principle (*Abstraktionsgrundsatz*), the *Verpflichtung* (obligation) of a *Rechtssubjekt* (legal subject or person) is strictly separated from his *Verfügung*, ie his transfer, release, burdening or variation of a (subjective) right (*Übertragung, Aufhebung, Belastung oder Änderung eines Rechtes*). Both are *Rechtsgeschäfte*, but are independent of each other.[58]

The sale of a book, for example, requires not only an obligatory contract, but also the transfer of ownership (*Übereignung*). Only when the latter (abstract) transaction is concluded, is the former performed (*erfüllt*).

By § 433(i) first sentence BGB the contract of sale (*Kaufvertrag*) of a *Sache* obliges the vendor to do two things:

- transfer physical possession of (ie hand over) the *Sache* = *Übergabe*; and
- ensure that *Eigentum* (ownership) over the *Sache* passes to the purchaser = *Verschaffung von Eigentum*.

The *Kaufvertrag* itself merely creates a *Verpflichtung* (obligation). The actual transfer of ownership (the *Übereignung* (a *Verfügung*)) is dealt with separately in Book III of the BGB according to whether movables (§§ 929-984) or immovables (§§ 873 and 925-928) are concerned.[59]

In this connection, it is vital to understand the construction of the BGB and its norms (the *Gesetzesaufbau*):

- whether or not a valid *Rechtsgeschäft* (eg a *Kaufvertrag*) has been concluded is the domain of the *Allgemeiner Teil* (Book I), which supplements the rest of the BGB and deals with general questions first (such matters are said to be *vor die Klammer gezogen* (drawn before the clasp);
- the usual pattern of German legal norms is that, first, the content (*Tatbestand*) of the norm – a particular *Voraussetzung* ((pre)condition; in § 433(i) first sentence the existence of a *Kaufvertrag*) – is stated and, second, a particular legal consequence (*Rechtsfolge*; in § 433(i) first sentence the *Verpflichtung* of the vendor) is laid down.[60]

3 *Schuldverhältnisse* (obligations) can arise either from (*aus*) a *Rechtsgeschäft* (so-called *rechtsgeschäftliche Schuldverhältnisse*, eg *Vertrag*)[61] or from statute.

---

58 See the diagrams in Klunzinger (*Einführung*), Part II, Chapter 2 (§ 9, Section II; *Kausale und abstrakte Rechtsgeschäfte* and *Abstraktionsprinzip*) and Chapter X *post*. See also Kallwass, Section 2, Chapter 5 (§ 25) and Schwab (*Einführung*), Part V, Chapter 2.

59 See Wesel (FR), Chapter 3 (Kauf). See also: Chapter X (the components of a transfer of ownership).

60 In order to assess whether the application (*Anwendung*) of a legal provision (*Rechtssatz*) or norm is possible in a particular case, one must interpret the relevant provision/norm (*Auslegung*) and establish whether the *Sachverhalt* (set of facts) involved can be subsumed under it (so-called *Subsumtion*).

See Baumann (ER), Part I, § 4; Engisch, Chapters III to V; Klunzinger (*Einführung*), Part I, § 3 I-II; Löwisch, §§ 4 and 5, pp 9-15; Rehbinder, Chapter II, § 12; Schwab (*Einführung*), Part I, Chapter 1 D. See also: Chapter X (Note 13); Chapter X (note 17; Chapter XV (note 13); Creifelds under *Auslegung* (Interpretation) I and *Rechtsanwendung*.

61 A *Schuldverhältnis aus Rechtsgeschäft* can be *einseitig begründet* (based on the declaration of (only) one participant) – the sole example being an *Auslobung* (public offer of reward; § 657 BGB) – or, usually, *zwei- oder mehrseitig begründet* (based on the declarations of two or more participants) – as in the case of a *Vertrag* (see § 305 BGB). ...

Examples of statutory obligations (*gesetzliche Schuldverhältnisse*) are torts (*unerlaubte Handlungen*)[62]

and unjust enrichment (*ungerechtfertigte Bereicherung*).[63]

Sections 1-7[64]

Section 1 (§§ 241-304 BGB)[65]

Section 1 of Book II (§§ 241-304) deals with the *Inhalt* (content) of *Schuldverhältnisse* (obligations) and is divided into two titles:

61...A *Vertrag* can be distinguished according to whether it is:

- contractual (*schuldrechtlich*). Such a *Vertrag* can be:
  - *einseitig verpflichtend* (unilaterally obliging), the sole example being a *Schenkungsversprechen* (promised gift; § 518 BGB);
  - usually, *zwei- oder mehrseitig verpflichtend* (bilaterally or multilaterally obliging). The latter type of *Vertrag* is, in turn, classified as either:
    — *gewöhnlich* (usual) or *unvollkommen* (incomplete); or
    — *gegenseitig* (reciprocal) or *synallagmatisch.* (synallagmatic).
- based on the law of property (*sachenrechtlich* or *dinglich*);
- based on family law (*familienrechtlich*);
- based on the law of succession (*erbrechtlich*); or
- based on public law (*öffentlich-rechtlich*), rather than on private law (*privatrechtlich*).

Regarding the fields in which a *Vertrag* can be found and the types of *Vertrag*, see Creifelds under *Vertrag* III, IV and V.

Whereas a *Rechtsgeschäft* requires *Geschäftsfähigkeit*, the parties to a *Schuldverhältnis* need only be *rechtsfähig*: see Creifelds under *Schuldverhältnis*.

Schuldverhältnisse are classified in detail in *Fikentscher*, Section 1, Subsection 2, §§ 10-13 and in Section 8, Introduction, § 64.

62 Dealt with in §§ 823-853 BGB. A detailed comparative study of the German law of tort is contained in Zweigert and Kötz, Part II C (Chapters 47-50).

63 Dealt with in §§ 812-822 BGB. A detailed comparative study of the German law of unjust enrichment is contained in Zweigert and Kötz, Part II B (Chapters 45 and 46; see also Chapter 36 IV).

64 The following description of the arrangement of Sections 1-7 of Book II of the BGB is broad and cursory. It is intended as a framework for the English-speaking beginner, for whose purposes I consider that it suffices.

In order to understand the system of Sections 1-7, the reader is recommended to compare my (unofficial) groupings of §§ 241-853 BGB with the text of the BGB itself. A study of each individual paragraph (in conjunction, if required, with a German textbook and/or commentary) is unavoidable, if further explanation is desired.

The content of this Note is similarly applicable not only to my coverage of the other parts of the BGB, but also to my treatment of other German statutes in this book.

65 See Klunzinger (*Einführung*), Part III, Chapter 2 (§§ 24-26).

Title 1: *Verpflichtung zur Leistung* **(duty (of the** *Schuldner* **(debtor)) to perform): §§ 241-292.**

The term *Leistung* has no equivalent usage in English. In German legal speech it expresses the content of a *Schuldverhältnis* (obligation), ie what is owed.

A *Schuldverhältnis* gives rise to a *Leistungsverpflichtung* or *-pflicht* (duty of performance) on the part of a *Schuldner* (debtor).

The counterpart of the *Leistung(-spflicht)* owed by the *Schuldner* is the right or entitlement (*das Recht/die Berechtigung*) of the *Gläubiger* (creditor) to demand (*fordern*) it/performance (§ 241). This right is, accordingly, referred to as a (*schuldrechtliche*) *Forderung* ((contractual) claim or demand). If the *Gläubiger* himself owes a reciprocal *Leistung*, it is referred to as a *Gegenleistung* (counter-performance), eg the price payable by a purchaser.

When using the term *Leistung* it should be borne in mind that it can be used to mean both the performance (result) owed by the *Schuldner* (debtor) – the *Leistungserfolg* – and the conduct (*Verhalten*) or omission (*Unterlassen*) due from him (the *Leistungshandlung*). The *Leistung* referred to in § 241 BGB is the *Leistungshandlung*.

Moreover, there is a basic difference in legal meaning between the term *Leistung* and the term *Erfüllung* (§ 362(i)), both of which can be translated as performance. When the BGB refers to *Erfüllung* it has the technical meaning of the (proper) fulfilment (performance) by the *Schuldner* of his *Leistungspflicht*,[66] as a result of which the individual claim (*Anspruch*) of the *Gläubiger* (creditor) against the *Schuldner* is extinguished.[67]

Title 2: *Verzug des Gläubigers* **(delay of the creditor); §§ 293-304.**

* * * * *

Arrangement of Titles 1 and 2

§§ 241-304 can be arranged into the following groups:

---

66 As § 362(i) BGB puts it, the *Bewirkung* (effecting) of the *Leistung*, ie the *Leistungserfolg*.

67 In § 362(i) BGB the word *Schuldverhältnis* is meant in this (narrow) sense: see Fikentscher, Section 4, § 38 I 3.

Regarding the meaning of the term *Schuldverhältnis*, see, for example, Brox (AS), Chapter 2, § 2, see eg Brox (AS), Chapter 2, § 2 and Fikentscher, Section 1, Subsection 1 (± 7 1).

A *Schuldverhältnis* is to be distinguished from a *Gefälligkeitsverhältnis* (a relationship of grace and favour), which is merely socially, but not legally, binding. See Chapter X (the term *Willenserklärung*).

Regarding the meaning of the term *Leistung*, see *Fikentscher*, Section 1, Subsection 1 (§ 8).

Regarding the special meaning of the term *Leistung* in §§ 812ff BGB and its meaning in § 326 BGB, see under *Leistung* in Appendix A.

A check-list for determining the content of a *Schuldverhältnis* (*aus Rechtsgeschäft*) is set out in Fikentscher, Section 3, § 26 V and X.

Title 1

§§ 241-242   *Leistungspflicht* (duty of performance)

§§ 243-245   *Leistungsgegenstand* (object of performance)

§ 243:   *Gattungsschuld* (generic debt)[68]

§§ 244-245:   *Geldschuld* (money debt)[69]

§§ 246-248   *Zinsen* (interest (on the debt))

§§ 249-255   *Schadensersatz* (damages)[70]

§ 249:   *Art und Umfang des Schadensersatzes* (type and extent of damages)

§ 250:   *Schadensersatz in Geld nach Fristsetzung* (damages in money after setting a time-limit)

§ 251:   *Schadensersatz in Geld ohne Fristsetzung* (damages in money without setting a time-limit)

§ 252:   *Entgangener Gewinn* (lost profit)

§ 253:   *Immaterieller Schaden* (non-financial loss)

§ 254:   *Mitverschulden* (contributory fault (on the part of the injured party))

§ 255:   *Abtretung der Ersatzansprüche* (assignment of compensation claims)

§§ 256-257   *Aufwendungsersatz* (compensation for expenditure)[71]

§ 258   *Wegnahmerecht (bei Herausgabepflicht)* (right of removal (from a thing which has to be returned))

§§ 259-261   *Auskunftspflicht* (duty of information)

§§ 262-265   *Wahlschuld* (selectable (alternative) debt)[72]

§ 266   *Teilleistungen* (partial performance)[73]

§§ 267-268   *Leistung durch Dritte* (performance by a third party)

§§ 269-270   *Leistungsort; Zahlungsort* (place of performance; place of payment)

§§ 271-272   *Leistungszeit* (time of performance)

§§ 273-274   *Zurückbehaltungsrecht* (right of retention (withholding))

§§ 275-283   *Leistungsstörungen* (disturbances in performance)[74]

---

68   See, for example, Brox (AS), Chapter 4, § 7 I.
69   *Ibid* Chapter 4, § 8 I.
70   See, for example, Brox (AS), Chapter 7, §§ 24-27.
71   *Ibid* Chapter 4, § 9.
72   See, for example, Brox (AS), Chapter 4, § 7 II.
73   *Ibid* Chapter 4, § 11 and § 12 I.
74   A *Schuldverhältnis* gives rise to a *Leistungsverpflichtung* on the part of the *Schuldner* (§ 241 BGB; see above). ...

§§ 284-290   *Verzug des Schuldners* (delay on the part of the debtor)

§§ 284-285:   *Voraussetzungen* (pre-conditions)

§§ 286-290:   *Rechtsfolgen* (legal consequences)

– replacement of damage resulting from delay (*Verzugsschaden*); § 286

74...If the *Schuldner* does not carry out the *Leistung* (performance) required of him – usually by *Erfüllung* – there is a *Leistungsstörung* (disturbance in performance).

The BGB only deals with two types of *Leistungsstörung*:

* *Unmöglichkeit* (impossibility); the BGB distinguishes between *anfängliche* (initial) and *nachträgliche* (subsequent) *Unmöglichkeit*; and

* *Verzug* (delay); the BGB distinguishes between *Verzug des Schuldners* (delay on the part of the debtor) and *Verzug des Gläubigers* (delay on the part of the creditor).

Outside the BGB, the principle of *positive Vertragsverletzung* (PVV; positive breach of contract) and the doctrine of the (*Wegfall der*) *Geschäftsgrundlage* ((falling-away (collapse) of the) basis of the transaction) were developed to handle situations requiring relief not falling within impossibility or delay.

A claim seeking a remedy for positive breach of contract (PVV) requires an existing *Schuldverhältnis* (obligation) – *rechtsgeschäftlich* or *gesetzlich* – and is mainly used in cases of *Schlechtleistung* (bad performance) and *Verletzung einer Nebenpflicht* (breach of an accessory duty). PVV is excluded, if a claim under a *Gewährleistungsvorschrift* (guarantee provision) of the BGB is available, as, for example, in a contract of sale (*Kauf*) or rental (*Miete*).

The liability (*Einstehenmüssen/Haftung*) of a *Schuldner* for a *Leistungsstörung* usually depends on the *Schuldners Verschulden* (also referred to as *Vertretenmüssen*). The question is: is the *Leistungsstörung* the fault of (due to) the *Schuldner* (*von ihm zu vertreten*)?

The civil law concept of *Verschulden* is defined in § 276 BGB: insofar as there is no different provision, a *Schuldner* is liable for *Vorsatz* (intent) and for *Fahrlässigkeit* (negligence).

Apart from being a component of most *Leistungsstörungen*, *Verschulden* is a condition for liability under the (unwritten) principle of *culpa in contrahendo* (cic; see notes 13 and 76 in this chapter) and also a requirement for a claim in tort (*unerlaubte Handlung*; §§ 823 ff BGB).

In certain cases, there is, exceptionally, *Haftung ohne Verschulden* (ie the *Schuldner* is liable without *Verschulden*/in any event), eg for faulty goods (under §§ 459 ff BGB) – so-called *Erfolgshaftung* (liability for the result) – or for the various situations in which *Gefährdungshaftung* (strict liability) is laid down by statute (eg in cases of road and rail traffic and cases of liability for damage caused by animals).

The BGB contains complex rules setting out the consequences for the *Schuldner* of a *Leistungsstörung* and the effect of a *Leistungsstörung* in the case of a *gegenseitiger Vertrag* (reciprocal/synallagmatic contract), ie the position (and rights) of the *Gläubiger* (creditor) and the fate of his *Gegenleistung* (counter-performance).

See generally: §§ 275-304, 306-309 and 320-327 BGB; Creifelds under *Leistungsstörungen*, *Unmöglichkeit der Leistung, Schuldnerverzug, Gläubigerverzug, Verschulden, Haftung, Positive Vertragsverletzung, Geschäftsgrundlage, Gefährdungshaftung* and *Gegenseitiger Vertrag*. Regarding *Gefährdungshaftung* see also the comments under *Strict Liability and Animals* in the *Sourcebook*, Chapter 6.

See also the very detailed coverage of the topic of *Leistungsstörungen* in Zweigert and Kötz, Part II A I (Chapter 43 (entitled *Breach of Contract*) and Chapter 44 (entitled *The Effect of Supervening Events*)) and the innumerable German textbooks and commentaries on *Schuldrecht* (*Allgemeiner Teil*), eg: Brox (AS), Chapter 6, §§ 18-23; Fikentscher, Section 5 (§§ 41-48); Kallwass, Section 3, Chapter 2 (§§ 41-45); Medicus (AT), Part 5 (§§ 28-46).

- extended liability during delay (*erweiterte Haftung*); § 287

- interest during delay (*Verzugszinsen*); §§ 288-290

§§ 291-292   *Lage des Schuldners nach Rechtshängigkeit* (position of the debtor once a matter is *sub judice*)

Title 2

§§ 293-304   *Verzug des Gläubigers* (delay on the part of the creditor)

§§ 293-299:   *Voraussetzungen* (pre-conditions)

§§ 300-304:   *Rechtsfolgen* (legal consequences)

Section 2 (§§ 305-361 BGB)

Section 2 of Book II (§§ 305-361) deals with obligations arising out of *Verträge* (contracts) (ie so-called *rechtsgeschäftliche Schuldverhältnisse*) and is divided into five titles:

Title 1:   *Begründung* (establishment (of a *rechtsgeschäftliche* obligation by means of a *Vertrag*); *Inhalt* ((content) of the *Vertrag*); §§ 305-319.

Title 2:   *Gegenseitiger Vertrag* (reciprocal/synallagmatic contract); §§ 320-327.

Title 3:   *Versprechen der Leistung an einen Dritten* (promise of performance for the benefit of a third party); §§ 328-335.

Title 4:   *Draufgabe* (bonus); *Vertragsstrafe* (contractual penalty); §§ 336-345.

Title 5:   *Rücktritt* (rescission); §§ 346-361.

Arrangement of Titles 1-5

§§ 305-361 can be arranged into the following groups:

Title 1

§ 305   *Begründung* (establishment)[75]

§§ 306-307   *Anfängliche Unmöglichkeit; Ersatz des Vertrauensschadens* (initial (objective) impossibility; compensation for damage suffered due to reliance on the validity of the contract)

§ 308   *Vorübergehende Unmöglichkeit* (temporary impossibility)

§ 309   *Gesetzwidriger Vertrag* ((corresponding application of §§ 307-308 to a contract contrary to statute)

§§ 310-312   *Verträge über künftiges oder gegenwärtiges Vermögen oder über den Nachlaß eines lebenden Dritten* (contracts regarding future or present assets or the estate of a living third party)

§ 313   *Form der Verpflichtung zur Veräußerung oder zum Erwerb eines Grundstücks* (form of an agreement for the sale or purchase of a piece of land)

---

75   See, for example, Brox (AS), Chapter 3, § 3 I and § 4 I.

§ 314   *Erstreckung auf Zubehör* (extension (of a contract) to accessories)

§§ 315-316   *Bestimmung der Leistung (Gegenleistung) durch eine Partei* (specification of performance (or counter-performance) by one party)[76]

§§ 317-319   *Bestimmung der Leistung durch einen Dritten* (specification of performance by a third party)

Title 2

§ 320   *Einrede des nichterfüllten Vertrags* (objection to (right to decline) performance until counter-performance is effected)

§ 321   *Vermögensverschlechterung* (right to decline performance where an obligation to perform in advance (*Vorleistungspflicht*) exists and there is a deterioration in the other party's assets)

§ 322   *Folgen der Einrede* (procedural consequences of the objection; judgment *Zug um Zug* (one against the other))

§§ 323-325   *Nachträgliche Unmöglichkeit* (subsequent impossibility – effect on the *Gegenleistung*; position of the other party)

§ 326   *Verzug; Fristsetzung mit Ablehnungsandrohung* (delay; setting of a time-limit with threat of rejection)

§ 327   *Anwendbarkeit der §§ 346-356 beim gesetzlichen Rücktritt* (application of §§ 346-356 to the statutory right of rescission)

Title 3

§ 328   *Vertrag zugunsten Dritter* (contract for the benefit of a third party)[77]

§§ 329-332   *Auslegungsregel* (rules of interpretation)

§ 329:   *Erfüllungsübernahme* ((internal) promise of performance)

---

76   See, for example, Brox (AS), Chapter 4, § 5 II.

77   *Ibid* Chapter 8, § 28. See also Zweigert and Kötz, Part II A I (Chapter 41 (entitled *Contracts for the Benefit of Third Parties*)).

A variation of the *Vertrag zugunsten Dritter* is the concept of the *Vertrag mit Schutzwirkung zugunsten Dritter* (contract with protective effect in favour of a third party). See Creifelds under *Vertrag zugunsten Dritter*.

In the *Fall in the Supermarket Case* (*Sourcebook*, Chapter 5) the defendant would have been liable under the principle of *culpa in contrahendo* to the mother of the plaintiff child, had the mother herself been injured. As it was, the plaintiff was able to base her (contractual) claim for breach of accessory duties (*vertragliche Nebenpflichten*) on her mothers (precontractual) position: there was a *Vertrag mit Schutzwirkung zugunsten Dritter*.

The motivation for this outcome lay in the different limitation periods for claims in contract and tort (§ 195 as against § 852 BGB) and the reversal of the burden of proof (§ 282 BGB).

The *Termination of Negotiations Case* (*Sourcebook*, Chapter 5) is an illustration of the application of the principle of *culpa in contrahendo* where precontractual negotiations are broken off without good reason.

Another fruitful area for claims based on *culpa in contrahendo* is negligent misrepresentation.

§ 330:	*Lebensversicherungsvertrag* (life insurance contract)
§ 331:	*Leistung nach Todesfall* (performance after death of the promisee)
§ 332:	*Änderung durch Verfügung von Todes wegen bei Vorbehalt* (substitution of the third party by the promisee is also possible in a *Verfügung von Todes wegen*, if the right is reserved)

§§ 333-335	Miscellaneous
§ 333:	*Zurückweisung des Rechts durch den Dritten* (rejection of the right by the third party)
§ 334:	*Einwendungen des Schuldners* (objections by the promisor (debtor))
§ 335:	*Forderungsrecht des Versprechensempfänger* (right of the promisee to demand performance)

Title 4

§§ 336-338	*Draufgabe* (bonus)
§§ 339-345	*Vertragsstrafe* (contractual penalty)[78]

Title 5

§§ 346-361 apply directly only in the case of a right of rescission being reserved in a contract (*Rücktrittsvorbehalt*). However, their main importance is their corresponding application (*entsprechende Anwendung*) to statutory rights of rescission (§§ 327, 467, 634(iv); also §§ 280(ii), 286(ii)).[79]

§§ 346-349	*Wirkung; Haftung; Erklärung* (effect of rescission; liability; requirement of an *Erklärung* (declaration))
§§ 350-353	*Ausschluß des Rücktritts* (exclusion of rescission)
§§ 354-355	*Fristsetzung für Rückgewähr; Fristsetzung für die Ausübung des Rücktrittsrechts* (setting of a time-limit for return of the relevant item; setting of a time-limit for the exercise of the right of rescission)
§ 356	*Mehrere Beteiligte* (exercise of the right of rescission by or against several persons)
§§ 357-361	*Rücktritt in besonderen Lagen* (rescission in special situations):
§§ 357-358	(*wegen Nichterfüllung* (for non-performance))
§ 359	(*gegen Reugeld* (on payment))
§ 360	(*Verwirkungsklausel* (in the case of a forfeiture clause))

---

78 See, for example, Brox (AS), Chapter 4, § 10.
79 *Ibid* Chapter 5, § 17.

§ 361   (in the case of a *relatives Fixgeschäft* (a (relative) time-related transaction)

* * * * *

Section 3 (§§ 362-397 BGB)[80]

Section 3 of Book II (§§ 362-397) deals with the *Erlöschen* (extinction/discharge/ ending) of obligations and is divided into four titles:

Title 1:   *Erfüllung* (fulfilment/performance); §§ 362-371.

Title 2:   *Hinterlegung* (deposit); §§ 372-386.

Title 3:   *Aufrechnung* (set-off); §§ 387-396.

Title 4:   *Erlaß* (remission of debt); § 397.

* * * * *

Arrangement of Titles 1-4

§§ 362-397 deal with the *Beendigung* (ending) of *Schuldverhältnisse* (and thereby the extinction of the relevant *Ansprüche* (claims)) by the *Befriedigung* (satisfaction) of the creditor's interest in performance.

Events which, broadly speaking, can also cause a *Schuldverhältnis* (or *Anspruch*) to end or which have other consequences are:

- §§ 142: *Anfechtung* (challenge)
- *Kündigung*: (termination by notice (for the future))
- § 158: *Eintritt einer auflösenden Bedingung* (occurrence of a resolutive condition)
- § 163: *Zeitablauf* (lapse of time)
- § 242: *Verwirkung* (forfeiture)
- § 305: *Aufhebungsvertrag* (contrary agreement) or *Novation* (novation)
- §§ 275ff, 323ff: *Leistungsstörung* (disturbance in performance)
- §346FF: *Rücktritt* (rescission).

Titles 1-4 can be arranged into the following groups:

Title 1: *Erfüllung*

§§ 362-363   *Wirkung* (effect); *Beweislast* (burden of proof)

§§ 364-365   *Leistung an Erfüllungs Statt* (performance in lieu)

§§ 366-367   *Anrechnung* (credit)

---

80   See: Klunzinger (*Einführung*), Part III, Chapter 3 (§§ 32-33); Brox (AS), Chapter 5, §§ 13-16; Fikentscher, Section 4 (§§ 38-40).

§§ 368-371   *Pflichten des Gläubigers* (duties of the creditor)

§§ 368-370:   *Quittung* (receipt)

§ 371:   *Rückgabe des Schuldscheins* (return of document confirming the debt)

Title 2: *Hinterlegung*

§§ 372-375   *Voraussetzungen* (pre-conditions); *allgemeine Vorschriften* (general conditions)

§§ 376-377   *Rücknahmerecht* (right of reclaim)

§§ 378-379   *Wirkung der Hinterlegung* (effect of deposit)

§§ 380-382   *Nachweis und Erlöschen des Gläubigerrechts; Kosten* (proof and extinction of the creditors right; costs)

§§ 383-386   *Selbsthilfeverkauf durch Versteigerung; Kosten* (self-help sale by auction; costs)

Title 3: *Aufrechnung*

§§ 387-388   *Voraussetzungen* (preconditions); *Erklärung* (declaration)

§ 389   *Wirkung* (effect)

§§ 390-395   *Ausschluß durch Gesetz* (exclusion (by statute))

§ 396   *Mehrere Forderungen* (several claims)

Title 4: *Erlaß*

§ 397   *Wirkung* (effect)

*   *   *   *   *

Section 4 (§§ 398-413 BGB)

Section 4 of Book II (§§ 398-413) deals with the *Übertragung* (transfer) of a *Forderung* (claim) by means of a contract of *Abtretung* (assignment).[81]

§§ 398-413 can be arranged into the following groups:

§ 398   *Begriff* (definition); *Wirkung* (effect)

§§ 399-400   *Ausschluß* (exclusion)

§ 401   *Übergang von Neben- und Vorzugsrechte* (transition of accompanying and preferential rights)

§§ 402-403   *Pflichten des (bisherigen) Gläubigers* (duties of the (previous) creditor)

§§ 404-411   *Schuldnerschutz* (protection of the debtor)

§ 412   *Gesetzlicher Forderungsübergang* (assignment by operation of law)

§ 413   *Übertragung anderer Rechte* (transfer of other rights)

---

81   See, for example, Brox (AS), Chapter 8, § 29. See also Zweigert and Kötz, Part II A I (Chapter 40 (entitled *Assignment*)).

Section 5 (§§ 414-419 BGB)

Section 5 of Book II (§§ 414-419) deals with *Schuldübernahme* (substitution).[82]

§§ 414-419 can be arranged into the following groups:

§§ 414-415	*Vereinbarung des Übernehmers entweder mit dem Gläubiger oder mit dem Schuldner* (agreement between the third party and either the creditor or the debtor)
§ 416	*Übernahme einer Hypothekenschuld* (assumption of a mortgage debt)
§ 417	*Einwendungen des Übernehmers* (objections by the third party)
§ 418	*Erlöschen von Sicherungs- und Vorzugsrechten* (extinction of security and preferential rights)
§ 419	*Vermögensübernahme* (assumption of assets); *Haftung des Übernehmers* (liability of the third party)

Section 6 (§§ 420-432 BGB)

Section 6 of Book II (§§ 420-432) is entitled *Mehrheit von Schuldnern und Gläubigern* (multitude of debtors and creditors).[83]

§§ 420-432 can be arranged into the following groups:

§ 420	*Teilbare Leistung* (divisible performance)
§ 421	*Gesamtschuldner* (joint debtors)
§§ 422-425	*Wirkung* (effect) of *Erfüllung* (performance), *Erlaß* (remission of debt), *Gläubigerverzug* (delay on the part of the creditor) and *anderer Tatsachen* (other facts) for or against joint debtors
§ 426	*Innenverhältnis* (internal relationship); *Ausgleich* (indemnity)
§ 427	*Auslegungsregel* (rule of interpretation) in the case of a *teilbaren Leistung* (divisible performance)
§§ 428-430	*Gesamtgläubiger* (joint creditors)
§§ 431-432	*Unteilbare Leistung* (indivisible performance); *Mitgläubiger* (co-creditors)

Section 7 (§§ 433-853 BGB)[84]

Section 7 of Book II (§§ 433-853) deals with the typical individual *Schuldverhältnisse* (both *rechtsgeschäftliche* and *gesetzliche*) and is arranged into 25 titles as follows:

Title 1:	*Kauf* (purchase); *Tausch* (exchange); §§ 433-515.
Title 2:	*Schenkung* (gift); §§ 516-534.

---

82 See, for example, Brox (AS), Chapter 8, § 30.

83 *Ibid* Chapter 9, §§ 31-33.

84 See generally: Creifelds; Kaiser, Parts III and IV; Klunzinger (*Einführung*), Part IV (§§ 43-57); Brox (BS); Medicus (BT); Model/Creifelds/Lichtenberger, Part 3 F (315-332).

Title 3:   *Miete* (tenancy/lease); *Pacht* (commercial lease); §§ 535-597.

Title 4:   *Leihe* (gratuitous loan); §§ 598-606.

Title 5:   *Darlehen* (loan); §§ 607-610.

Title 6:   *Dienstvertrag* (contract of services); §§ 611-630.[85]

Title 7:   *Werkvertrag* (contract of service); *Reisevertrag* (travel contract); §§ 631-651k.

Title 8:   *Maklervertrag* ((civil) agency contract); §§ 652-656.

Title 9:   *Auslobung* (public offer of reward); §§ 657-661.

Title 10:   *Auftrag* ((gratuitous) contract of instruction); §§ 662-676.

Title 11:   *Geschäftsführung ohne Auftrag* (transaction (of a matter) without instruction); §§ 677-687.

Title 12:   *Verwahrung* (deposit in custody); §§ 688-700.

Title 13:   *Einbringung von Sachen bei Gastwirten* (bringing in of things at a *Gastwirtschaft* (inn)); §§ 701-704.

Title 14:   *Gesellschaft* (company); §§ 705-740.

Title 15:   *Gemeinschaft* (community); §§ 741-758.

Title 16:   *Leibrente* (annuity, pension for life); §§ 759-761.

Title 17:   *Spiel* (game); *Wette* (bet); §§ 762-764.

Title 18:   *Bürgschaft* (contract of surety); §§ 765-778.

Title 19:   *Vergleich* (settlement); § 779.

Title 20:   *Schuldversprechen* (promise); *Schuldanerkenntnis* (acknowledgement of debt); §§ 780-782.

Title 21:   *Anweisung* (documentary instruction); §§ 783-792.

Title 22:   *Schuldverschreibung auf den Inhaber* (promissory note); §§ 793-808a.

Title 23:   *Vorlegung von Sachen* (presentation for inspection); §§ 809-811.

Title 24:   *Ungerechtfertigte Bereicherung* (unjust enrichment); §§ 812-822.

Title 25:   *Unerlaubte Handlungen* (torts); §§ 823-853.[86]

*   *   *   *   *

Arrangement of Title 1

§§ 433-515 are arranged as follows:

Allgemeine Vorschriften *(general provisions)*; *§§ 433-458*

§ 433:   *Grundpflichten des Verkäufers und Käufers* (basic duties of vendor and purchaser)

---

85 See Chapter XVII (note 43).

86 Regarding the law of torts, see generally: the comments under § 823 BGB in the *Sourcebook*, Chapter 6; Kötz; Schwab (Einführung), Part IV, Chapters 2-8; Kallwass, Section 3 (§§ 34-38).

§ 434:   *Gewährleistung wegen Rechtsmängel* (liability for legal faults (title))

§§ 435-436:   *Nicht bestehende Buchbelastungen; Öffentliche Lasten bei Grundstücken* (non-existent registered charges; public charges over land)

§§ 437-438:   *Verkauf einer Forderung oder sonstigen Rechtes* (sale of a claim or other right)

§ 439:   *Kenntnis des Käufers vom Rechtsmangel* (the purchaser's knowledge of a legal fault)

§§ 440-441:   *Rechte des Käufers* (rights of the purchaser)

§§ 442-444:   *Beweislast für Rechtsmängel; Ausschluß der Gewährleistung (für Rechtsmängel); Nebenpflichten des Verkäufers* (burden of proof of legal faults; exclusion of liability (for legal faults); the vendor's (statutory) accessory duties)

§ 445:   *Ähnliche Verträge* (similar contracts)

§§ 446-447:   *Übergang des Preisgefahrs; Nutzungen; Lasten* (transition of (price) risk; benefit; burden)

§§ 448-450:   *Nebenpflichten des Käufers* (the purchaser's (statutory) accessory duties)

§ 451:   *Entsprechende Anwendung von §§ 446-450 bei Rechtskauf* (corresponding application of §§ 446-450 to the sale of a right to a thing)

§ 452:   *Verzinsung des Kaufpreises* (interest on the purchase price)

§ 453:   *Marktpreis* (market price)

§ 454:   *Ausschluß des Rücktrittsrechts* (exclusion of the right of rescission)

§ 455:   *Eigentumsvorbehalt* (retention of title)

§§ 456-458:   *Kaufverbote* (forbidden purchases)

Gewährleistung wegen Mängel der Sache (*liability for faulty goods*): §§ 459-493

§ 459:   *Haftung für Sachmängel* (liability for faulty goods)

§ 460:   *Kenntnis des Käufers* (knowledge of the purchaser)

§ 461:   *Pfandverkauf* (sale on the basis of a lien: vendor's liability)

§§ 462-465:   *Rechtsfolgen* (legal consequences)

§ 466:   *Ausschlußfrist für Wandlung* (exclusion period for rescission)

§ 467:   *Anwendbare Vorschriften bei der Durchführung der Wandlung* (provisions applicable to rescission)

§§ 468-471:   *Wandlung in besonderen Lagen* (rescission in particular situations)

§ 472:   *Berechnung der Minderung* (calculation of reduction in price)

§§ 473-475:   *Minderung in besonderen Lagen* (reduction in price in particular situations)

               Sachleistungen als Kaufpreis (performance in kind); § 473

Mehrere Beteiligte (several parties); § 474

Mehrmalige Gewährleistung (repeated liability); § 475

§ 476: *Vertraglicher Ausschluß der Gewährleistung* (contractual exclusion of liability)

§ 476a: *Aufwendungen beim Recht auf Nachbesserung* (vendor's liability for costs where a right to request repair is substituted)

§ 477: *Verjährung* (limitation period)

§§ 478-479: *Lage nach Verjährung bei vorheriger Mängelanzeige* (supervening limitation)

§ 480: *Gattungskauf* (generic purchase)

§§ 481-492: *Viehkauf usw* (sale of cattle etc)

§ 493: *Kaufähnliche Verträge* (similar contracts)

Besondere Arten des Kaufes *(special types of purchase); §§ 494-514*

Kauf nach Probe, Kauf auf Probe (purchase by sample, purchase on approval)

§ 494: *Kauf nach Probe* (purchase by sample)

§§ 495-496: *Kauf auf Probe* (purchase on approval)

Wiederkauf (repurchase)
§§ 497-503

Vorkauf (pre-emption)
§§ 504-514

Tausch *(exchange); § 515*

*   *   *   *   *

Arrangement of Title 2
§§ 516-534 are arranged as follows:

§§ 516-517: *Begriff* (definition)

§§ 518-520: *Schenkungsversprechen* (promised gift)

§§ 521-524: *Haftung des Schenkers* (liability of the donor)

§§ 525-527: *Schenkung unter Auflage* (direction by the donor)

§§ 528-534: *Rückforderung; Widerruf der Schenkung* (claim to return of the gift; revocation)

*   *   *   *   *

Arrangement of Title 3
§§ 535-597 are arranged as follows:

Miete *(lease/tenancy); §§ 535-580a*

§§ 535-536: *Begriff; Pflichten der Parteien* (definition; duties of the parties)

§§ 537-541: *Haftung des Vermieters für Mängel* (lessor's liability for faults)

§§ 541a-541b: *Maßnahmen zur Erhaltung/Verbesserung* (tenant must tolerate measures of maintenance and improvement)

§§ 542-544: *Fristlose Kündigung durch den Mieter* (termination without notice by the lessee)

§ 545: *Mängelanzeige* (notice of faults)

§ 546: *Lasten der Mietsache* (lessors liability for charges)

§ 547: *Ersatz von Verwendungen* (compensation for lessees expenditure)

§ 547a: *Wegnahme von Einrichtungen* ((lessee's right of) removal of fixtures)

§ 548: *Abnutzung durch vertragsmäßigen Gebrauch* (wear and tear)

§ 549: *Untermiete* (sub-letting)

§ 550: *Vertragswidriger Gebrauch* (use in breach of agreement)

§ 550a: *Vertragsstrafe unwirksam* (invalidity of contractual penalty)

§ 550b: *Mietkaution* (deposit (for residential premises))

§§ 551-552a: *Entrichtung des Mietzinses* (payment of rent)

§§ 553-554b: *Fristlose Kündigung durch den Vermieter* (termination without notice by the lessor/landlord)

§ 556: *Rückgabe der Mietsache* (return of the rental object)

§§ 556a-556c: *Widerspruch des Mieters; Fortsetzung des Mietverhältnisses* (objection by the tenant (to termination of a tenancy of residential premises); continuation of the tenancy)

§ 557: *Ansprüche bei verspäteter Rückgabe* ((lessor's) rights in the event of delayed return of the rental object)

§ 558: *Verjährung* (limitation period (for claims))

§§ 559-563: *Vermieterpfandrecht* (landlord's lien)

§ 564: *Ende des Mietverhältnisses* (end of the lease/tenancy)

§§ 564a-564b: *Form und Voraussetzungen der Kündigung* (form of and requirements for termination (of tenancy of residential premises))

§ 564c: *Fortsetzung* (continuation (of a tenancy of residential premises))

§ 565: *(Ordentliche) Kündigungsfristen* (time-limits for (ordinary) termination (of tenancy of premises)/lease (of movables))

§ 565a: *Verlängerung* (extension (of tenancy of residential premises))

§§ 565b-565e: *Werkunterkünfte* (works accommodation)

§ 566: *Form des Mietvertrags* (form of tenancy agreement (of more than one year))

§ 567: *Kündigung bei Verträgen für mehr als 30 Jahre* (termination of agreements for more than 30 years)

§ 568: *Stillschweigende Verlängerung* (tacit extension (of lease))

§ 569: *Kündigung bei Tod des Mieters* (termination following death of tenant)

§§ 569a-569b: *Ehegatten; Familienangehörige* ((position of) married couples/family members (following death of tenant))

§ 570: *Versetzung des Mieters* (tenant's job transfer)

§ 570a: *Vereinbartes Rücktrittsrecht* ((corresponding application to) contractual right of rescission)

§§ 571-576: *Veräußerung (eines vermieteten Grundstücks)* (disposal of rented property)

§ 577: *Belastung des Mietgrundstücks* (incumbrances over rented property)

§ 578: *Veräußerung vor Überlassung* (disposal before rental)

§ 579: Weiterveräußerung (further disposal)

§§ 580-580a: *Zusätzliche Geltung der Vorschriften* (additional application of the provisions)

Pacht (commercial lease); §§ 581-584b
§§ 581-584b

Landpacht (agricultural lease); §§ 585-597
§§ 585-597

* * * * *

Arrangement of Title 4
§§ 598-606 are arranged as follows:

§ 598: *Begriff* (definition)

§§ 599-600: *Haftung des Verleihers* (liability of the lender)

§§ 601-604: *Rechte und Pflichten des Entleihers* (rights and duties of the borrower)

§ 605: *Kündigung* (termination)

§ 606: *Kurze Verjährung* (short limitation period)

* * * * *

Arrangement of Title 5
§§ 607-610

* * * * *

Arrangement of Title 6
§§ 611-630 are arranged as follows:

§ 611: *Begriff* (definition)

§§ 611a-611b: *Diskriminierung durch einen Arbeitgeber* ((prohibition of) discrimination (by an employer)

§ 612: *Vergütung* (reimbursement, payment)

§ 612a: *Weiteres Benachteiligungsverbot* (further prohibition of discrimination (by an employer))

§ 613: *Persönliche Rechte und Pflichte im Dienstvertrag* (personal rights and duties in a contract of services)

§ 614: *Fälligkeit der Vergütung* (time at which payment is due)

§§ 615-616: *Vergütung ohne Dienstleistung* (payment where services are not rendered)

§§ 617-619: *Schutzpflichten des Dienstherrn* (duties of protection)

§ 620: *Ende des Dienstverhältnisses* (end of the relationship)

§§ 621-622: *Ordentliche Kündigungsfristen* (time-limits for (ordinary) termination)

§ 624: *Kündigung bei Verträgen von mehr als 5 Jahren* (termination of contracts for more than five years)

§ 625: *Stillschweigende Verlängerung* (tacit extension)

§§ 626-628: *Fristlose Kündigung* (termination without notice)

§§ 629-630: *Rechte und Pflichte nach Beendigung* (rights and duties after expiry)

* * * * *

Arrangement of Title 7

§§ 631-651k are arranged as follows:

Werkvertrag *(contract of service)*

§§ 631-632: *Begriff* (definition); *Vergütung* (reimbursement)

§ 633: *Leistungspflicht des Herstellers* (duty of manufacturer); *Beseitigung des Mangels* (correction of the defect)

§§ 634-636: *Sekundäre Rechte bei erfolgloser Nachbesserung* (secondary rights in the event of unsuccessful repair)

§ 637: *Vertraglicher Ausschluß der Haftung* (contractual exclusion of liability)

§§ 638-639: *Kurze Verjährung* (short limitation period)

§§ 640-641: *Abnahme des Werkes* (acceptance of the work)

§§ 642-643: *Mitwirkung des Bestellers* (cooperation by the customer)

§ 644: *Übergang der Gefahr* (transition of risk)

§ 645: *Teilvergütungsanspruch* (claim to partial reimbursement)

§ 646: *Vollendung statt Abnahme* (completion instead of acceptance)

§§ 647-648: *Sicherung des Unternehmers* (security for the manufacturer)

§ 649: *Kündigung durch den Besteller* (termination by the customer)

§ 650:   *Überschreitung eines Kostenanschlags* (exceeded estimate)

§ 651:   *Werklieferungsvertrag* (contract for delivery of a work)

Reisevertrag *(travel contract)*

§§ 651a-651b: *Begriff* (definition); *Teilnahme eines Dritten* (participation of a third party)

§§ 651c-651g: *Rechte des Reisenden* (rights of the traveller)

§ 651h: *Haftungsbeschränkung* (restriction of liability)

§ 651i: *Rücktritt vor Reisebeginn* (rescission before commencement of travel)

§ 651j: *Kündigung wegen höherer Gewalt* (termination due to force majeure)

§ 651k: *Abweichende Vereinbarungen* (divergent agreements)

*   *   *   *   *

Arrangement of Title 8
§§ 652-656

*   *   *   *   *

Arrangement of Title 9
§§ 657-661

*   *   *   *   *

Arrangement of Title 10
§§ 662-676 are arranged as follows:

§ 662:   *Begriff* (definition)

§ 663:   *Anzeigepflicht bei Ablehnung* (duty to notify refusal)

§§ 664-668: *Rechte und Pflichte des Beauftragten* (rights and duties of the person instructed)

§§ 669-670: *Aufwendungen* (disbursements)

§§ 671-674: *Ende des Auftrags* (end of the contract of instruction)

§ 675:   *Entgeltliche Geschäftsbesorgung* (contract to transact business for reward)

§ 676:   *Keine Haftung für Rat oder Empfehlung* (no liability for advice or recommendation)

*   *   *   *   *

Arrangement of Title 11

§§ 677-687 are arranged as follows:

§ 677   *Pflichten des Geschäftsführers* (duties of the person transacting the matter)

§§ 678-679   *Unberechtigte Geschäftsführung* (unjustified transaction of a matter)

§ 680   *Haftung bei Notgeschäftsführung* (unjustified transaction of a matter)

§ 681   *Nebenpflichten des Geschäftsführers* (accessory duties of the person transacting the matter)

§ 682:   *Haftungsprivileg bei fehlender Geschäftsfähigkeit* (reduced liability where there is no *Geschäftsfähigkeit*)

§ 683:   *Aufwendungsersatzanspruch des berechtigten Geschäftsführers* (reimbursement of expenditure for a justified transaction)

§ 684:   *Lage bei nicht berechtigten Geschäftsführung* (position where transaction is not justified)

§ 685:   *Schenkungsabsicht* (intended gift)

§ 686:   *Irrtum über den Geschäftsherrn* (mistake as to principal)

§ 687:   *Eigengeschäftsführung* (self-transaction)

*   *   *   *   *

Arrangement of Title 12

§§ 688-700

*   *   *   *   *

Arrangement of Title 13

§§ 701-704

*   *   *   *   *

Arrangement of Title 14

§§ 705-740 are arranged as follows:

§ 705:   *Begriff* (definition)

§§ 706-707:   *Beiträge* (contributions)

§ 708:   *Erleichterte Haftung* (reduced liability)

§§ 709-712:   *Geschäftsführung* (management)

§§ 714-715:   *Vertretung* (representation)

§ 716:   *Kontrollrecht* (right of control)

§ 717:   *Übertragbarkeit von Rechten* (transferability of rights)

§§ 718-720:   *Gesellschaftsvermögen* (company assets)

§§ 721-722:   *Verteilung von Gewinn und Verlust* (distribution of profit and loss)
§§ 723-729:   *Auflösungsgründe* (grounds for termination)
§§ 730-735:   *Auseinandersetzung* (split-up)
§§ 736-740:   *Gesellschafterwechsel* (change of members)

*　*　*　*　*

Arrangement of Title 15
§§ 741-758 are arranged as follows:
§ 741:   *Begriff* (definition)
§§ 742-743:   *Anteile* (shares)
§§ 744-746:   *Verwaltung und Benutzung* (administration and use)
§§ 747-748:   *Rechte und Pflichten* (rights and duties)
§§ 749-751:   *Aufhebung* (termination)
§§ 752-754:   *Art der Aufhebung* (manner of termination)
§§ 755-757:   *Folgeansprüche bei Aufhebung* (claims consequent on termination)
§ 758:   *Unverjährbarkeit des Aufhebungsanspruchs* (the right to claim termination is not subject to limitation)

*　*　*　*　*

Arrangement of Title 16
§§ 759-761

*　*　*　*　*

Arrangement of Title 17
§§ 762-764

*　*　*　*　*

Arrangement of Title 18
§§ 765-778 are arranged as follows:
§§ 765-766:   *Begriff* (definition); *Form* (form)
§ 767:   *Umfang der Bürgschaftsschuld* (extent of the guarantor's debt)
§ 768:   *Einreden des Bürgen* (objections by the guarantor)
§ 769:   *Mitbürgschaft* (co-surety)
§§ 770-773:   *Einreden des Bürgen* (objections by the guarantor)
§ 774:   *Gesetzlicher Forderungsübergang* (transition of claim by operation of law)

§§ 775-777: *Befreiung des Bürgen* (release of the guarantor)

§ 778:   *Kreditauftrag* (instruction to provide credit)

*   *   *   *   *

Arrangement of Title 19
§ 779

Arrangement of Title 20
§§ 780-782

*   *   *   *   *

Arrangement of Title 21
§§ 783-792 are arranged as follows:

§§ 783-786: *Begriff* (definition); *Verpflichtung* (obligation)

§§ 787-791: *Rechtsverhältnisse* (legal relationships)

§ 792:   *Übertragung* (transfer)

*   *   *   *   *

Arrangement of Title 22
§§ 793-808a are arranged as follows:

§§ 793-797: *Begriff; Lage des Ausstellers; Voraussetzungen* (definition; position of the issuer; preconditions)

§§ 798-800: *Ersatzurkunde und Kraftloserklärung* (replacement document and declaration of nullity)

§§ 801-802: *Verjährung und Vorlegungsfrist* (limitation and presentation period)

§§ 803-808a: *Scheine; Umschreibung auf den Namen; Besondere Arten* (notes (coupons); alteration in favour of a named person; special types)

*   *   *   *   *

Arrangement of Title 23
§§ 809-811

*   *   *   *   *

Arrangement of Title 24
§§ 812-822 are arranged as follows:

§§ 812-813(i): *Grundtatbestände* (basic (substantive) provisions): *Leistungskondiktion* and *Nichtleistungskondiktion*

§§ 813(ii)-815: *Ausschluß der Rückforderung* (exclusion of the claim to return (of something received due to a *Leistung*))

§ 816: *Verpflichtung zur Herausgabe des Erlangten nach Verfügung eines Nichtberechtigten: Besonderer Fall der Eingriffskondiktion* (liability of an unauthorised person to hand out what he receives following his (valid) *Verfügung*: special case of the *Eingriffskondiktion*)

§§ 817 First sentence: *Verpflichtung des Empfängers, der gegen Gesetz oder gute Sitten verstößt* (liability of a recipient, who breaches statute or good morals)

Second sentence: *Ausschluß der Rückforderung, wenn dem Leistenden (gleichfalls) ein solcher Verstoß zur Last fällt* (exclusion of the claim to return, where the claimant is (similarly) in breach)

§ 818(i), (ii): *Umfang des Anspruchs: Gegenstand der Bereicherung* (extent of the claim: object of enrichment)

§ 818(iii): *Wegfall der Bereicherung* ((exclusion of the claim) where the enrichment falls away)

§ 818(iv)-820: *Verschärfte Haftung des Empfängers* (increased liability of the recipient)

§ 821: *Einrede der Bereicherung* (objection of unjust enrichment)

§ 822: *Dritthaftung* (liability of third parties)

Arrangement of Title 25

§§ 823-853 are arranged as follows:

§ 823: *Grundtatbestände* (basic (substantive) provisions)[87]

§§ 824-826: *Weitere Anspruchsgrundlagen* (further (legal) grounds for claiming (damages))[88]

---

87 § 823 BGB contains two heads of liability: one general (§ 823(i)) and the other based on breach of a protective statute (*Schutzgesetz*) (§ 823(ii)). For further details see note 85 above.
Liability under § 823(i) was successfully established in:
- The *Fowl Pest Case*;
- The *Publication of a Letter Case*; and
- The *Newspaper Delivery Obstruction Case*.
Liability under § 823(i) was also proven in:
- The *Air Traffic Controllers Strike Case*
together with liability under § 839 BGB (see *Sourcebook*, Chapter 6).

88 These further *Anspruchsgrundlagen* are directed towards compensation for
- harm to financial status (§ 824 BGB); and
- harm contrary to morality (§§ 825-826 BGB)
(*Sourcebook*, Chapter 6).

§§ 827-829:   *Deliktsfähigkeit* (capacity to commit a delict)

§ 830:   *Beteiligung mehrerer* (involvement of several persons)

§ 831:   *Haftung für den Verrichtungsgehilfen* ((presumed) (vicarious) liability for a person entrusted with a particular task)[89]

§ 832:   *Haftung des Aufsichtspflichtigen* (liability of the person who supervises)

§§ 833-834:   *Haftung für Schaden durch Tiere* (liability for (damage caused by) animals)

§§ 836-838:   *Haftung bei Einsturz eines Gebäudes* (liability in the event of collapse of a building)

§ 839:   *Beamtenhaftung* (civil servants liability for breach of his Amtspflicht (official duty))[90]

§§ 840-841:   *Haftung mehrerer* (liability of several persons)

§§ 842-843:   *Umfang des Schadensersatzes bei Verletzung einer Person* (extent of damages in the case of personal injury)

§§ 844-846:   *Ansprüche Dritter bei Tötung oder wegen entgangener Dienste* (third party claims where a person is killed or was obliged by statute to provide services)

§ 847:   *Schmerzensgeld* (damages for pain and suffering)

§§ 848-851:   *Haftung bei Entziehung einer Sache* (liability in the event of removal of a thing)

§§ 852-853:   *Verjährung* (limitation period); *Verweigerung der Erfüllung* (refusal of performance)

*   *   *   *   *

---

89   In the *Fallen Telegraph Pole Case* (*Sourcebook*, Chapter 6) the question was whether there had been a blameworthy omission by the defendant to observe a *Verkehrssicherungspflicht* (duty of safety).

The plaintiff alleged both delayed removal and defective maintenance of the fallen telegraph pole. In the context of the former argument, the exception to § 831 BGB was successfully invoked. A direct claim under § 823 BGB was also rejected, because there was no apparent organisational fault (*Organisationsverschulden*) or negligence.

On the question of defective maintenance, however, the facts still required to be clarified. The matter was, therefore, referred back (to the lower court) and the burden of proof reversed.

90   Liability under § 839 BGB was established in the *Air Traffic Controllers Strike Case* (*Sourcebook*, Chapter 6).

BOOK III: THE LAW OF PROPERTY
(§§ 854-1296 BGB)[91]

Introduction

Book III of the BGB (*Sachenrecht*/law of property; §§ 854-1296) is divided into nine Sections.

In the important first three Sections of Book III provisions are set out dealing with possession (*Besitz*; §§ 854-872), rights to land (*Rechte an Grundstücken*; §§ 873-902) and ownership (*Eigentum*; §§ 903-1011).

Sections 5-9 (§§ 1018-1296) contain a *numerus clausus* (fixed number) of so-called *beschränkte dingliche Rechte* (limited real rights, as opposed to *Eigentum* as the most comprehensive, unlimited real right).[92]

Beschränkte dingliche Rechte are classified as user rights (*Nutzungsrechte*, eg servitudes) and disposal or security rights (*Verwertungs- oder Sicherungsrechte*, eg mortgages and pledges).[93]

Book III distinguishes between movable (*bewegliche*) and immovable (*unbewegliche*) *Sachen*. The only *unbewegliche Sachen* are *Grundstücke* ((pieces of) land).

Dingliches Recht and *Verfügung*

With regard to the term *dingliches Recht* (real right), it is helpful to note the following:

(a) *Besitz* (possession) is not a *dingliches Recht* (real right) or *Recht an der Sache* (right with regard to a *Sache*), but merely *tatsächliche Sachherrschaft* (actual dominance over a *Sache*).

(b) *Dingliche Rechte* are absolute, ie have effect against everyone (*gegen jedermann*) and, for reasons of certainty, are restricted to the types set out in Sections 5-9 of Book III.

To be contrasted therewith are the rights of parties to a *Schuldverhältnis*, which are relative, ie effective only amongst the parties. The principles underlying Book II are the parties fundamental freedom of contract (*Vertragsfreiheit*) and choice of type of *Schuldverhältnis* (*Typenfreiheit*, ie the

---

91 For further information, see generally: Creifelds; Kaiser, Part V; Kallwass, Section 4, Chapters 1-6 (§§ 58-79); Klunzinger (*Einführung*), Part V (§§ 58-66); Model/Creifelds/Lichtenberger, Part 3 F (333-340); Westermann (*Grundbegriffe*), Chapters 14-18; Westermann (SR), Vol I (*General Principles and Movables*) and Vol II (*Immovables*); other textbooks, eg Schwab/Prütting; Wolf.

92 See Creifelds under *Grundstücksrechte* and the diagram in Klunzinger (*Einführung*), Part V, Chapter 1 (§ 58, Section III; *Regelungsbereiche des Sachenrechts*).

93 See the diagram in Klunzinger (*Einführung*), Part V, Chapter 3 (§ 64, Section II; *Sonstige dingliche Rechte*).

Regarding the various types of security over movables and immovables, see also: Kallwass, Section 4, Chapter 3 (§ 65); Wolf, Chapter 5 (*Sicherungsrechte*; §§ 28-35).

parties are not limited to the type or form of the *Schuldverhältnisse* listed in §§ 433-811), while in Book III the principle of *Typenzwang* (compulsory choice of type) prevails.

(c) Each *dingliches Recht* is *spezial* (special), ie exists only with reference to a specific, individual *Sache* (*Spezialitätsgrundsatz* or principle of speciality). A *Sachgesamtheit* (collection of *Sachen*) is not one *Sache*, but a multitude of *Sachen* (eg a herd or library).

(d) An *Anwartschaftsrecht* is a right of expectancy with regard to a *dingliches Recht*. It is a concept developed by the judiciary (*richterliche Rechtsfortbildung*) and, while not being expressly referred to in the BGB, is treated as essentially similar to (the *wesensgleiches Minus* of) the relevant *dingliches Recht*.

Thus, for example, in the case of an instalment purchase (*Abzahlungskauf*), it is common for a retention of title (*Eigentumsvorbehalt*) to be agreed in favour of the vendor. The purchaser acquires an *Anwartschaftsrecht*, which gradually strengthens (*erstarkt*) into the full right (*Vollrecht*) of *Eigentum* (ownership) on final payment of the last instalment. Until then, the real agreement between the parties (the so-called *Einigung*) is said to be conditional upon (*bedingt durch*) full payment of the price. Just as his future *Eigentum*, the purchasers *Anwartschaftsrecht* can be transferred, charged, enjoys the same protection and can also be the subject of *Zwangsvollstreckung* (enforcement) by a creditor.[94]

(e) The abstraction principle (*Abstraktionsgrundsatz*)

The *Rechtsgeschäfte* of Book III (eg transfer of ownership) are *Verfügungen* or *Verfügungsgeschäfte* and are abstract from the basic or causal transaction (eg purchase contract).

It is important to understand that, in German legal speech, the term *Verfügung* is used in various contexts. Thus, in court or administrative terminology, a *Verfügung* can refer to the decision of the presiding judge (*Verfügung des Vorsitzenden*), an injunction (*einstweilige Verfügung*) or an administrative order or ban (*Gebot oder Verbot*), eg from the police (*polizeiliche Verfügung*). In the BGB, it is important both for Book III (law of property) and Book V (law of succession).

In Book V, the term *Verfügung* is used to refer to the legal transaction (*Rechtsgeschäft*) of a person having effect in the event of that persons death, ie a so-called *Verfügung* (*Rechtsgeschäft*) *von Todes wegen*, eg a will (*Testament*) or contract of succession (*Erbvertrag*), including any direction (*Anordnung*) therein.

In Book III, the term *Verfügung* means a legal transaction which, in strict contrast to a *Verpflichtung* (obligation), has direct effect on the constitution of a

---

94 See: Creifelds under *Anwartschaft* and *Anwartschaftsrecht*; Rüthers, Chapter 2, § 5 IV.

Rüthers points out that an *Anwartschaftsrecht* can be directed not only to the acquisition of a *dingliches Recht*, but also to the acquisition of a relative right.

Regarding *Eigentumsvorbehalt* see generally: Brox (BS), Chapter 1, § 6 I; Fikentscher, Section 9, § 71 V 1-4; Schwab/Prütting, Chapter 3, Section 3 (§ 30); Wolf, Chapter 5, Section 1 (§ 29).

right by means of its transfer, release or burdening or a variation of its content (*ein Rechtsgeschäft, welches den Bestand eines Rechts unmittelbar beeinflusst durch Übertragung, Aufhebung, Belastung oder inhaltliche Änderung*). The use of the term *Verfügung* in this sense is apparent from the provisions of Book III regarding rights to land, which lay down the necessary components of a *Verfügung* over such rights (§§ 873, 875 and 877).

The validity of a *Verfügung* in the Book III (property) sense is dependent not only on the special pre-conditions laid down in the relevant paragraphs of Book III and on the general requirement of all *Rechtsgeschäfte – Geschäftsfähigkeit –* but also on the so-called *Verfügungsbefugnis* (entitlement to undertake a *Verfügung*).

By means of this important concept, a distinction is drawn between the usual case of a right being held by its owner (who is then referred to as the *Berechtigter* or *Inhaber des Rechts* (owner of the right)) and the case of an unauthorised third party (a so-called *Nichtberechtigter*), who purports to undertake a *Verfügung*.[95]

Statutory provisions limiting the *Verfügungsbefugnis* in various circumstances (so-called *Verfügungsbeschränkungen* or *Veräusserungsverbote*) can be absolute (ie effective as against all the world, eg § 1365 BGB or § 7(i) KO) or relative (§ 135 BGB) in effect. A court order (eg an *einstweilige Verfügung* (injunction)) forbidding a *Verfügung* is an example of a relative *Verfügungsbeschränkung*: a *Verfügung* undertaken despite the order is effective for all purposes except as against the person in favour of whom the order was granted.

A person cannot exclude or limit his *Verfügungsbefugnis* by means of a *Rechtsgeschäft*, but a purely contractual restriction (abstraction principle!) is possible (§ 137).

A *Verfügung* usually remains valid even if its causal/obligational transaction (*Verpflichtungsgeschäft*) is void. To rectify the position, a claim for unjust enrichment (*ungerechtfertigte Bereicherung*) can be made (within the Law of Obligations), for which complex provisions are contained in §§ 812-822 BGB.[96]

---

95 See §§ 185 and 816 BGB. See also: Creifelds under *Verfügung eines Nichtberechtigten, Ermächtigung* and *Unwirksamkeit eines Rechtsgeschäfts*; Wolf, Chapter 4, § 17 IV.

96 See: Chapter X pp 37 and 68; Appendix A under *Ungerechtfertigte Bereicherung, Leistungskondiktion* and *Nichtleistungskondiktion*. See also: Wolf, Chapter 4 (§ 17); Zweigert and Kötz, Part II A I (Chapter 36 IV) and Wesel (FR), Chapter 3 (*Eigentum*).

Wesel points out that the abstraction principle is the creation of the 19th century jurist Savigny. Wesel describes it as a high point of juristic acrobatics.

Sections 1-9[97]

Section 1 (§§ 854-872 BGB)

Section 1 (§§ 854-872) deals with the acquisition, types and protection of *Besitz* (possession).[98]

Section 2 (§§ 873-902 BGB)

Section 2 (§§ 873-902) sets out provisions dealing (*inter alia*) with:

* the acquisition, release and variation of rights to land (§§ 873-878);
* the rank of limited rights to land between themselves (§§ 879-881);
* the protection of the position of a person claiming a right to land by means of the entry of a so-called *Vormerkung* (priority notice) in the land register (*Grundbuch*) (§§ 883-888);
* the effect of entries in the land register (§§ 891-893);
* the correction of incorrect entries in the land register (§§ 894-899);
* the influence of expiry of time on rights to land (§§ 900-902).

Section 3 (§§ 903-1011 BGB)

Section 3 (§§ 903-1011) is divided into five titles:

Title 1 (§§ 903-924 BGB)

Title 1: *Inhalt des Eigentums* (content of ownership); §§ 903-924

Subject to certain exceptions, the owner of a *Sache* can deal with it as he pleases and exclude others from it (§ 903).

However, Article 14(ii) of the Basic Law makes it clear that he also has certain obligations in the public interest (*Eigentum verpflichtet*). The term *Eigentum* as used in Article 14 GG is wider than that of § 903 BGB (which is limited to *Sachen*) and includes all legal positions of value.[99] The content (*Inhalt*) and limits (*Schranken*) of *Eigentum* are set (*bestimmt*) by statute and only if *Eigentum* is removed by *Enteignung* (expropriation) or a similar interference (*Eingriff*) is compensation (*Entschädigung*) available.[100]

Title 2 (§§ 925-928 BGB) and Title 3 (§§ 929-984 BGB)

Title 2: *Erwerb und Verlust des Eigentums an Grundstücken* (acquisition and loss of ownership to land (immovables)); §§ 925-928.

---

97 See note 63 in this chapter.
98 Regarding *Besitz* see generally: Creifelds; Kaiser, Part V, 5; Klunzinger (*Einführung*), Part V, Chapter 2, § 60; Rehbinder, Chapter II, § 16; Schwab/Prütting, Chapter 1 (§§ 3-11); Westermann (*Grundbegriffe*), Chapter 14; Westermann (SR), Volume I, Book II (§§ 8-27); Wolf, Chapter 2, § 8.
99 However, Article 14 GG does not protect a person's *Vermögen* (wealth) as such: see the *Investment Aid Act Case* (*Sourcebook*, Chapter 3).
100 See the comments under Article 14 GG in the *Sourcebook*, Chapter 3.

Title 3: *Erwerb und Verlust des Eigentums an beweglichen Sachen* (acquisition and loss of ownership to movables); §§ 929-984.

The components of a transfer of ownership[101]

The transfer of ownership (*Übertragung des Eigentums* or *Übereignung*) of a *Sache* by means of a *Rechtsgeschäft* is composed of two elements:

- the so-called *Einigung* (a real agreement; known as the *Auflassung* in the case of immovables; § 925(i)); and

- the *Übergabe* (transfer of physical possession) in the case of movables (§ 929) or *Eintragung* (entry in the land register (*Grundbuch*)) in the case of immovables (§ 873).

An *Übergabe* (of movables) can in certain circumstances be unnecessary (ie where the transferee (*Erwerber*) is already in possession of the *Sache*; § 929, second sentence) or replaced *(ersetzt)*:

- by a so-called *Besitzkonstitut* (constructive possession, ie an arrangement whereby the (original) *Eigentümer* remains in possession of the *Sache*, but holds it for the proper (new) owner; § 930. This is the usual technical legal basis for a *Sicherungsübereignung* (transfer of ownership as security, ie a chattel mortgage);[102] or

- by an *Abtretung des Herausgabeanspruchs* (assignment of the right to claim return of the *Sache*; § 931).

Bona fide *acquisition of ownership to movables*

Normally, a transfer of ownership (of movables) is from the *Eigentümer* himself (§ 929). If, however, the transferor (*Veräusserer*) is (a person) not entitled to (transfer) the *Sache* (a so-called *Nichtberechtigter*), the *bona fide* acquisition of *Eigentum* by the transferee (*gutgläubiger Erwerb*) is possible (§ 932) unless:

- the *Erwerber* is not in good faith (*nicht in gutem Glauben* (*bösgläubig*), ie if he is aware of or grossly negligent as to the situation); or

---

101 See the diagram in Klunzinger (*Einführung*), Part V, Chapter 2 (§ 62, Section I; *rechtsgeschäftlicher Eigentumserwerb*). See also: Kaiser, Part V, 7; Schwab/Prütting, Chapter 3 (§§ 26 and 29); Westermann (*Grundbegriffe*), Chapter 15; Wolf, Chapter 4, Section 1 (§ 18) and Section 2 (§ 22).

A transferee can usually only acquire the same legal position as that of the transferor: *Nemo plus iuris ad alium transferre potest, quam ipse habet.* The right of the transferee is said to be *abgeleitet* (derived) from his predecessor (*Rechtsvorgänger*). A transfer of ownership is an example of a *Rechtsnachfolge* or *Sukzession* (succession).

See Creifelds under *Rechtsnachfolge*, *Rechtserwerb* and *Nemo plus iuris ...* and the discussion of § 929 BGB and the abstraction principle in Wesel (FR), Chapter 3 (*Eigentum*). See also Kallwass, Section 4, Chapter 5 (§ 74).

102 Regarding *Sicherungsübereignung* see generally: Schwab/Prütting, Chapter 3, Section 3 (§ 31); Westermann (SR), Volume I, Book IV (§ 44); Wolf, Chapter 5, Section 1 (§ 30). See also note 108 in this chapter.

- the *Sache* has been stolen, lost or has otherwise gone astray (*abhanden gekommen*; § 935).[103]

Bona fide acquisition of ownership is also possible in the event that a *Besitzkonstitut* or *Abtretung des Herausgabeanspruchs* is entered into/granted by a *Nichtberechtigter*.[104]

Statutory acquisition of ownership to movables[105]

Ownership of movables can be acquired not only in accordance with §§ 929-936 by means of a *Rechtsgeschäft*, but also by statute (so-called *gesetzlicher Erwerb*; dealt with in §§ 937-984), ie by

- *Ersitzung* (acquisition of ownership through the passage of time); §§ 937-945.
- *Verbindung*; *Vermischung*; *Verarbeitung* (connection; mixture; processing); §§ 946-952.
- *Erwerb von Erzeugnissen und sonstigen Bestandteilen einer Sache* (acquisition of products and other parts of a *Sache*); §§ 953-957.
- *Aneignung* (acquisition of ownership to ownerless movables (appropriation); §§ 958-964.
- *Fund* (finding of lost property); §§ 965-984.

Title 4 (§§ 985-1007 BGB)

Title 4: *Ansprüche aus dem Eigentum* (claims arising out of ownership); §§ 985-1007.

The owner of a *Sache*, whether movable or immovable, has various *dingliche Ansprüche* (real claims), eg to return (*Herausgabe*) of the *Sache* against a person with no right to possession (*Recht zum Besitz*) of it (so-called *Vindikation* under § 985) and to removal or stoppage of a disturbance (*Beseitigung oder Unterlassung einer Störung*); § 1004.[106]

---

103 Exceptions: money, bearer securities and things sold at public auction.

See Kallwass, Section 4, Chapter 4 (§ 70 I-III); Westermann (SR), Volume I, Book IV (§§ 45-50); Wolf, Chapter 4, Section 2 (§ 23).

Wesel (FR), Chapter 3 (*Eigentum*) is of the opinion that, due to the enactment of § 932 BGB on 1 January 1900, the abstraction principle underlying § 929 BGB has become superfluous.

104 See the complex provisions in §§ 933 and 934 BGB. See also Kallwass, Section 4, Chapter 4 (§ 71 I).

105 See the diagram in Klunzinger (*Einführung*), Part V Chapter 2 (§ 63, Section I; *gesetzlicher Eigentumserwerb*). See also Kallwass, Section 4, Chapter 2 (§§ 63-64); Westermann (SR), Volume I, Book IV (§§ 51-60).

106 §§ 987-1003 BGB deal with the so-called *Eigentümer-Besitzer-Verhältnis* (the relationship between the owner and the person in possession of a *Sache*).

Apart from the owners claim to return of the *Sache* under § 985 (the *Herausgabeanspruch*), a person in illegal possession (an *unrechtmäßiger Besitzer*) can also – unless he is in good faith (*gutgläubig*) – be subject to accessory claims (*Nebenansprüche*) from the owner for replacement of benefits (*Nutzungsherausgabe*) and damages (*Schadensersatz*); §§ 987-993. ...

Title 5 (§§ 1008-1011 BGB)

Title 5: *Miteigentum (nach Bruchteilen)*: joint ownership by shares (as opposed to *Gesamthandseigentum*);[107] §§ 1008-1011.

Section 4 (§§ 1012-1017 BGB)

Section 4 of Book III (§§ 1012-1017), which formerly dealt with the *Erbbaurecht* (right to erect a building on anothers land), has been replaced by the *Verordnung über das Erbbaurecht* of 15 January 1919.

Section 5 (§§ 1018-1093 BGB)

Section 5 (§§ 1018-1093) deals with *Dienstbarkeiten* (servitudes) and is divided into three titles:

Title 1:   *Grunddienstbarkeiten* (easements); §§ 1018-1029.

Title 2:   *Nießbrauch (usufruct)*; §§ 1030-1089.

Title 3:   *Beschränkte persönliche Dienstbarkeit* (limited personal servitude); §§ 1090-1093.

Section 6 (§§ 1094-1104 BGB)

Section 6 (§§ 1094-1104) deals with the *Vorkaufsrecht* (right of pre-emption). The *Vorkaufsrecht* referred to here is the *dingliches Vorkaufsrecht* (real right of pre-emption) and not the contractual one (dealt with in §§ 504-514).

Section 7 (§§ 1105-1112 BGB)

Section 7 (§§ 1105-1112) deals with the *Reallast* (successive duty of supply from a property).

Sections 8 and 9 (§§ 1113-1296 BGB)

Sections 8 and 9 of Book III deal with security/disposal rights over immovables and movables respectively (ie mortgages and pledges) and are set out as follows:

Section 8 (§§ 1113-1203) deals with *Grundpfandrechte* (security rights over land) and is divided into two titles:[108]

Title 1:   *Hypothek* (mortgage); §§ 1113-1190.

106...A person in possession (*Besitzer*), who has incurred expenditure (*Verwendungen*) on a *Sache*, can counter-claim against the owner for reimbursement (*Verwendungsersatz*; § 994) and has a right of retention (*Zurückbehaltungsrecht*) until he is satisfied (§ 1000).

See the diagram in Klunzinger (*Einführung*), Part V, Chapter 2 (§ 61, Section II; *Schutz des Eigentums*); Kaiser, Part V, Chapters 2, 3, 4 and 6; Kallwass, Section 4, Chapter 6 (§§ 78-79); Schwab/Prütting, Chapter 3, Section 4 (§§ 44-47); Wolf, Chapter 3 (§§ 10-14).

107 See §§ 741ff BGB, Creifelds under *Miteigentum* and Chapter XI.

108 Regarding *Grundpfandrechte* see: Creifelds under *Grundpfandrechte, Hypothek* and *Grundschuld*; Kaiser, Part V, 9; Klunzinger (*Einführung*), Part V, Chapter 3 (§ 66 II); Schwab/Prütting, Chapter 4, Section 1 (§§ 51-65); Westermann (*Grundbegriffe*), Chapter 17; Westermann (SR), Volume II, Book VI (§§ 107-136); Wolf, Chapter 5, Section 2 (§§ 32-35).

Title 2:   *Grundschuld. Rentenschuld* (land charge; regular land charge); §§ 1191-1203.

Section 9 (§§ 1204-1296) deals with the *Pfandrecht* (pledge) and is divided into two titles:[109]

Title 1:   *Pfandrecht an beweglichen Sachen* (pledge of movables); §§ 1204-1258.

Title 2:   *Pfandrecht an Rechten* (pledge of rights); §§ 1273-1296.

BOOK IV: FAMILY LAW (§§ 1297-1921 BGB)[110]

Book IV of the BGB (*Familienrecht*/family law); §§ 1297-1921) is divided into three sections (in turn subdivided into titles) as follows:

---

109 Section 9, Title 1 distinguishes between a *Pfandrecht* created (*bestellt*) by *Rechtsgeschäft* ((contract) a so-called *Faustpfandrecht*) and a statutory *Pfandrecht* (*gesetzliches Pfandrecht*).

The provisions regarding a *Pfandrecht* created by *Rechtsgeschäft* (§§ 1205-1256 BGB) are of corresponding application (*entsprechende Anwendung*) to a *Pfandrecht*, which has arisen by statute (*ein kraft Gesetzes entstandenes Pfandrecht*); § 1257 BGB.

Examples of statutory *Pfandrechte* are:

- in the BGB, the liens of the landlord (§ 559), the manufacturer (§ 647) and the innkeeper (§ 704);
- in the HGB, the liens of the *Spediteur* (carrier (forwarder); § 410) and the *Frachtführer* (freighter: § 440).

A *Pfandrecht* over movables is defined in § 1204(i) BGB as securing a contractual claim (*Forderung*) and entitling the creditor ((*Pfand*)*gläubiger*) to seek satisfaction (*Befriedigung*) out of the thing pledged (*aus der Sache*). Satisfaction is achieved by means of sale ((*Pfand*)*verkauf*) once the contractual claim is due (*fällig*); §§ 1228ff.

A *Pfandrecht* is strictly accessory (linked) to the contractual claim, which it secures (so-called *Akzessorietät*). Thus, it can only be transferred with the *Forderung* and ends (is discharged: *erlischt*) with it; § 1250(i) and § 1252.

Another type of lien is the *Pfändungspfandrecht* (distraint lien), which arises (under public law) where enforcement (*Zwangsvollstreckung*) in movable assets takes place; § 804(i) ZPO.

Where movables are concerned, the creation of a *Pfandrecht* usually requires actual delivery (*Übergabe*) of the *Sache* to the creditor. This has resulted in the institute of the *Pfandrecht* largely being displaced as a form of security by the more practical *Sicherungsübereignung*, where the debtor need not part with possession.

However, the contractual *Pfandrecht* is still of commercial significance in Lombard transactions (*Lombardgeschäft*) and pawnbroking (*Pfandleihe*).

See generally: Creifelds under *Lombardgeschäft, Pfandrecht, Pfandleiher, Pfändung* and *Pfändungspfandrecht*; the diagram in Klunzinger (*Einführung*), Part V, Chapter 3 (§ 66 I (*Pfandrechte*) and § 66 III-IV); Schwab/Prütting, Chapter 4, Section 2 (§§ 66-71); Westermann (SR), Volume I, Book V (§§ 61-73); Wolf, Chapter 5, Section 1 (§ 31).

110 For further information, see generally: Creifelds; Model/Creifelds/Lichtenberger, Part 3 F (341-352); Westermann (*Grundbegriffe*), Chapter 19; various textbooks, eg Beitzke/Lüderitz; Schwab (F).

Section 1: Bürgerliche Ehe *(civil marriage)*; §§ 1297-1588

Title 1:   *Verlöbnis* (engagement); §§ 1297-1302.

Title 2:*   *Eingehung der Ehe* (conclusion of marriage); §§ 1303-1322.

Title 3:*   *Nichtigkeit und Anfechtbarkeit der Ehe* (nullity and voidability of marriage); §§ 1323-1347.

Title 4:*   *Wiederverheiratung im Falle der Todeserklärung* (remarriage in the event of declaration of death); §§ 1348-1352.

* Titles 2, 3 and 4 above have been repealed (*aufgehoben*) and are dealt with in the *Ehegesetz* (Marriage Law) of 20 February 1946.

Title 5:   *Wirkungen der Ehe im allgemeinen* (effects of marriage in general); §§ 1353-1362.

Title 6:   *Eheliches Güterrecht* (marital property law); §§ 1363-1563.[111]

Title 7:   *Scheidung der Ehe* (divorce); §§ 1564-1587p.

Title 8:   *Kirchliche Verpflichtungen* (ecclesiastical obligations); §§ 1588.

Section 2: Verwandtschaft *(kinship)*; §§ 1589-1772

Title 1:   *Allgemeine Vorschriften* (general provisions); §§ 1589-1590.

Title 2:   *Abstammung* (descent); §§ 1591-1600o.

Title 3:   *Unterhaltspflicht* (duty of maintenance); §§ 1601-1615o.

Title 4:   *Rechtsverhältnis zwischen den Eltern und dem Kinde im allgemeinen* (legal relationship between parents and child in general); §§ 1616-1625.

Title 5:   *Elterliche Sorge für eheliche Kinder* (parental care for legitimate children); §§ 1626-1704.

Title 6:   *Elterliche Sorge für nichteheliche Kinder* (parental care for illegitimate children); §§ 1705-1718.

Title 7:   *Legitimation nichtehelicher Kinder* (legitimation of illegitimate children); §§ 1719-1740g.

Title 8:   *Annahme als Kind* (adoption); §§ 1741-1772.

Section 3: Vormundschaft *(guardianship)*; §§ 1773-1921

Title 1:   *Vormundschaft über Minderjährige* (guardianship over minors); §§ 1773-1895.

Title 2:   *Betreuung* (care and attendance over adults suffering from a psychological illness or a physical or mental handicap); §§ 1896-1908i.

Title 3:   *Pflegschaft* (appointment of an administrator (*Pfleger*) in special cases, eg where parents or a guardian cannot act; where an adult is absent and cannot be located; for a foetus); §§ 1909-1921.

---

111 See *Güterrecht*.

BOOK V: LAW OF SUCCESSION (§§ 1922-2385 BGB)[112]

Book V of the BGB (*Erbrecht*/law of succession; §§ 1922-2385) is divided into nine sections:

Section 1:   *Erbfolge* (succession); §§ 1922-1941.

Section 2:   *Rechtliche Stellung des Erben* (legal position of the heir); §§ 1942-2063.

Section 3:   *Testament* (will); §§ 2064-2273.

Section 4:   *Erbvertrag* (contract of succession); §§ 2274-2302.

Section 5:   *Pflichtteil* (compulsory portion (of the estate)); §§ 2303-2338.

Section 6:   *Erbunwürdigkeit* (unworthiness to inherit); §§ 2339-2345.

Section 7:   *Erbverzicht* (disclaimer of inheritance); §§ 2346-2352.

Section 8:   *Erbschein* (certificate of inheritance); §§ 2353-2370.

Section 9:   *Erbschaftskauf* (estate purchase); §§ 2371-2385.

---

112 For further information, see generally: Creifelds; Model/Creifelds/Lichtenberger, Part 3 F (353-362); Westermann (*Grundbegriffe*), Chapter 20; various textbooks, eg Brox (ER); Leipold.

CHAPTER XI

PRIVATE LAW: BGB COMPANY LAW AND THE COMMERCIAL CODE (HGB)[1]

CONTEXT AND DEFINITIONS

The German Commercial Code (*Handelsgesetzbuch* or HGB) of 10 May 1897 came into force with the BGB on 1 January 1900. It contains the special law (*Sonderrecht*) of a particular professional class (*Berufsstand*), namely of the *Kaufmann* (businessman; trader).

A person can conduct his business either alone (in which case, if he is a *Kaufmann*, as a so-called *Einzelkaufmann* (sole trader)) or together with others as a *Gesellschaft* (company).

A *Gesellschaft* can take one of the following main forms:[2]

- a *Gesellschaft des bürgerlichen Rechts* (GbR = *BGB-Gesellschaft*: civil law company or BGB-company, ie partnership; §§ 705-740 BGB).

- an *offene Handelsgesellschaft* (OHG: open trading company; §§ 105-160 HGB).

- a *Kommanditgesellschaft* (KG: limited partnership; §§ 161-177a HGB).

- a *Gesellschaft mit beschränkter Haftung* (GmbH: company with limited liability).

- an *Aktiengesellschaft* (AG: public limited company).

The last four are also known as *Handelsgesellschaften* (trading companies), although only the OHG and KG are dealt with in the HGB (§§ 105-177).

For the OHG and KG, the HGB builds on the primary provisions for the *BGB-Gesellschaft* contained in §§ 705-740 BGB (§§ 105(ii) and 161(ii) HGB). Separate statutes govern the GmbH and AG (the GmbHG and AktG).[3]

---

1   On *Handelsrecht* (commercial law) see generally: Baumann (ER), Part III, § 9; Capelle/Canaris; Hofmann; Klunzinger (*Grundzüge*) (HR); Model/Creifelds/Lichtenberger, Part III G (363-379).

   On *Gesellschaftsrecht* (company law) see generally: Eisenhardt, Chapters 1-6; Hueck, Sections 1 and 2 (§§ 1-19); Klunzinger (*Grundzüge*) (GR), Chapters 1, 2 and 4; Kraft/Kreutz, Parts A-G.

2   See Eisenhardt, Chapter 1, § 2 I; Kallwass, Section 7 (§ 107). See also the diagram in Klunzinger (*Einführung*), Part II, Chapter 1 (§ 4, Section I; *Personenzusammenschlüsse*) and Chapter XIX, note 54 B.

3   Not dealt with in this text.

   Another type of *Gesellschaft*, also governed by a separate statute, is the *Genossenschaft* (co-operative (association/society)), which is a form of trading *Verein* established for one of the purposes set out in § 1(i) of the *Genossenschaftsgesetz* (GenG; Law relating to *Genossenschaften*), eg acquisition, production and/or sale of agricultural and/or other products; banking. Its function is the advancement (*Förderung*) of the livelihood or commercial interests (*Erwerb oder Wirtschaft*) of its members (*Genossen*) by means of a communal business (*gemeinschaftlicher Geschäftsbetrieb*).

   A *Genossenschaft* requires registration in the *Genossenschaftsregister* (register of *Genossenschaften*) – kept at the *Amtsgericht* (District Court; § 10 GenG) – and is then referred to as a registered co-operative (*eingetragene Genossenschaft* (eG)).

The *BGB-Gesellschaft* (and the OHG and KG) is a so-called *Gesamthandsgemeinschaft* (a joint community), the assets of which (*Gesellschaftsvermögen*) are the joint property of the members (*Gesellschafter*) and can only be disposed of jointly (*gemeinschaftlich*; §§ 718(i) and 719(i) BGB). Other *Gesamthandsgemeinschaften* are the *Gütergemeinschaft* (community of property between spouses) and the *Erbengemeinschaft* (community between heirs).

The *Gesamthandsgemeinschaft* is to be distinguished from the *Gemeinschaft nach Bruchteilen* (a community by shares; §§ 741-758 BGB), where each *Teilhaber* (shareholder) can dispose of his *Anteil* ((ideal) share) in the asset(s) of the *Gemeinschaft*; the asset(s) as a whole can, however, only be disposed of jointly; § 747 BGB).

The *Gesamthandsgemeinschaft* is also to be strictly distinguished from the *juristische Person* or *Körperschaft* (juristic person or corporate body), of which the *Verein* (club, association) is the prototype (§§ 21-79 BGB).[4] Unlike the *Gesamthandsgemeinschaft*, the *juristische Person* or *Körperschaft*:

- is a *Rechtssubjekt* and, once registered, *rechtsfähig*;

- acts through its *Organe* (organs, eg its *Vorstand* (board of directors)) for whose acts it is liable (§ 31 BGB);

- can be non-capitalised (*Verein*) or capitalised (a *Kapitalgesellschaft*, eg a GmbH or AG).

As opposed to a *Kapitalgesellschaft*, the *BGB-Gesellschaft*, OHG and KG are also examples of a *Personengesellschaft* (a personal company),[5] which is characterised by the personal liability (*persönliche Haftung*) and personal direction (*Selbstorganschaft*) of its *Gesellschafter/Mitglieder* (members). In a *Kapitalgesellschaft*, the organs and members do not have to be identical (*Drittorganschaft* is permitted).

An OHG is based on the unlimited liability (*unbeschränkte Haftung*) of all its members (§ 105(i) HGB), while a KG has two types of member: the member(s) with unlimited liability (the *Komplementär(en)*) and the member(s) whose liability is limited to the amount of a particular investment (the *Kommanditist(en)*; § 161(i) HGB).[6]

---

4   Regarding juristic persons of public law, see Chapter II (Note 6).

5   A *stille Gesellschaft* (silent partnership) is also a *Personengesellschaft*, but not a *Handelsgesellschaft*.

   Regarding *Personengesellschaften*, see Hueck, Section 2, Chapters 1-4 (§§ 5-19); Klunzinger (*Grundzüge*) (GR), Chapter 2 (§§ 4-7) and Kraft/Kreutz, Parts D-G.

   Regarding *Kapitalgesellschaften*, see Klunzinger (*Grundzüge*) (GR), Chapter 3 (§§ 8 and 11) and Kraft/Kreutz, Parts K and M.

   Regarding the fundamental distinction BGB-*Gesellschaft/Verein* see: Eisenhardt, Chapter 2 (§§ 4-5); Hueck, Section 1, § 1 III and § 2; Kallwass, Section 7, Chapter 1 (§ 108); Kraft/Kreutz, Part J

6   See Eisenhardt, Chapter 5 (§ 19).

A *juristische Person* (eg a GmbH) can also be a member of an OHG or the *Komplementär* of a KG (so in the GmbH & Co KG).[7]

All *Gesellschaften* are based on a *Gesellschaftsvertrag* (company agreement), which, in the case of a *juristische Person/Körperschaft* is known as the *Satzung* (§ 25 BGB). The *Gesellschaftsvertrag/Satzung* of a GmbH or AG must be notarially documented (§§ 2 GmbHG and 23(i) AktG).

THE HGB IN DETAIL

Introduction

The HGB is divided into five books:

Book I (§§ 1-104):	*Handelsstand* (classification)[8]
Book II (§§ 105-237):	*Handelsgesellschaften* (non-capitalised commercial companies)
Book III (§§ 238-339):	*Handelsbücher* (bookkeeping)
Book IV (§§ 343-460):	*Handelsgeschäfte* (commercial transactions)[9]
Book V (§§ 476-905):	*Seehandel* (sea trade).[10]

Book I (§§ 1-104 HGB): *Handelsstand*

Book I is divided into eight sections:

1 *Kaufleute* (businessmen; §§ 1-7).

2 *Handelsregister* (commercial/trade register; §§ 8-16).

3 *Handelsfirma* (trade firm; §§ 17-37).

4 (Repealed).

5 *Prokura* and *Handlungsvollmacht* (*procura* and authority to trade; §§ 48-58).

6 *Handlungsgehilfen* and *Handlungslehrlinge* (trading assistants and apprentices; §§ 59-83).

7 *Handelsvertreter* (commercial agents; §§ 84-92c).

8 *Handelsmakler* ((trade) broker; §§ 93-104).

Section 1 (§§ 1-7 HGB)[11]

A person, who engages in one of the basic trading activities (*Grundhandelsgewerben*) listed in § 1(ii) HGB, is a so-called *Mußkaufmann*

---

7 See Eisenhardt, Chapter 5 (§ 20); Klunzinger (*Grundzüge*) (GR), Chapter 4 (§ 13).

8 See generally Baumann (ER), Part III, § 9 and Capelle/Canaris, Part 1.

9 See generally Capelle/Canaris, Part 2.

10 Not dealt with in this text.

11 See: Capelle/Canaris, Part 1, Section 1 (§§ 2-3); Gierke/Sandrock, Section 1, Chapter 1 (§§ 6-8, 10); Hofmann, Part B; Kallwass, Section 5 (§§ 83-86); Klunzinger (*Grundzüge*) (HR), Chapter 2, § 6.

(compulsory businessman), whether or not he is registered. Depending on the extent of his business activities, the *Mußkaufmann* can be either a *Vollkaufmann* or *Minderkaufmann* (full or lesser businessman). Various provisions of the HGB are inapplicable to the *Minderkaufmann* (eg firm registration, bookkeeping, grant of *procura*; § 4(i)).

A trading company, whether or not capitalised, is a so-called *Formkaufmann* (businessman by reason of its form; § 6 HGB).

By § 2 HGB, a so-called *Sollkaufmann* is a person, who does not fall within § 1(ii), but the type and extent of whose activities require a properly organised business (*dessen Unternehmen nach Art und Umfang einen kaufmännisch eingerichteten Geschäftsbetrieb erfordert*), eg a builder or hotelier). A *Sollkaufmann* becomes a *Kaufmann* by registration, which he is obliged to procure.

Sections 2 and 3 (§§ 8-37 HGB)[12]

The name under which a *Vollkaufmann* engages in commercial activities is known as the *Firma* (firm) and must be registered in the *Handelsregister* (commercial/trade register), which is kept at the *Amtsgericht* (district court) (§§ 8, 17 and 29 HGB).

Section 5 (§§ 48-58 HGB)[13]

The non-independent representatives and assistants (*unselbstständige Vertreter und Hilfspersonen*) of a *Kaufmann* are dealt with in §§ 48-83 HGB.

The widest power of representation (*Vertretungsmacht*) that can be granted by a *Vollkaufmann* is the *Prokura*, which enables the procurist effectively to undertake any transactions, which a (not the!) trading activity (*Handelsgewerbe*)

---

12 See Capelle/Canaris, Part 1, Section 2 (§ 4) and Section 4 (§ 10 I); Gierke/Sandrock, Section 1, Chapters 2 and 3 (§ 17); Hofmann, Parts C and D; Klunzinger (*Grundzüge*) (HR), Chapter 3, § 11 and § 13.

§ 15 HGB sets out certain important rules regarding the effect (or lack) of an *Eintragung* (registration) and *Bekanntmachung* (publication) of a particular fact, which requires registration (an *einzutragende Tatsache*) in the *Handelsregister*, and of an incorrect publication (*unrichtige Bekanntmachung*) in the necessary journals (see § 10 HGB):

- by § 15 (ii) HGB a third party is bound by the (proper) registration and publication of a (correct) fact (except within 15 days of publication, provided the third party proves that he neither knew nor should have known the fact);
- by § 15 (i) HGB a fact which is not registered and published cannot be held against a third party acting in good faith (so-called *negative Publizität* (negative publicity): one can rely on the silence of the *Handelsregister*);
- by § 15 (iii) HGB a fact which is *unrichtig bekanntgemacht* (incorrectly published) can be relied upon in the form of its publication by a third party acting in good faith (so-called *positive Publizität* (positive publicity): one can rely on the information as published in the relevant journal(s) unless one knows it is incorrect).

See Capelle/Canaris, Section 2, § 5; Klunzinger (*Grundzüge*) (HR), Chapter 3, § 13 III and IV. See also Creifelds under *Handelsregister*.

13 See: Capelle/Canaris, Part 1, Section 6 (§§ 14-15); Gierke/Sandrock, Section 1, Chapters 4 and 5 (§§ 21-25); Hofmann, Part F; Klunzinger (*Grundzüge*) (HR), Chapter 2, § 8.

involves. The grant of *procura* (*Erteilung der Prokura*) must be registered and is unlimited (*unbeschränkt*) as far as third parties are concerned (§§ 49(i), 50(i) and 53(i) HGB).

A *Kaufmann* can also grant a so-called *Handlungsvollmacht* (trading power of attorney), which is limited to those transactions, which are usual (*gewöhnlich*) for that type of *Handelsgewerbe* (§ 54 HGB).

Section 6 (§§ 59-83 HGB)[14]

The staff (*Personal*) of a *Kaufmann* are his *Handlungsgehilfen* or *kaufmännische Angestellten* (§ 59 HGB). A *Lehrling* is a trainee.

Sections 7 and 8 (§§ 84-104 HGB)[15]

The *Handelsvertreter* (commercial agent) is an independent *Hilfsperson* of a *Kaufmann*. As opposed to the *Handelsmakler* (a broker (§ 93 HGB), eg an insurance or stockbroker),[16] the *Handelsvertreter* is constantly (*ständig*) engaged in the referral (*Vermittlung*) or conclusion (*Abschluß*) of business to or for another entrepreneur (*Unternehmer*); § 84(i) HGB. The *Handelsvertreter* acts as agent for his principal (*Geschäftsherr*), unlike the commissioneer (*Kommissionär*; § 383 HGB), who acts in his own name (*im eigenen Namen*).

A *Handelsvertreter* or *Kommissionär* receives commission (*Provision*; §§ 87 and 396 HGB). A *Handelsmakler* receives a fee (*Maklerlohn/Courtage*).

The *Handelsvertreter*, *Handelsmakler* and *Kommissionär* are all *Kaufleute* (§ 1(ii) Nos 6 and 7 HGB).

Book II (§§ 105-237 HGB): *Handelsgesellschaften*

Content

Book II is divided into three sections:

1 *Offene Handelsgesellschaft* (open trading company; §§ 105-160).[17]
2 *Kommanditgesellschaft* (limited partnership; §§ 161-177a).[18]
3 *Stille Gesellschaft* (silent partnership; §§ 230-237).[19]

---

14 As note 12 in this chapter.
15 See: Capelle/Canaris, Part 1, Section 7 (§ 17 and § 19); Gierke/Sandrock, Section 1, Chapter 6 (§§ 26, 27 and 29); Hofmann, Part G; Klunzinger (*Grundzüge*) (HR), Chapter 2, § 9.
16 But not an estate agent, who is a so-called *Zivilmakler* under § 652 BGB.
17 See generally Eisenhardt, Chapter 4 (§§ 10-17).
18 *Ibid* Chapter 5 (§§ 18-23).
19 See note 4 in this chapter.

Section 1 (§§ 105-160 HGB)[20]

Section 1 contains six titles:

Title 1:   *Errichtung der Gesellschaft* (formation of the company; §§ 105-108).

Title 2:   *Rechtsverhältnis der Gesellschafter untereinander* (legal relationship of the members amongst each other; §§ 109-122).

Title 3:   *Rechtsverhältnis der Gesellschafter zu Dritten* (legal relationship of the members towards third parties; §§ 123-130b).

Title 4:   *Auflösung der Gesellschaft und Ausscheiden von Gesellschaftern* (termination (dissolution) of the company and departure of members; §§ 131-144).

Title 5:   *Liquidation der Gesellschaft* (liquidation of the company; §§ 145-158).

Title 6:   *Verjährung* (limitation period; §§ 159-160).

Title 1 (§§ 105-108 HGB)

§ 105(i) defines the OHG as a company whose purpose (*Zweck*) is directed to the engagement in (*Betrieb*) a trading activity (*Handelsgewerbe*) under a joint firm (name; *Firma*), the liability of its members towards company creditors being unlimited. The OHG is the trading version of the *BGB-Gesellschaft* (civil law company); thus, unless stated to the contrary in Section 1, the provisions of the BGB regarding the *Gesellschaft* (§§ 705-740 BGB) additionally apply to the OHG (§ 105(ii)).

By § 106(i) a notification (*Anmeldung*) to register an OHG must be made to the (district) court (*Amtsgericht*) for the area in which it has its registered address (*Sitz*). Any change in its *Firma* (firm name), *Sitz* or the entry of a new member into the company must also be notified (§ 107).[21]

Title 2 (§§ 109-122 HGB)

§ 109 HGB contains the basic rule that, in the first instance (*zunächst*), the (internal) legal relationship of the *Gesellschafter* (members) of an OHG amongst each other is governed by the *Gesellschaftsvertrag* (company agreement) and that §§ 110-122 only apply insofar as the *Gesellschaftsvertrag* does not otherwise provide. The company agreement, therefore, has priority (*Vorrang*).

§§ 110-122 contain provisions dealing with:

- compensation for expenditure and losses incurred by a member (*Ersatz für Aufwendungen und Verluste*; §§ 110-111);
- restraint of competition by a member (*Wettbewerbsverbot*; §§ 112-113);
- the members right of management (*Geschäftsführungsbefugnis*), its extent (*Umfang*) and withdrawal (*Entziehung*) by the court (§§ 114-117).

---

20 See Klunzinger (*Grundzüge*) (GR), Chapter 2, § 5; Kraft/Kreutz, Part E.
21 See also §§ 29 and 31 HGB.

By § 115(i), a member is entitled to act alone, a veto from another member only having internal effect.[22]

The company agreement can require the members to act together and with mutual consent, but not in a case of urgency (*Gefahr im Verzug*; § 115(ii)).

§ 116 provides that, unlike the members very extensive external power to represent the OHG (*Vertretungsmacht*; laid down in § 126), their *Geschäftsführungsbefugnis* only entitles them to engage in usual trading activities (*Handlungen, die der gewöhnliche Betrieb des Handelsgewerbes der Gesellschaft mit sich bringt*). Anything beyond that requires a resolution (*Beschluß*) of all members (§ 116(ii)).

- the members right of control (*Kontrollrecht*; § 118);
- the passing of resolutions (*Beschlüsse*; § 119). No particular form is required and majority resolutions can be permitted by the company agreement.
- the establishment and division of profit and loss (*Gewinn und Verlust*; §§ 120-122).

Title 3 (§§ 123-130b HGB)

The HGB sharply divides the legal relationship between the members of an OHG internally (*nach innen*; §§ 109-122) from their relationship to third parties (externally (*nach außen*; §§ 123-130b).

For the protection (*Schutz*) of its business partners, §§ 123-130b contain essentially compulsory provisions dealing with:

- the time of effective creation of the OHG (*Wirksamkeit*; § 123);
- the legal status of the OHG and enforcement against its property (§ 124);
- the members power to represent the OHG (*Vertretungsmacht*; §§ 125-125a), its extent (*Umfang*; § 126) and its withdrawal by the court (*Entziehung*; § 127);
- the personal liability (*persönliche Haftung*) of the members of the OHG towards creditors (§§ 128-129a) and the liability of new members following entry (*Eintritt*; § 130);
- the duty to apply for the opening of bankruptcy or composition proceedings in the event of the insolvency of an OHG having no human members (§§ 130a-130b).

Towards third parties, the OHG becomes effective (*wirksam*) from the moment of registration in the *Handelsregister* or from the time it commences business, if this takes place before registration (§ 123(i) and (ii)).

Title 4 (§§ 131-144 HGB)

§ 131 sets out various grounds for the termination (*Auflösung*) of an OHG, eg commencement of insolvency or bankruptcy proceedings, death, notice (*Kündigung*) or court decision (so-called *Auflösungsklage*; § 133).

A member can only apply for termination by court decision, if an important reason exists (*wenn ein wichtiger Grund vorliegt*), eg if another member is guilty

---

22 However, the vetoing member can sue for a restraining order (*Unterlassung*).

of a breach of a fundamental obligation of his under the company agreement (whether deliberately or through his gross negligence) or if the performance of such an obligation becomes impossible (§ 133(i) and (ii)).

Instead of applying to the court for termination of the OHG, the remaining members can apply to the court for the exclusion (*Ausschließung*) of a member if an important reason, as laid down in § 133, exists (§ 140). The company agreement can itself provide for such exclusion in certain circumstances (so-called *Hinauskündigungsklausel*).

The company agreement can provide for an OHG to be continued among the remaining members on departure (*Ausscheiden*) of a member (so-called *Fortsetzungsklausel*; § 138) or with the heirs of a deceased member (so-called *Nachfolgeklausel*; § 139). A departing member is entitled to a pay-out (*Abfindung*) on the same basis as is laid down in the BGB for the composition (*Auseinandersetzung*) between the members of a *BGB-Gesellschaft*.[23]

Within three months of knowledge of his inheritance, an heir has a right to request that the other members allow him to remain in the company as a limited partner (*Kommanditist*) or to declare his departure (§ 139).

The termination of an OHG and the departure of a member must be notified to the trade registry (§ 143).

Title 5 (§§ 145-158 HGB)

Unless the members agree a different form of *Auseinandersetzung* or insolvency proceedings are commenced, the liquidation (*Liquidation*) of an OHG follows its termination (*Auflösung*; § 145(i)). The liquidation procedure is set out in §§ 146-155 HGB. After completion of the liquidation, the liquidators have to notify the extinction of the firm (*Erlöschen der Firma*) to the trade registry (§ 157(i)).

Title 6 (§§ 159-160 HGB)

By § 159 HGB, claims against a former member for company obligations expire five years after the termination of the OHG or the departure of the member unless the claim against the company is subject to a shorter period of limitation. The five year period begins with the end of the day on which the termination or departure is registered in the trade register or, if later, from the time at which the claim against the company becomes due (*fällig*).

Section 2 (§§ 161-177a HGB)[24]

Section 2 of Book II (§§ 161-177a HGB) deals with the *Kommanditgesellschaft* (limited partnership). It contains:

- a definition of the KG and declaration that the OHG provisions of the HGB find supplementary application, except as otherwise provided in Section 2 (§ 161);
- a paragraph dealing with trade registry notification and publication of the entry (§ 162);

---

23 See §§ 105(ii) HGB and 730-740 BGB.
24 See Klunzinger (*Grundzüge*) (GR), Chapter 2, § 6; Kraft/Kreutz, Part F.

- certain special norms regarding the relationship of the members amongst each other (in particular the position of the *Kommanditist* (limited partner)), which only apply in the absence of alternative provisions in the company agreement (§§ 163-169);

- a paragraph forbidding a *Kommanditist* from representing the KG externally (§ 170);

- provisions dealing with the liability (*Haftung*) of the *Kommanditist* to creditors of the KG (§§ 171-176);

- a paragraph stating that the death of a *Kommanditist* does not lead to the termination of a KG (§ 177); and

- a paragraph regarding obligations to provide details on business letters and the duty of application on insolvency (§ 177a).

Section 3 (§§ 230-237 HGB)

Section 3 deals with the *stille Gesellschaft* (silent partnership; §§ 230-237).

Book III (§§ 238-339 HGB): *Handelsbücher*[25]

Book III is divided into three sections:

1   *Vorschriften für alle Kaufleute* (provisions for all businessmen; §§ 238-263).

2   *Ergänzende Vorschriften für Kapitalgesellschaften (Aktiengesellschaften, Kommanditgesellschaften auf Aktien und Gesellschaften mit beschränkter Haftung)* (supplementary provisions for capitalised companies (public companies, partnerships limited by shares and limited companies); §§ 264-335).

3   *Ergänzende Vorschriften für eingetragene Genossenschaften* (supplementary provisions for registered co-operative societies; §§ 336-339).

Book IV (§§ 343-460 HGB): Handelsgeschäfte[26]

Book IV is divided into seven sections:

Allgemeine Vorschriften *(general provisions; §§ 343-372)*[27]

This Section contains the general provisions relating to *Handelsgeschäfte*.

Handelsgeschäfte are defined in § 343(i) HGB as all business belonging to the trading activity of a *Kaufmann* (*alle Geschäfte...die zum Betriebe seines Handelsgewerbe gehören*).

By § 344(i), in the event of doubt it is (rebuttably) presumed that a *Rechtsgeschäft* concluded by a *Kaufmann* is a *Handelsgeschäft*. Moreover, by § 344(ii), it is (irrebuttably) presumed that a *Handelsgeschäft* is involved, if a

---

25 See: Capelle/Canaris, Part 1, Section 5 (§§ 12-13); Hofmann, Part E; Klunzinger (*Grundzüge*) (HR), Chapter 3, § 10.

26 See: Creifelds under *Handelsgeschäft*; Hofmann, Parts H and J; Kallwass, Section 5, Chapter 2 (§§ 87-88); Klunzinger (*Grundzüge*) (HR), Chapter 4, §§ 14-17.

27 See Capelle/Canaris, Part 2, Sections 1-4 (§§ 20-28).

Kaufmann signs a *Schuldschein* (a document confirming a debt (including cheques and bills of exchange)), unless indicated to the contrary in the *Schuldschein*.

§ 345 provides that the provisions on *Handelsgeschäfte* in Book IV HGB also apply to transactions where only one party is a *Kaufmann*. However, there are various exceptions. Thus, in so-called *beiderseitigen Handelsgeschäften* (ie where each party is a *Kaufmann*):

* account must be taken of commercial customs and usages (*Handelsbräuche*); § 346;[28]

* the statutory interest rate is 5% per annum; § 352(i);[29]

* interest on contractual claims can already be demanded from the due date of payment (*Fälligkeit*); § 353;[30]

* a *Kaufmann* with a due contractual claim against another *Kaufmann* has a right to retain and satisfy himself from movables or securities belonging to the other party in his possession; §§ 369-372.

The HGB also increases the protection of persons dealing with a *Kaufmann*, whatever their status:

* by § 347(i), the duty of care (*Sorgfaltspflicht*) of a *Kaufmann* is stricter than in § 276(i) BGB;

* by § 348, a contractual penalty (*Vertragsstrafe*) promised by a *Kaufmann* cannot be reduced;[31]

* by § 349, a *Kaufmann*, who gives a guarantee (*Bürgschaft*), cannot require the creditor to sue the debtor first;

* by § 350, a guarantee, acknowledgement of debt (*Schuldanerkenntnis*) or promise (*Schuldversprechen*) given by a *Kaufmann* does not require a particular form;

* by § 366(i), where a *Kaufmann* disposes of a movable not belonging to him, the other party can acquire ownership, if he (the other party) is in good faith regarding the *Kaufmann's* entitlement to undertake the transaction (his *Verfügungsbefugnis*): he does not need to regard the *Kaufmann* as the owner.[32]

Handelskauf *(trade purchase; §§ 373-382)*[33]

---

28 These include trade terms (*Handelsklauseln*), eg Incoterms. See Creifelds under *Handelsbrauch* and *Handelsklauseln*.

29 Cf § 246 BGB.

30 Cf § 288 BGB. Normally, a *Mahnung* (warning) and *Verschulden* (fault) on the part of the debtor are also necessary.

31 Cf § 343(i) BGB.

32 Cf § 932 BGB.

33 See Capelle/Canaris, Part 2, Section 5 (§ 29).

Kommissionsgeschäft *(commissioneer business; §§ 383-406)*[34]

Speditionsgeschäft *(forwarding agency business; §§ 407-415)*[35]

Lagergeschäft *(storage business; §§ 416-424)*[36]

Frachtgeschäft *(freight business; §§ 425-452)*[37]

Beförderung von Gütern und Personen auf den Eisenbahnen des öffentlichen Verkehrs *(transport of goods and persons by public railways; §§ 453-460)*[38]

Sections 2-7 deal with individual types of *Handelsgeschäfte*.

§§ 373-382 (which are dispositive!) amend the provisions of the BGB regarding sale of goods in the interests of clarity and speed of trade.

Thus, for example, a trader, who purchases goods *(Waren)* from another trader, must examine them and notify any apparent faults *(Mängel)* without delay *(unverzüglich)* after delivery, otherwise the goods are regarded as approved and the purchaser loses his guarantee rights *(Gewährleistungs-ansprüche*; §§ 377(i) and 377(ii)).

Where, however, one of the parties is not a *Kaufmann*, the ordinary sale of goods law of the BGB applies and claims only become statute-barred after six months (§ 477 BGB).[39]

---

34 See Capelle/Canaris, Part 2, Section 5 (§ 30).
35 *Ibid* Part 2, Section 5 (§ 31).
36 See Capelle/Canaris, Part 2, Section 5 (§ 32).
37 *Ibid* Part 2, Section 5 (§ 33).
38 See Capelle/Canaris, Part 2, Section 5 (§ 34).
39 See Creifelds under *Mängelrüge* and *Untersuchungspflicht*.

CHAPTER XII

CIVIL PROCEDURE

THE *ZIVILPROZEßORDNUNG* (ZPO)

German civil procedure (*Zivilprozeß*) is based on the *Zivilprozeßordnung* (ZPO; Civil Procedure Order) of 30 January 1877. The ZPO is divided into 10 Books:

Book I   *Allgemeine Vorschriften* (general provisions; §§ 1-252)

Book II   *Verfahren im ersten Rechtszuge* (first instance proceedings; §§ 253-510b)

Book III   *Rechtsmittel* (legal remedies/appeals; §§ 511-577)

Book IV   *Wiederaufnahme des Verfahrens* (resumption of proceedings; §§ 578-591)

Book V   *Urkunden- und Wechselprozeß* (procedure in the case of documents and bills of exchange; §§ 592-605a)

Book VI   *Familien-, Kindschaft- und Unterhaltssachen* (family, children and maintenance matters; §§ 606-644)[1]

Book VII   *Mahnverfahren* (default notice procedure; §§ 688-703d)

Book VIII   *Zwangsvollstreckung* (enforcement; §§ 704-945)

Book IX   *Aufgebotsverfahren* (claims notification procedure; §§ 946-1024)

Book X   *Schiedsrichterliches Verfahren* (arbitration proceedings; §§ 1025-1048).

THE MAXIMS OF CIVIL PROCEDURE[2]

Civil procedure is governed by certain basic principles or maxims (*Grundsätze*):

1   *Grundrecht des rechtlichen Gehörs* (the basic right to be heard). The parties are entitled under the Basic Law to be given an opportunity to be heard in the proceedings (Article 103(i) GG).

2   *Verhandlungsgrundsatz (Beibringungsgrundsatz)*. It is for the parties to proceedings to introduce facts (*Tatsachen*) and applications (*Anträge*). The opposite of this principle is the so-called *Untersuchungsgrundsatz* or *Inquisitionsprinzip* (examination maxim or inquisition principle), which applies, for example, in criminal and administrative proceedings.

The *Verhandlungsgrundsatz* is restricted by:

(a)   § 138 ZPO: the parties factual statements must be complete (*vollständig*) and truthful (*wahrheitsgemäß*);

---

1   As from 1 January 1992, §§ 645-687 ZPO, which formerly dealt with matters relating to *Entmündigung* (tutelage), have been repealed, as has § 6 BGB in which *Entmündigung* was defined. Adults can now be placed under *Betreuung* (care and attendance). See §§ 1896-1908i BGB.

2   See: Baumann (ER), Part VI, § 18 II; Baur/Grunsky, § 4; Jauernig (ZP), Book 2, Chapter 4 (§§ 24-29); Model/Creifelds/Lichtenberger, Part III C (234).

(b) § 139 ZPO: the judicial duty to clarify and ask questions (*die richterliche Aufklärungs- und Fragepflicht*).

3 *Dispositionsgrundsatz (Verfügungsgrundsatz;* disposition principle). The proceedings are at the disposition of the parties; they can settle or acknowledge claims, make or withdraw applications.

4 *Mündlichkeitsgrundsatz* (oral principle). The *Verhandlung* (hearing) must be oral. However, by §§ 128(ii) and 128(iii) ZPO, written proceedings are possible in certain cases, eg if both parties agree.

5 *Unmittelbarkeit und Öffentlichkeit* (directness and publicity). Only those judges, who are present at the oral hearing, can pass judgment (§ 309 ZPO). With certain exceptions, the hearing must take place in public (§ 169 *Gerichtsverfassungsgesetz* (GVG): Constitution of the Courts Law).

6 *Beschleunigung und Konzentration des Verfahrens* (acceleration and concentration of the proceedings). The dispute must usually be dealt with in one comprehensively prepared hearing (*in einem umfassend vorbereiteten Termin*), the so-called *Haupttermin* (main hearing), which must take place as early as possible (§§ 272(i) and 272(iii)).

7 *Freie Beweiswürdigung* (free assessment of evidence). The court must decide as to the truth or otherwise of the facts presented to it according to its own free conviction (*nach freier Überzeugung*) and only those rules of evidence (*Beweisregeln*) laid down by statute bind it (§§ 286(i) and 286(ii)).

To convince the court, it suffices to establish such a degree of probability as to silence reasonable doubts (*ein so hoher Grad von Wahrscheinlichkeit, daß vernünftige Zweifel schweigen*).[3]

---

3 (1) Whether or not a particular alleged fact is true can be assessed freely by the court. It can consider the proceedings as a whole and (not only) any evidence presented to it: see Jauernig (ZP), Book 2, Chapter 8, § 49 V 1;

(2) To be distinguished from the (normal) requirement of the (full) conviction ((*volle*) *Überzeugung*) of the court is the *Glaubhaftmachung* (substantiation) of a particular alleged fact.

This applies only if permitted by statute (eg in *Arrest* or injunction proceedings: §§ 920, 936 ZPO) and means that a lesser degree of proof – namely, mere *Wahrscheinlichkeit* (probability) – suffices, whereby any *Beweismittel* (means by which evidence is presented) can be used (§ 294 ZPO).

(3) In civil procedure, it is a basic rule (*Grundregel*) that the party alleging that the factual conditions for a particular *Anspruchsgrundlage* or *Gegennorm* (counter-norm) are fulfilled must allege and prove them (the *Behauptungslast* or *Beweislast*).

The evidence of that party (the *beweisbelastete Partei*) is referred to as the *Hauptbeweis* (main evidence), while that of the other party is the *Gegenbeweis* (counter-evidence).

(4) If, following its *Beweiswürdigung*, there is a *non liquet* (ie, something remains unclear) and the court is not convinced of the truth or otherwise of a particular *Tatsache* (fact), the question is then: who (still) has the *Beweislast*?

That person is referred to as remaining *beweisfällig* (liable to supply proof) and bears the consequences (*Folgen*) of the failure of proof (*Beweislosigkeit*). ...

POINTS TO NOTE

One should be aware of the following:

1   There is a basic distinction between the so-called *Erkenntnisverfahren* (judgment proceedings), in which the court reaches its decision (*Entscheidung*) – usually an (*End-*)*Urteil* ((final) judgment; § 300 ZPO) – and the *Vollstreckungsverfahren* (enforcement proceedings; dealt with in Book VIII), in which enforcement (*Zwangsvollstreckung*) takes place.

2   A court can decide not only by means of an *Urteil*, but also in the form of a *Beschluß* (order) or *Verfügung* (direction). These are normally for decisions during the proceedings. The form of appeal against a *Beschluß* is the *Beschwerde* (complaint).[4]

3   After conclusion of the oral hearing, the *Urteil* is pronounced (*verkündet*; § 310 ZPO). The court is then bound by its decision (§ 318), which becomes *formell rechtskräftig* when it can no longer be challenged (*angefochten*) by a *Rechtsmittel*. The *formelle Rechtskraft* of an *Urteil* is a condition of its so-called *materielle Rechtskraft*, whereby the inner content of the decision on the claim becomes binding on the parties and the court. The matter in dispute

---

3... (5)   The *Beweislast* can be eased by *prima facie* evidence (*Beweis des ersten Anscheins or Anscheinsbeweis*).

Anscheinsbeweis is a special type of circumstantial evidence (*Indizienbeweis*). Both are so-called *tatsächliche Vermutungen* (actual presumptions (not to be confused with the term *Tatsachenvermutung* (presumption of fact)).

However, unlike *Indizienbeweis*, *Anscheinsbeweis* is merely provisional (*vorläufig*) and can be destroyed (*zerstört*) or shaken (*erschüttert*) by facts indicating the serious possibility of a different course of events (*die ernsthafte Möglichkeit eines anderen Geschehensablaufes*).

(6)   The *Beweislast* can also be regulated or reversed (*Umkehr der Beweislast*) in cases where statutory presumptions (*gesetzliche Vermutungen*) apply or where presumptions have been developed by the courts (for example, in actions involving alleged medical negligence (*Arzthaftung*) or product liability (*Produkthaftung*), eg in the *Allergy to Hair Tonic Case* (*Sourcebook*, Chapter 5) and the *Fowl Pest Case* (*Sourcebook*, Chapter 6).

See generally Creifelds under *Beweis, Beweislast, Glaubhaftmachung, Non liquet, Anscheinsbeweis, Indizienbeweis* and *Produzentenhaftung*.

See also: Bergerfurth, Part 3 (15-18); Jauernig (ZP), Book 2, Chapter 8 (§§ 49-50); Schellhammer (ZP), Book 1, Part 3, Chapter 7 (Note: the numbering in Schellhammer (ZP) has changed since I consulted the 3rd edn (1987), Book 2, Part 3, Chapter 7, Sections 6, 9 and 10.3-10.6).

(7)   In criminal proceedings, where the inquisition principle (*Inquisitionsprinzip*) applies, the term *Beweislast* is not used in the above manner. The consequence of a *non liquet* is that the accused always has the benefit of any remaining doubt: the unwritten principle *in dubio pro reo* (in case of doubt, for the accused (on issues of fact)). The principle of *freie Beweiswürdigung* again applies and the court must be convinced (of the guilt of the accused) on the basis of the totality of the hearing; § 261 StPO. There are no presumptions of guilt (*Schuldvermutungen*). See Creifelds under *non liquet* and *in dubio pro reo*.

4   See Chapter XII, p 112.

(*Streitgegenstand*) or procedural claim (*prozessualer Anspruch*) cannot be decided upon again (§ 322(i) ZPO).[5]

4   By Articles 97(i) and 20(iii) GG, the judiciary is independent and only bound by statute and law. Previous decisions in other cases (*Präjudizien*: precedents) are not binding on the courts. This principle applies with certain exceptions, eg among the supreme courts where the interest in maintaining unified decisions prevails.[6]

5   Instead of commencing proceedings by writ (*Klage*), an application (*Antrag*) can be made to the plaintiff's local *Amtsgericht* (district court)[7] for the issue of a *Mahnbescheid* (default notice) where a specific amount is due in German currency (the so-called *Mahnverfahren* (default (warning) procedure)).

The defendant has two weeks from service (*Zustellung*) of the Mahnbescheid to pay or dispute the claim. In the event of an objection (*Widerspruch*) from the defendant, the matter is passed to the appropriate court on application (§ 696(i) ZPO). Otherwise, a so-called *Vollstreckungsbescheid* (enforcement notice) can be issued (§ 699). However, a further two weeks are available to the defendant to lodge an *Einspruch* (objection) against the *Vollstreckungsbescheid* (§§ 338 and 700 ZPO).[8]

---

5   *Bis de eadem re ne sit actio* (no action lies twice in the same matter; *ne bis in idem* is the equivalent expression in the field of criminal law). See: Baur, § 13 A and § 17; Bergerfurth, Part 4 (24); Jauernig (ZP), Book 2, Chapter 9 (§§ 61-65). See also Chapter VIII (Note 15).

   Exceptionally, the *Rechtskraft* of a decision can be *beseitigt* (disposed of, overturned) by means of:

   • an application for *Wiedereinsetzung in den vorigen Stand* (reinstitution of the previous position); §§ 233-238 ZPO;

   • an *Abänderungsklage* (writ to adjust a judgment for the payment of regular sums (eg maintenance) due to a change of circumstances); § 323 ZPO;

   • a *Wiederaufnahme des Verfahrens* (resumption of proceedings); §§ 578-591 ZPO.

   The *Rechtskraft* of a decision can also be *durchbrochen* (breached), if grounds for a claim under § 826 BGB can be proven.

   See Creifelds under *Rechtskraft, Wiedereinsetzung in den vorigen Stand, Abänderungsklage* and *Wiederaufnahmeverfahren*.

6   See Creifelds under *Präjudizien, Bindungswirkung* and Jauernig (ZP), Book 1, Chapter 2 (§ 8 V 2).

7   A foreign plaintiff must apply to the *Amtsgericht Schöneberg* in Berlin (§ 689(ii) ZPO).

8   See Baur/Grunsky, § 18 B; Bergerfurth, Part 6 (34); Jauernig (ZP), Book 3, Chapter 14 (§ 90); Model/Creifelds/Lichtenberger, Part III C (249).

THE ZPO IN DETAIL[9]

Book I (§§ 1-252 ZPO): General provisions

Content

Book I of the ZPO (*Allgemeine Vorschriften*; §§ 1-252) is divided into three sections:

Section 1:   *Gerichte* (courts; §§ 1-49)

Section 2:   *Parteien* (parties; §§ 50-127a)

Section 3:   *Verfahren* (proceedings; §§ 128-252).

Section 1 (§§ 1-49 ZPO)

Section 1 contains four titles:

Title 1:   *Sachliche Zuständigkeit der Gerichte und Wertvorschriften* (substantive jurisdiction and value provisions; §§ 1-11).

Title 2:   *Gerichtsstand* (local jurisdiction; §§ 12-37).

Title 3:   *Vereinbarung über die Zuständigkeit der Gerichte* (agreement as to jurisdiction; §§ 38-40).

Title 4:   *Ausschließung und Ablehnung der Gerichtspersonen* (exclusion of and objection to court personnel; §§ 41-49).

Section 2 (§§ 50-127a ZPO)

Section 2 contains seven titles:

Title 1:   *Parteifähigkeit und Prozeßfähigkeit* (capacity to be a party and to take steps in the proceedings; §§ 50-58).

Title 2:   *Streitgenossenschaft* (joinder of parties; §§ 59-63).

Title 3:   *Beteiligung Dritter am Rechtsstreit* (involvement of third parties in proceedings; §§ 64-77).

Title 4:   *Prozeßbevollmächtigte und Beistände* (authorised persons in proceedings and parties assistants; §§ 78-90).

Title 5:   *Prozeßkosten* (costs; §§ 91-107).

Title 6:   *Sicherheitsleistung* (security for costs; §§ 108-113).

Title 7:   *Prozeßkostenhilfe und Prozeßkostenvorschuß* (legal aid and payment on account of costs; §§ 114-127a).[10]

---

9   Books of the ZPO and, as appropriate, their sections are not subdivided into sections or, as appropriate, into titles except where stated in this text.

10   It would extend beyond this text to consider Book I, Section 2, Titles 5-7 ZPO (§§ 91-127a ZPO) in detail. For further information, see: Baur/Grunsky, § 20; Bergerfurth, Part 4 (22); Jauernig (ZP), Book 4, Chapter 16 (§ 95). See also Chapter XIX (note 20) and (note 90) below.

Section 3 (§§ 128-252 ZPO)

Section 3 contains five titles:

Title 1:   *Mündliche Verhandlung* (oral hearing; §§ 128-165).

Title 2:   *Verfahren bei Zustellungen* (procedure for service of documents; §§ 166-213a).

Title 3:   *Ladungen, Termine und Fristen* (summonses to attend, hearing dates and time-limits; §§ 214-229).

Title 4:   *Folgen der Versäumung. Wiedereinsetzung in den vorigen Stand* (consequences of failure to observe time-limits, reinstitution of the previous position; §§ 230-238).

Title 5:   *Unterbrechung und Aussetzung des Verfahrens* (interruption and suspension of the proceedings; §§ 239-252).

Section 1 in detail (§§ 1-49 ZPO)[11]

It is important to note that the GVG (and not the ZPO) governs the substantive (factual) jurisdiction (*sachliche Zuständigkeit*) of the courts (§ 1 ZPO). The ZPO only deals with the local jurisdiction of the courts (*örtliche Zuständigkeit* or *Gerichtsstand*; §§ 12-37 ZPO). Courts without statutory *Zuständigkeit* are forbidden: Article 101(i) GG.

Thus, by § 71(i) GVG, the *Zivilkammer* (civil chamber) of the *Landgericht* (county court (LG)) has jurisdiction (ie is *zuständig*) in the first instance in all civil disputes, which are not within the jurisdiction of the *Amtsgericht* (district court (AG)).

The *Amtsgericht* is the appropriate court for disputes with a value (*Streitwert*) of up to DM 10,000, in landlord and tenant disputes and family matters (*Familiensachen*; § 23b GVG) and in default notice and enforcement proceedings (§§ 689(i) and 764(i) ZPO).

The *Streitwert* of a dispute is relevant both for the *Zuständigkeit* of the court – the so-called *Zuständigkeitsstreitwert*, which is dealt with in §§ 2-9 ZPO – and for the purpose of court fees and costs – the so-called *Gebührenstreitwert* or *Kostenstreitwert*, which is dealt with in §§ 12-34 of the *Gerichtskostengesetz* (GKG: Court Fees Law) (see below: Chapter XIX, p 175).

The *Kammer für Handelssachen* (chamber for commercial matters) at the *Landgericht* deals on application, *inter alia*, with claims between *Kaufleute*, actions between members of a *Handelsgesellschaft* and trade mark and unfair competition matters (§ 95 GVG).

The jurisdiction of the *Oberlandesgericht* (county court of appeal (OLG)) and the *Bundesgerichtshof* (Federal Supreme Court (BGH)) in civil matters is laid down in §§ 119 and 133 GVG. An appeal (*Rechtsmittel*) to the former is known as a *Berufung*, while an appeal (on a point of law) to the latter is a *Revision*.

---

11 See: Baur/Grunsky, § 5; Jauernig (ZP), Book 1, Chapter 2 (§§ 9-12); Model/Creifelds/ Lichtenberger, Part 3 C (236-237).

Section 2 in detail (§§ 50-127a ZPO)

Title 1 (§§ 50-58 ZPO)[12]

A party to civil proceedings is *eine Partei*.[13]

The ZPO distinguishes between the capacity to be a *Partei* – so-called *Parteifähigkeit* – and the capacity to take steps in the proceedings (*Prozeßhandlungen*) – so-called *Prozeßfähigkeit*. *Parteifähigkeit* and *Prozeßfähigkeit* are both pre-conditions for being able to take steps in the proceedings (*Prozeßhandlungsvoraussetzungen*) and pre-conditions for a judgment (so-called *Sachurteilsvoraussetzungen*; also referred to as *Prozeßvoraussetzungen, Zulässigkeitsvoraussetzungen* or *Verfahrensvoraussetzungen*).

It is important to note here that, in all jurisdictional branches, the relevant *Prozeßvoraussetzungen* are checked by the court itself (*von Amts wegen*) as a preliminary point. Their fulfilment means that the action is *zulässig* (admissible).[14]

Prozeßvoraussetzungen can be grouped according to whether they relate to the parties, the court or the object of the action (*Streitgegenstand*)[15] and include, for example:

- the question of the parties being *parteifähig* and *prozeßfähig* and having the right to conduct the action (*Prozeßführungsbefugnis* or *Prozeßführungsrecht*);[16]
- the question of the *Rechtsweg* (legal route, ie court) chosen for the dispute being *zulässig* (used here in the sense of permissible);[17]
- the question of the *Streitsache* (matter in dispute) not already being *sub judice* (*rechtshängig*) and not being the subject of a previous decision finally binding between the parties (*materiell rechtskräftig*);
- the question of the plaintiff having a need for legal protection (*Rechtsschutzbedürfnis* or *Rechtsschutzinteresse*);
- the question of the writ having been correctly issued (*Ordnungsmäßigkeit der Klageerhebung*), ie by the correct (authorised) person and with the correct content.

By § 50 ZPO, a person is *parteifähig* if he is *rechtsfähig*, ie any person, natural or legal, who is capable of being a carrier of rights and obligations. On the other

---

12 See: Bergerfurth, Part 1 (3); Jauernig (ZP), Book 1, Chapter 3 (§§ 18-20) and generally Baur/ Grunsky, § 6.

13 A party in non-contentious matters (*freiwillige Gerichtsbarkeit*): and in administrative, social and finance proceedings (see Chapter XIX, pp 168 and 169) is referred to as *ein Beteiligter* (a person involved).

14 See: Baur/Grunsky, § 10; Bergerfurth, Part 1 (7); Jauernig (ZP), Book 2, Chapter 5 (§ 33); Creifelds under *Zulässigkeit*; note 15 in this chapter.

15 See Creifelds under *Prozeßvoraussetzungen* and Chapter XII, p 108.

16 See Chapter XII, p 103.

17 The basic provision governing the *Rechtsweg* in civil and criminal proceedings is § 13 GVG: see Chapter XIX, p 169.

hand, a person is only *prozeßfähig* so far as he can bind himself by a *Vertrag* (contract; § 52), ie so far as he is *geschäftsfähig*.

Unlike a natural person, a legal person is not itself *geschäftsfähig*, but acts through its legal representatives (*gesetzliche Vertreter*) and is, therefore, technically *prozeßunfähig*. Any procedural fault on the part of a legal representative (which term includes, *inter alia*, parents of minors[18] and company representatives) is equated with that of the party itself (§ 51(ii)).

Title 2 (§§ 59-63 ZPO)[19]

Parties can sue or be sued jointly (*gemeinschaftlich*) and are then known as *Streitgenossen*.

In the case of (normal) so-called *einfache Streitgenossenschaft* (simple joinder of parties), the *Streitgenossen* are, for procedural purposes, treated individually (*als einzelne*, eg accident victims), whereas in the case of so-called *notwendige Streitgenossenschaft* (necessary joinder of parties) only a united decision (*einheitliche Entscheidung*) by the court is possible. The members of a *Gesamthandsgemeinschaft* are *notwendige Streitgenossen* and the presence at a hearing or observation of a time-limit by one of them is effective for all (§§ 61 and 62(i)).

Title 3 (§§ 64-77 ZPO)[20]

A third party can become involved in proceedings in the following ways:

- by means of so-called *Hauptintervention* (direct intervention) where the third party herself claims the thing or right in dispute (§ 64);

- by means of so-called *Nebenintervention* or *Streithilfe* (assistance to one of the parties in the dispute) where the third party has a legal interest (*rechtliches Interesse*) in the success of one of the main parties (*Hauptparteien*) (§ 66(i)).

The third party (*Nebenintervenient* (intervener)) must take the proceedings as he finds them at the time of his accession (*Beitritt*): § 67. He is entitled to use means of attack and defence (so-called *Angriffs- und Verteidigungsmittel*)[21] and generally to take all steps in the proceedings (*Prozeßhandlungen*) so long as the means used and steps taken do not contradict those of the main party he is assisting. Thus, the third party can plead matters in support of or by way of objection to the action, but he cannot extend, amend or withdraw the *Klage* nor can he acknowledge the *Klage* or lodge a counterclaim (*Widerklage*).

The court's decision is binding for the purpose of any subsequent proceedings between the *Hauptpartei* and the *Nebenintervenient* (so-called *Interventionswirkung*) and the latter only has a limited right of complaint if he alleges that the *Hauptpartei* has improperly conducted the action (§ 68);

---

18 See Zweigert and Kötz, Part II A I (Chapter 39 III) on the different position of minors in English and German law. See also: Chapter X, notes 20 and 23; note 25 in this chapter.

19 See Bergerfurth, Part 1 (8) and Jauernig (ZP), Book 3, Chapter 13 (§§ 81-82).

20 See Jauernig (ZP), Book 3, Chapter 13 (§§ 83-85) and Baur/Grunsky, § 9.

21 See also §§ 146, 282 and 296 ZPO.

- by means of so-called *Streitverkündung* (notification of dispute/third party notice) where one of the parties to the dispute believes (*glaubt*) that, in the event of an outcome unfavourable to him, he can make a claim for guarantee or indemnity against a third party (*einen Anspruch auf Gewährleistung oder Schadloshaltung gegen einen Dritten*) or fears (*besorgt*) a claim from a third party (§ 72(i)).

  If the third party accedes to the party giving the notice (the *Streitverkünder*), he has the position of a *Nebenintervenient* and can, in his own interest, assist in the action; otherwise, the proceedings continue without regard to him. However, whether or not the third party accedes to the *Streitverkünder*, the so-called *Interventionswirkung*[22] takes effect between them (§ 74(iii));

- where the third party alleges that he is the rightful creditor (*Gläubigerstreit*: dispute between creditors; § 75) or the defendant alleges that he is in possession of a *Sache* not for the plaintiff, but for a third party (*Urheberbenennung*; § 76).

Title 4 (§§ 78-90 ZPO)[23]

Generally speaking, parties can either conduct their legal proceedings themselves, give any person, who is *prozeßfähig*, written authority (*schriftliche Vollmacht/Prozeßvollmacht*) to take steps in the proceedings (*Prozeßhandlungen*) on their behalf as a *Bevollmächtigte* (authorised person) or allow such a person to appear with them as an assistant (*Beistand*): a so-called *Parteiprozeß* (party action; §§ 79 and 90 ZPO).

However, before certain courts and in certain matters, legal representation (*Vertretung durch Anwälte*) is required (*geboten*), in which case the lawyer instructed must be admitted (*zugelassen*) at the court involved: a so-called *Anwaltsprozeß* (lawyer's action). Thus, for example, in civil cases before a *Landgericht* (county court) or a higher court, as well as in family matters (*Familiensachen*), appropriate lawyers have to be instructed (*Anwaltszwang*); § 78 ZPO.[24]

The term Vollmacht

When considering the term *Vollmacht* (authority/power of attorney), it is important to realise that it is a technical term of the German law of agency (*Vertretung*) set out in §§ 164-181 BGB.[25]

The agent or representative of a person is referred to as a *Stellvertreter* or *Vertreter* and must fulfil two requirements before he can be regarded as such:

---

22 See the previous paragraph in the text.

23 See Jauernig (ZP), Book 1, Chapter 3 (§§ 21 and 22).

24 But not in proceedings before an Amtsgericht (§§ 495-510b ZPO). See also Chapter XIX, note 54.

25 See: Creifelds under *Vollmacht* (*cf Ermächtigung* and *Treuhandeigentum*); Kaiser, Part I (17); Köhler, Part 5 (§ 18); Klunzinger (*Einführung*), Part II (§§18-20); Löwisch, Part 2, § 8; Zweigert and Kötz, Part II A I (Chapter 39 (entitled *Representation*)); see also Chapter X, note 21. For the position regarding minors, see Chapter X, notes 20 and 23 and note 18 in this chapter.

- he must have *Vertretungsmacht* (power to represent/authority); and
- he must act *im Namen des Vertretenen* (in the name of the person represented) or, as is usually said, *im fremdem Namen* (in someone else's name).

A *Vollmacht* is defined in § 166(ii) BGB as *eine durch Rechtsgeschäft erteilte Vertretungsmacht* (a power of representation granted by *Rechtsgeschäft* (legal transaction)). A *Vollmacht* is, therefore, a power of representation granted by means of a *Willenserklärung*/on a voluntary basis, as opposed to a power of representation granted by statute, ie the (*gesetzliche*) *Vertretungsmacht* ((statutory) authority) of a *gesetzlicher Vertreter* (statutory representative).[26]

German law distinguishes strictly between:

(a) the so-called *Innenverhältnis* (internal relationship) between the grantor of a *Vollmacht* (the *Vollmachtgeber*) and the grantee/authorised person/attorney (*Bevollmächtigte*) and

(b) the so-called *Aussenverhältnis* (external relationship) between the *Bevollmächtigte* and third parties.

It is vital to understand that a *Vollmacht* only has effect *im Aussenverhältnis*, ie externally, and is completely independent from the (underlying) internal legal relationship (usually a contract). Thus, a breach of any internal (contractual) restrictions does not affect the validity of (external) acts under the *Vollmacht*.

The extent (*Umfang*) of a *Vollmacht* in proceedings (*Prozeßvollmacht*) is laid down in § 81 ZPO (ie by statute) and a limitation (*Beschränkung*) thereof is only valid externally insofar as it relates to the resolution of the action by means of a settlement (*Vergleich*), a renunciation of the matter in dispute (*Verzichtsleistung auf den Streitgegenstand*) or an acknowledgement of the other party's claim (*Anerkennung des von dem Gegner geltend gemachten Anspruch*); § 83(i). Internal limitations on the *Bevollmächtigter* are, however, always possible.

The *Prozeßhandlungen* of a *Prozeßbevollmächtigter* are just as binding as if they had been taken by the party/*Vollmachtgeber* himself (the *Bevollmächtigter* is the latter's *alter ego*)[27] and any *Verschulden* (fault) on the part of the *Bevollmächtigten* is equated with that of the *Vollmachtgeber*; § 85.[28]

A person who purports to take steps in proceedings without a *Vollmacht* is referred to as a *vollmachtloser Vertreter* or *Vertreter ohne Vertretungsmacht* (unauthorised representative).

The court is only obliged to check whether a *Vollmacht* exists on objection by the other party, in which case the *Vollmacht* must be lodged at the court (§§ 88 and 80(i)).

---

26 See Chapter X, note 20.

27 However, the *Vollmachtgeber* can immediately withdraw or correct admissions or factual statements made by the *Bevollmächtigten* in his presence.

28 See also § 164(i) BGB.

Other relevant terms

It remains necessary to clarify and distinguish the following terms:

• *Prozeßführungsbefugnis* or *Prozeßführungsrecht* (permission (or right) to conduct an action (in one's own name)).

Unlike a *Vollmacht*, which is a pre-condition for being able to take steps in the proceedings (*Prozeßhandlungsvoraussetzung*), the *Prozeßführungsbefugnis* is a precondition of the admissibility of the proceedings (a *Prozeßvoraussetzung*). Its absence results in the action being rejected as *unzulässig* (inadmissible).

The *Prozeßführungsbefugnis* is to be distinguished from the active or passive legitimation (*Sachlegitimation*) of the person whose right or liability is alleged, the lack of which results in the action being dismissed as *unbegründet* (unfounded).

The *Prozeßführungsbefugnis* usually belongs to the person actively or passively legitimated (*sachlich legitimiert*), but it can be transferred to someone who has no *Sachlegitimation* (so-called *Prozeßstandschaft*, where a person is a party to proceedings in his own name although he is not the owner of the right or liability involved).

• *Postulationsfähigkeit*. This is the capacity of a person to appear before a particular court and take steps in the proceedings (right of audience). Thus it is a *Prozeßhandlungsvoraussetzung* and, where *Anwaltszwang* prevails, is restricted to appropriate lawyers.

Titles 5-7 (§§ 91-127a ZPO)

Within Title 5 (§§ 91-107) two separate matters should be distinguished:

• in §§ 91-101, the courts decision on costs (*Kostenentscheidung*), ie the question of the parties liability for costs (*Kostenhaftung*); and

• in §§ 103-107, the procedure for the fixing of costs (*Kostenfestsetzung*), which takes place after the hearing, ie the question of the actual amount of costs due.

Section 3 in detail (§§ 128-252 ZPO)

Title 1 (§§ 128-165 ZPO)

Apart from the fundamental oral principle (*Grundsatz der Mündlichkeit*), this Title contains provisions regarding:

1 (*vorbereitende*) *Schriftsätze* ((preparatory) pleadings), ie content, enclosures, time-limits and additional copies (§§ 129-133).[29] Such pleadings are compulsory where lawyers are involved;

2 deposit and discovery of documents referred to in the pleadings (§§ 134-135);

---

29 See also § 283 ZPO.

3   the course of the oral hearing (*Gang der mündlichen Verhandlung*) and the duties (*Pflichten*) of the parties and the presiding judge (*Vorsitzender*); §§ 136-140.[30]

In particular:

- the parties must give a full and truthful account of the facts (they have a *Wahrheitspflicht*; § 138(i)).[31]

- each party must declare its position regarding facts (*Tatsachen*) alleged by the other party (§ 138(ii). Facts are deemed to be admitted unless objected to (*bestritten*) and a declaration of ignorance (*Erklärung mit Nichtwissen*) is only permissible in certain circumstances; §§ 138(iii) and (iv).

- in restriction of the *Verhandlungsgrundsatz* and in modification of the *Dispositionsgrundsatz*,[32] the presiding judge has a duty to work towards the parties giving a full account of all significant facts and making appropriate applications (*sachdienliche Anträge*) to the court. He can discuss the facts and law with the parties, ask questions (as can other members of the court) and express any reservations (*Bedenken*) regarding matters which have to be checked by the court (eg whether the action is admissible); § 139.[33]

4   the various *Anordnungen* (directions) that can be given by the court, eg the personal appearance (*persönliches Erscheinen*) of the parties, the presentation (*Vorlegung*) of documents (*Urkunden*) and files (*Akten*), the suspension of the proceedings (*Aussetzung des Verfahrens*); §§ 141-155.[34]

5   the protocol of the hearing (*Verhandlungsprotokoll*) that must be kept; §§ 159-165.

Title 2 (§§ 166-213a ZPO)

This title is sub-divided into two blocks:

I   *Zustellung auf Betreiben der Parteien* (service at the instance of (and on and between) the parties; §§ 166-207;

II   *Zustellungen von Amts wegen* (service by the court; also called *Amtsbetrieb* (official conduct (of service)); §§ 208-213a).[35]

---

30   See Creifelds under *Mündliche Verhandlung* and Chapter XII, p 109. See also §§ 272 and 278 ZPO.

31   See Chapter XII, p 93.

32   *Ibid*.

33   See Creifelds under *Aufklärungspflicht des Richters* and Chapter XII, p 94. By § 279(i) ZPO the court must, at all stages of the proceedings, consider and work towards a possible amicable settlement of the dispute in whole or in part.

34   See also §§ 246*ff* ZPO.

35   The provisions relevant to the issue of a *Klage* (writ) are dealt with in Chapter XII, p 107).

Title 3 (§§ 214-229 ZPO)

To be noted here are that:

- a distinction is drawn between normal time-limits (*Fristen*), time-limits set by a judge (*richterliche Fristen*), time-limits set by statute (*gesetzliche Fristen*) and so-called *Notfristen* (time-limits specified as such in the ZPO).

  Notfristen run at all times and cannot be shortened in any event, while the others can in certain circumstances be shortened or extended (§§ 223-224);

- on application, a *Termin* (hearing (date)) can be changed or postponed (*vertagt*) on significant grounds (*aus erheblichen Gründen*); § 227(i). Where a case is not postponed and neither party appears or makes submissions, the court can either decide the matter on the basis of the file (*nach Aktenlage*) or direct the resting (*Ruhen*) of the proceedings; § 251a.

Title 4 (§§ 230-238 ZPO)[36]

To be distinguished are the following terms:

- a *Versäumung*,[37] which refers to a partys failure to observe the time-limit for or to carry out a *Prozeßhandlung* (step in the proceedings) and leads to the party being excluded (*ausgeschlossen*) with the *Prozeßhandlung*; and

- a *Versäumnis*,[38] which refers to a party's failure to attend a *Termin* (*Nichterscheinen*) or to make submissions at a *Termin* (*Nichtverhandeln*)[39] and leads to a possible *Versäumnisurteil* (judgment in default) against him (§§ 330 and 331). A defendant who fails to notify his intention to defend (*Verteidigungsabsicht*) is also open to this risk; § 331(iii).

Title 5 (§§ 239-252 ZPO)

Unterbrechung is the interruption of proceedings *ipso iure*, for example due to the *Prozeßunfähigkeit* of a party, his death or that of his *gesetzlicher Vertreter*. Where, however, a party becomes *prozeßunfähig* or he or his *gesetzlicher Vertreter* dies and the party is represented in the action (by a *Prozeßbevollmächtigter*), it is only possible to achieve the suspension of the proceedings (*Aussetzung des Verfahrens*) on application (§ 246).[40]

Time-limits commence anew (*von neuem*) after any interruption or suspension (§ 249).

Proceedings can not only be interrupted or suspended, but can merely rest. Thus, if both parties so apply and the court considers it expedient (*zweckmäßig*) due to pending negotiations for a settlement or for other important reasons, a *Ruhen des Verfahrens* (resting of the proceedings) can be ordered (§ 251).[41]

---

36 See Baur/Grunsky, § 13.

37 Dealt with here; §§ 230-231 ZPO.

38 Dealt with in Book II of the ZPO (§§ 253ff).

39 See § 333 ZPO.

40 See also §§ 148-155 ZPO.

41 See also § 251a ZPO.

Book II (§§ 253-510b ZPO): Proceedings at first instance

Content

Book II of the ZPO (*Verfahren im ersten Rechtszuge*; §§ 253-510b) is divided into two sections:

Section 1   *Verfahren vor den Landgerichten* (proceedings before the county courts; §§ 253-494).

Section 2   *Verfahren vor den Amtsgerichten* (proceedings before the district courts; §§ 495-510b).

First instance proceedings can be commenced at an *Amtsgericht* or a *Landgericht* by writ (*Klage*). In the absence of any special provisions in Book I, §§ 496-510b or in provisions regarding the constitution of the *Amtsgerichte*, the proceedings in both cases are governed by Book II, Section 1 (§§ 253-494; § 495).

Section 1 (§§ 253-494 ZPO): In the Landgericht

Section 1 contains 12 titles:

Title 1:   *Verfahren bis zum Urteil* (proceedings up to judgment; §§ 253-299a).

Title 2:   *Urteil* (judgment; §§ 300-329).

Title 3:   *Versäumnisurteil* (judgment in default; §§ 330-347).

Title 4:   *Verfahren vor dem Einzelrichter* (proceedings before a single judge; §§ 348-350).

Title 5:   *Allgemeine Vorschriften über die Beweisaufnahme* (general provisions regarding the taking of evidence; §§ 355-370).

Title 6:   *Beweis durch Augenschein* (evidence by inspection; §§ 371-372a).

Title 7:   *Zeugenbeweis* (witness evidence; §§ 373-401).

Title 8:   *Beweis durch Sachverständige* (expert evidence; §§ 402-414).

Title 9:   *Beweis durch Urkunden* (documentary evidence; §§ 415-444).

Title 10:   *Beweis durch Parteivernehmung* (evidence by examination of the parties; §§ 445-455).

Title 11:   *Abnahme von Eiden und Bekräftigungen* (the taking of oaths and confirmations; §§ 478-484).

Title 12:   *Sicherung des Beweises* (securing of evidence; §§ 485-494).[42]

---

42   A more detailed consideration of Titles 2-12 (§§ 300-494 ZPO) would extend beyond the scope of this text.

However, for information regarding
- Title 2, see *Urteil* in Appendix A;
- Title 3, see Chapter XII, p 105;
- Title 4, see Chapter XII, p 105;
- Titles 5-12, see Chapter XII, pp 93 and 105 and the entries between *Beweis* and *Beweiswürdigung* in Appendix A.

Section 1, Title 1 (§§ 253-299a ZPO)

Issue and service of a *Klage*[43]

The issue (*Erhebung*) of a *Klage* requires two acts:

- the lodging (*Einreichung*) of a particular form of pleading (*Schriftsatz*) – the *Klageschrift* – at the court; and
- the service (*Zustellung*) of the *Klageschrift* on the defendant (§ 253(i) ZPO).

When a matter is before the court, it is referred to as being *anhängig* (pending). The proceedings become *rechtshängig* (*sub judice*) once they are served on the other party.

The relevant provisions regarding the procedure of service are contained in:

- § 270(i) ZPO, whereby service is usually undertaken by the court (*von Amts wegen*);
- § 271 ZPO, whereby service must be carried out *unverzüglich* (forthwith) together with a direction to the defendant to appoint an appropriate lawyer, if he intends to defend himself, and to state via his lawyer (ie in cases before a *Landgericht*), within a time-limit of at least two weeks after service, whether there are any reasons why the *Zivilkammer* should not transfer the matter to a single judge (*Einzelrichter*), ie if the case involves particular factual or legal difficulties or is of fundamental significance; § 348(i);
- §§ 208-213a ZPO (together with § 170 ZPO), whereby the *Geschäftsstelle* (business office) of the court is responsible for service of a *beglaubigte Abschrift* (certified copy) of the *Klageschrift* by means of its *Übergabe* (handing-over) by a court bailiff (*Gerichtsvollzieher*)[44] or through the post (§§ 170 and 211).[45]

A certificate of service (*Zustellungsurkunde*) must be returned to the *Geschäftsstelle*, although, where the person to be served is a lawyer, notary, court bailiff, authority or public corporation, a written and dated *Empfangsbekenntnis* (acknowledgement of receipt) suffices to prove service (§§ 212 and 212a).

Where a person has been appointed as a *Bevollmächtigter*, he must be served (§§ 173-178); and

- § 65(i) GKG, whereby in civil actions the *Klage* can only be served after prepayment (*Vorauszahlung*) of the court's fee (*Gebühr*) and disbursements (*Auslagen*).[46]

A *Rechtsanwalt* can ask his client for a fair payment on account of costs (*Kostenvorschuß*): § 17 BRAGO.[47]

---

43 See: Baur/Grunsky, § 7; Bergerfurth, Part 1 (2 and 6); Jauernig (ZP), Book 2, Chapter 6 (§§ 38-40 I); Model/Creifelds/Lichtenberger, Part 3 C (240).

44 For the bailiff's involvement in enforcement proceedings, see Chapter XII, p 118.

45 Other forms of *Zustellung* are available where the circumstances require: *Ersatzzustellung* (substituted service; §§ 181-185 ZPO); *öffentliche Zustellung* (service by public notice: §§ 203-206 ZPO).

46 Certain exceptions are set out in § 65(vii) GKG.

47 See also Chapter XIX, p 175.

Types of *Klage*[48]

A *Klage* is customarily distinguished according to whether it is a:

* *Leistungsklage*, whereby an enforceable judgment requiring a *Tun, Unterlassen oder Dulden* (act, omission or sufferance = a *Leistung*) from the defendant is sought (eg payment of a debt).

* *Gestaltungsklage*, whereby a judgment is sought reshaping a legal situation on the basis of particular legal provisions (eg divorce, company dissolution). The judgment brings about an automatic rearrangement (*Umgestaltung*) of the position and requires no enforcement.

* *Feststellungsklage*, whereby a judgment establishing/declaring the existence or non-existence of a legal relationship (*das Bestehen oder Nichtbestehen eines Rechtsverhältnisses*; § 256(i) ZPO) is sought.

A *Feststellungsklage* can be brought to establish/declare absolute rights (eg ownership, succession, family status, patent or copyrights) and is also useful in accident cases to establish a claim for liability only (*dem Grunde nach*) when a figure for damages is not yet available.[49]

The *Streitgegenstand*[50]

The controversial concept of the *Streitgegenstand* (object of the action) is not used directly as such in the ZPO. However, § 253(ii) No 2 ZPO states that the necessary content of a *Klageschrift* must include the specific statement of the object and ground of the claim raised, as well as a specific application (to the court).[51]

Accordingly, the term *Streitgegenstand* is generally regarded as having the meaning of a procedural as opposed to a merely material *Anspruch* and as consisting of two elements:

* a particular *Klagegrund* (factual basis for the *Klage*); and

* a particular *Klageantrag* (application to the court) in the *Klage*).

When the plaintiff's *Klageantrag* is justified by the *Klagegrund*, the *Klage* is referred to as being *schlüssig* (apparently well-founded).[52]

---

48 See Jauernig (ZP), Book 2, Chapter 5 (§ 34) and Creifelds under *Klagearten*.

49 See § 304(i) ZPO, Jauernig (ZP), Book 2, Chapter 5 (§ 34) and Creifelds under *Leistungsklage, Gestaltungsklage* and *Feststellungsklage*. See also Chapter XIV (note 6).

50 See Jauernig (ZP), Book 2, Chapter 5 (§ 37).

51 *Die bestimmte Angabe des Gegenstandes und des Grundes des erhobenen Anspruchs, sowie einen bestimmten Antrag.*

52 (1) The court compares the submissions in the *Klage* (the *Klagevortrag*) and defence (the *Verteidigungsvortrag*) with the requirements of the relevant *Anspruchsgrundlage* or *Gegennorm* (counter-norm): the so-called *doppelte Schlüssigkeitsprüfung* (double check of apparent well-foundedness).

   See Schellhammer (ZP), Book 1, Part 3, Chapter 6 (Note: the numbering in Schellhammer (ZP) has changed since I consulted the 3rd edn (1987), Book 2, Part 3, Chapter 6). ...

Whether or not the plaintiff's *Klage* (and the *Anspru(e)ch(e)* (claim(s)) made therein) is ultimately actually well-founded (*begründet*) is for the court to decide,[53] following the defendant's response (his so-called *Einlassung*) and any necessary taking of evidence (*Beweisaufnahme*).[54]

The concept of the *Streitgegenstand* is of relevance when the question is raised

- whether the same matter is already *sub judice* (*rechtshängig*);
- whether an amendment of the writ (*Klageänderung*) has taken place;
- whether a court judgment has become finally (and not merely formally) binding on the parties (*materiell rechtskräftig*) and the court has to consider whether the new *Streitgegenstand* is identical, in which case it must be rejected, or is an *anderer* (different) *Streitgegenstand*, which is permissible.[55]

After the *Klage* is lodged[56]

The presiding judge (*Vorsitzender*) has two means to progress the matter once the writ has been lodged. He can either (§ 272(ii)):

52... (2) If both the *Klage* is *schlüssig* and the defence *erheblich*, this can only mean that one or other *Tatsache* is streitig (disputed/contentious).

Facts which are disputed are *beweisbedürftig* (ie require evidence) and form the *Beweisgegenstand* (subject of evidence; also referred to as the *Beweisthema* (evidence theme)). A fact, which is *offenkundig* ((patently) obvious) is never *beweisbedürftig*. See Jauernig (ZP), Book 2, Chapter 4, § 25 IV and Chapter 8, § 49 VII.

(3) The *Schlüssigkeitsprüfung*, therefore, enables the court to establish whether it is necessary to take evidence and, if so, on what points (the *Beweisgegenstand* or *Beweisthema*).

(4) Whether the submission of a party (the *Parteivortrag*) is regarded by the court as *schlüssig* has nothing to do with the *Behauptungslast*, ie the question of which party has the burden of alleging that the factual conditions for a particular *Anspruchsgrundlage* or *Gegennorm* are fulfilled. See Chapter XII, p 93, and Schellhammer (ZP), Book 1, Part 3, Chapter 7 (Note: the numbering in Schellhammer (ZP) has changed since I consulted the 3rd edn (1987), Book 2, Part 3, Chapter 7, Section 8).

(5) There is no *Schlüssigkeitsprüfung* in proceedings where the *Untersuchungsgrundsatz Inquisitionsprinzip* (inquisition principle)) applies: see Jauernig (ZP), Book 2, Chapter 4, § 25 V. In that case it is the court which alone decides the *Beweisbedürftigkeit*: see Jauernig (ZP), Book 2, Chapter 8, § 49 VII 1.

53 *Iura novit curia*: the court knows the law.

54 (1) By § 355(i) ZPO, the *Beweisaufnahme* must take place before the court hearing the case (the *Prozeßgericht*): the principle of *Unmittelbarkeit* (directness). *Beweisaufnahme* can only be placed in the hands of a member of the court – the *beauftragter Richter* (appointed judge) – in certain (exceptional) cases. See Creifelds under *Beweis* and *Beauftragter Richter*.

(2) By § 357(i) ZPO, the parties have the right to be present during the *Beweisaufnahme*: the principle of *Parteiöffentlichkeit* (party openness). See Creifelds under *Beweis* and Chapter XII, p 94.

55 See §§ 261(iii) No 1, 263, 264 and 322(i) ZPO. A proper demarcation (*Abgrenzung*) can be problematical: see Jauernig (ZP), Book 2, Chapter 5 (§ 37), Chapter 6 (§§ 40 II and 41) and Chapter 9 (§ 62 III). The concept is also used in other jurisdictional branches: see Creifelds under *Streitgegenstand*.

56 See Bergerfurth, Part 2 (10); Jauernig (ZP), Book 2 (§ 23).

(a) set a so-called *frühen ersten Termin* (*zur mündlichen Verhandlung*) (initial oral hearing) not less than two weeks after service (§§ 275 and 274(iii)).

The period between service of the writ and an oral hearing is a so-called *Einlassungsfrist* (period for engagement). To prepare this hearing, the presiding judge can require the defendant to lodge a (written) defence (*Klageerwiderung*) within at least two weeks; §§ 275(i) and 277(iii); or

(b) initiate the so-called *schriftliches Vorverfahren* (preliminary written procedure), which the presiding judge must do, if he does not set an initial oral hearing.

In the event of a *schriftliches Vorverfahren*, the presiding judge must (together with service of the writ) require the defendant (*Beklagte*):

- to notify the court (within a *Notfrist* of two weeks) in writing if he intends to defend (*wenn er sich ... verteidigen wolle*); and

- (within at least two further weeks) to lodge his (written) defence (*Klageerwiderung*); § 276(i).[57]

It must be drawn to the defendants attention that:

- if he intends to defend himself, he must appoint an appropriate lawyer (if necessary) to notify the court of his intention (§§ 276(ii) and 271(ii));

---

57 Cf § 275(i) ZPO.

A defendant can react to a *Klage* in various ways, all of which come under the general heading of the defendants *Einlassung* (engagement (in the action)).

The defendant can:

- acknowledge the claim (*Anerkenntnis*; see §§ 307(i) and 93 ZPO);

- take no action at all, possibly resulting in a judgment in default (*Versäumnisurteil*) against him;

- assert that the *Klage* is inadmissible (*unzulässig*) on the ground that one or more *Prozeßvoraussetzungen* (preconditions for a judgment) are not fulfilled or because certain *Prozeßhindernisse* (obstructions to the proceedings) exist;

- dispute the plaintiff's factual submissions (*Bestreiten*);

- admit the plaintiff's factual submissions (*Geständnis*; see §§ 288-290 ZPO), but submit that they are not *schlüssig* (apparently well-founded);

- assert the existence of objections to the claim (*Einwendungen* or *Einreden*);

- lodge a counter-claim (*Widerklage*).

In all but the first two situations, the defendant's (main) application (*Antrag*) is for dismissal (*Abweisung*) of the *Klage*.

See respectively:

- regarding a *Versäumnisurteil*: Chapter XII (note 38);

- regarding *Prozeßvoraussetzungen*: Chapter XII (note 14);

- regarding *Schlüssigkeit*: Chapter XII (note 52);

- regarding *Einwendungen* and *Einreden*: Chapter X (note 15).

See also: Baur/Grunsky, § 11; Bergerfurth, Part 1 (9); Jauernig (ZP), Book 2, Chapter 7 (§§ 43-48); Model/Creifelds/Lichtenberger, Part 3 C (241).

- a failure (*Versäumung*) by the defendant to notify his intention to defend within the *Notfrist* can lead to a judgment in default against him (§§ 276(ii) and 331(iii))[58]
- the defence must be lodged by an appropriate lawyer (if necessary) and that, if the time-limit set is missed, the defence can be rejected as out of time (*verspätet*) (§§ 277(ii) and 296(i)).

The court can require the plaintiff to give his written comments on the defence within at least two weeks (a so-called *Replik*); §§ 275(iv), 276(iii) and 277(iv).

The court's preparation for the hearing[59]

Whether an initial oral hearing (*früher erster Termin*) is set or the main hearing (*Haupttermin*) is to take place, the court must:

- at all stages of the proceedings work towards the parties making their submissions in good time and fully (*rechtzeitig und vollständig*); and
- take necessary preparatory measures (*erforderliche vorbereitende Maßnahmen*) in good time (*rechtzeitig*), eg require the parties to supplement or explain (points in) their pleadings, obtain official information and summon witnesses and experts (§ 273; so-called *prozeßleitende Verfügungen*).

The hearing[60]

Once a hearing date is set (*bestimmt*) by the court, the parties (and any witnesses and experts) are summoned to attend by means of a *Ladung*; § 274(i).

The period between service of the *Ladung* and the date of the hearing (the *Ladungsfrist*) amounts to at least one week where lawyers are instructed, otherwise at least three days; § 217.

The main hearing (*Haupttermin*) proceeds as follows:[61]

1 the matter is announced (*Aufruf der Sache*; § 220(i));

2 the persons present are established (*Feststellung der Anwesenheit*);

3 the court leads the parties into a consideration of the subject-matter (facts) of the case (*Sachverhalt*), both non-contentious and contentious (*Sach- und Streitstand*; § 278(i));[62]

4 the parties make their applications (*Anträge*) to the court with (or without) reference to the pleadings (= *Stellung der Anträge*; §§ 137(i) and 297(ii));[63]

---

58 See also Chapter XII, p 106.

59 See Bergerfurth, Part 2 (10).

60 See Bergerfurth, Part 2 (11); Jauernig (ZP), Book 2, Chapter 12 (§ 78).

61 See note 30 in this chapter and Schellhammer (ZP), Book 1, Part 5, Chapter 2 (Note: the numbering in Schellhammer (ZP) has changed since I consulted the 3rd edn (1987), Book 2, Part 5, Chapter 2).

62 This is the *Verhandlung zur Hauptsache* (see, for example, § 39 ZPO).

63 This is the start of the *streitige Verhandlung* (contentious proceedings) proper.

5 the parties' submissions (*die Vorträge der Parteien*) on the facts and law are made, usually merely by reference to the pleadings (§ 137(ii) and (iii));

6 if necessary, the court orders the taking of evidence (*Beweisaufnahme*) by means of a *Beweisbeschluß* (§ 278(ii), first sentence and § 284);[64]

7 both the evidence and (again) the non-contentious and contentious subject-matter is considered (§ 285 and § 278(ii), second sentence);[65]

8 the court reaches its decision (*Entscheidung*): either in the form of an *Urteil* or *Beschluß*.

The parties must not delay the proceedings (which they have a duty to further (*Prozeßförderungspflicht*)). Thus:

• if the parties do not submit or notify their *Angriffs- und Verteidigungsmittel* (eg facts, allegations, objections, evidence)[66] in time (*rechtzeitig*); or

• if an objection from the defendant to the admissibility of the *Klage* (a so-called *Rüge*) is not raised in time;

the relevant *Angriffs- und Verteidigungsmittel* or *Rüge* stands at risk of being rejected by the court as *verspätet* (too late/out of time); §§ 282(iii) and 296(i)-(iii).

Section 2 (§§ 495-510b ZPO): In the Amtsgericht

Unlike the position before the *Landgericht*, writs or applications can be made to an *Amtsgericht* orally. Moreover, where the *Streitwert* (value in dispute) does not exceed DM 1,200, the *Amtsgericht* has discretion to decide upon the form of the proceedings itself (*nach billigem Ermessen* (in accordance with fair discretion)): an oral hearing is only required if applied for (§§ 495a and 496).

Book III (§§ 511-577 ZPO): Remedies[67]

Book III of the ZPO (*Rechtsmittel*) (legal remedies/appeals) is divided into three sections:

Section 1: Berufung (§§ 511-544 ZPO)[68]

In connection with a *Berufung* (general appeal) in civil proceedings, one should note that

• a *Berufung* against a final judgment (*Endurteil*) of the *Amtsgericht* is dealt with by the *Landgericht* and a *Berufung* against a final judgment of a *Landgericht* by the *Oberlandesgericht* (§§ 511 ZPO, 72 and 119(i) GVG);

---

64 See Chapter XII, p 106.

65 See Chapter XII, p 93.

66 See §§ 146 and 282(i) ZPO for a definition of *Angriffs und Verteidigungsmittel*.

67 See: Baur/Grunsky, § 16; Bergerfurth, Part 5; Jauernig (ZP), Book 2, Chapter 11 (§§ 72-75); Model/Creifelds/Lichtenberger, Part 3 C (245).

68 See Creifelds under *Berufung*.

- the general principle governing proceedings before the *Landgericht* (ie §§ 253-494 ZPO) apply, except as otherwise provided in §§ 511-544 (§ 523 ZPO). Thus, the *Berufung* is a full, second rehearing of the case (§ 525 ZPO);
- the *Berufungssumme* (appeal value) must exceed DM 1,500 (§ 511a ZPO);
- the *Berufungsfrist* (time-limit for lodging the notice of appeal (*Berufungsschrift*)) is one month from service of the judgment and, at the latest, five months after the judgment was pronounced (the *Verkündung* (pronouncement); § 516 ZPO)
- the appellant (*Berufungskläger*) has a further month after lodging his *Berufungsschrift* to lodge his particulars of appeal (*Berufungsbegründung*, consisting of an appeal application (*Berufungsantrag*) and a factual and/or evidential basis for the appeal (*Berufungsgrund*)), but this period can be extended on application (§ 519 ZPO);
- *Angriffs- und Verteidigungsmittel* and *Rügen* (eg new facts, evidence, objections) not submitted by the appellant or respondent (*Berufungsbeklagter*) in time (*rechtzeitig*) can be rejected (§§ 527-529 ZPO).

Section 2: Revision (§§ 545-566a ZPO)[69]

A *Revision* is an appeal on a point of law only to the BGH (Federal Supreme Court) following a final judgment on a *Berufung* to an *Oberlandesgericht* (OLG).

A *Revision* can only be lodged:

- in disputes concerning monetary claims (*vermögensrechtliche Ansprüche*), if the amount at stake exceeds DM 60,000; or
- in the case of a dispute involving a lesser amount or a non-monetary claim (*nichtvermögensrechtlicher Anspruch*), if the OLG grants leave to do so in its judgment on the ground that cither:
  - the case has fundamental significance; or
  - its judgment departs from a decision of the BGH or of the *Gemeinsamer Senat der obersten Gerichtshöfe des Bundes* (Joint Senate of the Supreme Federal Courts) and is based on such departure.

The BGH is bound by the leave of the OLG (*Zulassung*); § 546(i).

A *Revision* can only be based on an alleged breach of federal law or of a provision extending beyond the area of an *Oberlandesgericht* (§ 549(i)). A breach consists of the non-application or incorrect application of a particular legal norm (§ 550) and is always deemed to exist on the seven absolute grounds set out in § 551.

The *Revision* must be lodged within one month of service of the OLGs complete judgment and, at the latest, within five months after the pronouncement (*Verkündung*) of the judgment (§ 552).

---

69 See Creifelds under *Revision*.

Section 3: Beschwerde (§§ 567-577 ZPO)[70]

A *Beschwerde* (complaint) is a form of appeal, which cannot be used against judgments (*Urteile*) or against decisions of an *Oberlandesgericht*, but only in those cases specified in the ZPO, in particular against *Beschlüsse* (decisions/orders) and *Verfügungen* (directions) (§ 329).

The *einfache Beschwerde* (simple complaint) is to be distinguished from the *sofortige Beschwerde* (immediate complaint), which must be lodged within two weeks (§ 577).

Book IV (§§ 578-591 ZPO): *Wiederaufnahme des Verfahrens*[71]

Book IV of the ZPO (*Wiederaufnahme des Verfahrens*; §§ 578-591) deals with the resumption (reopening) of proceedings after final judgment by means of a so-called *Nichtigkeitsklage* (action for nullity in the case of certain procedural errors) or a so-called *Restitutionsklage* (action for reinstitution in the case of certain material errors); §§ 579 and 580.[72]

Book V (§§ 592-605a ZPO): *Urkunden- und Wechselprozeß*[73]

Book V of the ZPO (*Urkunden- und Wechselprozeß*; §§ 592-605a) provides for particular speedy forms of action for claims based on documents, bills of exchange or cheques.

Book VI (§§ 606-644 ZPO): Family matters[74]

Content

Book VI of the ZPO (*Familien-, Kindschafts- und Unterhaltssachen*; §§ 606-644) is divided into three sections:

Section 1:   *Verfahren in Familiensachen* (proceedings in family matters; §§ 606-638).

Section 2:   *Verfahren in Kindschaftssachen* (proceedings in (certain) matters concerning children; §§ 640-641k).

Section 3:   *Verfahren über den Unterhalt Minderjähriger* (proceedings regarding the maintenance of minors; §§ 641l-644).

The former Section 4 (§§ 645-687) has been repealed.[75]

---

70   See Creifelds under *Beschwerde*.

71   See: Jauernig (ZP), Book 2, Chapter 11 (§ 76); Model/Creifelds/Lichtenberger, Part 3 C (246).

72   Such actions breach the *Rechtskraft* of the judgment.

73   See Model/Creifelds/Lichtenberger, Part 3 C (247).

74   *Ibid* Part 3 C (248).

75   See Chapter XII at note 1.

Section 1 (§§ 606-638 ZPO)

Section 1 contains four titles:

Title 1: *Allgemeine Vorschriften für Ehesachen* (general provisions for marriage matters; §§ 606-620g).

Title 2: *Verfahren in anderen Familiensachen* (proceedings in other family matters; §§ 621-621f).

Title 3: *Scheidungs- und Folgesachen* (divorce and ancillary matters; §§ 622-630).

Title 4: *Verfahren auf Nichtigerklärung und auf Feststellung des Bestehens oder Nichtbestehens einer Ehe* (proceedings for declaration of nullity and for establishment of the existence or non-existence of a marriage; §§ 631-638).

Section 3 (§§ 641l-644 ZPO)

Section 3 contains two titles:

Title 1: *Vereinfachtes Verfahren zur Abänderung von Unterhaltstiteln* (simplified proceedings for the alteration of maintenance judgments; §§ 641l-641t).

Title 2: *Verfahren über den Regelunterhalt nichtehelicher Kinder* (proceedings regarding standard maintenance for illegitimate children; §§ 642-644).

Book VII (§§ 688-703d ZPO): The *Mahnverfahren*

Book VII of the ZPO (*Mahnverfahren*; §§ 688-703d) deals with the default notice procedure.[76]

Book VIII (§§ 704-945 ZPO): *Zwangsvollstreckung*[77]

Content

Book VIII of the ZPO (*Zwangsvollstreckung*; enforcement) is divided into five sections:

Section 1: *Allgemeine Vorschriften* (general provisions; §§ 704-802).

Section 2: *Zwangsvollstreckung wegen Geldforderungen* (enforcement of money claims; §§ 803-882a).

Section 3: *Zwangsvollstreckung zur Erwirkung der Herausgabe von Sachen und zur Erwirkung von Handlungen oder Unterlassungen* (enforcement for the purpose of achieving the release of things and the undertaking of actions or omissions; §§ 883-898).

---

76 See Chapter XII, p 96.

77 The subject of enforcement is fully covered in Jauernig (ZVS), Part I. See also: Creifelds under *Zwangsvollstreckung*; Kallwass, Section 8 (§ 120); Model/Creifelds/Lichtenberger, Part 3 C (250-255 and 260-261).

Section 4:   *Eidesstattliche Versicherung und Haft* (assurance in lieu of oath and custody; §§ 899-915).

Section 5:   *Arrest und einstweilige Verfügung* (arrest and injunction; §§ 916-945).

Section 1 (§§ 704-802 ZPO)

Section 1 contains a complex mixture of provisions and terminology of great practical importance. However, the scattering of relevant paragraphs makes an understanding of the system difficult.

The topics dealt with in Section 1 can be set out in the following main groups:

1   Enforcement of (final) judgments ((*End)urteile*); § 704.

2   Other titles capable of enforcement (*Vollstreckungstitel*); §§ 794-801.

3   Formal legal force (*formelle Rechtskraft*) of judgments; §§ 705-706.[78]

4   Provisional enforceability (*vorläufige Vollstreckbarkeit*) of judgments (§§ 708-720a):[79]

   • deposit of security (*Sicherheitsleistung*) by the creditor; §§ 708-710;

   • protection of the debtor against enforcement (*Vollstreckungsschutz*):

      – in the court hearing the case (*Prozeßgericht*); §§ 711-714;

      – in the enforcement court (*Vollstreckungsgericht*); § 765a.

   • temporary suspension of enforcement (*einstweilige Einstellung*); § 719 (707);

   • when provisional enforceability ends; liability of the plaintiff; § 717;

   • preventive enforcement (*Sicherungsvollstreckung*); § 720a (750(iii)).

5   Application for a period to give up possession of residential premises (*Räumungsfrist für Wohnraum*); § 721 (794a).

6   Enforcement of foreign judgments; §§ 722-723.[80]

7   The enforcement duplicate (*vollstreckbare Ausfertigung*) and enforcement clause (*Vollstreckungsklausel*); §§ 724-734.

8   Enforcement in the assets of particular persons (eg unregistered associations, partnerships, married and deceased persons); §§ 735-745, 747-749, 778-785.

---

78   See Chapter XII, p 95 at 3.

79   See Chapter XIII (note 14).

80   Where court decisions from an EU (EEC) country in civil or commercial matters are to be enforced, application can be made for an enforcement clause to be appended to the decision (see the EuGVU and the *Ausführungsgesetz* thereto in Sartorius II Nos 160 and 160a).

   To be distinguished from such cases is enforcement by means of a *Vollstreckungsurteil* (§§ 722-723 ZPO) or by means of a *Vollstreckbarerklärung*. The latter remains necessary under various international conventions in those areas of law where the EuGVU is not applicable (see Article 56 EuGVU).

9   Commencement of enforcement: title (*Titel*), clause (*Klausel*), specification of the parties (*Parteibezeichnung*), service (*Zustellung*) and fulfilment of other conditions; §§ 750-751.

10 The enforcement organs (*Vollstreckungsorgane*); §§ 753-765, 802.

11 Legal remedies during enforcement (*Rechtsbehelfe in der Zwangsvollstreckung*); §§ 766-777, 793 ZPO, 11 RPflG.

12 Costs of enforcement and help from other authorities; §§ 788-792.

Section 2 (§§ 803-882a ZPO)

What can be enforced

Section 2 details the procedure of enforcement of titles directed to the payment of money claims (*Geldforderungen*). To be strictly distinguished therefrom is enforcement of claims to the release of things (*Herausgabe von Sachen*) or to the undertaking of actions or omissions (*Handlungen oder Unterlassungen*), dealt with in Section 3.

Content

Section 2 contains four titles:

Title 1:   *Zwangsvollstreckung in das bewegliche Vermögen* (enforcement in movable assets; §§ 803-863).

Title 2:   *Zwangsvollstreckung in das unbewegliche Vermögen* (enforcement in immovable assets; §§ 864-871).

Title 3:   *Verteilungsverfahren* (distribution procedure; §§ 872-882).

Title 4:   *Zwangsvollstreckung gegen juristische Personen des öffentlichen Rechts* (enforcement against public corporations; § 882a).

Against what can be enforced

Titles 1 and 2 of Section 2 distinguish the manner of enforcement in movable and immovable assets. Against which assets a creditor chooses to enforce is up to him.[81]

Enforcement against assets of the *Bund*, a *Land* or other public corporations or institutions is, however, subject to restrictions; § 882a.

Das bewegliche Vermögen: movable assets

Title 1 (enforcement in movable assets) is divided into three parts:

I   General provisions; §§ 803-807.

II   Enforcement in corporeal things (*körperliche Sachen*); §§ 808-827.

III Enforcement in claims (*Forderungen*) and other valuable rights (*andere Vermögensrechte*); §§ 828-863.

The term *bewegliches Vermögen* (movable assets), accordingly, includes claims and other valuable rights belonging to the debtor. He may, for example, have

---

81 The only exception is contained in § 777 ZPO.

money claims (*Geldforderungen*, eg debts or income) or claims to release of a *Sache* (*Herausgabeansprüche*), against which claims the creditor can enforce.[82]

Pfändung and Verwertung

§ 803(i) states that enforcement in movable assets takes place by way of *Pfändung* (distraint). The following points should be noted:

- the term *Pfändung* is used with regard to *körperliche Sachen, Forderungen* and *andere Vermögensrechte* (ie throughout Title 1);

- while the *Pfändung* of *körperliche Sachen* is undertaken by the *Gerichtsvollzieher* (court bailiff), it is the *Amtsgericht* (district court) acting as enforcement court (*Vollstreckungsgericht*), which deals with the *Pfändung* of the debtor's claims and other valuable rights.[83]

  The responsible officer in the court is the *Rechtspfleger* (§ 20 No 17 RPflG).

  Applications for enforcement by court bailiff are distributed to the appropriate *Gerichtsvollzieher* by the *Gerichtsvollzieherverteilungsstelle* (bailiff's distribution office) of the relevant *Amtsgericht*.

- enforcement involves not merely *Pfändung*, but also, as a further stage, the *Verwertung* (realisation) of the movable asset. The manner of realisation is distinguished according to whether *Sachen* or *Forderungen* are involved.[84]

Das unbewegliche Vermögen: immovable assets

A creditor can choose between three means of enforcement in a piece of land (*Grundstück*):

- registration in the land register of a *Sicherungshypothek* (security mortgage)[85] for an amount of more than DM 500;

- *Zwangsversteigerung* (compulsory sale by auction);

- *Zwangsverwaltung* (compulsory administration).[86]

  Zwangsversteigerung and *Zwangsverwaltung* are dealt with in the *Gesetz über die Zwangsversteigerung und Zwangsverwaltung* (ZVG) of 24 March 1897.[87]

The Verteilungsverfahren

This is a court procedure for the distribution amongst creditors of an amount of money insufficient to satisfy all of them following enforcement in the debtor's movable assets.

---

82 See §§ 829-845 and 846-849 ZPO. See also Model/Creifelds/Lichtenberger, Part 3 C (251-254).

83 See §§ 808 and 828 ZPO and also §§ 753 and 764 ZPO.

84 See §§ 814-825 and 835-839 ZPO.

85 Also referred to as a *Zwangshypothek* (compulsory mortgage). See Model/Creifelds/Lichtenberger, Part 3 C (255).

86 See § 866 ZPO.

87 See § 869 ZPO.

Section 3 (§§ 883-898 ZPO)[88]

Section 4 (§§ 899-915 ZPO)[89]

Section 5 (§§ 916-945 ZPO)[90]

Book IX (§§ 946-1024 ZPO): The *Aufgebotsverfahren*[91]

Book IX of the ZPO (*Aufgebotsverfahren*; §§ 946-1024) sets out the procedure for the issue of court notices requesting the notification of claims or rights where their exclusion is sought, eg in the case of estate creditors (§§ 989ff).

Book X (§§ 1025-1048 ZPO): *Arbitration*[92]

Book X of the ZPO (*Schiedsrichterliches Verfahren*; §§ 1025-1048) deals with the procedure for arbitration pursuant to an arbitration agreement (*Schiedsvertrag*).

---

88 Exposition planned. See Model/Creifelds/Lichtenberger, Part 3 C (256-257).

89 Exposition planned.

90 Exposition planned. See Model/Creifelds/Lichtenberger, Part 3 C (258-259).

91 See Model/Creifelds/Lichtenberger, Part 3 C (262).

92 *Ibid* Part 3 C (263).

CHAPTER XIII

ADMINISTRATIVE LAW

INTRODUCTION

The administration of federal laws is largely in the hands of the *Länder* and administration by the *Bund* (*Bundeseigene Verwaltung*) is the exception (Articles 83 and 86 GG). The federal ministries only have authorities (*Behörden*) beneath them in certain limited areas (eg the *Auswärtiger Dienst* (service of the Foreign Office (*Auswärtiges Amt*)), the *Bundesgrenzschutz* (Federal Border Guard), the *Luftfahrt-Bundesamt* (Federal Office of Aviation) and (before their conversion into public limited companies) the *Bundespost* (Federal Post Office) and the *Bundesbahn* (Federal Railway). Federal ministries normally have no *Verwaltungsunterbau* (administrative sub-construction).

Administrative law in Germany is complicated by the existence of a hierarchy of numerous legal sources (*Rechtsquellen*) for the activities of the executive (*Verwaltung*) on federal, state and local level, not to speak of European Community and public international law (*Recht der Europäischen Gemeinschaft und Völkerrecht*):[1]

1   *Das Grundgesetz* (Basic Law)/*Verfassung des Landes* (state constitution);

2   (*Einfache*) *Gesetze* ((simple) statutes);

3   *Rechtsverordnungen* (statutory instruments);

4   *Satzungen* (by-laws) of the *öffentlich-rechtlichen Körperschaften* (public corporations);

5   *Gewohnheitsrecht* (customary law);

6   *Allgemeine Grundsätze des Verwaltungsrechts* (general principles of administrative law);

7   *Verwaltungsvorschriften* ((internal) administrative regulations).

Federal law always prevails over state law (Article 31 GG).[2]

---

1   Whether *Richterrecht* (judge-made law) is (also) a *Rechtsquelle* is questionable. See: Giemulla/ Jaworsky/Müller-Uri, Book I, Chapter 1; Maurer, Part 1, § 4 and Erichsen, Part II, §§ 6-9; Wolff/Bachof/Stober, Part 3, Section 2, §§ 24 ff.

Regarding the history and development of administrative law see: Bull, Section I, § 2 1-5 and § 5; Maurer, Part 1, § 2 and § 3 I.

For a general summary of administrative law see Baumann (ER), Part IV, § 14.

2   See Chapter II (The Passing of Laws).

THE *VERWALTUNGSVERFAHRENSGESETZ* (VWVFG)[3]

Introduction

The two main statutes at federal level regarding general administrative law are the *Verwaltungsverfahrensgesetz* (VwVfG: Administrative Procedure Law) and the *Verwaltungsgerichtsordnung* (VwGO: Administrative Courts Order).

Before the VwVfG came into force on 1 January 1977, the general principles of administrative law were largely unwritten. The VwVfG basically applies to the administrative activity (*Verwaltungstätigkeit*) of federal authorities (*Bundesbehörden*; § 1(i)). Where federal law is carried out (*ausgeführt*) by state and local authorities (as is the usual case), the federal VwVfG is displaced by the Vw*Vf Gesetze* of the *Länder*, which are practically mirror-images of the VwVfG (§ 1(iii) VwVfG).

The VwVfG does not apply where the activity of the executive is in the form of private law (*Verwaltungsprivatrecht*) nor, for example, to the activities of the tax authorities (*Finanzbehörden*, where the *Abgabenordnung* (AO) 1977 applies), to the area of criminal prosecutions and minor offences (where the StPO and the OWiG apply) nor to the foreign activities of the *Bund* (§ 2).

Content

The VwVfG is divided into eight Parts of which the first six are as follows:

Teil I: *Anwendungsbereich, örtliche Zuständigkeit, Amtshilfe* (application, local jurisdiction, official assistance; §§ 1-8)

Teil II: *Allgemeine Vorschriften über das Verwaltungsverfahren* (general provisions regarding administrative proceedings; §§ 9-34)

Teil III: *Verwaltungsakt* (administrative act; §§ 35-53)

Teil IV: *Öffentlich-rechtlicher Vertrag* (public contract; §§ 54-62)

Teil V: *Besondere Verfahrensarten* (special types of administrative proceedings; §§ 63-78)

Teil VI: *Rechtsbehelfsverfahren* (remedy proceedings; §§ 79-80).[4]

The *Verwaltungsverfahren*[5]

The VwVfG applies to *Verwaltungsverfahren* (administrative proceedings), which is defined by § 9 as the activity (*Tätigkeit*) of a *Behörde* (authority), which:

- has external effect (*Wirkung nach aussen*); and
- is directed either

---

3   See Maurer, Part 1, § 5.

4   Teil VII contains provisions regarding *Ausschüsse* (committees/boards) and honorary activity in the *Verwaltungsverfahren*. Teil VIII contains final provisions.

5   See: Bull, Section II, § 8; Maurer, Part 5, § 19; generally Erichsen, Part IV, §§ 36-42.

(a) to the examination of the conditions for, the preparation and issue of a *Verwaltungsakt* (VA: administrative act; the large majority of cases) or

(b) to the conclusion of an *öffentlich-rechtlicher Vertrag* (public contract).

A *Behörde* is defined for the purpose of the VwVfG as every *Stelle* (point), which undertakes functions of public administration (§ 1(iv)).

A *Verwaltungsverfahren* can be and is, as a rule, conducted informally (*formlos*; § 10).[6]

Formal proceedings can, however, be required by statute, in which case certain supplementary provisions apply (§§ 63-71).

The parties to (and conduct of) a *Verwaltungsverfahren* are dealt with in §§ 11-30 VwVfG.

The relevant *Behörde* has discretion whether and when to conduct the *Verwaltungsverfahren* and investigates the facts itself (§§ 22, first sentence and 24(i)). The parties are referred to as *Beteiligte* (persons involved) and have rights to:

- information (*Auskunft*) as to their rights and duties (§ 25);
- a hearing (*Anhörung*; § 28);
- inspection of the file(s) (*Akteneinsicht*; § 29);
- secrecy (*Geheimhaltung*; § 30).

THE *VERWALTUNGSAKT* (VA)[7]

Definition

The important concept of the *Verwaltungsakt* is defined in § 35, first sentence VwVfG and consists of the following elements:[8]

(a) *jede Verfügung, Entscheidung oder andere hoheitliche Maßnahme* (every direction, decision or other official measure)

(b) *von einer Behörde* (by an authority)

---

6   The *Verwaltungsverfahren* must be conducted simply and expediently (*einfach und zweckmäßig*; § 10, 2nd sentence VwVfG) in German (§ 23(i) VwVfG).

7   See: Giemulla/Jaworsky/Müller-Uri, Book I, Chapters 5-6 and Maurer, Part 3, §§ 9-12; Erichsen, Part III, Section I, §§ 11-20; Wolff/Bachof/Stober, Part 5, Section 2, § 45.

8   See Giemulla/Jaworsky/Müller-Uri, Book I, Chapter 4 B-G.

   To be distinguished from the formal *Verwaltungsakt* is the pure administrative order (*schlichtes Verwaltungsgebot*), which can be issued by the executive in the case of civil servants (*Beamte*) and other persons, who are subject to direction (*weisungsabhängig*, eg schoolchildren and soldiers): see Bull, Section III, § 10.

   For a classification of the various types of administrative legal relationships (*Verwaltungsrechtsverhältnisse*) see Bull, Section IV, § 14.

   See also Creifelds under *Gewaltverhältnis, öffentlich-rechtliches*.

(c) *zur Einzelfallregelung auf dem Gebiet des öffentlichen Rechts* (to regulate an individual case in the area of public law)

(d) *mit unmittelbarer Rechtswirkung nach aussen* (with direct external legal effect).

Where a VA is addressed to a particular or distinguishable group of persons (*Personenkreis*) or relates to the public quality of a *Sache* or its use by the general public, it is known as an *Allgemeinverfügung* (general direction; § 35, second sentence).

Content

The content of a VA must be sufficiently specific (*hinreichend bestimmt*). It can be issued orally, in writing or in other form, but, if in writing, reasons (*Gründe*) must be given.[9]

A VA can be supplemented or limited by a so-called *Nebenbestimmung* (collateral provision), eg a *Bedingung* (condition) or *Auflage* (requirement).[10]

Validity and legality

A VA becomes *wirksam* (effective/valid) on its *Bekanntgabe* (notification) to the person to whom it is directed or who is affected by it and remains valid for so long and insofar as it is not withdrawn, revoked, otherwise (ie judicially) quashed or settled by lapse of time or otherwise.[11]

Exceptionally, however, a VA can be *nichtig* (void *ab initio*), in which case it is *unwirksam*.[12]

A VA is presumed valid, but the executive is bound by Article 20(iii) GG to act in accordance with law (the principle of the *Rechtmäßigkeit der Verwaltung* (*Vorbehalt des Gesetzes*)).

A VA, which is not *rechtmäßig* (legal), is, therefore, *rechtswidrig* (illegal) or *fehlerhaft* (faulty). Once it has been challenged (*angefochten*), it can be rescinded (*aufgehoben*) by the (administrative) court; until then, the VA is known as being *anfechtbar* (challengeable) or *aufhebbar* (voidable).[13]

---

9   See §§ 37 and 39 VwVfG.

10 See § 36 VwVfG. See also: Giemulla/Jaworsky/Müller-Uri, Book I, Chapter 7; Maurer, Part 3, § 12; Wolff/Bachof/Stober, Part 5, Section 2, § 47.

11 See § 43(ii) VwVfG: *Ein Verwaltungsakt bleibt wirksam, solange und soweit er nicht zurückgenommen, widerrufen, anderweitig aufgehoben oder durch Zeitablauf oder auf andere Weise erledigt ist.*
    See also: Bull, Section III, §§ 11 and 12; Giemulla/Jaworsky/Müller-Uri, Book I, Chapter 6 A I.

12 See §§ 43(iii), 44(i) and 44(ii) VwVfG. See also Giemulla/Jaworsky/Müller-Uri, Book I, Chapter 5 C I.

13 See Giemulla/Jaworsky/Müller-Uri, Book I, Chapter 5 C II and the diagram (*Prüfungsschema (Fehlerlehre)*) in Book I, Chapter 5 F.

With certain exceptions, a *Widerspruch* (formal objection) and *Anfechtungsklage* (writ of challenge) against a VA have suspensive effect (*aufschiebende Wirkung*); § 80(i) VwGO.[14]

Accordingly, whether or not a VA is *wirksam* (valid) is a strictly separate question from that of its *Rechtmäßigkeit* (legality).

The criteria for establishing the legality of a VA are:

* formal: was the issuing *Behörde zuständig* (competent)? Did it conduct the correct procedure (*Verfahren*)? Was the VA issued in the correct form?

* material: did the *Behörde* observe the general principles of administrative law and, in accordance with the principle of the *Rechtmäßigkeit der Verwaltung*, act on the basis of and properly apply a valid norm?[15]

---

14 Once one of these *Rechtsmittel* (legal remedies) is lodged, no steps can be taken to enforce the VA. *Vollziehung* (enforcement) of the VA is *gehemmt* (prevented from running).

This is unlike the position in civil proceedings, where the lodging of a *Rechtsmittel* does not usually prevent a judgment from being declared provisionally enforceable (*vorläufig vollstreckbar*).

By § 80(ii) VwGO the suspensive effect (*aufschiebende Wirkung*) of a *Widerspruch* and *Anfechtungsklage* is inapplicable:

(1) where public levies and costs are demanded;

(2) where orders (*Anordnungen*) and measures (*Maßnahmen*) are given or taken by *Polizeivollzugsbeamten* ((executive) police officers), which are *unaufschiebbar* (ie cannot be postponed);

(3) in (other) cases prescribed by federal law;

(4) where the *Behörde* orders immediate enforcement (*sofortige Vollziehung*) of the VA.

In the case of no 4 above:

* the *Behörde* must give written reasons for the particular interest (*das besondere Interesse*) in immediate enforcement, unless there is *Gefahr im Verzug* (danger in delay); § 80(iii) VwGO;

* an application can be made to the administrative court for the *aufschiebende Wirkung* to be fully or partially restored (*wiederhergestellt*); § 80(v) VwGO. This can be done without having to involve the *Widerspruchsbehörde* (next higher authority) and before lodging an *Anfechtungsklage*. It is a form of *vorläufiger Rechtsschutz* (provisional legal protection).

When it deals with an application under § 80(v) VwGO, the administrative court has discretion (*Auf Antrag kann das Gericht...*). Unless the VA is clearly legal or illegal, the court must weigh the public interest in enforcement of the VA against the applicants interest in its suspension: see Drews/Wacke/Vogel/Martens, Part 7, § 30 no 5.

In the case of § 80(ii) nos 1-3, the administrative court can order that the *aufschiebende Wirkung* takes effect fully or partially.

Once a *Widerspruch* has been lodged, enforcement of the VA can also be suspended by the *Behörde* itself on application; § 80(iv) VwGO.

See: Bull, Section VI, § 19 8; Creifelds under *Aufschiebende Wirkung, Vollziehung, sofortige* I and *Vorläufige Vollstreckbarkeit*. See also Chapter XII (note 77) and Chapter XVII (note 39) below.

15 Ie was there a *gesetziche Grundlage* (statutory basis) for the issue of the VA? See Chapter II, p 8 above and Chapter XIV, note 12 below. See also: Erichsen, Part III, Section I, § 15; Giemulla/Jaworsky/Müller-Uri, Book I, Chapter 5 B III; Wolff/Bachof/Stober, Part 5, Section 2, §§ 48-49.

Bestandskraft, Rücknahme and *Widerruf*

A VA becomes *bestandskräftig* (finally binding) when it can no longer be challenged.

The parallel of the concept of *Bestandskraft* is, in civil procedure, the concept of the *Rechtskraft* of a judgment (*Urteil*).[16]

However, unlike the position after judgment in a civil case, the *Rücknahme* (withdrawal) and *Widerruf* (revocation) of a VA or the *Wiederaufgreifen des Verfahrens* (reconsideration of the proceedings) by the *Behörde* are possible in certain circumstances.[17]

Types[18]

Administrative acts (VAs) are distinguished according to whether they:

* are *befehlend* (require or forbid particular action, eg police orders, notices for payment of fees or taxes)
* are *rechtsgestaltend* (create or amend particular legal relationships, eg naturalisation, appointments, permissions)
* are *feststellend* (effect a declaration as to particular circumstances, eg as to status or claims)
* are *begünstigend* (favourable/advantageous)
* are *belastend* (burdensome/disadvantageous)
* are *Verwaltungsakte mit Drittwirkung* (have effect on third parties, eg building consent).

---

16 See Chapter XII, p 95 at 3.

As in civil procedure, one distinguishes the *formelle Bestandskraft* (formal authority) or *Unanfechtbarkeit* (non-challengeability) of a VA and its *materielle Bestandskraft* (material authority), which arises only insofar as the VA is not withdrawn or revoked by the issuing *Behörde*.

Once a VA becomes *formell und materiell bestandskräftig*, it becomes *vollziehbar* (enforceable).

See: Giemulla/Jaworsky/Müller-Uri, Book I, Chapter 6 A II; Maurer, Part 3, § 11 I 3 and 4; Wolff/Bachof/Stober, Part 5, Section 2, § 50.

17 See §§ 48-51 VwVfG.

See also: Erichsen, Part III, Section I, §§ 16-19; Giemulla/Jaworsky/Müller-Uri, Book I, Chapter 6 B-E; Maurer, Part 3, § 11 II-VII; Wolff/Bachof/Stober, Part 5, Section 2, § 51

Rücknahme and *Widerruf* are subsidiary terms to *Aufhebung* (annulment). When a VA is *rechtswidrig* (illegal) one speaks of *Rücknahme* (§ 48 VwVfG), whereas when a VA is *rechtmäßig* (legal) one speaks of *Widerruf* (§ 49 VwVfG).

18 See Giemulla/Jaworsky/Müller-Uri, Book I, Chapter 4 K; Maurer, Part 3, § 9 V; Wolff/ Bachof/Stober, Part 5, Section 2, § 46.

Grant of an *Erlaubnis* or *Genehmigung*

A particular example of a *rechtsgestaltende* and *begünstigende* VA is the (grant (*Erteilung*) of an) *Erlaubnis* (permission),[19] the usual basis for which is a *Verbot mit Erlaubnisvorbehalt* ((preventive) prohibition with the right to grant an *Erlaubnis* reserved).

The *Erlaubnis* is to be distinguished from the so-called *Ausnahmebewilligung*, *Dispens* or *Befreiung*, which grants the applicant an exception from the normal (repressive) prohibition of particular conduct.

The grant of an *Erlaubnis* can either be *gebunden* (compulsory: where terms such as *muß* or *ist zu* (*erteilen*) are used) or *frei* (free, ie the authority has *Ermessen* (discretion): where terms such as *kann* or *darf* are used).

Decisions of a *Behörde* on the basis of *Ermessen* (*Ermessensentscheidungen*) can be examined by the administrative court:

- if the exercise of the *Ermessen* exceeds the *gesetzlichen Grenzen* (statutory limits; *Ermessensüberschreitung*);

- if the *Ermessen* is not (fully) exercised (*Ermessensnichtgebrauch / Ermessensunterschreitung*); or

- if its exercise is abused (*Ermessensmißbrauch*).

Ermessen must be exercised *pflichtgemäß* (in accordance with (legal) obligation) and *fehlerfrei* (free of faults).[20]

It is important to contrast *Ermessen*, which is part of the consequence (*Rechtsfolge*) of a norm and can only be controlled by the administrative court in certain circumstances,[21] with the concept of the *unbestimmter Rechtsbegriff* (indefinite legal term), which is part of the norm itself, part of its *Tatbestand*. The interpretation by a *Behörde* of an *unbestimmter Rechtsbegriff* can always be fully reexamined by the court, except where the *Behörde* has so-called *Beurteilungsspielraum* (room for judgment).[22]

A *Behörde* can sometimes be compelled (*verpflichtet*) to take action in the event of a reduction of its *Ermessen* to zero (*Ermessensreduzierung auf Null*) where there is a particularly intensive threat to individual interests.[23]

---

19 Also referred to as a *Genehmigung* (approval). See Creifelds under *Erlaubnis (behördliche)* and *Gewerbezulassung*.

20 The executive must observe the principles of appropriateness/expediency (*Zweckmäßigkeit*) and proportionality (*Verhältnismäßigkeit*). See § 40 VwVfG, § 114 VwGO and Creifelds under *Ermessen, Zweckmäßigkeitsgrundsatz* and *Verhältnismäßigkeit(sgrundsatz)*. See also Chapter VIII, note 9.

21 See the previous paragraph in the text.

22 This is only the case in certain limited areas when internal value-judgments are involved, eg decisions regarding exams or civil service matters. See Creifelds under *Ermessen*.

23 See: Bull, Section II, § 7 7; Giemulla/Jaworsky/Müller-Uri, Book I, Chapter 2 D; Maurer, Part 2, § 7. If the executive exercises its *Ermessen* in a particular way, it can become bound (*Selbstbindung der Verwaltung*). In a similar subsequent case, it cannot then depart from its existing practice without a substantial reason (*ohne sachlichen Grund*).

CHAPTER XIV

ADMINISTRATIVE PROCEDURE

AVAILABLE REMEDIES:
THE *VERWALTUNGSGERICHTSORDNUNG* (VWGO)

The addressee of a *Verwaltungsakt* can defend himself by informal *Rechtsbehelfen* (namely by a *Gegenvorstellung* (counter-response), by an *Aufsichtsbeschwerde* (complaint to the next higher *Behörde*) or even by a parliamentary petition,[1] or by formal *Rechtsmitteln* (namely by *Widerspruch* (objection) and, usually thereafter, by proceedings before the *Verwaltungsgericht* (VG: administrative court).

Administrative court procedure is governed by the (federal) *Verwaltungsgerichtsordnung* (VwGO: Administrative Court Order) of 21 January 1960. There are three instances: the VG, the *Oberverwaltungsgericht* (OVG; administrative court of appeal)[2] and, on the federal level, the *Bundesverwaltungsgericht* (BVerwG; Federal Administrative Court) in Berlin. Legal representation by a *Rechtsanwalt* is only compulsory before the BVerwG.[3]

The OVG is not only *zuständig* (competent) on an appeal (*Berufung*) from the VG, but also for the so-called *Normkontrollverfahren* (norm control procedure),[4] in which, on application, the OVG can examine the validity of norms below a *Landesgesetz* (state statute), eg local building plans (*Bebauungspläne*), which are passed by the *Gemeinden* in the form of *Satzungen* (by-laws).[5]

TYPES OF WRIT

The main types of *Klage* (writ) issued at the VG are:

- the *Gestaltungsklagen* (actions to (re)organise a legal relationship, eg the *Anfechtungsklage* (directed to the *Aufhebung* (annulment or quashing) of a VA));
- the *Leistungsklagen* (actions claiming a *Leistung* (performance), eg the *Verpflichtungsklage* (directed to the *Erlaß* (issue) of a VA)); and
- the *Feststellungsklagen* (actions to establish/declare a particular right or legal relationship; a special example is the so-called *Fortsetzungsfeststellungsklage* (an action to establish/declare that, after the event, a particular VA was illegal).[6]

---

1   See Creifelds under *Beschwerde- und Petitionsrecht* and *Gegenvorstellungen*.
2   The OVG is sometimes called the *Verwaltungsgerichtshof* (VGH).
3   See § 67 VwGO.
4   See § 47(i) VwGO.
5   See: Bull, Section VI, § 19 9; Stern, Part 1, § 5.
6   See § 42(i) VwGO, § 43(i) VwGO and § 113(i), fourth sentence VwGO. See also: Bull, Section VI, § 19 6; Creifelds under *Verwaltungsstreitverfahren* 1 (a)-(c).

PRELIMINARY REQUIREMENTS

Before an *Anfechtungsklage* or *Verpflichtungsklage* can be lodged, it is usually necessary for a *Widerspruchsverfahren/Vorverfahren* (objection proceedings/ preliminary proceedings) to have been conducted (on initiation by the complainant) and for a so-called *Widerspruchsbescheid* (objection notice, normally from the next higher *Behörde*) to have been issued.[7]

The *Widerspruchsverfahren* is no judicial proceeding, but part of the *Verwaltungsverfahren*, ie dealt with internally by the *Widerspruchsbehörde*, which examines not only the *Rechtmäßigkeit* (legality) of the VA (as does the VG), but also its *Zweckmäßigkeit* (expediency).[8]

The general clause § 40(i) VwGO grants access to the administrative court (*Verwaltungsrechtsweg*) in all public law disputes of a non-constitutional nature, so long as jurisdiction is not expressly granted to another court by federal law.[9]

The conduct of the *Widerspruchsverfahren* and the availability of the *Verwaltungsrechtsweg* under § 40(i) are only two of the preliminary requirements (conditions) for the admissibility (*Zulässigkeit*) of a *Klage* to the VG.[10]

The *Kläger* (plaintiff) must also:

- claim (at least the possibility) that he is injured in his (subjective) rights (*in seinen Rechten verletzt*) by the VA, its refusal or the failure to grant it, ie he must have so-called *Klagebefugnis* (authority to sue); a popular action (*Popularklage*) is thereby excluded;[11]

- choose the correct type of *Klage* (*Klageart*);

---

7 See §§ 68 and 73 VwGO.

8 See § 68(i) VwGO.

   A *Widerspruch* must be lodged within one month of the *Bekanntgabe* (notification) of the VA; § 70(i) VwGO. If the issuing *Behörde* considers the *Widerspruch* to be justified (*begründet*) – because, for example, the VA was *rechtswidrig* (illegal) – the *Behörde* must remedy the situation (so-called *Abhilfe* (redress)) and decide on costs; § 72 VwGO. Otherwise, a *Widerspruchsbescheid* must be issued; § 73(i) VwGO.

9 *Cf* Chapter VII (Note 5). See also: Creifelds under *Enumerationsprinzip, Öffentlich-rechtliche Streitigkeiten* and *Ordentlicher Rechtsweg*; Bull, Section VI, § 19 2

10 Such conditions are known as the *Sachurteilsvoraussetzungen* (conditions for a substantive judgment). See: Stern, Part I, §§ 2-16; Giemulla/Jaworsky/Müller-Uri, Book III, Chapters 2 and 3; Bull, Section VI, § 19 4.

11 See § 42(ii) VwGO.

   To be distinguished from a *Popularklage* is the action by a federation (*Verbandsklage*), which, for example, in issues concerning environmental law (*Umweltrecht*), has the right to sue before the administrative court in certain *Länder*. See Creifelds under *Popularklage, Verbände* and *Verbandsklage*.

   On the question of *Klagebefugnis*, see also the good example given in Wesel (JW), Chapter IX and Wesel (FR), Chapter 5 (a neighbour's *Anfechtungsklage* against a *Baugenehmigung* (planning permission)). See also Bull, Section VI, § 19 5 and 7.

- lodge his *Klage* in the correct form and within the appropriate time-limit (*Frist*; usually one month from service of the *Widerspruchsbescheid*).[12]

The question of the *Zulässigkeit* of a *Klage* must be strictly separated from the question whether it is well-founded (its *Begründetheit*). An *Anfechtungsklage* or *Verpflichtungsklage* is only *begründet* (well-founded), if the VA (or, in the case of a *Verpflichtungsklage*, its refusal or the failure to grant it) is illegal (*rechtswidrig*) and the plaintiff is thereby injured in his rights (*in seinen Rechten verletzt*).[13]

The protection of the administrative court is not only available against VAs, but also against pure administrative action (*schlichtes Verwaltungshandeln*) in the form of so-called *Realakte* (real acts). Stoppage (*Unterlassung*) or disposal (*Beseitigung*) can be claimed.[14]

As in criminal procedure, the *Untersuchungsgrundsatz* (inquisition maxim) applies before the VG.[15]

---

12 See §§ 74, 81 and 82 VwGO.
13 See § 113(i) and § 113(iv) VwGO. A VA is illegal, if it is not *rechtmäßig* (lawful): see Chapter XIII, p 123.
14 § 1004 BGB analogously.
15 See § 86(i) VwGO.

CHAPTER XV

CRIMINAL LAW

INTRODUCTION

German criminal law is governed by the *Strafgesetzbuch* (StGB: Criminal Code) of 15 May 1871, variously reformed, amended and reissued. Criminal offences are also contained in numerous collateral statutes (*Nebengesetze*).[1]

The StGB is divided into two *Teile* (parts):[2]

1 The *Allgemeiner Teil* (AT: General Part; §§ 1-79b), in turn divided into five *Abschnitte* (Sections). The AT contains general provisions and principles for all offences (*Straftaten* or *Delikte*).

2 The *Besonderer Teil* (BT: Special Part; §§ 80-358), in turn divided into 29 *Abschnitte*. The BT contains a catalogue of individual *Straftaten* and their permissible punishment.

The StGB is based on the principle (*Grundsatz*) that an act (*Tat* or *Handlung*) can only be punished, if its punishability (*Strafbarkeit*) is fixed by statute (*gesetzlich bestimmt*) before the act is committed, ie there can be no crime (or punishment) without law: *nullum crimen (nulla poena) sine lege*.[3]

This principle is laid down in § 1 StGB, which repeats Article 103(ii) GG, and means that

1 the conditions for (*Voraussetzungen*) and consequences (*Rechtsfolgen*) of offences must be defined (*bestimmt*) by the legislature as exactly as possible (*Bestimmtheitsgrundsatz*);

2 the retrospective application of offences to acts committed before the offence existed is forbidden (*Rückwirkungsverbot*); and

3 an act cannot be punished by analogy to a particular offence (*Analogieverbot*).

---

1   See: Baumann (ER), Part V, § 16 II 1; Model/Creifelds/Lichtenberger, Part H (393-394, 404); Naucke, § 4 II.

2   See Naucke, § 6.

3   See Baumann (GBS), Chapter 3 II; Creifelds under *nullum crimen sine lege*; Naucke, § 2 II. See also Chapter VIII (note 15).

When considering Article 103(ii) GG, the fact that acts are committed on state instructions (*im staatlichen Auftrag*) can give rise to problems. Was punishability fixed by statute before the act was committed?

In the *Shootings at the Berlin Wall Case* (*Sourcebook*, Chapter 7), the court concluded that: 'It is not arbitrary treatment, if the accused, so far as the unlawfulness of his action is concerned, is judged in the way in which he ought to have been treated on the correct interpretation of GDR law at the time of the act.'

Following barbaric orders did not properly constitute a justification and, accordingly, Article 103(ii) GG was no defence.

TYPES OF OFFENCE[4]

The offences (*Straftaten*) of the StGB are divided into two categories (§ 12):

1 *Verbrechen*, being those offences attracting a minimum punishment of one year's imprisonment (*Freiheitsstrafe*);

2 *Vergehen*, being those offences attracting a minimum punishment of a lesser period of imprisonment or a fine (*Geldstrafe*).

The main importance of the distinction is that an attempted *Verbrechen* is always punishable, whereas an attempted *Vergehen* only if expressly provided for.[5]

Lesser offences have been removed from the StGB and decriminalised (*entkriminalisiert*). They are termed *Ordnungswidrigkeiten* and are punishable merely by a so-called *Geldbuße* (fine).[6]

The basis for an understanding of the BT is the concept of *Rechtsgüterschutz* (protection of *Rechtsgüter*, ie assets of social (literally, legal) importance). It is a central principle that the function of criminal law is to protect *Rechtsgüter* against injury (*Verletzung*) or threat (*Gefährdung*).

The BT contains three main groups of offences categorised according to the relevant *Rechtsgut* protected:[7]

1 offences against the state[8] and community values (*Gemeinschaftswerte*);[9]

---

4 See: Creifelds under *Straftat II*; Model/Creifelds/Lichtenberger, Part H (395, 403); Naucke, § 6 III and IV; Otto (AS), Part 1 (§§ 1-4).

5 See § 23(i) StGB. The punishment for an attempted offence can be reduced: see § 23(ii) StGB (§ 49 StGB).

6 See the *Gesetz über Ordnungswidrigkeiten* (OWiG; Minor Offences Law) of 24 May 1968 as amended and reissued from time to time. See also: Creifelds under *Bußgeld, -verfahren, Geldbuße* and *Ordnungswidrigkeiten*; Baumann (ER), Part V, § 16 II 2; Jakobs, Book 1, Chapter 1 (Section 3 I); Naucke, § 4 V.

Most traffic offences under the *Straßenverkehrsgesetz* (Road Traffic Law) are *Ordnungswidrigkeiten*.

The prosecution of an *Ordnungswidrigkeit* is at the discretion of the relevant authority, which can decide merely to give a warning (*Verwarnung*) together with a *Verwarnungsgeld* (penalty); § 47(i) and § 56 OWiG.

If a *Bußgeldbescheid* (notice of fine) is issued, an objection (*Einspruch*) can be lodged within two weeks, in which case the matter has to be dealt with by the *Amtsgericht* (district court); § 67(i) and § 68(i) OWiG.

7 A classification of the most important offences in the BT according to the relevant *Rechtsgut* protected can be found in Naucke, § 6 III 3.

8 See §§ 80-165 StGB. Regarding *Delikte gegen staatliche Rechtsgüter* see Otto (ED), Part 3, Chapter 2 (§§ 83-100).

9 See §§ 166-184 StGB. Regarding offences against (other) *Rechtsgüter der Gesamtheit (nicht-staatliche überindividuelle Rechtsgüter)* see Otto (ED), Part 3, Chapter 1 (§§ 60-82).

2   offences against the person;[10]
3   offences against property (*Eigentum* and *Vermögen*).[11]

ELEMENTS OF AN OFFENCE[12]

The construction of norms in German criminal law follows the usual pattern of:

* *Tatbestand* (content); and
* *Rechtsfolge* (legal consequence).[13]

However, an act, which can be subsumed (*subsumiert*) under a (*Straf-*) *Tatbestand*, is not of itself punishable. Independently of fulfilling the *Tatbestand*, the act must also be *rechtswidrig* (illegal) and *schuldhaft* (blameworthy). These three elements of *Tatbestandsmäßigkeit* (*Tatbestandserfüllung*), *Rechtswidrigkeit* and *Schuld* form the crux of German criminal legal theory. The existence of a *Straftat* depends on the fulfilment of each of these elements.[14]

---

10   See: §§ 185-241 StGB; Otto (ED), Part 2, Chapter 1 (§§ 2-37).

Four cases involving offences within this category are contained in the *Sourcebook*, Chapter 7:

* The *Insult of Soldiers Case* § 185 StGB, *Ehre* (honour);
* The *Base Motive Case* § 211 StGB, *Leben* (life);
* The *Shootings at the Berlin Wall Case* §§ 212, 213 StGB;
* The *Rough Ill-Treatment Case* § 223b StGB, *Körperliche Unversehrtheit* (bodily integrity).

11   See §§ 242-358 StGB (Sections 19-29). Section 27 covers certain *gemeingefährliche Straftaten* (offences involving danger to the public) and includes § 323c.

In the *Neglected Assistance Case* (*Sourcebook*, Chapter 7) there was a subsequent prosecution under what is now § 323c StGB. The court passed a guilty verdict (*Schuldspruch*), but could not, due to the *Verbot der reformatio in peius* rule, impose a punishment: see § 358 (ii) StPO.

See also Otto (ED), Part 2, Chapter 2 (§§ 38-59). *Rechtsgüterschutz* as the legitimate function of criminal law is criticised by Jakobs (Book 1, Chapter 1 (Section 2)).

12   See: Baumann (GBS), Chapter 2 2; Creifelds under *Straftat I*, *Schuld* and *Rechtswidrigkeit*; Model/Creifelds/Lichtenberger, Part H (397, 401); Naucke, § 7; Otto (AS), Part 2 (§§ 5-17); Wesel (FR), Chapter 4 (*Rechtswidrigkeit und Schuld*): Wesel points out that *Rechtswidrigkeit* and *Schuld* were first distinguished as separate elements 100 years ago.

13   See Chapter X, note 17 and note 60.

14   These elements form part of the German system of criminal offences and must be examined individually in each case. In particular, in German criminal law there can be no punishment without *Schuld* (*nulla poena sine culpa*), whereas in civil law liability is not always dependent on blame (*Verschulden*; eg cases of *Gefährdungshaftung* (strict liability))

Tatbestand and *Rechtswidrigkeit* are objective elements; *Schuld* is subjective.

In certain special cases, the following additional elements can also become relevant:

* *Objektive Bedingungen der Strafbarkeit* (objective conditions of punishability);
* *Persönliche Strafausschließungs- und Strafaufhebungsgründe* (personal grounds for the exclusion of punishment and personal grounds for the lifting of punishment);
* *Prozeßvoraussetzungen* (preconditions for a hearing). ...

Tatbestandsmäßigkeit of the *Handlung*

When an act is *tatbestandsmäßig*

To be *tatbestandsmäßig*, an act must:

- be a *Handlung* (ie *vom Willen getragenes menschliches Verhalten*: human conduct carried by (free) will);[15]
- fall within the catalogue of criminal offences in the BT or in a *Nebengesetz* (collateral law);
- fulfil all the *Merkmale* (elements) of the *Tatbestand*.

A *Handlung* can be punishable either according to the activity (*Tätigkeit*), which is described as forbidden, – a so-called *schlichtes Tätigkeitsdelikt* – or according to the result (*Erfolg*) caused (*verursacht*) by it – a so-called *Erfolgsdelikt*. In the latter case, there has to be a causal link between the *Handlung* and the *Erfolg*. By the dominant theory of causation (*Kausalität*) – the so-called *Äquivalenztheorie* (equivalence theory) –[16] every condition without which the *Erfolg* would fall away[17] is regarded as (equivalent/) causal for the *Erfolg*.

Crimes by omission

A *Tatbestand* can be fulfilled not only by a *Handlung* (giving rise to a so-called *Begehungsdelikt* (crime by active conduct)), but also by an *Unterlassung* (omission), which is regarded as the equivalent of a *Handlung*.

It is important to note here that a German criminal norm may be one of two types: either a norm, which requires certain action to be carried out (a so-called *Gebotsnorm*) or, more usually, a norm, which forbids certain action or injury to a particular *Rechtsgut* (a so-called *Verbotsnorm*).

14...See: Baumann (ER), Part V, § 15 I; Baumann (GBS), Chapter 1 II 2 b; Jakobs, Book 2, Title 1, Chapter 1 (Sections 7-10); Otto (AS), Part 2, Chapter 1, Section 1 (§ 5); Naucke, § 7 (*Das Straftatsystem*); Creifelds under *Bedingungen der Strafbarkeit*; note 52 in this chapter.

15   Baumann understands the term *Handlung* in this sense.

   The finale *Handlungslehre* (developed by Welzel) regards a *Handlung* as final, ie directed to a particular aim (*Ziel*). The perpetrators will is incorporated as a subjective element in his conduct. The theory, therefore, incorporates a subjective element in the *Tatbestand*.

   The *kausaler (normativer) Handlungsbegriff*, on the other hand, regards conduct as significant for the purposes of criminal law, if it is caught by the provisions of a criminal norm and causes a particular consequence. The perpetrators will causes his conduct, but is not part of it.

   See Baumann (ER), Part V, § 15 I 1 b; Baumann (GBS), Chapter 4 I; Creifelds under *Finale Handlungslehre*, Wesel (JW), Chapter X and Wesel (FR), Chapter 4 (*Tat und Tatbestand*).

16   This theory dominates in criminal law, but not in civil law, where the theory of foreseeability (*Adäquanztheorie* (adequacy theory)) applies.

   See Creifelds under *Schadensersatz* I (a); Jakobs, Book 2, Title 1, Chapter 1 (Section 7); Kallwass, Section 3, Chapter 1 (§ 39).

17   *Jede Bedingung, die nicht hinweggedacht werden kann, ohne daß der Erfolg entfiele: conditio sine qua non.*

The breach of a *Gebotsnorm* by omission is called an *echtes Unterlassungsdelikt* (genuine crime by omission), while the breach of a *Verbotsnorm* by omission is referred to as an *unechtes Unterlassungsdelikt* (artificial crime by omission).

An *unechtes Unterlassungsdelikt* is only punishable, if:

* the *Erfolg* in a *Tatbestand* has arisen;
* the *Täter* (perpetrator) omitted to prevent the *Erfolg*, although it was possible for him to do so;
* the *Täter* had a special legal duty to act, a so-called *Garantenpflicht*.[18]

A *Garantenpflicht* can arise in four (unwritten) circumstances:

* *aus Rechtssatz* (when it is provided for by law);
* *aus Rechtsgeschäft* (when a *Schutzpflicht* (duty of protection) is assumed by *Vertrag* (contract));
* *aus vorangegangenem Tun* (when it flows from prior conduct); or
* *aus einer Lebensbeziehung* (when a close personal relationship exists).

An *Unterlassungstäter* (perpetrator by omission) is punishable, as if he had fulfilled the *Tatbestand* of a *Begehungsdelikt*, but the punishment (*Strafe*) can be reduced.[19]

Rechtswidrigkeit of the *Handlung*

When a Handlung is rechtswidrig

The mere fact that a *Handlung* fulfills the *Tatbestand* of a criminal norm does not, of itself, make the *Handlung rechtswidrig* (illegal). However, unless the *Handlung* is justified (*gerechtfertigt*) by another norm or principle, the fulfilment of the *Tatbestand* is, as a rule, regarded as indicating the illegality of the *Handlung*: *die Tatbestandserfüllung indiziert die Rechtswidrigkeit*.

Rechtfertigungsgründe[20]

Whether or not a person has acted illegally is dependent on a further consideration: the (non-)existence and (non-)fulfilment of so-called *Rechtfertigungsgründe* (justifying reasons). *Rechtfertigungsgründe* supplement (*ergänzen*) the *Tatbestand*; they are so-called *negative Tatbestandsmerkmale*

---

18 See § 13 StGB, which states that the *Täter* must legally have to answer for (*rechtlich einstehen für*) preventive action.

An *echtes Unterlassungsdelikt* is subsidiary to a *Begehungsdelikt*. Thus, in the *Neglected Assistance Case* (*Sourcebook*, Chapter 7) the court considered and distinguished the position where a crime is committed by means of an *unechte Unterlassung* from § 323c StGB, which penalises a genuine omission.

Regarding crimes by omission see: Creifelds under *Garantenstellung* and *Unterlassungsdelikt*; Jakobs, Book 2, Title 2, Chapter 6 (Sections 28-30); Otto (AS), Part 2, Chapter 1, Section 3 (§ 9).

19 See §§ 13(ii) and 49(i) StGB.

20 See: Creifelds under *Rechtswidrigkeit*; Otto (AS), Part 2, Chapter 1, Section 2 (§ 8).

(negative elements of a *Tatbestand*) and can be both written (eg in the StGB, StPO or BGB) and unwritten.[21]

The most important *Rechtfertigungsgründe* in practice are:

- *Einwilligung*: consent (*volenti non fit iniuria*)[22]
- *mutmaßliche Einwilligung*: presumed consent;[23]
- *Notwehr*: self-defence;[24]
- *defensiver Notstand*: defensive emergency;[25]
- *aggressiver Notstand*: offensive emergency;[26]
- *rechtfertigender Notstand*: justifying emergency;[27]
- *Ausübung von Dienstrechten oder Ausführung von rechtmäßigen Befehlen*: exercise of official rights or implementation of legal orders;[28]
- *Wahrnehmung berechtigter Interessen*: pursuit of just interests;[29]
- *soziale Adäquanz*: social adaquacy;[30]
- *sonstige Eingriffsrechte*: other intervention rights.[31]

Schuld

Meaning of Schuld

Although it is clear that a *Handlung* is not a *Straftat* and is not punishable without the *Schuld* (blame/guilt) of the *Täter*, the concept of *Schuld* itself is far from simple or clear.

---

21 See Baumann (GBS), Chapter 5 I 1 and Chapter 5 IV.

22 For example, § 226a StGB. See also Jakobs, Book 2, Title 1, Chapter 2 (Section 14).

23 See Jakobs, Book 2, Title 1, Chapter 2 (Section 15 IV).

24 See: § 32 StGB; Jakobs, Book 2, Title 1, Chapter 2 (Section 12).

25 See § 228 BGB.

26 See § 904 BGB.

27 See § 34 StGB.

  Notstand can also exclude *Schuld*: see 3 (d) below and § 35 StGB. See also Jakobs, Book 2, Title 1, Chapter 2 (Section 13).

28 See Jakobs, Book 2, Title 1, Chapter 2 (Section 16 II).

  In the *Shootings at the Berlin Wall Case* (*Sourcebook*, Chapter 7) the *Grenzgesetz* (Border Act) of the former GDR did not, in the final analysis, amount to a justifying reason. Moreover, the argument that they acted *auf Befehl* (on orders) did not help the accused either.

  However, on the issue of *Schuld*, § 5(i) *Wehrstrafgesetz* (Military Crime Act) was applied analogously in favour of the accused, enabling the court to assess a milder punishment.

29 In the case of a prosecution for *Beleidigung* (insult). See § 193 StGB.

30 Social adaquacy or acceptability is also relevant in employment law as a precondition for the legality of industrial action. See Creifelds under *Soziale Adäquanz*.

31 See § 127 StPO and § 1631 BGB.

The dominant normative definition of *Schuld* regards *Schuld* as such a relationship (*Beziehung*) of the *Täter* to his *Tat* as can, on evaluation, be deemed *vorwerfbar* (reproachable).[32]

Schuldfähigkeit

In the normal case, the *Täter* is assumed to be *schuldfähig* (capable of blame). However, children (*Kinder*) under 14 are *schuldunfähig*[33] and youths between 14 and 18 (*Jugendliche*) are *schuldfähig* depending on their moral and intellectual development.[34]

Those between the age of majority (18) and 21 are referred to as *Heranwachsende* and can be treated as *Jugendliche* or as *Erwachsene* (adults) depending on the circumstances.

The absence or reduction in *Schuldfähigkeit* due to physical or emotional defects is dealt with in §§ 20 and 21 StGB.[35]

Forms of Schuld[36]

Schuld can arise in two forms:

- *Vorsatz* (intent), the usual form of *Schuld*, known as *Vorsatzschuld*;
- *Fahrlässigkeit* (negligence).

Acts (*Handlungen*) are usually only punishable if they are committed with *Vorsatz* (*vorsätzliches Handeln*). The law must expressly say so, if negligent conduct (*fahrlässiges Handeln*) is punishable.[37]

Vorsatz may be defined as the knowledge of and desire for those (objective and subjective) circumstances/elements, which belong to the *Tat*: *das Wissen und Wollen der Tatumstände/Tatbestandsmerkmale, die zum gesetzlichen Tatbestand gehören*. The *Täter* need not know the statutory details of the offence, provided, as a layman, he has evaluated his conduct as wrong (so-called *Parallelwertung in der Laiensphäre*).[38]

Vorsatz is classified as either:[39]

---

32 This is to be compared with the (formerly dominant) psychological definition of *Schuld*; see: Baumann (GBS), Chapter 6 I 1; Jakobs, Book 2, Title 1, Chapter 3 (Section 17 II); Otto (AS), Part 2, Chapter 2 (§ 12).

   Another (subjective) definition of *Schuld* (formulated by Stratenwerth) is: *persönliche Verantwortung* (personal responsibility). See Creifelds under *Schuld* and Wesel (FR), Chapter 4 (*Rechtswidrigkeit und Schuld*).

33 See § 19 StGB and Creifelds under *Strafmündigkeit*.

34 See the JGG (Juvenile Courts Law).

35 See Baumann (GBS), Chapter 6 I 4 a.

36 See: Creifelds under *Schuld*; Jakobs, Book 2, Title 1, Chapter 1 (Sections 8 and 9); Otto (AS), Part 2, Chapter 1, Section 2 (§ 7); Model/Creifelds/Lichtenberger, Part H (397).

37 See: § 15 StGB; Baumann (GBS), Chapter 6 II 1 a; Naucke § 6 IV 5 (a) (§ 15).

38 See Baumann (GBS), Chapter 6 II 1 b.

39 *Ibid* Chapter 6 II 1 c.

- *dolus directus* (*unmittelbarer Vorsatz*). This is the usual form of *Vorsatz*: the *Täter* knows that he is committing an offence and wants to do so. It is to be distinguished from *Absicht* (pure intention), which requires more than just *Wissen und Wollen der Tatumstände* ie where the particular *Erfolg* itself is the prime motive of the *Täter*;[40]

- *dolus eventualis* (*bedingter* (eventual) *Vorsatz*; the *Täter* does not want to commit an offence, but, for the purpose of his *Handlung*, takes such a possibility into account (*nimmt die Möglichkeit in Kauf*). It is to be distinguished from *bewußte Fahrlässigkeit* (conscious negligence), where the *Täter* hopes that things will go well and relies on (*vertraut auf*) the possible offence not occurring.[41]

Fahrlässigkeit is the exceptional form of *Schuld*. It can be *bewußt* (conscious) or *unbewußt* (unconscious), *leicht* (slight) or *grob* (gross). A person is *fahrlässig*, if he fails to act with care (*Sorgfalt*), despite the fact that, due to his personal abilities and qualities, he is in a position (*in der Lage*) to know that he should do so and that he can avoid the (foreseeable) *Erfolg*; he has the capacity of *Wissenkönnen und Vermeidenkönnen*.[42]

Exclusion of Schuld

Schuld can be excluded if a (written or unwritten) *Schuldausschließungsgrund* (ground for exclusion of *Schuld*) exists.[43]

Thus, if the *Täter* is unaware of one of the *Tatumstände* (§ 16(i) StGB: so-called *Tatumstands-* or *Tatbestandsirrtum*), his *Vorsatz* and, therefore, unless there is *Fahrlässigkeit* on his part, his *Schuld* are excluded.[44]

---

40 *Absicht and sonstige spezielle subjektive Merkmale* (other special subjective elements (of a *Straftat*)) form a separate, differentiated subcategory under the general heading of *Schuld*. See Naucke, § 7 IV.

41 See the *Sourcebook*, Chapter 7, Footnote 5.

42 See: Baumann (GBS), Chapter 6 III; Otto (AS), Part 2, Chapter 1, Section 4 (§ 10).

43 Creifelds lists five *Schuldausschließungsgründe* (grounds for the exclusion of *Schuld*):
    - *Tatbestandsirrtum* (§ 16 StGB);
    - *Entschuldigter (unvermeidbarer) Verbotsirrtum* (§ 17 StGB);
    - *Schuldunfähigkeit* (§ 19, § 20 StGB);
    - *Überschreitung der Notwehr* (§ 33 StGB; so-called *Notwehrexzeß*); and
    - *Entschuldigender Notstand* (§ 35 StGB).

    Even if *Schuld* is excluded, the *Handlung* of the *Täter* remains *rechtswidrig*. See Creifelds under *Schuldausschließungsgründe*; Model/Creifelds/Lichtenberger, Part H (401).

    Regarding *Verbotsirrtum*, see Baumann (GBS), Chapter 6 II 3.

    Regarding *Schuldunfähigkeit* and *Notwehrexzeß* see Jakobs, Book 2, Title 1, Chapter 3 (respectively Sections 18 II and 20 III).

    See also Otto (AS), Part 2, Chapter 2 (§§ 13-14).

44 See Creifelds under *Irrtum* II. To be distinguished is the situation where the *Täter* knows that what he is doing is wrong, but makes a mistake as to its punishability (*Irrtum über die Strafbarkeit*). That is a *Rechtsfolgeirrtum* (mistake as to the legal consequence), which is always irrelevant.

The same applies, if the *Täter* mistakenly believes that his *Handlung* is justified by a *Rechtfertigungsgrund* (so-called *Putativrechtfertigung*).[45]

A *Putativ-* or *Wahndelikt* describes the non-punishable conduct of a *Täter*, who believes he is committing an offence, which, in fact, does not exist.[46]

Where there is a change in the course of events (*Abweichung im Kausalverlauf*) leading to the *Erfolg*, the *Handlung* of the *Täter* remains *vorsätzlich*, unless the change is significant (*erheblich; aberratio ictus*). However, an error *in obiecto* or *in persona* has no effect on the *Vorsatz* of the *Täter*.[47]

If the *Täter* had no *Unrechtsbewußtsein* (consciousness of the illegality of his conduct),[48] *Schuld* can be excluded. *Unrechtsbewußtsein* is not, however, an element of *Vorsatz*: it goes to the question of *Schuld*.

If a *Täter* has no *Unrechtsbewußtsein* due to an avoidable mistake (eg he could be expected to inform himself about the illegality), his punishment can be reduced,[49] but he has still acted *vorsätzlich*. *Schuld* is only excluded, if the mistake was unavoidable. Both types of mistake (avoidable and unavoidable) are cases of so-called *Verbotsirrtum* (§ 17 StGB).

The *Schuld* of a *Täter* can also be excluded, if, in an immediate emergency, in which he has no other choice, a person commits an illegal act in order to ward off a danger to the life, limb or freedom of himself or persons near to him; he acts without *Schuld* (§ 35(i) StGB; so-called *entschuldigender Notstand*). If he acts mistakenly (so-called *Putativnotstand*), he is only punishable, if his mistake (*Irrtum*) was avoidable (*vermeidbar*), but his punishment can be reduced (§ 35(ii) StGB).[50]

To be distinguished from *Rechtfertigungsgründe* and *Schuldausschließungsgründe*, the presence of either of which excludes the existence of a *Straftat*,[51] are the *Strafausschließungs-* or *Strafaufhebungsgründe*, which exclude or lift the possibility of *Strafe* (punishment).[52]

---

45   For example, *Putativnotwehr*: see Creifelds under *Notwehr* I 3. For *Putativnotstand* see below and Creifelds under *Notstand* I 2.

46   See Creifelds under *Wahndelikt*.

47   See Creifelds under *Irrtum* II.

48   Referred to in § 17 StGB as *die Einsicht, Unrecht zu tun*.

   Regarding *Unrechtseinsicht* and *Verbotsirrtum* see Jakobs, Book 2, Title 1, Chapter 3 (Section 19). See also Englisch, Chapter VIII, note 246a.

49   See § 17, second sentence StGB.

   Punishment was reduced on this ground in the *Shootings at the Berlin Wall Case* (*Sourcebook*, Chapter 7).

50   Regarding the exclusion of *Schuld* in cases of *unvermeidbarer Verbotsirrtum* (§ 17 StGB) and *entschuldigender Notstand* (§ 35 StGB), see Wesel (FR), Chapter 4 (*Rechtswidrigkeit und Schuld*). See also Jakobs, Book 2, Title 1, Chapter 3, (Section 20 I).

51   An act is not *rechtswidrig* (illegal) in the former case and is carried out without *Schuld* (guilt) in the latter.

52   Due to personal circumstances existing at the time of, or arising after, the *Tat*. See Creifelds under *Strafausschließungs (aufhebungs) -gründe*.

CONSEQUENCES OF AN OFFENCE[53]

The *Rechtsfolgen der Tat* (legal consequences of the offence) are dealt with in the third *Abschnitt* (section) of the AT (§§ 38-76a StGB).

Strafen

§§ 38-45 set out the possible *Strafen* (punishments), which can be imposed (*verhängt*). To be distinguished is the *Hauptstrafe* (a main punishment, which can be imposed by itself) and the *Nebenstrafe* (an accessory punishment).[54] *Hauptstrafen* are the *Freiheitsstrafe* (imprisonment)[55] and the *Geldstrafe* (fine).[56]

The *Freiheitsstrafe* can be either *lebenslang* (a life sentence) or *zeitig* (for a particular period between one month and 15 years).[57]

The *Geldstrafe* is the appropriate punishment for less serious crimes and is imposed in (a minimum of five and a maximum of 360) *Tagessätzen* (daily rates) of between DM 2 and DM 10,000.[58]

A *Freiheitsstrafe* of less than six months is only imposed in exceptional cases (*Ausnahmefällen*), if essential (*unerläßlich*) as an *ultima ratio* (final measure) to impress the *Täter* (*zur Einwirkung auf den Täter*) or to defend the legal system (*zur Verteidigung der Rechtsordnung*).[59]

A *Geldstrafe* is the preferred punishment in practice.

Where a *Freiheitsstrafe* imposed does not exceed one year, suspension of the sentence is possible for between two and five years (*Strafaussetzung zur Bewährung*).[60]

The suspension of the rest of a *zeitiger* or *lebenslanger Freiheitsstrafe* is also possible where at least two-thirds of the sentence (or, as appropriate, 15 years) has been served.[61]

Where a *Geldstrafe* of not more than 180 *Tagessätze* has been imposed, the court can, under certain circumstances (eg first offence), merely issue a warning and fix the punishment, but reserve actual sentence for a probationary period

---

53 See Creifelds under *Strafen* and *Maßregeln der Besserung und Sicherung*; Model/Creifelds/Lichtenberger, Part H (396); Wesel (FR), Chapter 4 (*Dogmatik und Strafe*).

54 The main example of a *Nebenstrafe* is the *Fahrverbot* (driving ban) in § 44 StGB. See Creifelds under *Nebenstrafen* and note 72 in this chapter below. See also Baumann (ER), Part V, § 15 IV 3.

55 See §§ 38-39 StGB.

56 See §§ 40-43 StGB.

57 See § 38 StGB.

58 See § 40 StGB.

59 See § 47(i) StGB.

60 See § 56 StGB.

61 See §§ 57 and 57a StGB.

(*Bewährungszeit*) of between one and three years (*Verwarnung mit Strafvor-behalt*).[62]

The court can also disregard imposing a *Strafe* altogether, if the consequences of the *Tat* for the *Täter* are so severe as to make the imposition of punishment obviously wrong (*offensichtlich verfehlt*): so-called *Absehen von Strafe*.[63]

The type and extent of the appropriate *Strafe* are dependent on the *Schuld* of the *Täter*: the *Strafe* must be *schuldangemessen* (appropriate to (the) *Schuld*).[64]

Maßregeln der Besserung und Sicherung

Regardless of his *Schuld*, a *Täter* may pose a danger to society or require particular attention. This is the domain of the so-called *Maßregeln der Besserung und Sicherung* (measures of improvement and security).[65]

The German criminal legal system is, therefore, *zweispurig* (two-tracked): a *Täter* can be sentenced to a *Strafe* and/or to a *Maßregel*.[66]

The *Maßregel* must be proportionate (*verhältnismäßig*).[67]

The possible *Maßregel* are:

- placement in a psychiatric hospital;[68]
- placement in a rejection institution (*Entziehungsanstalt*);[69]
- placement in secure custody (*Sicherungsverwahrung*);[70]
- supervision of conduct (*Führungsaufsicht*);[71]
- withdrawal of driving licence (*Entziehung der Fahrerlaubnis*)[72]
- occupational ban (*Berufsverbot*);[73]

---

62 See §§ 59(i) and 59a(i) StGB.

63 See § 60 StGB.

64 See § 46(i) StGB.

65 See §§ 61-72 StGB. A Maßregel is also a *Maßnahme* (measure) as defined in § 11(i) No 8 StGB. Regarding *Maßregel* see: Baumann (ER), Part V, § 15 IV 4; Jakobs, Book 1, Chapter 1 (Section 1 VI).

66 See: Baumann (ER), Part V, § 15 IV; Naucke, § 3; Creifelds under *Zweispurigkeit im Strafrecht*.

67 See § 62 StGB.

68 See § 63 StGB.

69 See § 64 StGB.

70 See § 66 StGB.

71 See § 68 StGB.

72 See § 69 StGB; to be distinguished from the Fahrverbot of § 44 StGB: see note 54 in this chapter above.

73 See § 70 StGB.

Apart from the above, the court can also order other *Maßnahmen*, ie *Verfall* (forfeiture of a pecuniary advantage), *Einziehung* (confiscation of *Gegenstände*) and *Unbrauchbarmachung* (neutralisation (rendering useless) of associated equipment).[74]

---

74   See §§ 73-76 StGB.

CHAPTER XVI

CRIMINAL PROCEDURE[1]

INTRODUCTION

German criminal procedure is governed by the *Strafprozeßordnung* (StPO: Criminal Procedure Order) of 1 February 1877, variously amended and reissued. The StPO is supplemented by the provisions of the GVG concerning the criminal courts (§ 1 StPO) and the *Staatsanwaltschaft* (public prosecutor's office).[2]

The StPO is divided into seven books:

Book I: *Allgemeine Vorschriften* (general provisions; §§ 1-150)

Book II: *Verfahren im ersten Rechtszug* (proceedings at first instance; §§ 151-295)

Book III: *Rechtsmittel* (legal remedies/appeals; §§ 296-358)

Book IV: *Wiederaufnahme eines Verfahren*s (reopening of proceedings; §§ 359-373a)

Book V: *Beteiligung des Verletzten am Verfahren* (involvement of the injured party in the proceedings; §§ 374-406h)

Book VI: *Besondere Arten des Verfahrens* (special types of proceedings; §§ 407-448)

Book VII: *Strafvollstreckung und Kosten des Verfahrens* (enforcement of punishment and costs of the proceedings; §§ 449-473).

The general public can notify the authorities (the court, the *Staatsanwaltschaft* or the police) of a *Straftat* in two ways,[3] namely either:

• by means of a *(Straf-)Anzeige* (notice of an offence), which anyone can lodge, orally or in writing (*mündlich oder schriftlich*); or

---

1   See generally: Creifelds under *Strafprozeß(recht)*; Baumann (ER), Part VI (§ 19); Model/Creifelds/Lichtenberger, Part 3 D (267-292); Naucke, § 5; Roxin.

2   The relevant §§ of the GVG are:
   • in accordance with their respective *Zuständigkeit* (competence/jurisdiction):
      –   for the *Strafrichter* (single criminal judge): § 25 GVG;
      –   for the AG: § 24 GVG;
      –   for the LG: §§ 73-74 GVG;
      –   for the OLG: §§ 120-121 GVG;
      –   for the BGH: § 135 GVG; and
   • for the *Staatsanwaltschaft*: §§ 141-152 GVG.
   See Naucke, § 5 II-IV. Regarding the sources of the law of criminal procedure, see Roxin, Introduction (§ 3).

3   See § 158 StPO. Regarding the German criminal courts and the *Staatsanwaltschaft* see Roxin, Book I, Chapter 1 (§§ 6-10). See also Model/Creifelds/Lichtenberger, Part 3 D (277).

- by means of a (*Straf-*)*Antrag* (application for prosecution), which can only be lodged by a *Verletzten* (injured party) within three months of his *Kenntnis* (knowledge) of the *Tat* and the identity of the *Täter*.[4]

It must be lodged in writing.[5]

No judicial investigation (*gerichtliche Untersuchung*) of a criminal matter can take place without an (*öffentliche*) *Klage* ((public) complaint): the so-called *Anklagegrundsatz*.[6]

THE *STAATSANWALTSCHAFT*

The *Staatsanwaltschaft* is the competent prosecution authority (*Anklagebehörde*) and possesses a so-called *Anklagemonopol* (prosecution monopoly).[7]

A *Privatklage* (private prosecution) is possible, however, in certain cases, eg trespass, damage to property or libel.[8]

The *Staatsanwaltschaft* is independent from the courts[9] and has a hierarchical structure. Depending on the court to which they are attached,[10] the officers of the *Staatsanwaltschaft* are variously described as:

- *Amtsanwälte* (district public prosecutors) (AG);
- *Staatsanwälte* (state prosecutors) (AG and LG);
- *Oberstaatsanwälte* (senior state prosecutors) (LG);
- *Generalstaatsanwälte* (general state prosecutors) (OLG); and
- *Bundesanwälte* (federal prosecutors) (BGH).

The most senior officer at the BGH is the *Generalbundesanwalt* (general federal prosecutor).

The *Staatsanwaltschaft* is obliged to intervene (*einzuschreiten*) with regard to all *Straftaten* capable of prosecution, so far as *zureichende tatsächliche Anhaltspunkte* (sufficient factual clues) exist[11] (the so-called *Legalitätsgrundsatz* (legality principle), as opposed to the *Opportunitätsgrundsatz* (opportunity principle), whereby, in certain cases, the *Staatsanwaltschaft* has a discretion not to pursue the matter).[12]

---

4   See §§ 77 and 77b StGB.
5   See § 158(ii) StPO.
6   See § 151 StPO.
7   See § 152 StPO.
8   See § 374 StPO.
9   See § 150 GVG.
10 The relevant courts are shown in brackets.
11 See § 152(ii) StPO.
12 See § 153ff StPO and, in this chapter, note 25.
    The maxims of criminal procedure are set out in Baumann (ER), Part VI, § 19 II and in Roxin, Book I, Chapter 2 (§§ 11-16).

As soon as the *Staatsanwaltschaft* receives notice (*Kenntnis*) of a suspected *Straftat* whether by *Anzeige* or in another manner, it must investigate the facts (*den Sachverhalt erforschen*) in order to decide whether to lodge a *Klage* (the so-called *Ermittlungsverfahren* (investigation procedure)).[13]

The *Staatsanwaltschaft* can require *Auskunft* (information) from all public authorities (*öffentlichen Behörden*) and either itself conduct enquiries of any kind (*Ermittlungen jeder Art*) or arrange for the police to do so.[14]

The *Staatsanwaltschaft* can apply to the local *Amtsgericht* (district court), if it considers that a particular *richterliche Untersuchungshandlung* (judicially ordered investigative act) is necessary (*erforderlich*),[15] eg an *Untersuchung* (bodily search),[16] *Beschlagnahme* (seizure),[17] *Durchsuchung* (search of premises), or, subject to the issue of a *Haftbefehl* (arrest warrant), *Untersuchungshaft* (remand in custody).[18]

---

13 See § 160(i) StPO. See also: Model/Creifelds/Lichtenberger, Part 3 D (278) and Roxin, Book I, Chapter 7 (§ 37).

   Regarding the procedure and methods of questioning (*Vernehmung*) in the *Ermittlungs-verfahren* see Creifelds under *Vernehmungen im Strafverfahren* I.

14 See § 161 StPO.

15 See § 162(i) StPO.

16 See § 81a StPO.

17 See §§ 94*ff* StPO.

18 See §§ 112*ff* StPO.

   In accordance with the *Verhältnismäßigkeitsgrundsatz*, *Untersuchungshaft* cannot be ordered, if it is out of proportion to the importance of the matter and to the expected *Strafe* or *Maßregel*: § 112(i), second sentence StPO.

   § 116 StPO enables the judge to suspend execution of an arrest warrant, if the purpose of *Untersuchungshaft* can be achieved by less incisive measures.

   In the *Arrested Admiral Case* (*Sourcebook*, Chapter 3), on the basis of the *Verhältnismäßigkeitsgrundsatz*, the possible *Haftverschonung* (exemption from custody) under § 116 StPO was applied by analogy to a warrant based on § 112(iv) (now § 112(iii)) StPO, ie in a case alleging murder.

   Regarding the various powers of search and seizure (*Zwangsmaßnahmen*) see Roxin, Book I, Chapter 6 (§§ 33-35). Regarding *Untersuchungshaft* see Roxin, Book I, Chapter 6 (§ 30)

THE POLICE[19]

It is also[20] a function of the police to investigate *Straftaten* (not merely on instruction by the *Staatsanwaltschaft*) and take all immediately necessary steps (*alle keinen Aufschub gestattenden Anordnungen*) to prevent the obscuring of the matter (*die Verdunkelung der Sache zu verhüten*).[21]

---

19 In Germany, police law is governed by separate statutes in each of the *Länder*.

Although there is no general federal police force in Germany, various federal authorities engage (broadly speaking) in police activities. Well-known are the *Bundesgrenzschutz* (federal border guard), the *Bundeskriminalamt* (federal office of criminal investigation; located in Wiesbaden) and the *Bundesamt für Verfassungsschutz* (federal office of constitutional protection; located in Cologne).

It is important to understand that the German term *Polizei* is used in two senses. The function (*Aufgabe*) of the police in the classic, so-called material sense is *die Abwehr von Gefahren für die öffentliche Sicherheit und Ordnung* (the warding-off of dangers for public security and order) or just *Gefahrenabwehr*.

In the so-called formal or institutional sense, the term *Polizei* is understood according to whether it acts as *Verwaltungspolizei* (administrative police) – in which case the authorities involved are referred to as *Polizeibehörden* (police authorities) or *Ordnungsbehörden* (order authorities) – or as *Vollzugspolizei* (executive police) – also referred to as the *Polizeivollzugsdienst* (executive police service) or just *Polizei*.

The prevention and investigation of crime is the domain of separate branches of the *Vollzugspolizei*, known respectively as the *Schutzpolizei* (protective police) and *Kriminalpolizei* (criminal police).

Drews/Wacke/Vogel/Martens broadly describe the difference between the *Verwaltungspolizei* and the *Vollzugspolizei* as follows: '*Vollzugspolizei ist Gefahrenabwehr vor Ort, Verwaltungspolizei Gefahrenabwehr vom Schreibtisch aus*' (*Vollzugspolizei* is the warding-off of dangers locally, *Verwaltungspolizei* the warding-off of dangers from the desk; see Drews/Wacke/Vogel/Martens, Part 2, § 4 No 3).

Thus, the *Vollzugspolizei* usually becomes involved in situations where action needs to be taken immediately (*sofort*).

Although the *Verwaltungspolizei* is no longer generally referred to as the police in everyday speech, the same legal principles apply to the *Verwaltungspolizei* and the *Vollzugspolizei* and they are often governed by one and the same law in the various *Länder*. The strict terminological distinction must, however, be borne in mind when one refers to these laws.

See generally: Drews/Wacke/Vogel/Martens, Part 1, §§ 1-3 and Part 2, §§ 4-6; Model/Creifelds/Lichtenberger, Part 2 C (158-177); Schmidt-Aßmann, Section 2. See also Creifelds under *Polizei, Polizeirecht, Ordnungsbehörden, Kriminalpolizei, Bundesgrenzschutz, Bundeskriminalamt* and *Verfassungsschutz*.

20 The police has a double function (*Doppelfunktion*). It is competent both to deal, on a preventive basis, with *Gefahrenabwehr* (the warding-off of dangers, including crime) and to act in *Strafverfolgung* (the pursuit of crime).

While the authority of the police in the former case is the police law of the relevant *Land*, in the latter case federal law (the StPO) applies.

See Drews/Wacke/Vogel/Martens, Part 3, § 9 and Wesel (FR), Chapter 5 (*Polizeirecht*).

21 See § 163(i) StPO.

The police must then pass its file to the *Staatsanwaltschaft* without delay or, if it seems that *richterliche Untersuchungshandlungen* need to be carried out speedily, direct to the *Amtsgericht* (district court).[22]

Without the decision of a judge, the police itself has no right to detain a person in custody (ie cause a deprivation of freedom (*Freiheitsentziehung*)) longer than until the end of the day following the person's seizure (Article 104(ii) GG).

A person suspected of an offence must be brought before the judge (the *Vorführung vor den Richter*) at the latest the day after his *vorläufige Festnahme* (provisional arrest; Article 104(iii) GG). The competent court is the *Amtsgericht* for the area in which the suspect was arrested (§ 128(i) StPO). The judge must forthwith (*unverzüglich*) either issue an arrest warrant (*Haftbefehl*) or placement order (*Unterbringungsbefehl*) or otherwise release the suspect (Article 104(iii), second sentence GG and § 128(ii) StPO).[23]

---

22 See § 163(ii) StPO.

23 A person caught in the act or being pursued (*auf frischer Tat betroffen oder verfolgt*) can be provisionally arrested by *jedermann* (anyone), provided the person is suspected of being on the run (*der Flucht verdächtig*) and cannot be immediately identified; § 127(i) StPO.

Usually, however, where there is no existing *Haftbefehl* or *Unterbringungsbefehl*, a *vorläufige Festnahme* is undertaken by the *Staatsanwaltschaft* or police; § 127(ii) StPO.

There are two pre-conditions (*Voraussetzungen*) for the issue of a *Haftbefehl*:

(i)   there must be a high suspicion that the suspect (*Beschuldigter*) committed the offence (*dringender Tatverdacht*); and

(ii) there must be a *Haftgrund* ((factual) ground for detaining the suspect in custody).

There are four main *Haftgründe*: *Flucht* (ie the suspect is fugitive); *Fluchtgefahr* (ie there is a danger of flight); *Verdunkelungsgefahr* (ie there is a danger of an obstruction of justice (eg possible tampering with evidence or collusion)); *Wiederholungsgefahr* (ie there is a danger of repetition (in the case of certain serious crimes)). See § 112 StPO. (See also §§ 112a, 114, 116-126 StPO and note 18 in this chapter above).

A person arrested *auf Grund eines Haftbefehls* (on the basis of an arrest warrant) must *unverzüglich* (without delay):

•   receive details of the warrant (§ 114a StPO);

•   be brought before the competent judge (§ 115(i) StPO); and

•   be examined by the judge, at the latest the day after the *Vorführung* (§ 115(ii) StPO).

If an arrest warrant or placement order already exists, a *Steckbrief* (warrant of apprehension) can be issued (§ 131 StPO).

Regarding *Vorläufige Festnahme* and *Vorführung* see Roxin, Book I, Chapter 6 (§ 31). See also Creifelds under *Haftbefehl*, *Steckbrief* and *Festnahme*.

ACTION FOLLOWING INVESTIGATION

If the investigations of the *Staatsanwaltschaft* provide sufficient cause (*genügender Anlaß*), the *Staatsanwaltschaft* can apply to the competent court by means of an *Anklageschrift* (= *Anklage* = *Klage*) for the opening of the main proceedings (*Eröffnung des Hauptverfahrens*).[24]

Otherwise, it must terminate the investigation (*Einstellung des Verfahrens*).[25]

Alternatively, the *Staatsanwaltschaft* can apply for the issue of a *Strafbefehl* (punishment order) where a *Vergehen* is involved and a main hearing is not considered necessary.[26]

Before a *Klage* is lodged, the suspect is known as the *Beschuldigter*. Thereafter (and before the main proceedings are opened) he is referred to as the *Angeschuldigter*.[27]

If, from the results of the preparatory investigation, the *Angeschuldigter* appears sufficiently suspect of a *Straftat* (*einer Straftat hinreichend verdächtig*), the competent court decides to open the *Hauptverfahren*.[28]

---

24 See §§ 170(i) and 199(ii) StPO. The *Anklageschrift* must specify the accused, the alleged offence, the time and place of its commission, the statutory elements of the offence and the applicable legal provisions; § 200(i) StPO.

25 See § 170(ii) StPO.

In various types of case the *Legalitätsgrundsatz* gives way and the *Opportunitätsgrundsatz* applies, enabling a prosecution to be dropped or, where proceedings have begun, for these to be terminated by the court (*eingestellt*).

Thus, with the consent of the court, the *Staatsanwaltschaft* can refrain from a prosecution (*von der Verfolgung absehen*) on grounds of insignificance (*Geringfügigkeit*) where a *Vergehen* is involved, the perpetrator's *Schuld* is negligible and there is no public interest involved in the matter: § 153(i) StPO.

Further, with the consent of the court, the *Staatsanwaltschaft* can provisionally disregard raising an indictment (*vorläufig von der Erhebung der öffentlichen Klage absehen*), if imposition of *Auflagen und Weisungen* (conditions and directions) on the perpetrator would be appropriate, the perpetrator's *Schuld* is negligible and the public interest in a prosecution can thereby be disposed of: § 153a(i) StPO.

Absehen von Strafverfolgung and *Einstellung* are also possible, for example, where crimes with a foreign element are involved, where state security takes precedence or where the accused has already been (or is expected to be) sentenced for another offence and the relevant *Strafe* or *Maßregel* he could receive if prosecuted would not be of such significance by comparison. See §§ 153c, 153d and 154(i) StPO.

See generally Creifelds under *Bagatellstrafsachen* and *Geringfügigkeit*; Roxin, Book I, Chapter 2 (§ 14) and Chapter 7 (§ 38).

26 See § 407 StPO.

27 See § 157 StPO.

28 See § 203 StPO. This is the so-called *Eröffnungsverfahren* or *Zwischenverfahren* (interim proceedings). See: Creifelds under *Anklageerhebung und -zulassung* and *Eröffnungsverfahren*; Model/Creifelds/Lichtenberger, Part 3 D (279); Roxin, Book I, Chapter 7 (§ 40).

The decision (which cannot be challenged by the accused, who is then referred to as the *Angeklagter*)[29] is known as the *Eröffnungsbeschluß*.[30]

Once the *Hauptverfahren* is opened, the *Klage* cannot be withdrawn.[31]

If the court rejects the application for *Eröffnung* from the *Staatsanwaltschaft* or passes the matter to a lower court, the *Staatsanwaltschaft* can raise immediate objection (*sofortige Beschwerde*).[32]

The *Angeklagter* must be notified at least one week before the *Hauptverhandlung* (main hearing (date)) by a *Ladung* (notice to attend).[33]

The *Hauptverhandlung* is dealt with in Section 6 of Book II (§§ 226-275) StPO.

THE MAIN PROCEEDINGS AND THEREAFTER (BOOK II (SECTION 6) – BOOK IV STPO) (§§226-373A)[34]

INVOLVEMENT OF THE INJURED PARTY (BOOK V STPO)[35]

Book V (§§ 374-406h) is divided into four sections:

Section 1: *Privatklage* (private prosecution; §§ 374-394)

Section 2: *Nebenklage* (collateral prosecution; §§ 395-402)

Section 3: *Entschädigung des Verletzten* (compensation for the injured party; §§ 403-406c)

Section 4: *Sonstige Befugnisse des Verletzten* (other powers of the injured party; §§ 406d-406h)

SPECIAL TYPES OF PROCEEDINGS (BOOK VI STPO)[36]

Book VI (§§ 407-448) is divided into four sections:

Section 1: *Verfahren bei Strafbefehlen* (procedure in the case of punishment orders; §§ 407-412)

---

29 See §§ 210(i) and 157 StPO.

30 See § 207 StPO.

31 See § 156 StPO.

32 See § 210(ii) StPO.

33 See §§ 214 and 217 StPO.

34 Exposition planned. See: Model/Creifelds/Lichtenberger, Part 3 D (280-283); Roxin, Book I, Chapter 8 (§§ 41-45).

35 See: Model/Creifelds/Lichtenberger, Part 3 D (284); Roxin, Book I, Chapter 13 (§§ 61-63).

36 *Ibid* Part 3 D (285-287); Roxin, Book I, Chapter 14 (§§ 64-66).

Section 2: *Sicherungsverfahren* (security proceedings; §§ 413-416)

Section 3: *Verfahren bei Einziehungen und Vermögensbeschlagnahmen* (procedure in the case of forfeiture and seizure of assets; §§ 430-443)

Section 4: *Verfahren bei Festsetzung von Geldbußen gegen juristische Personen und Personenvereinigungen* (procedure in the case of fines being set against juristic persons and associations; § 444)

ENFORCEMENT OF PUNISHMENT AND COSTS OF THE PROCEEDINGS (BOOK VII STPO)[37]

Book VII (§§ 449-473) is divided into two sections:

Section 1: *Strafvollstreckung* (enforcement of punishment; §§ 449-463d)

Section 2: *Kosten des Verfahrens* (costs of the proceedings; §§ 464-473).

---

37 See: Model/Creifelds/Lichtenberger, Part 3 D (288-289); Roxin, Book I, Chapter 11 (§§ 56-57).

CHAPTER XVII

EMPLOYMENT LAW

INTRODUCTION

The three main fields of German employment law are *Arbeitsvertragsrecht* (individual employment contract law), *kollektives Arbeitsrecht* (collective employment law) and *Arbeitsschutzrecht* (work protection law). The latter two largely developed after 1900, due to the fact that the BGB only concerned itself with *Dienstvertragsrecht* (law relating to contracts of services).[1]

An employment relationship (*Arbeitsverhältnis*) is usually based on a contract of employment (*Arbeitsvertrag*) between an *Arbeitgeber* (employer) and an *Arbeitnehmer* (employee).

The term *Arbeitnehmer* includes *Arbeiter* (workers) and *Angestellte* (employees).[2]

FORM AND TERMINATION OF A CONTRACT OF EMPLOYMENT[3]

An *Arbeitsvertrag* requires no particular form and can end by:

* *Zeitablauf* (effluxion of time);
* *Tod des Arbeitnehmers* (death of the employee);
* *Aufhebungsvertrag* (annulment agreement); or
* *Kündigung* (dismissal).

The *Kündigung* of an employee can be either *ordentlich* (in proper form), ie *befristet* (with notice), or *außerordentlich* (summary), ie *fristlos aus wichtigem Grund* (without notice for an important reason).

By § 626(ii) BGB, a *Kündigung aus wichtigem Grund* must be declared within two weeks of knowledge of the facts (upon which the important reason is based). The employee will, usually, have received a prior warning (*Abmahnung*).[4]

The *befristete Kündigung* is the usual means of terminating an *Arbeitsverhältnis* with no specific date of expiry (*auf eine unbestimmte Zeit*

---

1   An *Arbeitsvertrag* is an example of a *Dienstvertrag* and the provisions in the BGB regarding *Dienstverträge* (§§ 611-630) are of subsidiary application.

See note 43 in this chapter; Baumann (ER), Part III, § 12 and Model/Creifelds/ Lichtenberger, Part 6 A (601-637).

Relevant statutes in the field of employment law are listed in Hanau/Adomeit, Part B IV.

2   See Creifelds under *Arbeitsverhältnis*, *Arbeitsvertrag* and *Arbeitnehmer*.

3   See: Brox (GBA), Chapter 7 A I-III and Chapter 7 B I-IV; Hanau/Adomeit, Parts E and J; Söllner, Part 4 (§§ 28, 34-36); Creifelds under *Kündigung* and *Kündigungsschutz für Arbeitnehmer*.

4   See Brox (GBA), Chapter 7 II 2 and Söllner, Part 4, § 35 III 2.

geschlossen). The applicable *Fristen* (notice periods) are laid down in § 622 BGB, which generally requires six weeks to the end of a quarter for *Angestellte* and two weeks for an *Arbeiter*. Longer *Fristen* apply after at least five years' employment. Provision for one month's notice to the end of a calendar month for *Angestellte* is possible by individual agreement.[5]

If an employee has been employed for at least six months, he is protected against *Kündigung* by the *Kündigungsschutzgesetz* (KSchG; Employment Protection Law) of 10 August 1951, provided at least ten persons are employed in the relevant business.

§ 1(i) KSchG declares that an (*ordentliche*) *Kündigung* which is *sozial ungerechtfertigt* (socially unjustified) is *rechtsunwirksam* (of no legal effect).

A *Kündigung* is *sozial ungerechtfertigt*, if it is not based on (*bedingt durch*) reasons in the person or conduct of the employee (*Gründe in der Person oder in dem Verhalten des Arbeitnehmers*) or on urgent requirements of the business (*dringende betriebliche Erfordernisse*: the so-called *betriebsbedingte Kündigung*). When selecting employees for *Kündigung* due to *dringende betriebliche Erfordernisse*, the employer must still give sufficient consideration (*ausreichende Rücksicht*) to social aspects (*soziale Gesichtspunkte*), otherwise the dismissal is socially unjustified.[6]

If an employee considers his *Kündigung* as socially unjustified, he can lodge an *Einspruch* (objection) within one week at the *Betriebsrat* (works council), which can then attempt to reach a *Verständigung* (understanding) with the employer.[7]

If this remains unsuccessful, the employee must within three weeks of his receipt of the *Kündigung* issue a *Klage* at the *Arbeitsgericht* (employment court) for a declaration (*Feststellung*) that the *Arbeitsverhältnis* was not dissolved by the *Kündigung* (a so-called *Kündigungsschutzklage*). The *Kündigung* becomes effective, if no *Klage* is issued.[8]

Even if the *Arbeitsgericht* concludes that the *Arbeitsverhältnis* was not dissolved by the *Kündigung*, the employee (or employer) can apply to the court to dissolve the *Arbeitsverhältnis* and order the employer to pay an appropriate settlement (*eine angemessene Abfindung*).[9]

THE *BETRIEB* AND *BETRIEBSRAT*

The *Betriebsrat* (works council) is the elected representative of the employees of a *Betrieb* and is the most important institution of the constitution of a *Betrieb*

---

5   See § 622(i) BGB.

6   See § 1(iii) KSchG.

7   See § 3 KSchG.

8   See § 7 KSchG. The alleged invalidity of an *außerordentliche Kündigung* must be claimed in the same way: § 13(i) KSchG.

9   See §§ 9 and 10 KSchG. Regarding the *Arbeitsgericht*, its jurisdiction and procedure see Brox (GBA), Chapter 12; Hanau/Adomeit, Part K and Söllner, Part 5.

(*Betriebsverfassung*). The applicable law is the *Betriebsverfassungsgesetz* of 15 January 1972 (BetrVG).

The equivalent of the *Betriebsrat* in the public sector is the *Personalrat*; the applicable laws being the *Personalvertretungsgesetze* of the *Bund* and the *Länder*.[10]

The term *Betrieb* is to be distinguished from the wider term *Unternehmen* (enterprise). Both describe an organisational business unit and are used interchangeably in daily speech. However, while an *Unternehmen* refers to a business in the general sense, a *Betrieb* is technically the individual business unit, the direct (place of) business. An *Unternehmen* can consist of various *Betriebe*.

The involvement (*Beteiligung*) of employees in a *Betrieb* is commonly referred to as *betriebliche Mitbestimmung*, while their involvement in the organs of an *Unternehmen* as *Mitbestimmung in den Unternehmensorganen*.[11]

A *Betriebsrat* can be elected in all *Betrieben* with at least five permanent *Arbeitnehmer*. Usually, only employees who have belonged to the *Betrieb* for six months are eligible for election (*wählbar*).[12]

The number of members of a *Betriebsrat* is dependent on the total number of adult employees in the *Betrieb*.[13]

The BetrVG does not apply to *leitende Angestellte* (leading employees),[14] nor to so-called *Tendenzbetriebe*, ie businesses which directly and predominantly serve political, confessional, charitable, educational, scientific or artistic provisions or the purposes of reporting or the expression of opinion.[15]

CO-OPERATION BETWEEN EMPLOYER AND *BETRIEBSRAT*[16]

By § 2(i) BetrVG, the employer and *Betriebsrat* must work together in confidence and in co-operation with the trade unions (*Gewerkschaften*) and employer associations (*Arbeitgebervereinigungen*) for the benefit of the employees and the *Betrieb* (the *Grundsatz der vertrauensvollen Zusammenarbeit* (confidential co-operation principle)).

---

10 See also § 130 BetrVG.

11 For the *Mitbestimmungsrecht* (right of co-decision) of the *Betriebsrat* see Chapter XVII, p 157. See also Hanau/Adomeit, Part D III and IV and Söllner, Part 2, Section 4 (§§ 19-24).

12 See § 8 BetrVG.

13 See § 9 BetrVG.

14 See § 5(iii) BetrVG.

15 *Betriebe, die unmittelbar und überwiegend 1. politischen ,.. konfessionellen, karitativen, erzieherischen, wissenschaftlichen oder künstlerischen Bestimmungen oder 2. Zwecken der Berichterstattung oder Meinungsäußerung ... dienen.* See § 118(i) BetrVG.

16 See generally Hanau/Adomeit, Part D II.

The employer and *Betriebsrat* are *Betriebspartner* (business partners). Thus:

(a) they must negotiate regarding contentious questions with the serious desire (*mit dem ernsten Willen*) to reach an agreement (*Einigung*) and must make suggestions (*Vorschläge*) to settle differences of opinion (*Meinungs-verschiedenheiten*);[17]

(b) they are not entitled to take any measures of industrial action (*Maßnahmen des Arbeitskampfes*). However, industrial action between *tariffähigen Parteien* (parties capable of reaching a tariff agreement (*Tarifvertrag*), ie trade unions and employer organisations) is still possible;[18]

(c) they must desist from actions which interfere with the course of work or the peace of the *Betrieb* (*Betätigungen ..., durch die der Arbeitsablauf oder der Frieden des Betriebs beeinträchtigt werden*: the so-called *Pflicht zur Wahrung des Betriebsfriedens* or *Friedenspflicht*;[19]

(d) they must desist from any party-political action (*jede parteipolitische Betätigung*) in the *Betrieb*.[20]

Employer and *Betriebsrat* can co-operate in various forms. They can reach a written *Betriebsvereinbarung* (business agreement)[21] or merely settle the matter by oral consent (*betriebliche Einigung, Betriebsabsprache* or *Regelungsabrede*).

Differences of opinion (*Meinungsverschiedenheiten*) can be referred to an internal standing or *ad hoc Einigungsstelle* ((compulsory) arbitration body), usually on the application or with the approval of both parties.[22]

It consists of equal numbers of representatives from each side, with an impartial chairman.[23]

The decision (*Spruch*) of the *Einigungsstelle* is usually only suggestive in nature, but can in certain cases replace the agreement between employer and *Betriebsrat* and is then binding.[24]

---

17 See § 74(i), second sentence BetrVG.

18 See § 74(ii), first sentence BetrVG.

19 *Ibid*, second sentence BetrVG.

20 See § 74(ii), third sentence BetrVG.

21 See Hanau/Adomeit, Part D II 3, Creifelds under *Betriebsvereinbarung* and § 77 BetrVG.

   A *Betriebsvereinbarung* is only applicable on the level of the *Betrieb*. It is of direct and compulsory effect (*gilt unmittelbar und zwingend*).

   Like a *Tarifvertrag*, a *Betriebsvereinbarung* can contain a normative and contractual part (see note 37 in this chapter). However, in the event of a conflict with a *Betriebsvereinbarung*, a tariff agreement takes precedence (*Vorrang des Tarifvertrags*).

22 See Hanau/Adomeit, Part D II 4 and § 76(vi) BetrVG.

   The *Einigungsstelle* is competent to deal with regulatory questions (*Regelungsfragen*) between employer and *Betriebsrat*, whereas the *Arbeitsgericht* (employment court) handles legal questions (*Rechtsfragen*).

23 See § 76(ii) BetrVG.

24 See § 76(v), first sentence and § 87 BetrVG.

THE RIGHTS OF THE *BETRIEBSRAT*[25]

The *Betriebsrat* has rights of involvement (*Beteiligung*) and co-operation (*Mitwirkung*) in three main areas: in social, personnel and commercial matters (*sozialen, personellen und wirtschaftlichen Angelegenheiten*). Such rights are commonly classified, in ascending order of intensity, as including:

- an *Informationsrecht* (right of information), ie the *Unterrichtung* of the *Betriebsrat* is required;

- a *Mitspracherecht* (right of consultation), ie the *Anhörung* or *Beratung* of the *Betriebsrat* is required;

- a *Widerspruchsrecht* (right of objection) of the *Betriebsrat* (typically in cases of *personellen Einzelmaßnahmen* (measures regarding individual members of staff);

- a *Mitbestimmungsrecht* or *betriebliche Mitbestimmung* in the narrow sense (right of co-decision), ie the positive *Zustimmung* (approval) of the *Betriebsrat* is required.

The *Mitbestimmungsrecht* is the strongest right of the *Betriebsrat* and exists, for example, in social matters (ie broadly in the field of collective working conditions) in the absence of a provision in a statute or tariff agreement.[26]

The rights of the *Betriebsrat* in commercial matters are set out in §§ 106-113 BetrVG. Most important here is the right of the *Betriebsrat* (in a *Betrieb* consisting of more than 20 employees) to be informed regarding any planned *Betriebsänderung* (change in the *Betrieb*), which could involve significant disadvantages (*wesentliche Nachteile*) for staff. The *Betriebsrat* is then entitled to negotiate regarding the practicalities and conclude a so-called *Interessenausgleich* (settlement of interests) and a *Sozialplan* (social plan) for those affected.

The rights of the *Betriebsrat* in personnel matters are set out in §§ 92-105 BetrVG:

1   In a *Betrieb* with more than 20 adult employees, the *Betriebsrat* can, for example, on certain grounds refuse its approval to a recruitment (*Einstellung*) or transfer (*Versetzung*): it has a *Widerspruchsrecht* (right of objection).[27]

2   The *Betriebsrat* must be heard before any dismissal (*Kündigung*) by the employer. A dismissal declared without such hearing (*Anhörung*) is ineffective (*unwirksam*).[28]

The *Betriebsrat* can inform the employer of its doubts (*Bedenken*) regarding an ordinary dismissal within one week and regarding an extraordinary dismissal within three days.[29]

---

25   See generally Hanau/Adomeit, Part D III and Creifelds under *Mitbestimmung*.

26   See § 87(i) BetrVG.

27   See § 99(i) and (ii) BetrVG.

28   See § 102(i) BetrVG.

29   See § 102(ii) BetrVG.

Further, it has a right of objection (*Widerspruchsrecht*) on certain grounds against an ordinary dismissal within the same period.[30]

In the event of a valid objection from the *Betriebsrat* and a *Kündigungsschutzklage* from the employee (within three weeks), the employee has a right to continue to be employed (*Recht auf Weiterbeschäftigung*) on unchanged terms until conclusion of the dispute.[31]

Apart from *Mitwirkung* by the *Betriebsrat*, the individual employee also has rights to be informed and heard (*Unterrichtungs- und Anhörungsrechte*) and to lodge a complaint (*Beschwerderecht*).[32]

MITBESTIMMUNG IN LARGE *UNTERNEHMEN*[33]

There are special provisions in the BetrVG 1952 for *Mitbestimmung* in the *Aufsichtsräten* (supervisory boards) of *Unternehmen* (enterprises) with more than 500 employees.[34]

The *Mitbestimmungsgesetz* 1976 applies to *Unternehmen* having more than 2,000 employees.

THE COALITIONS[35]

Collective employment law deals not only with organisational questions and rights to *Mitbestimmung* (BetrVG and *Mitbestimmungsgesetz*), but also with the relationship between trade unions (*Gewerkschaften*) and employer associations (*Arbeitgeberverbände*), each of which is referred to as a *Koalition* (coalition). The importance of coalitions in German employment law lies in the fact that only they can conclude a *Tarifvertrag* (tariff agreement) and engage in an *Arbeitskampf* (industrial action).[36]

A tariff agreement can contain a normative and contractual part.[37]

---

30 See § 102(iii) BetrVG.

31 See § 102(v) BetrVG.

32 See §§ 81-86 BetrVG.

33 See Hanau/Adomeit, Part D, Section IV; Söllner, Part 2, Section 4 (§ 24) and Chapter XVII, p 155.

34 See § 129(i) BetrVG 1952.

35 See: Brox (GBA), Chapter 8 and Chapter 9 I-II; Hanau/Adomeit, Part C I; Söllner, Part 2, Section 2 (§§ 9-10).

36 The main means by which an *Arbeitskampf* (industrial action) can be conducted are *Streik* (strike) and *Aussperrung* (lock-out).

   See: Brox (GBA), Chapter 10; Hanau/Adomeit, Part C III; Söllner, Part 2, Section 2 (§§11-13).

37 See: Brox (GBA), Chapter 9 III-IV; Hanau/Adomeit, Part C II; Söllner, Part 2, Section 3; Creifelds under *Koalitionsfreiheit* and *Tarifvertrag*.

   Tariff agreements are governed by the *Tarifvertragsgesetz* (TVG) of 9 April 1949.

Measures of industrial action (*Kampfmaßnahmen*) during the currency of a tariff agreement constitute a breach of the *Friedenspflicht* and can give rise to a claim for damages.[38]

ARBEITSSCHUTZRECHT

Various statutory provisions govern safety at work in Germany and give protection against accident (*Unfallschutz*) and protection of health (*Gesundheitsschutz*). They are part of the field of employment law known as *Arbeitsschutzrecht* (work protection law) and are of a compulsory, public law nature (*öffentlich-rechtlich*).

The observance of the norms of *Arbeitsschutzrecht* is subject to state control by the *Gewerbeaufsichtsbehörden* (business (trade) supervisory authorities) either alone or in conjunction with the police authorities of the relevant *Bundesland* (federal state). The *Berufsgenossenschaften* (occupational cooperatives) also have rights of supervision.

Provisions of *Arbeitsschutzrecht* include:

• § 120a of the *Gewerbeordnung* (GewO; Business (Trade) Order)

This provision obliges *Gewerbeunternehmer* (business (trade) enterprises) to take such steps as are necessary to maintain *Betriebssicherheit* (safety at the workplace). Thus, for example, they must provide and maintain workrooms, equipment, machines and tools in such a way and generally see to it that employees are protected against dangers to life and health as far as the nature of the business permits.

• § 120d GewO

The appropriate authorities are empowered to issue (*ordnungsbehördliche*) *Verfügungen* ((official) directions) ordering such measures as are necessary and appear practicable to be carried out.

---

38 See: Brox (GBA), Chapter 10 III 1 (b); Hanau/Adomeit, Part C III; Söllner, Part 2, Section 2, § 12 II 3.

By way of enforcement, the authorities can resort to various *Zwangsmittel* (compulsory measures),[39] which must usually first be threatened (*angedroht*) in writing.[40]

Orders from the authorities are administrative law sanctions, which, in the first instance, fall within the jurisdiction of the administrative courts.

Additionally, however, a deliberate or negligent contravention of an enforceable order (*vollziehbare Anordnung*) from the *Gewerbeaufsichtsbehörde* constitutes a minor offence (*Ordnungswidrigkeit*).[41]

A fine of up to DM 10,000 can be imposed.[42]

- § 9 of the *Gesetz über Ordnungswidrigkeiten* (OWiG; Minor Offences Law)

  Organs (representatives) of a company, statutory representatives or persons instructed to direct a business by the owner can also themselves be the subject of regress.

39　*Zwangsmittel* are set out in the *Verwaltungsvollstreckungsgesetz* (Administrative Enforcement Law) of the relevant *Land* and are distinguished according to whether:

(1)　money is claimed; or

(2)　something is required to be done, tolerated or omitted (ie the administrative act (VA) is directed to a *Handlung, Duldung oder Unterlassung*).

Where a VA in category 2 is to be enforced, *Zwangsmittel* usually comprise:

－　*Ersatzvornahme* (substituted execution (of the measure) by the authority); or

－　*Zwangsgeld* ((compulsory) fine).

Another *Zwangsmittel*, restricted largely to the police, is the exercise of so-called *unmittelbarer Zwang* (direct force).

Administrative acts are normally only enforceable (*vollstreckbar*) if:

－　they are *befehlend* (require or forbid particular action); and

－　they have become *unanfechtbar* (unchallengable (before an administrative court)); or

－　immediate enforcement (*sofortige Vollziehung*) has been ordered; or

－　in other cases where a legal remedy would not have any suspensive effect (*aufschiebende Wirkung*).

However, in a case of urgency (*Eilfall*), administrative force (*Verwaltungszwang*) can be exercised, if immediate enforcement (*sofortige Vollziehung/sofortiger Vollzug*) is necessary (*notwendig*):

－　to prevent an act, which is illegal and falls within the *Tatbestand* (content) of a crime or minor offence (*zur Verhinderung einer mit Strafe oder Bußgeld bedrohten Handlung*); or

－　to avert a danger, which is (directly) threatening (*zur Abwendung einer (unmittelbar) drohenden Gefahr*);

and the authority acts within its statutory powers (*innerhalb ihrer gesetzlichen Befugnisse*).

See Creifelds under *Verwaltungsvollstreckungsgesetz* and *Verwaltungszwang* and Chapter XIII (note 14) and p 126. See also: Bull, Section V, § 17; Erichsen, Part 3, Section 1, § 20; Giemulla/Jaworsky/Müller-Uri, Book I, Chapter 8; Maurer, Part 5, § 20.

40　Both the threat of a *Zwangsmittel* and the basic order (*Grundverfügung*) it is meant to carry out are *Verwaltungsakte* (administrative acts) and can be challenged before an administrative court. See Creifelds under *Zwangsmittel*.

41　See § 147(i) No 1 GewO.

42　See § 147(iv) GewO.

- § 618(i) of the *Bürgerliches Gesetzbuch* (BGB; Civil Code)

  This provision contains a private law obligation to take measures similar to those mentioned in § 120a GewO to protect the life and health of persons, who have contracted to provide their services under a *Dienstvertrag* (contract for services).[43]

  The person entitled to the services (the *Dienstberechtigter*) has a non-excludable duty of protection (*Schutzpflicht*) and care (*Fürsorgepflicht*)[44]

  A blameworthy, so-called positive breach of contract (*positive Vertragsverletzung*) by the *Dienstberechtigter* can give rise to a claim for damages (*Schadensersatz*).[45]

- The *Verordnung über Arbeitsstätten (Arbeitsstättenverordnung*; ArbStättVO; (Work Places Order)

  The ArbStättVO of 20 March 1975 is a *Rechtsverordnung* passed in accordance with § 120e GewO. It contains comprehensive rules regarding the state of work places.

  § 53(i) ArbStättVO provides that an employer must maintain the work place and ensure that defects which are established, are rectified, if possible forthwith. If this cannot be done at once in the case of defects involving immediate danger, the relevant work must be discontinued.

  § 53(ii) ArbStättVO provides (*inter alia*) that security installations for the prevention or removal of dangers must be regularly examined and tested.

- § 5 and § 6 of the *Arbeitssicherheitsgesetz* (ASiG; Work Safety Law)

  These provisions oblige an employer to appoint qualified work safety personnel (*Fachkräfte für Arbeitssicherheit*) and set out their functions.

- § 636 of the *Reichsversicherungsordnung* (RVO; Imperial Insurance Order)

  An employee who sustains personal injuries (*Personenschäden*) due to an accident at work (*Arbeitsunfall*) has social insurance claims against the *Berufsgenossenschaft*. He cannot claim damages directly against the employer. However, an employers liability is not excluded, if the accident was caused deliberately or if it arose in the course of the employees *Teilnahme am allgemeinen Verkehr* (participation in general traffic).

- § 708 RVO

  The *Berufsgenossenschaft* can issue regulations for the prevention of accidents (*Unfallverhütungsvorschriften*).

---

43 A *Dienstvertrag* (contract for services) is to be distinguished from a *Werkvertrag* (contract of service) and, indeed, from an *Arbeitsvertrag* (contract of employment), to which the provisions in the BGB regarding the *Dienstvertrag* (§ 611 ff) have only subsidiary application (*hilfsweise Anwendung*). See Creifelds under *Dienstvertrag* and Chapter X, p 64.

44 An employer has a similar *Fürsorgepflicht* towards his *Handlungsgehilfen* (trading assistants and *Handlungslehrlinge* (trainees); § 62 HGB.

   Corresponding with an employer's *Fürsorgepflicht* is the employee's duty of loyalty (*Treuepflicht*). See Creifelds under *Fürsorgepflicht* and *Treuepflicht*.

45 See § 618(iii) BGB.

- § 714(i) RVO

  If, on an inspection by officials of a *Berufsgenossenschaft*, defects are discovered establishing an immediate threat of danger (*eine unmittelbar drohende Gefahr*), they can make immediately enforceable orders for the removal of the danger. Fines can be imposed.

- § 719 RVO

  This provides (*inter alia*) that in enterprises with more than 20 employees one or more safety officers (*Sicherheitsbeauftragte*) must be appointed.

CHAPTER XVIII

PRIVATE INTERNATIONAL LAW

The German rules governing conflicts of laws (private international law) are set out in Articles 3-38 of the Introductory Law to the Civil Code (the *Einführungsgesetz zum BGB* (EGBGB)). They specify the applicable legal system (law) where a case has a connection to the law of a foreign state (Article 3(i), first sentence).

Articles 3-38 are contained in Part I (general provisions) of the EGBGB and are divided into five sections:

Section 1: References (*Verweisungen*): Articles 3-6;

Section 2: Law of natural persons and legal transactions *(Recht der natürlichen Personen und Rechtsgeschäfte)*: Articles 7-12;

Section 3: Family law: Articles 13-24;

Section 4: Law of succession: Articles 25-26;

Section 5: Law of obligations: Articles 27-38.

Section 5 deals both with the position regarding contractual and non-contractual obligations (eg tort).

The position regarding the law applicable to contractual relationships is, broadly, as follows:-

By Article 27(i), first sentence EGBGB, the parties are free to choose the law applicable to their contract. The choice can be express or, if implication is possible with sufficient certainty, can be implied from the terms of the contract or the circumstances of the case: Article 27(i), second sentence.

In the absence of a choice, the contract is governed by the law of the state with which it has the closest connections (*engste Verbindungen*): Article 28(i), first sentence EGBGB.

By Article 28(ii), first sentence, it is presumed that the contract has the closest connections to the state in which:

- the party having to undertake the characteristic (act of) performance required by the contract (*die charakteristische Leistung*) usually resides; or

- if a company, association or juristic person is involved, its centre of administration (*Hauptverwaltung*) is situated.

Contracts with private consumers in another state (*Verbraucherverträge*) are subject to special rules: Article 29.

By Article 30(ii) EGBGB, in the absence of a particular choice of law, contracts of employment and employment relationships are governed either:

1 by the law of the state in which the employee usually undertakes his work in performance of the contract, even if he is sent temporarily to another state; or

2 insofar as the employee does not usually perform his duties in one and the same state, by the law of the state in which the employing branch is situated.

If, however, it appears from the totality of the circumstances that the contract of employment or employment relationship has closer connections to another state, the law of that state applies.

By Article 32(i) EGBGB, the above-mentioned applicable law is, in particular, decisive regarding (*inter alia*):

- interpretation of the contract;
- performance of contractual obligations; and
- consequences of full or partial non-performance of those obligations.

By Article 32(ii) EGBGB, in considering the manner of performance and the steps to be taken by a plaintiff in the event of faulty performance, account is to be taken of the law of the state in which performance takes place.

As for the position regarding non-contractual obligations (eg tort), the EGBGB only deals with torts committed by a German outside Germany. In such cases, the liability of the perpetrator cannot extend beyond the maximum laid down by German law: Article 38 EGBGB.

Torts committed in Germany by a German person fall to be dealt with according to German law.

Torts committed in Germany by other persons are also subject to German law, if a plaintiff choses to bring proceedings before the German courts.

CHAPTER XIX

THE LEGAL PROFESSION AND COURT SYSTEM[1]

THE JUDGES[2]

The position of judges in Germany is governed by the *Deutsches Richtergesetz* (DRiG: German Judges Law) of 8 September 1961, which is divided into four parts:

Part I: The office of judge in the *Bund* and in the *Länder* (§§ 1-45a)

Part II: Judges in service of the *Bund* (§§ 46-70)

Part III: Judges in service of a *Land* (§§ 71-84)

Part IV: Transitional and final provisions (§§ 85-126).

Judges can be either *Berufsrichter* (professional judges) or *ehrenamtliche Richter* (honorary (lay) judges).[3]

Where honorary judges take part in criminal matters, they are referred to as *Schöffe*.[4]

Civil matters are practically only dealt with by *Berufsrichter*. However, in the *Handelskammer* (chamber for commercial matters) in the *Landgericht*, a *Berufsrichter* presides with two honorary *Handelsrichter* (commercial judges).

In accordance with Article 101(i) second sentence GG (*Grundsatz des gesetzlichen Richters*), *ehrenamtliche Richter* (honorary judges) can only take part in a court hearing, if and as permitted by statute.[5]

They are selected on the basis of lists (*Vorschlagslisten*)[6] and enjoy similar independence to that of the *Berufsrichter*.[7] While they cannot preside over the hearing,[8] they basically have the same rights as a *Berufsrichter*.[9]

The capacity to be a judge (*Befähigung zum Richteramt*) in the *Bund* and in every German *Land* is acquired simultaneously with the capacity to be a *Rechtsanwalt* by passing the first state examination (*erste Staatsprüfung*), serving a *Vorbereitungsdienst* (preparatory period of service) of two and a half years as

---

1   See generally Baur, § 2.
2   See Article 98 GG; Jauernig (ZP), Book 1, Chapter 2 (§ 8) and Model/Creifelds/ Lichtenberger, Part 3 A (209).
3   See § 1 DRiG.
4   See § 45a DRiG.
5   See § 44(i) DRiG. See also Chapter VIII (note 15).
6   See §§ 36 and 108 GVG.
7   See §§ 44(ii) and 45 DRiG.
8   See § 28(ii) DRiG.
9   See §§ 30 and 112 GVG. See also Creifelds under *Ehrenamtliche Richter*.

Referendar, and then passing the second state examination *(zweite Staatsprüfung)*.[10]

Professors of law at a German university can be judges.[11]

In his position as a judge *(Richterverhältnis)*, a judge stands in the service of the *Bund* or a *Land*;[12] he is not a *Beamter* (civil servant).

The appointment *(Ernennung)* of a judge is usually for life *(auf Lebenszeit)*, although an appointment for a particular period or on probation *(auf Probe)* is possible.[13]

Judges in the supreme federal courts *(Bundesrichter)* are appointed by the *Bundespräsident* on the recommendation of the Federal Minister of Justice or other competent minister together with a *Richterwahlausschuß* (judicial selection council).[14]

Judges in the *Länder* are usually appointed merely by the competent minister of the relevant *Land*.

In the *Bundesverfassungsgericht* (Federal Constitutional Court), the 16 judges are chosen half by the *Bundesrat* and half by the *Bundestag*.[15]

Judges are independent *(unabhängig)* and only subject to the law *(nur dem Gesetz unterworfen)*.[16]

The transfer or removal *(Versetzung/Amtsenthebung)* of a judge without his agreement is only possible in certain limited cases.[17]

Supervisory and disciplinary measures are subject to final decision by a *Dienstgericht*.

THE *RECHTSPFLEGER*[18]

In order to relieve the judges, certain judicial business is transacted by civil servants *(Beamte)* known as *Rechtspfleger* (legal executives). §§ 3, 20-24a and 29-31 of the *Rechtspflegergesetz* of 5 November 1969 (RPflG) transfer to the

---

10 See §§ 5(i) and 9 DRiG. Lawyers from other EU (EEC) countries do not have the *Befähigung zum Richteramt*, even if they pass the new *Eignungsprüfung*. Moreover, passing the *Eignungsprüfung* does not enable such lawyers to become a notary *(Notar)*. See Chapter XIX note 92.

11 See § 7 DRiG.

12 See § 3 DRiG.

13 See §§ 10-13 DRiG.

14 See Article 95(ii) GG; § 1 *Richterwahlgesetz*.

15 See Article 94(i) GG; § 5 BVerfGG; Creifelds under *Richterwahl*. See also the comments above Article 93 GG in the *Sourcebook*, Chapter 2.

16 See § 25 DRiG and Article 97(i) GG. Withdrawal of appointment *(Rücknahme der Ernennung)* is also possible on certain grounds: § 19 DRiG.

17 See § 30 DRiG.

18 See: Jauernig (ZP), Book 1, Chapter 2 (§ 15); Model/Creifelds/Lichtenberger, Part 3 A (210); Creifelds under *Rechtspfleger*.

Rechtspfleger various types of business (so-called *übertragene Geschäfte*), for example:

- matters concerning *Vereine* (*Vereinssachen*);
- land register matters (*Grundbuchsachen*) and proceedings for *Zwangs-versteigerung* and *Zwangsverwaltung*;
- the *Verteilungsverfahren* (distribution procedure);[19]
- guardianship, family and care matters (*Vormundschafts-, Familien- und Betreuungssachen*);*
- probate and division matters (*Nachlaß- und Teilungsssachen*) and official custody of wills and *Erbverträgen*;*
- commercial matters (*Handelssachen*);*
- bankruptcy and composition proceedings (*Konkurs- und Vergleichsverfahren*);*
- default notice procedure (*Mahnverfahren*);
- enforcement of judgments (*Zwangsvollstreckung*); and
- fixing of costs (*Kostenfestsetzung*).[20]

Certain of the above matters[21] are subject to exceptions, which are reserved to be dealt with by the judge (*dem Richter vorbehaltene Geschäfte*).[22]

A *Rechtspfleger* is not empowered to administer an oath, to threaten or order a person's detention (with certain exceptions) or to decide on an application to amend a decision taken by a clerk of the *Geschäftsstelle* (business office) of the court.[23]

Moreover, only a judge can order a search of premises.[24]

The *Rechtspfleger* must submit a matter to the judge:

- if he wishes to deviate from an opinion of the judge of which he is aware;
- if the conduct of the matter gives rise to legal difficulties;
- if foreign law is involved; or
- if a close connection with a matter to be dealt with by a judge makes the submission expedient.[25]

---

19   See Chapter XII, p 118.
20   And the remuneration of a *Rechtsanwalt* under § 19 BRAGO.
21   Those marked with an * above.
22   See §§ 14-19b RPflG.
23   See § 4(ii) RPflG.
24   See Article 13(ii) GG.
25   See § 5(i) RPflG. Whilst a judge can effectively carry out a matter transferred to a *Rechtspfleger*, a judge's matter undertaken by a *Rechtspfleger* contrary to the RPflG is invalid (see § 8(i) and (iv) RPflG).

The appropriate legal remedy against the decision of a *Rechtspfleger* is the *Erinnerung* (reminder).[26]

The *Rechtspfleger* has power to correct his decision; otherwise, he must lay the *Erinnerung* before the judge. If the judge takes no action, he must in turn pass it to the next competent court (a so-called *Durchgriffserinnerung* (piercing *Erinnerung*)).[27]

THE COURT SYSTEM

The *Gerichtsbarkeiten*[28]

The German judicature or judicial power (*rechtsprechende Gewalt*) is divided into various branches (*Zweige*), known as *Gerichtsbarkeiten* (jurisdictions). The types of *Gerichtsbarkeit* are

- the *ordentliche Gerichtsbarkeit* (ordinary jurisdiction);
- the *besondere Gerichtsbarkeit* (special jurisdiction);
- the *Verwaltungsgerichtsbarkeit* (administrative jurisdiction); and
- the *Verfassungsgerichtsbarkeit* (constitutional jurisdiction).

The *ordentliche Gerichtsbarkeit*[29]

The *ordentliche Gerichtsbarkeit* comprises civil and criminal matters and the so-called *freiwillige Gerichtsbarkeit* (voluntary jurisdiction) in non-contentious civil matters.

A particular example of the *freiwillige Gerichtsbarkeit* is the activity of the *Amtsgericht* as the court responsible for guardianship, probate and trade and land register matters.

The basic statute governing the *freiwillige Gerichtsbarkeit* is the *Gesetz über die Angelegenheiten der freiwilligen Gerichtsbarkeit* (FGG) of 17 May 1898.[30]

Where a matter of *freiwillige Gerichtsbarkeit* is involved, the court is responsible for undertaking the necessary investigations itself (*von Amts wegen*).

A decision in a matter of *freiwillige Gerichtsbarkeit* is pronounced not as an *Urteil* (judgment), but in the form of a *Beschluß* or *Verfügung* (order or direction) and the hearing is not open to the public. An oral hearing is at the discretion of the court.[31]

---

26 To be distinguished is the so-called *Vollstreckungserinnerung* under § 766 ZPO against a measure (*Maßnahme*) taken by a *Rechtspfleger* or judge in enforcement proceedings. This is decided upon by the judge.

27 See § 11(i) and (ii) RPflG.

28 See Article 95(i) GG; Baumann (ER), Part VI, § 17 II.

29 See Model/Creifelds/Lichtenberger, Part 3 B (215-229).

30 See also the *Grundbuchordnung* (GBO) regarding land registration matters.

31 See Creifelds under *freiwillige Gerichtsbarkeit*.

The *ordentliche Gerichtsbarkeit* itself is dealt with in the *Gerichtsverfassungsgesetz* (GVG) of 27 January 1877.

Apart from the *Bundesgerichtshof* (BGH; Federal Supreme Court) in Karlsruhe, all other courts of the *ordentliche Gerichtsbarkeit* (the *ordentliche Gerichte*) are courts of the *Länder*. The hierarchy is as follows:[32]

- the *Amtsgericht* (district court: AG);
- the *Landgericht* (county court: LG);
- the *Oberlandesgericht* (County Court of Appeal: OLG);
- the *Bundesgerichtshof* (Federal Supreme Court: BGH).

In Bavaria, above the OLG an *Oberstes Landesgericht* (Supreme County Court) exists.[33]

The competence (*Zuständigkeit*) of the *ordentliche Gerichte* is laid down in § 13 GVG, whereby all civil disputes and criminal matters (*alle bürgerlichen Rechtsstreitigkeiten und Strafsachen*) belong before the *ordentliche Gerichte*.

The *besondere Gerichtsbarkeit*

Article 101(ii) GG provides that courts for special subject areas (*besondere Sachgebiete*) can only be formed by statute (*Gesetz*). The main example[34] of such *besondere Gerichte* are the *Arbeitsgerichte* (employment courts), where the hierarchy is as follows:

- the *Arbeitsgericht* (employment court (ArbG));
- the *Landesarbeitsgericht* (county employment court (LAG)); and
- the *Bundesarbeitsgericht* (federal employment court (BAG)); in Erfurt).[35]

Special federal courts exist for patent and disciplinary matters.[36]

To be distinguished from the *besondere Gerichte* are *Ausnahmegerichte* (exceptional courts for particular cases); these are forbidden by Article 101(i) GG and § 16, first sentence GVG.

The *Verwaltungsgerichtsbarkeit*

The *Verwaltungsgerichtsbarkeit* comprises three main areas:

- the *allgemeine Verwaltungsgerichtsbarkeit* (general administrative jurisdiction, ie the jurisdiction of the *Verwaltungsgerichte* (administrative courts));
- the *Sozialgerichtsbarkeit* (the jurisdiction of the social (security) courts);
- the *Finanzgerichtsbarkeit* (the jurisdiction of the finance courts).

---

32 See § 12 GVG.
33 See § 8 EGGVG.
34 The European Court of Justice also appears to have the status of such a court: see the comments under Article 101(ii) GG in the *Sourcebook*, Chapter 2.
35 See § 1 *Arbeitsgerichtsgesetz* (ArbGG); Article 95(i) GG. See also Chapter XVII (note 9) above.
36 See Article 96(i) and (iv) GG.

Apart from the *Finanzgerichtsbarkeit* (which comprises only two instances – the *Finanzgericht* and the *Bundesfinanzhof* (BFH; Federal Finance Court in Munich)), the court hierarchy of the administrative and social (security) courts is three-tiered:

respectively

- the *Verwaltungsgericht* (VG);
- the *Oberverwaltungsgericht* (OVG);[37]
- the *Bundesverwaltungsgericht* (BVerwG (in Leipzig));

and

- the *Sozialgericht* (SG);
- the *Landessozialgericht* (LSG);
- the *Bundessozialgericht* (BSG; in Kassel).

The competence of and procedure before the above-mentioned administrative, social and finance courts are, respectively, dealt with by the *Verwaltungsgerichtsordnung* (VwGO), the *Sozialgerichtsgesetz* (SGG) and the *Finanzgerichtsordnung* (FGO).[38]

Rechtspflege[39]

The term *Gerichtsbarkeit* is used not only in an organisational sense to refer to its various branches, but also in a functional sense as meaning the exercise of the administration of justice (*die Ausübung der Rechtspflege*).

Rechtspflege is not only the domain of the judiciary (the activity of which is referred to as *Rechtsprechung*),[40] but includes:

- the *freiwillige Gerichtsbarkeit* (voluntary jurisdiction in non-contentious civil matters);[41]
- the activity of the *Staatsanwalt* (public prosecutor);[42]
- the enforcement of judgments (*Zwangsvollstreckung*);[43]
- the grant of legal advice (*Rechtsberatung*) under the *Beratungshilfegesetz* (BerHG) of 18 June 1980;
- the activities of the *Notar* (notary) and the *Rechtsanwalt* (lawyer).[44]

---

37 An OVG is sometimes known as a *Verwaltungsgerichtshof* (VGH).

38 Regarding the VwGO see Chapter XIV above.

39 See Model/Creifelds/Lichtenberger, Part 3 A (204).

40 *Rechtsprechung* can also just mean case-law, the proper term for which is, however, *Fallrecht*.

41 See Chapter XIX, p 168.

42 See Chapter XVI, p 146.

43 See Chapter XII, p 115.

44 See Chapter XIX, pp 171 and 178.

THE *RECHTSANWALT*[45]

Introduction

The law relating to German lawyers (*Rechtsanwälte*) is set out in the *Bundesrechtsanwaltsordnung* (BRAO; Federal Lawyers Order) of 1 August 1959 and the *Richtlinien* (directives) laid down by the *Bundesrechtsanwaltskammer* (Federal Lawyers Chamber (BRAK)) on 21 June 1973.

The BRAO is divided into 12 parts, of which the following are the most important:

Part I: The status of the *Rechtsanwalt* (§§ 1-3)

Part II: The admission (*Zulassung*) of the *Rechtsanwalt* (§§ 4-42)

Part III: The rights (*Rechte*) and duties (*Pflichten*) of the *Rechtsanwalt* (§§ 43-59)

Part IV: The *Rechtsanwaltskammern* (Lawyers Chambers) (§§ 60-91)

Parts V-VII: Disciplinary provisions (*ehrengerichtliche Vorschriften*) (§§ 92-161a)

Part VIII: The *Rechtsanwälte* at the *Bundesgerichtshof* (Federal Supreme Court) (§§ 162-174)

Part IX: The *Bundesrechtsanwaltskammer* (Federal Lawyers Chamber) (§§ 175-191).

By § 1 BRAO, the *Rechtsanwalt* is an independent organ of the administration of justice (*ein unabhängiges Organ der Rechtspflege*).

The *Rechtsanwalt* exercises a free profession (*übt einen freien Beruf aus*) and is not a trader (*seine Tätigkeit ist kein Gewerbe*).[46]

He is the appointed independent adviser and representative in all legal matters (*der berufene unabhängige Berater und Vertreter in allen Rechtsangelegenheiten*).[47]

Within the framework of the relevant legal provisions, everyone has the right to be advised and represented by a lawyer of his choice (*durch einen Rechtsanwalt seiner Wahl*).[48]

Admission as a *Rechtsanwalt*

By § 4 BRAO, the admission (*Zulassung*) of a *Rechtsanwalt* is dependent on the acquisition of the *Befähigung zum Richteramt* (capacity to be a judge) or the passing of the aptitude test (*Eignungsprüfung*) for lawyers from other EEC countries under the *Gesetz über die Eignungsprüfung für die Zulassung zur Rechtsanwaltschaft* of 6 July 1990, in force since 1 January 1991.

---

45 See: the *Grundsätze des anwaltlichen Standesrechts* (BRAK *Richtlinien*); Jauernig (ZP), Book 1, Chapter 2 (§ 16); Model/Creifelds/Lichtenberger, Part 3 A (211).

46 See § 2 BRAO.

47 See § 3(i) BRAO.

48 See § 3(iii) BRAO.

The *Rechtsanwalt* enjoys professional freedom of movement (*Freizügigkeit*) within Germany,[49] but must be admitted at a particular court (*bei einem bestimmten Gericht*) of the *ordentliche Gerichtsbarkeit*.[50]

Admission is granted (*erteilt*) on application (*auf Antrag*).[51]

A *Rechtsanwalt* must reside within the area (*Bezirk*) of the *Oberlandesgericht* of his admission[52] and, if admitted at an OLG, cannot be admitted at another court.[53]

Usually, therefore, a *Rechtsanwalt* is admitted either at a *Landgericht* or at an OLG (the so-called principle of single admission (*Singularzulassung*)), although, in certain *Länder* (Baden-Württemberg, Bavaria, Berlin, Bremen, Hamburg and Saarland), the *Rechtsanwalt* is entitled to simultaneous admission (*Simultanzulassung*) at the OLG after five years' admission at a court of first instance[54]

---

49 See § 5 BRAO.

50 See § 18(i) BRAO.

51 See § 19(i) BRAO.

52 See § 27(i) BRAO.

53 See § 25 BRAO.

54 See § 226 BRAO.

A On 8 September 1994, the *Gesetz zur Neuordnung des Berufsrechts der Rechtsanwälte* was published, envisaging that a *Rechtsanwalt* admitted at a particular *Landgericht* will be entitled to appear (throughout Germany) before the civil chamber of any other *Landgericht* and before all *Familiengerichte* (Family Courts; these are divisions of the *Amtsgerichte*: see § 23b GVG).

The new rule will apply as from 1 January 2000 in the *Länder* of former West Germany and will come into force in the new *Länder* on 1 January 2005.

For further details, see the article by Jörn Loewer in BRAK-*Mitteilungen* 4/1994, at p 186.

B On 10 June 1994, a *Gesetz zur Schaffung von Partnerschaftsgesellschaften* (in force since 1 July 1995) was passed, enabling a *Partnerschaftsgesellschaft* (partnership (company)) to be registered at the local *Amtsgericht*.

The *Partnerschaftsgesellschaft* is a special type of *Personengesellschaft* for members of the *freie Berufe* (free professions), such as *Rechtsanwälte*.

The new law is supplemented by the provisions of the BGB regarding civil law partnerships (§§ 705 ff BGB) and contains various references (*Verweisungen*) to the HGB.

The *Partnerschaftsgesellschaftsgesetz* (PartGG) is set out, broadly, as follows:

§ 1 Definition of the *Partnerschaftsgesellschaft*; who can be a partner.

§ 2 Name of the partnership.

§ 3 Partnership agreement (*Partnerschaftsvertrag*).

§ 4 Notification (*Anmeldung*) for registration.

§ 5 Content of the entry in the register.

§ 6 Internal relationship (*Innenverhältnis*) between the partners.

By § 6(ii) individual (but not all) partners can be excluded from (internal) management (*Geschäftsführung*). ...

Admission as a *Rechtsanwalt* at the *Bundesgerichtshof* (Federal Supreme Court) is dependent on selection by a *Wahlausschuß* on the basis of *Vorschlagslisten* (lists). Admission to the BGH restricts practice to that court, the other supreme federal courts and the *Bundesverfassungsgericht* (Federal Constitutional Court).[55]

Position of the *Rechtsanwalt*

§§ 43-59 BRAO deal with the rights and duties (*Rechte und Pflichten*) of the *Rechtsanwalt*. Of particular importance is § 43 (which is repeated in § 1 of the *Richtlinien* (Directives) of the *Bundesrechtsanwaltskammer*):

§ 43 *Allgemeine Berufspflicht. Der Rechtsanwalt hat seinen Beruf gewissenhaft auszuüben. Er hat sich innerhalb und ausserhalb des Berufes der Achtung und des Vertrauens, welche die Stellung des Rechtsanwalts erfordert, würdig zu erweisen.*

§ 43 General professional duty. The *Rechtsanwalt* must exercise his profession conscientiously. Both within and outside the profession, he must show himself to be worthy of the respect and trust which the position of *Rechtsanwalt* demands.

The relationship of the *Rechtsanwalt* to his client (*Mandant* or *Auftraggeber*) is a so-called *Geschäftsbesorgungsvertrag* within § 675 BGB (an agreement of instruction for reward (*entgeltlich*), as opposed to a mere *Auftrag* ((contract of) instruction without payment).

If a *Rechtsanwalt* does not wish to accept instructions, he must notify his refusal (*Ablehnung*) forthwith.[56]

54...§ 7 External position (*Außenverhältnis*) of the partnership.

By § 7(i) the partnership (*Partnerschaftsgesellschaft*) arises (*entsteht*) on registration. Beforehand, it is treated as a GbR.

§ 7(ii) refers to § 124 HGB, meaning that like the OHG, but unlike the GbR, the *Partnerschaftsgesellschaft* is a *Rechtssubjekt* and *rechtsfähig*, ie capable of suing and being sued in its own name. The *Partnerschaftsgesellschaft* is a *Gesamthandsgemeinschaft* (joint community), but is approximated (*angenähert*) to a juristic person.

By § 7(iii) each partner has an unlimitable right of representation (*Vertretungsbefugnis*) in relation to third parties.

§ 8 Liability (*Haftung*).

Basically, all partners are personally liable, as joint debtors, for the obligations of the partnership. A contractual restriction of liability (*Haftungsbeschränkung*) to the partner assuming responsibility for the particular matter is possible (also in standard business terms).

In accordance with § 51a BRAO, liability for simple negligence (*einfache Fahrlässigkeit*) can be limited to four times the minimum amount of professional liability insurance (currently DM 500,000). Additionally, however, standard business terms can restrict liability in cases of gross negligence (*grobe Fahrlässigkeit*).

§ 9 Termination (*Auflösung*) of the partnership; departure (*Ausscheiden*) of a partner.

§ 10 Liquidation and limitation period for claims (*Verjährung*).

For further details, see the article by Dr Fritz Kempter in BRAK-*Mitteilungen* 3/1994, p 122.

55 See § 172(i) BRAO.

56 See § 44 BRAO.

In certain circumstances, he is forbidden from acting, eg where he would breach his professional duties or in cases of previous conflicting involvement in the same matter.[57]

Where a *Rechtsanwalt* is in continuous employment (*in einem ständigen Dienstverhältnis*) for an employer, he cannot represent that employer before a court in his capacity as *Rechtsanwalt* (he is a so-called *Syndikusanwalt*).[58]

A *Rechtsanwalt* can be appointed as a compulsory defence lawyer (*Pflichtverteidiger*).[59]

A *Rechtsanwalt* can decline to hand out his file (*Handakte*) until his fees (*Gebühren*) and disbursements (*Auslagen*) are paid; he must usually retain his file for five years after completion of the retainer.[60]

A clients claim for damages against the *Rechtsanwalt* out of their contractual relationship becomes statute-barred (*verjährt*) at the latest three years after the end of the retainer.[61]

The *Rechtsanwaltskammer*

The *Rechtsanwälte* admitted in the *Bezirk* (area) of an OLG comprise a *Rechtsanwaltskammer* (RAK; Lawyers' Chamber).[62]

The RAK is a public corporation (*Körperschaft des öffentlichen Rechts*) and is supervised in the observance of law and its rules and in the performance of its duties by the Ministry of Justice of the respective *Land*.[63]

Its organs are the *Vorstand* (board, elected by the *Kammerversammlung* (chamber assembly)) and the *Präsidium* (elected by the *Vorstand*).[64]

The *Rechtsanwälte* admitted at the BGH comprise a separate RAK.[65]

The Lawyers' Chambers are united in a *Bundesrechtsanwaltskammer* (BRAK; based in Bonn), which is supervised by the Federal Minister of Justice.[66]

Its organs are the *Präsidium* and *Hauptversammlung* (main assembly), where each RAK is represented by its president.[67]

---

57 See § 45 BRAO.
58 See § 46 BRAO.
59 See § 49(i) BRAO.
60 See § 50(i) and (ii) BRAO.
61 See § 51 BRAO.
62 See § 60(i) BRAO.
63 See § 62(ii) BRAO.
64 See §§ 63 and 78 BRAO.
65 See § 174 BRAO.
66 See §§ 175-176 BRAO.
67 See §§ 179 and 187 BRAO.

By § 177(ii) No 2 BRAO, the BRAK is responsible for establishing the general opinion (*die allgemeine Auffassung*) on questions of professional practice in the form of *Richtlinien* (directives). The *Richtlinien* supplement § 43 BRAO[68] and set out the basic principles of professional conduct (*die allgemeine Grundsätze des anwaltlichen Standesrechts*).

Legal fees

German lawyer's fees (*Gebühren*) are governed by the *Bundesgebührenordnung für Rechtsanwälte* (BRAGO) of 26 July 1957. Except as otherwise provided in BRAGO, they are calculated according to the value of the matter (*Gegenstandswert*).[69]

In civil court proceedings and preparatory work therefor, the *Gegenstandswert* follows the value established for court fee purposes (referred to as the *Streitwert*).[70]

To assess the court fee value, the applicable provisions are §§ 12-34 of the *Gerichtskostengesetz* (GKG: Court Fees Law), which refer to §§ 3-9 ZPO.

In the absence of an applicable valuation provision in the GKG or ZPO, the *Gegenstandswert* follows (for valuation purposes only) the so-called *Geschäftswert* (business value), which is the principle for calculation of court and notary costs in non-contentious civil matters (under the *Kostenordnung* (KostO), also of 26 July 1957).[71]

If, in turn, the provisions of the KostO do not assist and BRAGO does not contain a more special provision, the *Gegenstandswert* is to be calculated by the *Rechtsanwalt* according to fair discretion (*nach billigem Ermessen*).

Thus, the value of the matter in contentious civil matters is referred to:

* in matters where the GKG or ZPO contain an applicable valuation provision, as *Streitwert*. The actual scale fees of lawyers are set out in § 11(i) BRAGO and in the *Gebührentabelle* (fee table) annexed and the fees of the court in § 11(ii) GKG and in the *Gebührentabelle* (fee table) annexed;

* in matters where the KostO applies, as *Geschäftswert*. The actual scale fees of the court in matters of *freiwillige Gerichtsbarkeit* (voluntary jurisdiction) and the fees of notaries are set out in § 32 KostO and in the *Gebührentabelle* annexed. The fees of lawyers in cases where the KostO applies are based on the *Geschäftswert*, but are due in accordance with the BRAGO fee table.

Each individual fee is referred to as *eine (volle) Gebühr* (one (full) fee). It is divided into tenths (*Zehntel*).

In contentious civil matters, the fees of a *Rechtsanwalt* can be made up of one or more of several full *Gebühren*:[72]

---

68   See Chapter XII, p 98.
69   See § 7(i) BRAGO.
70   See § 8(i), first sentence BRAGO and §§ 11(i) and (ii) *Gerichtskostengesetz* (GKG).
71   See § 8(i), third sentence and § 8(ii) BRAGO and § 18 KostO.
72   See § 31(i) BRAGO.

1   a *Prozeßgebühr* (procedure fee) for dealing with the matter generally;

2   a *Verhandlungsgebühr* (hearing fee) for the oral hearing;

3   a *Beweisgebühr* (evidence fee) if evidence is taken;

4   an *Erörterungsgebühr* for merely raising the matter, eg where an attempt to reach a settlement is made. This fee and the *Verhandlungsgebühr* are mutually exclusive.

In other (non-contentious) civil matters, a *Rechtsanwalt* can claim five to 10 *Zehntel* of several full *Gebühren*: [73]

1   a *Geschäftsgebühr* (business fee) for dealing with the matter generally;[74]

2   a *Besprechungsgebühr* (discussion fee) for being involved in certain activities;[75]

3   a *Beweisaufnahmegebühr* (taking of evidence fee) for being involved in the taking of evidence required by a court or authority.

The *Gebühren* compensate a *Rechtsanwalt* for the whole of his activity in a particular matter and can only be claimed once in the same matter. In court proceedings, fees can be claimed in every instance. [76]

The fees before administrative and finance courts follow those for civil proceedings.[77]

All administrative proceedings preliminary to court proceedings count as one matter.[78]

Fees higher than those in BRAGO can (only) be demanded by a *Rechtsanwalt*, if this is agreed in writing.[79]

An *Erfolgshonorar* (fee based on the success of the matter) or *quota litis* (proportion of any amount recovered) is not permitted.[80]

---

73   See § 118(i) BRAGO. If proceedings before a court or authority follow, the *Geschäftsgebühr* is credited towards the *Gebühren* then due; § 118(ii) BRAGO.

74   This includes information to the client, the drafting, lodging or signing of pleadings (*Schriftsätze*) or letters (*Schreiben*) and the drafting of documents (*Urkunden*).

75   Such as: negotiations or discussions before a court or authority or with the other side or a third party; the drafting of a *Gesellschaftsvertrag* (company agreement/articles of association).

     If a *Rechtsanwalt* is involved in the reaching of a settlement (*Vergleich*; for meaning see § 779 BGB), he can (also) charge a *Vergleichsgebühr*. The *Vergleichsgebühr* amounts to fifteen-tenths of a *Gebühr* where no court proceedings are pending. See § 23(i) BRAGO.

76   See § 13(i) and (ii) BRAGO. Fees are due in accordance with § 16 BRAGO and can only be demanded following the delivery of a signed *Berechnung* (bill of costs); § 18 BRAGO. For VAT (MwSt) and disbursements (*Auslagen*: postage, typing, travel expenses) see §§ 25-30 BRAGO.

77   See § 114(i) BRAGO.

78   See § 119(i) and § 119(ii) BRAGO.

79   See § 3(i) BRAGO.

80   See § 52 of the BRAK *Richtlinien*.

Fees can be left to be established at the discretion of the board of the RAK[81] or can, on application by the *Rechtsanwalt* or the client, be set by the court.[82]

The fees set out in § 11(i) BRAGO increase in the event of an appeal (*Berufung* or Revision).[83]

For verbal or written advice (*Rat*) or (brief) information (*Auskunft*) unconnected to another chargeable activity, the *Rechtsanwalt* can charge (in civil matters) between one-tenth and ten-tenths of a full *Gebühr* and, where the matter relates to a fine or criminal matter, between DM 25 and DM 335.

The fee for a first consultation (*Erstberatung*) is limited to not more than DM 350.[84]

For simple letters (*einfache Schreiben*), the *Rechtsanwalt* is only entitled to two-tenths of a full *Gebühr*.[85]

The fees set out in BRAGO can be merely banded (so-called *Rahmengebühren* (framework fees)).[86]

In that case, the fee is calculated by the *Rechtsanwalt nach billigem Ermessen* (at his fair discretion) on consideration of all the circumstances, in particular:

- the importance of the matter (*die Bedeutung der Angelegenheit*);
- the extent and difficulty of the work involved (*der Umfang und die Schwierigkeit der anwaltlichen Tätigkeit*); and
- the capital (*Vermögen*) and income (*Einkommen*) of the client.

In criminal and social security matters *Rahmengebühren* apply, scaled according to the court involved and the length of the hearing. In criminal matters, fees are differentiated according to whether the defence lawyer is privately selected or appointed by the court.[87]

For the completion of a written opinion with legal reasoning (*Gutachten mit juristischer Begründung*), the *Rechtsanwalt* is entitled to a fair fee (*eine angemessene Gebühr*) and the criteria for *Rahmengebühren* apply.[88]

Where no court proceedings are pending, the provision of assisted legal advice and representation (*Beratungshilfe*) to persons with a low income is governed by the *Beratungshilfegesetz* (BerHG). Lower *Gebühren* apply.[89]

---

81 See § 3(ii) BRAGO.
82 See § 19(i) BRAGO.
83 See § 11(i), sentences 2 and 3 BRAGO.
84 See § 20(i) BRAGO.
85 See § 120(i) BRAGO.
86 See § 12(i) BRAGO.
87 See §§ 83-108 and § 116 BRAGO.
88 See § 21 BRAGO.
89 See § 132 BRAGO. Application must be made to the local *Amtsgericht*; § 4 BerHG.

Again different scale fees apply where legal aid for court proceedings (*Prozeßkostenhilfe*) is granted.[90]

THE *NOTAR*[91]

Notaries are governed by the *Bundesnotarordnung* (BNotO; Federal Notaries Order) of 24 February 1961. They are appointed by the justice ministries of the *Länder* and hold an independent public office. Notaries provide impartial assistance (*unparteiische Betreuung*) to both sides in the area of so-called *vorsorgende Rechtspflege* (precautionary administration of justice).[92]

A *Notar* is competent to undertake the matters set out in §§ 20-25 BnotO. The principal responsibility of the *Notar* is the (public) documentation ((*öffentliche*) *Beurkundung*) of various transactions, such as:

- the conclusion of a contract for the sale or purchase of land (§ 313 BGB);
- the making of an *öffentliches Testament* (public will; § 2232 BGB);
- the making of a *Schenkungsversprechen* ((contractual) promise of a gift; § 518 BGB);
- the conclusion of an *Erbvertrag* (estate contract; § 2276 BGB);
- the establishment of a GmbH (limited company) or AG (public company) (§ 2(i) GmbHG and § 23(i) AktG).

The *Beurkundungsgesetz* (BeurkG) of 28 August 1969 contains the procedural rules regarding documentation. A *Niederschrift* (written record) of the proceedings must be made. The original of the *Niederschrift* is normally kept by the *Notar* and listed in an annual *Urkundenrolle* (roll of documents).[93]

The copies (*Ausfertigungen*) are distributed as required.

When undertaking a *Beurkundung*, notaries have certain duties (so-called *Prüfungs- und Belehrungspflichten*; §§ 17-21 BeurkG), in particular:

- to check the facts and to check that the transaction is legal and accords with the true will of those involved;
- to take care that a person involved is not prejudiced through inexperience;
- to advise those involved of the legal effect of the transaction (*die rechtliche Tragweite des Geschäfts*); and
- to ensure that declarations are documented clearly and in no uncertain terms (*klar und unzweideutig*).

---

90 See § 123 BRAGO and §§ 114-127a ZPO (Chapter XII, note 10 above). See also Jauernig (ZP), Book 4, Chapter 17 (§ 96).

91 See Model/Creifelds/Lichtenberger, Part 3 A (213) and Creifelds under *Notar*, *Anwaltsnotar* and *Form* 1, 2 and 3.

92 See §§ 1, 12 and 14 BNotO. Only persons, who are German citizens and have the *Befähigung zum Richteramt*, may be appointed; § 5 BNotO.

93 See §§ 8, 36 and 45 BeurkG and § 25 BNotO.

Notaries can also provide certifications (*Beglaubigungen*) of signatures and copy documents and certificates (*Bescheinigungen*) of entries in public registers by means of a *Vermerk* (note under seal).

The taking of oaths (*Eide*) and assurances in lieu of oath (*eidesstattliche Versicherungen*) by a notary is limited, respectively, to cases requiring this abroad and circumstances in which an allegation of fact or a statement needs to be substantiated to a *Behörde* (authority) or *sonstige Dienststelle* (other public office).[94]

A breach of the notary's official duties (*Amtspflichtverletzung*) can lead to a claim for damages against him.[95]

Like the *Rechtsanwälte*, the notaries of a particular *Bezirk* (area) comprise a *Notarkammer* (Notaries Chamber).[96]

Notaries' costs (fees and disbursements) are dealt with in the *Kosten-ordnung*.[97]

---

94 See §§ 20-22 BNotO and §§ 39-43 BeurkG.
95 See § 19 BNotO.
96 See §§ 65-91 BNotO.
97 See Chapter XIX, p 175 and §§ 140-157 KostO.

VOCABULARY
selected German and Latin words and phrases
(with their English/legal meanings)

Abänderungsklage	writ claiming the adjustment of a judgment for payment of a regular sum (eg maintenance). See Creifelds under *Abänderungsklage* and Chapter XII (note 5)
Aberratio ictus	(significant) aberration in a criminal act, ie it goes seriously wrong; it excludes *Vorsatz*; cf *Error in persona* and *Error in obiecto*. See Chapter XV, p 141
Abfindung	pay-off; redemption payment. See: Creifelds under *Abfindung* and *Abfindungsguthaben*; Chapter XI, p 88 and Chapter XVII (note 9)
Abgabe	the giving away of something, delivery; placement into circulation (of a *Willenserklärung*); casting (of a vote); levy, tax. See Chapter X, p 38
Abgabenordnung (AO)	(Federal) Collection of Taxes Order. See Creifelds under *Abgabenordnung* and Chapter XIII, p 122
Abgeben	to give something away, deliver; to place into circulation (eg a *Willenserklärung*); to cast (a vote)
Abgrenzen	to separate, demarcate
Abgrenzung	separation, demarcation. See Chapter XII (note 55)
Abhanden kommen	to go astray. See Chapter X, p 76 (*Bona fide* acquisition of ownership to movables)
Abhilfe	redress (where a *Behörde* regards a *Widerspruch* against a VA as justified). See Creifelds under *Abhilfe* and Chapter XIV (note 8)
Ablehnen	to refuse, object to
Ablehnung	refusal, objection (to)
Abmahnung	prior warning (before summary dismissal of an employee). See Chapter XVII, p 153
Abschluß	conclusion (of a matter or contract). See Chapter XI, p 85
Abschnitt	section (part of statute). Cf *Vorschrift*: an individual provision in a statute, which incorporates the terms Paragraph (§) and *Artikel* (eg in the GG)

Abschrift	copy. Can be *einfach* (normal, simple) or *beglaubigt* (certified). See Chapter XII, p 107 and *cf Ausfertigung*
Absehen von Strafe	to disregard imposing (non-imposition of) a *Strafe*. See Creifelds under *Absehen von Strafe* and Chapter XV, p 143
Absicht	(pure) intent. See Chapter XV, p 140
Absichtlich	deliberately
Absolutes Recht	absolute right. *Cf Relatives Recht* and see Chapter X, p 33
Abstammen	to descend from
Abstammung	descent (from). See Chapter X, p 79
Abstimmung	vote, ballot; plebiscite. See Chapter II (note 11) and also *Volksabstimmung*
Abstrakt	abstract
Abstrakte Normkontrolle	see *Normkontrolle*
Abstraktionsgrundsatz	abstraction principle. See Chapter X, pp 48 and 72
Abtretung	assignment. See Creifelds under *Abtretung* and *cf Schuldübernahme*. See also Chapter X, pp 57 and 58
Abwägung	balancing. See Creifelds under *Abwägungsgebot* and Chapter VIII, p 24
Abwehr	warding-off, repulsion
Abwehrrecht(e)	defensive right(s). See Chapter VIII, p 23
Abweisen	to dismiss, reject (an application or *Klage*)
Abweisung	dismissal, rejection (of an application or *Klage*). See Chapter XII, note 57
Abzahlungskauf	instalment (hire) purchase. See Creifelds under *Abzahlungsgeschäft* and Chapter X, p 72. See also the *Verbraucherkreditgesetz* (Consumer Credit Law) of 17 December 1990
Adäquanztheorie	theory of foreseeability (adequacy theory). It is the dominant theory of causation in civil law. See Chapter XV (note 16) and *cf Äquivalenztheorie*
Adressat	addressee. See Chapter VIII, p 24
Aequitas	fairness; equity. See Chapter I (note 5)
Akte	file
Akteneinsicht	inspection of the file(s). See Chapter XIII, p 123

Aktiengesellschaft (AG)	public limited company. See *Gesellschaft* and *Vorstand*
Aktiengesetz (AktG)	Law relating to public limited companies. See Chapter XI, p 81
Akzessorietät	accessory relationship. See Creifelds under *Akzessorietät* I and Chapter X (note 109)
Alle Angelegenheiten der örtlichen Gemeinschaft	all local matters. See Chapter VI
Allgemein	general
Allgemeine Geschäftsbedingungen	general terms, (standard) conditions of business; also: *Vertragsbedingungen*. See Chapter X, p 45, Creifelds under *Allgemeine Geschäftsbedingungen* and the AGBG
Allgemeiner Teil (AT)	general part. See Chapter X, p 31
Allgemeines Bürgerliches Gesetzbuch (AGBGB)	General Civil Code (for Austria; 1811). See Chapter I (note 11)
Allgemeines Landrecht für die Staaten (ALR)	General Law for the Prussian States *preußischen* (1794). See Creifelds under *Allgemeines Landrecht* and Chapter I (note 11)
Allgemein verbindlich	of general effect; generally binding. See Chapter VII (note 8)
Allgemeinverfügung	a VA giving a general direction. See Chapter XIII, p 124
Als eigene Angelegenheit	as one's (its) own matter. See Chapter V, p 16
Amtsanwalt	district public prosecutor (at the AG). See Chapter XVI, p 146
Amtsbetrieb	conduct of a matter by the court (rather than by the parties: *Parteibetrieb*). See Chapter XII, p 104
Amtsenthebung	removal from office. See Chapter XIX (note 17)
Amtsgericht (AG)	district court. See: Creifelds under *Amtsgericht*; Chapter XII, p 112 and Chapter XIX, p 168
Amtshilfe	official assistance (between *Behörden*). See Creifelds under *Amtshilfe*
Amtspflicht	official duty. See § 839 BGB and Creifelds under *Staatshaftung* 1. See also Chapter XIX, p 179
Analog	analogously
Analogie	analogy. See Creifelds under *Analogie*, Chapter XV, p 133 and also *entsprechende Anwendung*
Änderung	variation, amendment
Aneignung	acquisition of ownership to ownerless movables (appropriation). See Chapter X, p 76

Anerkenntnis	acknowledgment (of a claim). See Chapter XII (note 57)
Anerkennung	acknowledgment
Anfechtbar(keit)	voidable, challengeable; voidability, challengability. See Chapter XIII, p 124. See also *Anfechtung*
Anfechten	to challenge, contest
Anfechtung	challenge, contestation. See Creifelds under *Anfechtung von Willenserklärungen* and Chapter X, p 24 (Title 2)
Anfechtungsklage	writ of challenge (against a VA). See Creifelds under *Verwaltungsstreitverfahren* I (a), Chapter XIII, p 125 and Chapter XIV, p 129
Angedroht	threatened. See Chapter XVII, p 159 (note 40)
Angebot	offer. See Chapter X, p 43 (Title 3)
Angeklagter	defendant, accused (after the opening of proceedings). *Cf Beschuldigter* and see Chapter XVI, p 151
Angemessen	fair
Angeschuldigter	person charged. *Cf Beschuldigter* and see Chapter XVI, p 150
Angestellter	employee. See *Arbeitnehmer*
Angriffs- und Verteidigungsmittel	means of attack and defence. See Chapter XII, p 112
Anhängig	pending (before a court). See Chapter XII, p 107 and *cf Rechtshängig*
Anhörung	hearing, listening. See Creifelds under *Anhörung* and Chapter XIII, p 123. *Cf Vernehmung*
Anklagebehörde	prosecution authority. See Chapter XVI, p 146
Anklagegrundsatz	principle that a public prosecution is necessary before a judicial investigation of an alleged crime can take place. See Chapter XVI, p 146
Anklagemonopol	prosecution monopoly. See Chapter XVI, p 146
Anklagen	to prosecute, accuse; cf *Beschuldigen* and *Vorwerfen*
Anklageschrift	(bill of) indictment. See Creifelds under *Anklageschrift*. See also *Angeschuldigter*, *Angeklagter* and Chapter XVI, p 150
Anlaß	cause, reason, occasion (for). See Chapter XVI, p 150
Anmelden	to notify, report. Also: to announce or register (oneself or something).

Anmeldung	notification, report. See Chapter XI, p 86
Annähern	to become close (approximate) to. See Chapter XIX (note 55)
Annahme	acceptance. See Chapter X, p 43 (Title 3)
Annahme als Kind	adoption. See Chapter X, p 79 and Creifelds under *Adoption*
Anordnung	order (direction) eg of a court during proceedings. See Chapter X, p 72 and Chapter XII, p 104
Anscheinsbeweis	*prima facie* evidence. It can ease the burden of proof (*Beweislast*). *Cf Indizienbeweis*
Anspruch	claim; right (to). See Chapter X, p 33 and *Exposé*
Anspruch auf einen gesetzlichen Richter	right to a proper (statutory) judge. See Creifelds under *Gesetzlicher Richter* and Chapter VIII (note 15)
Anspruch auf rechtliches Gehör	right to be heard; right to a proper hearing (in accordance with law). See Creifelds under *Rechtliches Gehör* and Chapter VIII (note 15)
Anspruchsgrundlage	(legal) basis (ground) for an *Anspruch*. See Chapter X, p 33
Anspruchsnorm	a norm containing an *Anspruchsgrundlage*. *Cf Hilfsnorm*
Anstalt	institution. See Chapter II, p 6
Anteil	part, share. See Chapter XI, p 82
Antrag	application (for). See Chapter XII (note 57)
Anwalt	see *Rechtsanwalt*
Anwaltsprozeß	lawyer's action. *Cf Parteiprozeß*. See Chapter XII, p 101
Anwaltszwang	compulsory instruction of lawyer. See Chapter XII, p 101 and Chapter XIX (note 55)
Anwartschaft(srecht)	(right of) expectancy. See Chapter X, p 46 and pp 71-72
Anweisung	documentary instruction. See Chapter X, p 59 (Title 21)
Anwendung	(practical) application. See Chapter X (note 60)
Anwendungsbereich	area of application
Anzahlung	deposit (on a transaction). *Cf Hinterlegung*
Äquivalenztheorie	equivalence theory (of causation); dominant in criminal, but not in civil law, where the theory of foreseeability (*Adäquanztheorie*) applies. See Chapter XV, p 136

Arbeit	work
Arbeiter	(manual) worker. See *Arbeitnehmer*
Arbeitgeber	employer. See Chapter XVII, p 153
Arbeitgebervereinigung (-verband)	employer association, federation. See Chapter XVII, p 155
Arbeitnehmer	employee; can be *Arbeiter* or *Angestellter*. See Chapter XVII, p 153
Arbeitsgericht (ArbG)	employment court. See Chapter XVII, p 154
Arbeitsgerichtsbarkeit	employment jurisdiction. See Creifelds under *Arbeitsgerichtsbarkeit* and Chapter XIX, p 169
Arbeitsgerichtsgesetz (ArbGG)	Law Relating to the Employment Courts. See Chapter XIX (note 34)
Arbeitskampf	industrial action. Conducted in two main forms: *Streik* and *Aussperrung*. See Creifelds under *Arbeitskampf* and Chapter XVI, p 156
Arbeitsplatz	work place; job
Arbeitsschutzrecht	work protection law. See Creifelds under *Arbeitsschutz* and Chapter XVII, p 159
Arbeitssicherheitsgesetz (ASiG)	Work Safety Law. See Chapter XVII, p 161
Arbeitsstätte	work place. See Chapter XVII, p 161
Arbeitsstättenverordnung (ArbStättVO)	Work Places Order. See Chapter XVII, p 161
Arbeitsunfall	accident at work. See Chapter XVII, p 161
Arbeitsverhältnis	employment relationship. Also *Dienstverhältnis*
Arbeitsvertrag	contract of employment. See Chapter XVII, p 153 and also *Dienstvertrag*
Arglist	craftiness; fraud. See *Arglistige Täuschung*
Arglistige Täuschung	fraudulent deceit. See Chapter X, p 42 (Nullity and challengeability of a *Willenserklärung*)
Arrest	summary means of securing the enforcement of a *Geldforderung* by seizure of assets. It can be personal. See Creifelds under *Arrest*, §§ 916-945 ZPO and Chapter XII, p 118. *Cf Festnahme*
Arzthaftung	medical liability (negligence). See Chapter XII (note 3)
Asylrecht	right of asylum. See Creifelds under *Asylrecht* und *Asylverfahren* and Chapter VIII (Article 16a GG)
Auctoritas non veritas facit legem	authority, not the truth, makes law. See Chapter I (note 9)
Auf Befehl	on orders. See Chapter XV (note 28)

Auffassung	opinion
Aufgabe	function. See Chapter XVI (note 19)
Aufgebot	public notification of a claim. See Chapter XII, p 119
Aufgrund	on the basis of, due to. See Chapter VIII, p 24
Aufheben	to repeal, quash, annul, terminate
Aufhebung	quashing, annulment; termination (eg of a *Gemeinschaft nach Bruchteilen*). See Chapters X, p 59 (Title 15), XIII, p 124, XIV, p 129 and XVII, p 153
Aufklärung	clarification; enlightenment. See Chapter I (at note 11) and Chapter XII, p 93
Auflage	binding direction, requirement (laid down by a person or *Behörde*); also: edition (of book)
Auflassung	*Einigung* in the case of immovables. See Chapter X, p 75 and § 925(i) BGB
Auflösung	termination (dissolution) (of a company), eg through *Kündigung*
Auflösungsklage	writ claiming *Auflösung* by court decision. See Chapter XI, p 87
Aufrechnung	set-off. See Chapter X *Exposé* and p 56 (Title 3)
Aufruf der Sache	announcement of the matter (in court). See Chapter XII, p 111
Aufschiebende Wirkung	suspensive effect. See Chapter XIII, p 124
Aufsicht	supervision
Aufsichtsbeschwerde	complaint to the next higher (supervisory) *Behörde*. It can relate to conduct of a *Beamter*. See Chapter XIV, p 129 (*Dienstaufsichtsbeschwerde*)
Aufsichtsrat	supervisory board. It is a compulsory organ of an AG, *Kommanditgesellschaft auf Aktien* and *Genossenschaft*; in a GmbH it is voluntary, except when there are more than 500 employees. See Creifelds under *Aufsichtsrat* and Chapter XVII, p 159
Auftrag	(gratuitous) (contract of) instruction (without payment). *Cf Geschäfts-besorgungsvertrag.* See Creifelds under *Auftrag* and Chapter X, p 59 (Title 10)
Auftraggeber	instructing person. See *Mandant*

Auftragsangelegenheiten	matters to be carried out on behalf of the transferor. Also: *Übertragene Aufgaben*. See Creifelds under *Auftragsangelegenheiten* and Chapter VI
Auftragsbestätigung	confirmation (acceptance) of order. See Chapter X (note 50): Rules governing offer and acceptance
Auftragsverwaltung	administration by a/the *Land/Länder* on instruction by the *Bund*. See Chapter II, p 6
Aufwenden	to expend (for), spend (on)
Aufwendung	expenditure, disbursement. See Chapter X, p 59 (Title 10) and Creifelds under *Aufwendungen*. Cf *Verwendung*
Augenschein	(evidence by) inspection. See *Beweis*
Ausbildung	training, education. See Chapter VII (note 13)
Aus erheblichen Gründen	on significant grounds. See Chapter XII, p 105
Aus wichtigem Grund	for (an) important reason. See Chapter XVII, p 153
Ausbürgerung	removal of citizenship (against ones will). It is forbidden by Article 16(i) GG. See Creifelds under *Entlassung aus der Staatsangehörigkeit* and Chapter VIII, p 26
Auseinandersetzung	composition, split-up (between). See Chapters X, p 59 (Title 14) and XI, p 88
Ausfertigen	to draw up, issue (a document)
Ausfertigung	drawing-up, issue; duplicate, (official) copy. It replaces the original (*Urschrift*) for legal purposes. See §§ 47 and 49(i) BeurkG and Chapter XIX, p 178. See also Creifelds under *Ausfertigung einer Urkunde*
Ausführung	the administration, carrying out, execution, implementation (of); version. See Creifelds under *Ausführung von Gesetzen* and Chapters V, p 16 and VII, p 19
Auskunft	information. See Creifelds under *Auskunft, behördliche* and Chapter XIII, p 123
Auslage(n)	disbursement(s). See Chapter XIX (note 76)
Auslegen	to interpret (a meaning)
Auslegung	interpretation (of a meaning). See Chapter X (note 60)
Auslegungsregel	rule of interpretation. See Chapter X, p 44 (Failure to reach an *Einigung*)

Auslieferung	extradition. See Creifelds under *Auslieferung* and Chapter VIII (Article 16(ii) GG)
Auslobung	public offer of reward. See Creifelds under *Auslobung* and Chapter X, p 59 (Title 9)
Ausnahme	exception
Ausnahmebewilligung	(special) approval by way of exception. See also *Befreiung* and *Dispens*
Ausnahmefall	exceptional case
Ausnahmegericht	exceptional court for a particular case. See Creifelds under *Ausnahmegerichte* and *Sondergericht* and Chapter XIX, p 169
Ausnahmsweise	by way of exception, exceptionally. See Chapter VII (note 11)
Ausscheiden	to leave; departure of member from a company. See Chapter XI, p 88
Ausschließlich	exclusive(ly). See Creifelds under *Ausschließliche Gesetzgebung* and Chapter II, p 5
Ausschließung	exclusion. See Chapter XI, p 88
Ausschuß	committee; board
Aussetzen	to suspend (proceedings)
Aussetzung	suspension (of proceedings). See Creifelds under *Aussetzung eines Verfahrens* and Chapter XII, p 104
Aussperrung	lock-out. See *Arbeitskampf*
Ausüben	to exercise. See Chapter XIX (note 46)
Ausübung	exercise (of)
Auswärtiges Amt	Foreign Office. See Chapter XIII, p 121
Auszubildender	a person requiring training. See *Lehrling*
Außenverhältnis	external relationship. See Chapter XII, p 102 (The term *Vollmacht*)
Außenwirkung	external effect. Also *Wirkung nach außen*
Außergerichtlich	extrajudicial. See *Prozeßkosten*
Außerordentlich	extraordinar(il)y; summary. See *Kündigung*
Baugenehmigung	building consent, planning permission. See Chapter XIII (note 19)
Bayern	Bavaria. See Chapter V, p 11 and Chapter XIX C 2 (note 33)

Beamter	civil servant. See Chapter XIII (note 8) and Chapter XIX, p 166
Beauftragen	to appoint, instruct
Bebauungsplan	(local) building plan. See Chapter XIV, p 129
Bedenken	reservation (regarding)
Bedeutung	importance, meaning
Bedingt durch	conditional on; due to. See Chapter X, p 72
Bedingung	condition (future uncertain event); can be *aufschiebend* (suspensive) or *auflösend* (resolutive). See Creifelds under *Bedingung* and Chapter X, p 45
Befähigung	capacity (to hold an office or exercise a profession). See Chapter XIX (note 10) and Creifelds under *Befähigung*
Befehl	order
Befehlend	(a VA) requiring or forbidding particular action. See Chapter XVII (note 39)
Beförderung	transport(ation); promotion
Befreiung	exemption. See *Dispens*
Befristet	limited to a particular period. See *Kündigung*
Befugnis	authority, power
Begehungsdelikt	crime by active conduct. See Chapter XV, p 136
Beglaubigen	to certify
Beglaubigte Abschrift	certified copy. See *Abschrift*
Beglaubigung	certification. See Chapter XIX, p 179
Begriffsjurisprudenz	conceptual jurisprudence. *Cf Interessenjurisprudenz* and see Chapter I, p 4
Begründet(heit)	(actual(ly) well-founded(ness). *Cf Zulässig(keit)*, *Schlüssig(keit)* and see Chapter XII, p 109
Begründung	establishment (of); reasoning, reasons for
Begünstigen	to favour
Begünstigend	favourable, advantageous. See Chapter XIII, p 127
Behauptung	allegation
Behauptungslast	(the) burden of allegation. See Chapter XII (note 3)
Behörde	authority. See Chapter II, p 6 and Creifelds under *Behörden*

Beibringungsgrundsatz	see *Verhandlungsgrundsatz*
Beistand	partys assistant; aid
Beitritt	accession. See Chapter V, p 15. See also *Schuldbeitritt*
Bekanntgabe	notification. See Chapter XIII, p 124 and *cf Bekanntmachung*
Bekanntmachung	publication, announcement, notification. See Chapter XI (note 12). See also *Verkündung*, *Veröffentlichung* and Creifelds under *Bekanntmachung*
Bekenntnis	confession, creed. See Chapter VIII (Article 4(i) GG)
Bekräftigung	confirmation (of a statement before a court)
Belasten	to burden, encumber; incriminate; debit. See Chapter X, p 73
Belastend	burdensome, disadvantageous. See Chapter XIII, p 126
Belehren	to advise, instruct
Belehrung	advice, instruction. See Chapter XIX, p 178
Beleidigung	insult; defamation. See: Chapter XV (note 10 and note 28); Creifelds under *Beleidigung*
Bellum omnium contra omnes	a war of all against all. See Chapter I (note 9)
Benachteiligung	discrimination. See §§ 611a-612a BGB
Benennen	to name
Beraten	to advise
Beratung	consultation. See Chapter XIX, p 178
Beratungshilfe	assisted legal advice (support) (for less well-off persons). *Cf Prozeßkostenhilfe*
Beratungshilfegesetz (BerHG)	Law relating to (the grant of) assisted legal advice. See Chapter XIX, pp 170 and 177
Berechtigter	person entitled; also: *Inhaber des Rechts* (owner of the right). See Chapter X, p 73) and *Verfügungsbefugnis*
Berechtigung	entitlement. See also *Inhaberschaft*
Beruf	occupation, profession. See Creifelds under *Beruf (freie Wahl und Ausübung)* and Chapter VIII, p 26
Berufsausübung	exercise of a profession. See Chapter VII (note 13)
Berufsgenossenschaft	occupational co-operative. See Chapter XVII, p 159

Berufspflicht	professional duty. See Chapter XIX, p 173
Berufsrichter	professional judge. See Chapter XIX, p 165
Berufsstand	professional class. See Chapter XI, p 81
Berufsverbot	occupational ban. See Creifelds under *Berufs-verbot* and *Rechtsanwalt* IV
Berufung	(general) appeal. See Chapter XII, p 112
Berufungsantrag	appeal application. See Chapter XII, p 113
Berufungsbegründung	particulars of appeal. See Chapter XII, p 113
Berufungsbeklagter	respondent. See Chapter XII, p 113
Berufungsfrist	time-limit for lodging *Berufungsschrift*. See Chapter XII, p 113
Berufungsgrund	factual and/or evidential basis for a *Berufung*. See Chapter XII, p 113
Berufungskläger	appellant. See Chapter XII, p 113
Berufungsschrift	notice of appeal. See Chapter XII, p 113
Berufungssumme	appeal value, amount. See Chapter XII, p 113
Beschlagnahme	seizure. See Chapter XVI, p 147
Beschleunigung	acceleration. See Creifelds under *Mündliche Verhandlung* and Chapter XII, p 94
Beschluß	(company) resolution; (court) order, decision. See Creifelds under *Beschluß*, *Beschlußverfahren* and Chapter XII
Beschränkte persönliche Dienstbarkeit	limited personal servitude. See Chapter X, p 77
Beschränkung	limitation
Beschuldigen	to accuse, charge (with). See Chapter XVI, p 150; *cf Anklagen* and *Vorwerfen*
Beschuldigter	suspect, person accused (of). See also *Verdächtigter* and Chapter XVI, p 150. After an *Anklageschrift* is lodged: *Angeschuldigter*; after proceedings opened: *Angeklagter*
Beschwerde	complaint; can be *einfache Beschwerde* (simple complaint) or *sofortige Beschwerde* (immediate complaint). See Chapter XII
Beseitigen	to remove, dispose of, overturn. See Chapter X, p 77; Chapter XII (note 5); Chapter XIV, p 130 (note 14)
Besitz	possession(s). See Chapter X, p 71 and *cf Recht zum Besitz*. See also Chapter X (note 98)
Besitzkonstitut	constructive possession (arrangement). See Chapter X, p 75 and *Sicherungsübereignung*

Besonderer Teil (BT)	special part. See Chapters X, p 47 and XV, p 133
Bestandskraft	finally binding nature, legal force (authority) of a VA. See Chapter XIII, p 126 and cf *Rechtskraft*
Bestandskräftig	possessing *Bestandskraft*. See Chapter XIII, p 126
Bestandteil	part (of a *Sache*). See Creifelds under *Bestandteil*
Bestätigen	to confirm. See Chapter X (note 50) (Rules governing offer and acceptance)
Bestehen	to exist, existence; to pass (test)
Bestellen	to order
Besteller	person who orders something, client, customer. See Chapter X, p 58 (Title 7)
Bestimmen	to specify
Bestimmt	specific; definite(ly). See Chapter XIII, p 124
Bestimmtheitsgrundsatz	principle that a matter must be defined as exactly as possible. See *Spezialitätsgrundsatz*, Chapter X, p 71 and Chapter XV, p 133
Bestimmung	provision, term; specification, setting (of). See Chapter X, p 54 (Title 1)
Bestreiten	to dispute (facts). See Chapter XII (note 57)
Beteiligter	person involved; participant. See Chapter XII (note 13), Chapter XIII, p 123 and Creifelds under *Beteiligter*
Beteiligung	involvement, participation
Betreiben	to engage in, run (a business). See Chapter XI, p 81
Betreuung	care (and attendance). Replaced *Entmündigung* after 1.1.1992. See Chapter XII (note 1)
Betrieb	actual business unit (trading or manufacturing); workplace. See Chapter XVII, p 154 and cf *Unternehmen*
Betriebsbedingt	due to circumstances in the *Betrieb*. See Chapter XVII, p 154
Betriebspartner	business partner. See Chapter XVII, p 155
Betriebsrat	works council. See Creifelds under *Betriebsrat*, Chapter XVII, p 154 and cf *Personalrat*
Betriebssicherheit	safety at the workplace. See Chapter XVII, p 159
Betriebsvereinbarung	(written) business agreement (relating to a *Betrieb*). See Chapter XVII, p 156

Betriebsverfassungsgesetz (BetrVG)	Law Relating to the Constitution of a *Betrieb* (1952 and 1972). See Chapter XVII, pp 154 and 157
Beurkunden	to document, authenticate, legalise. See Chapter XIX, p 177
Beurkundung	documentation, authentication, legalisation. See Chapter XIX, p 177
Beurkundungsgesetz (BeurkG)	law relating to *Beurkundungen*. See Chapter XIX, p 178
Beurteilungsspielraum	room for judgment. See Chapter XIII, p 127
Bevollmächtigte beim Bund	minister of a *Land* responsible for federal matters. See Chapter V, p 16
Bevollmächtigter	authorised person; attorney. See Chapter XII, p 102
Bevorzugung	preference
Bewährung	probation. See Chapter XV, p 142
Bewährungszeit	period of probation. See Chapter XV, p 143
Beweglich	movable (*adj*). See Chapter X, p 71
Beweis	evidence. It can be direct (*unmittelbar*) or indirect (*mittelbar*). See Baur/Grunsky, § 14 A 1 2, Creifelds under *Beweis* and *Indizienbeweis*. See also Chapter XII, pp 94 and 106
Beweisaufnahme	(the) taking of evidence. If immediate evidence is available, the *Beweisaufnahme* is ordered (*angeordnet*) informally. Otherwise, it requires a formal *Beweisbeschluß* (§ 358 ZPO). See Jauernig (ZP), Book 2, Chapter 8, § 51 and, in this text, Chapter XII, p 106 and (note 54)
Beweisbedürftig(keit)	requiring (to be proved by) evidence (requirement). See Chapter XII (note 52)
Beweisbeschluß	(formal) order directing the taking of evidence (*Beweisaufnahme*). By § 359 ZPO, it must indicate the *Beweisthema*, the *Beweismittel* and the *Beweisführer*
Beweis des ersten Anscheins	see *Anscheinsbeweis*
Beweisfällig	liable to supply proof. See Chapter XII (note 3)
Beweisführer	the party bringing evidence (*beweisführende Partei*)
Beweisgebühr	evidence fee. See Chapter XIX, p 176
Beweisgegenstand	subject of evidence. Also: *Beweisthema*
Beweislast	the burden of evidence (proof). See Chapter XII (note 3)

Beweislosigkeit	lack (failure) of proof. See Chapter XII (note 3)
Beweismittel	the means by which evidence can be brought. In civil proceedings, the ZPO lays down (§§ 371-484 ZPO) five different types of *Beweismittel*:

- *Augenscheinsbeweis* (visual evidence);
- *Zeugenbeweis* (witness evidence);
- *Sachverständigenbeweis* (expert evidence);
- *Urkundenbeweis* (documentary evidence); and
- *Parteivernehmung* (examination of a party).

The *Beweismittel* can be introduced – in accordance with the principle of *Strengbeweis* (strict evidence) – into the part of the proceedings known as the *Beweisverfahren*.

To be compared with the principle of *Strengbeweis* is the principle of *Freibeweis* (free evidence), where the court is not bound to particular *Beweismittel*.

See Creifelds under *Freibeweis* and Jauernig (ZP), Book 2, Chapter 8, § 49 III and §§ 51-56

Beweisregel	rule of evidence. See Chapter XII, p 94
Beweisthema	see *Beweisgegenstand*
Beweisverfahren	proceedings for the taking of evidence (by means of which a party introduces a particular *Beweismittel* into the proceedings).

In civil proceedings, the *Beweisverfahren* commences with a *Beweisantritt* (*Beweisangebot*), also referred to as a *Beweisantrag*. A *Beweisantrag* can only exceptionally be refused: see Baur/Grunsky, § 14 A III 3

Beweiswürdigung	assessment of evidence. See Chapter XII, p 94
Bewilligung	licence, allowance. See Chapter XIII, p 127
Bewirkung	the effecting of. See Chapter X (note 66)
Bewußt	conscious. See Chapter XV, p 140
Bezirk	area. See Chapter V, p 16
Binden	to bind
Bindung	binding, tie, restriction, fetter. See Chapter II, p 9, Chapter XII (note 6) and Chapter XIII (note 23)
Bis de eadem re ne sit actio	no action lies twice in the same matter. See Chapter XII (note 5). In criminal law: *Ne bis in idem*

Bösgläubig(keit)	(in) bad faith. See: Chapter X, p 75 (*Bona fide* acquisition of ownership to movables); Creifelds under *Böser Glaube*
Buch	Book (of a law). See for example Chapter X, p 31
Bund	see *Bundesrepublik*
Bundesamt für ...	Federal Office for/of...; see *Bundesoberbehörde*
Bundesamt für Verfassungsschutz	Federal Office of Constitutional Protection; in Cologne. See Chapter XVI (note 19)
Bundesanstalt für Arbeit	Federal Office of Employment (in Nürnberg). See Chapter II (note 6)
Bundesanwalt	federal prosecutor (at the BGH). See Chapter XVI, p 146
Bundesarbeitsgericht (BAG)	Federal Employment Court. See Chapter XIX, p 169
Bundesbahn	Federal Railway(s). Now a public limited company: *Deutsche Bahn* AG)
Bundesbahndirektion	Federal Railway Directorate. See Chapter IV
Bundesbank	Federal Bank (located in Frankfurt am Main). See Chapter II (note 6)
Bundesbehörde	(middle) federal authority, eg *Direktion*. See Chapter IV
Bundeseigene Verwaltung	(own) administration by the *Bund*. See Chapter II, p 6
Bundesfinanzhof (BFH)	Federal Finance (Tax) Court. See Chapter XIX, p 169
Bundesgebiet	federal territory. See Chapter II (note 11)
Bundesgebührenordnung für Rechtsanwälte (BRAGO)	Federal Lawyers Fee Order. See Chapter XIX, p 175
Bundesgerichtshof (BGH)	Federal Supreme Court. See Chapter XIX, p 169
Bundesgesetz	federal statute. *Cf Landesgesetz*
Bundesgrenzschutz (BGS)	Federal Border Guard. See Chapter XVI (note 19)
Bundeskanzler	Federal Chancellor. See Chapter III
Bundeskanzleramt	Federal Chancellor's Office; Chancellery. See Chapter IV
Bundeskriminalamt (BKA)	Federal Office of Criminal Investigation; in Wiesbaden. See Chapter XVI (note 19)
Bundesminister	federal minister(s). See Chapter III
Bundesministerium	federal ministry. See Chapter IV

Bundesnotarordnung (BNotO)	Federal Notaries Order. See Chapter XIX, p 178
Bundesoberbehörde	upper federal authority. See Chapter IV and *Bundesamt für...*
Bundespost	Federal Post Office. (Now a public limited company: *Deutsche Post AG*).
Bundespräsident	Federal President. See Chapter III
Bundespräsidialamt	Federal Presidential Office. See Chapter IV
Bundesrat	Federal Council. See Chapter III
Bundesrechnungshof	Federal Accounts Court. See Chapter IV
Bundesrecht bricht Landesrecht	federal law takes precedence (literally, breaks) the law of a *Land* (Article 31 GG). See Chapters II, p 6 and VIII, p 23
Bundesrechtsanwaltskammer (BRAK)	Federal Lawyers Chamber. It issues a magazine (the BRAK *Mitteilungen*) containing professional information, which is sent quarterly to members of the (regional) *Rechtsanwaltskammern*. See also Chapter XIX, p 174
Bundesrechtsanwaltsordnung (BRAO)	Federal Lawyers Order. See Chapter XIX, p 173
Bundesregierung	Federal Government. See Chapter III
Bundesrepublik (Deutschland)	Federal Republic (of Germany). See Chapter II, p 6
Bundesrichter	judge of one of the supreme federal courts (see Article 95 GG)
Bundessozialgericht (BSG)	Federal Social (Security) Court. See Chapter XIX, p 170
Bundesstaat	federal state. See Chapter VII, p 19
Bundestag	Federal Parliament. See Chapter III
Bundesunterbehörde	(lower) federal authority. See Chapter IV
Bundesverfassungsgericht	Federal Constitutional Court. See Chapter III and Chapter VII
Bundesverfassungsgerichtsgesetz (BVerfGG)	Law relating to the Federal Constitutional Court. See Chapter III and Chapter VII
Bundesversammlung	Federal Assembly. See Chapter III
Bundesverwaltungsgericht (BVerwG)	Federal Administrative Court. See Chapter XIX, p 170
Bürge	guarantor. See Chapter X, p 59 (Title 18)
Bürgerliches Gesetzbuch	Civil Code. See Chapter X
Bürgerliches Recht	civil law. See Chapter IX, p 29
Bürgermeister	Mayor. See also *Oberbürgermeister*

Bürgschaft	contract of surety, guaranty. See Creifelds under *Bürgschaft* and Chapter X, p 59 (Title 18). *Cf* also Creifelds under *Garantievertrag*
Bußgeldbescheid	notice of (a) fine. See *Geldbuße*
Conditio sine qua non	an essential condition (for); literally, a condition without which (the result is) not (possible). See *Äquivalenztheorie*
Corpus iuris civilis	body (collection) of civil law. See Chapter I
Culpa in contrahendo (cic)	fault/blame during (in the course of (preliminary)) negotiations. It is an (unwritten) principle developed outside the BGB and provides a remedy for fault up to the time of conclusion of a contract. Also called *Verschulden bei Vertragsschluß*. See Chapter X (note 13) and (note 73)
Da mihi factum, dabo tibi ius	see *Verhandlungsgrundsatz*
Darlehen	loan. See Creifelds under *Darlehen* and Chapter X, p 59 (Title 5)
Daseinsvorsorge	(future) welfare provision (for members of the public). See *Leistungs-verwaltung*
Datenschutz	data protection
Deckungsverhältnis	primary (covering) relationship. See Creifelds under *Deckungsverhältnis* and *cf Valutaverhältnis*
Delikt	*delict* (civil or criminal). See Creifelds under *Delikt*
Deliktsfähigkeit	capacity to commit a delict. See Creifelds under *Deliktsfähigkeit* and, for the position in criminal law, Chapter XV, p 139
Dem Grunde nach	(claim) on the basic question, issue (of liability). See *Zwischenurteil*
Deutscher Bund	German Confederation. See Chapter I (note 6)
Deutsches Richtergesetz (DRiG)	German Judges Law. See Chapter XIX, p 165
Dienstaufsichtsbeschwerde	see *Aufsichtsbeschwerde*
Dienstbarkeit	servitude. See Chapter X, p 77
Dienstberechtigter	person entitled to (the) services. See Chapter XVII, p 161
Dienstvertrag	contract for services. *Cf Werkvertrag* (contract of service), *Arbeitsvertrag* (contract of employment) and see Chapter X, p 59 (Title 6) and Chapter XVII, p 160

Dinglicher Anspruch	real claim. See Chapter X, p 77
Dingliches Recht	real right. See Chapter X, p 71
Direktion	directorate. See *Bundesbehörde*
Dispens	dispensation. See Chapter XIII, p 127 and also *Ausnahmebewilligung* and *Befreiung*
Dispositionsgrundsatz	principle that the parties are masters of the proceedings; also *Verfügungsgrundsatz*. See Chapter XII, p 93
Dispositiv	dispositive. See Chapter IX, p 30
Dissens	see *Einigungsmangel*
Dolus directus	direct intent. See Chapter XV, p 140
Dolus eventualis	eventual intent. See Chapter XV, p 140
Doppelfunktion	double (dual) function. See Chapter V, p 16 and Creifelds under *Doppelfunktion von Verwaltungsbehörden*. See also Chapter XVI (note 20)
Draufgabe	bonus. See Chapter X, p 55 (Title 4)
Dringender Tatverdacht	high (urgent) suspicion that the suspect committed the offence. See Chapter XVI (note 23)
Dritter	third party. See, for example, Chapter X, pp 53 and 54
Drittorganschaft	(principle of the) direction (of a company) by a third party. See Chapter XI, p 82
Drittwirkung	effectiveness in third party relations; effect on third parties. See Chapter VIII, p 23
Dulden	to allow, suffer to happen; can also mean sufferance (noun). See Chapter XII, p 108
Durch	through. See Chapter VIII, p 24
Durchbrechen	to break through, pierce, breach. See Chapter XII (note 5)
Durchgriffserinnerung	piercing *Erinnerung*, ie one passed by the judge to the court. See Chapter XIX, p 168
Durchsetzung	the carrying out, enforcement, prevailing (of). See Chapter IX, p 30
Durchsuchung	search (of premises). See Creifelds under *Durchsuchung* and Chapter XVI, p 147
Echt	genuine. See Chapter XV, p 137

Ehe	(state of) marriage. See Creifelds under *Ehe*, Chapter VIII, p 26 and Chapter X, p 79
Ehegesetz	Marriage Law (20 February 1946). See Chapter X, p 79
Ehelich	legitimate (child). See Chapter X, p 79 and Creifelds under *Eheliche Kinder*
Ehesache	marriage matter (eg *Scheidung*). See *Familiensache* and Creifelds under *Ehesachen*
Ehevertrag	(matrimonial) agreement (by which spouses can regulate their property status). See *Güterrecht*
Ehrenamtlich	honorary, lay. See Chapter XIX, p 165
Eid	oath. See Chapter XIX, pp 167 and 179
Eidesstattliche Versicherung	assurance, declaration in lieu of oath. See Creifelds under *Eidesstattliche Versicherung* and Chapter XIX, p 179
Eigentum	ownership; property. See: Article 14(i) GG; Creifelds under *Eigentum, Eigentumserwerb, Eigentumsgarantie, Eigentumsherausgabe-anspruch, Eigentumsstörungen* and *Eigentums-übertragung*; Chapter VII, p 26 and Chapter X, p 71 and 74
Eigentum verpflichtet	ownership obliges (Article 14(ii) GG). See Chapter VIII, p 26 and Chapter X, p 74
Eigentumsvorbehalt	reservation of title. See Creifelds under *Eigentumsvorbehalt* and Chapter X, p 72
Eigentümer-Besitzer-Verhältnis	relationship between the owner and person in possession of a *Sache*. See Chapter X (note 106)
Eignungsprüfung	aptitude test (for lawyers from other EEC (EU) countries enabling admission as a *Rechts-anwalt*). See Chapter XIX (note 10) and p 171
Einberufen	to convene (a meeting). See *Vermittlungs-ausschuß*
Einbringung	bringing in. See Chapter X, p 59 (Title 13)
Einfach	simple; simply
Einführungsgesetz zum BGB (EGBGB)	Introductory Law to the BGB. See Chapter XVIII, p 163
Einführungsgesetz zum GVG (EGGVG)	Introductory Law to the GVG. See Chapter XIX (note 33)
Eingehen	to go into, conclude (a matter or relationship)
Eingetragener Verein (eV)	see *Verein*

Eingriff(e)	attack(s); interference; infringement; intervention. See Chapters VII, p 21 and VIII, p 23
Eingriffsbefugnis	see *Gesetzesvorbehalt*
Eingriffskondiktion	type of *Nichtleistungskondiktion*, where the recipient obtains a benefit by infringing the claimants rights. See Chapter X, p 59 (Title 24)
Eingriffsverwaltung	intervention administration. See Chapter II (note 7) and *cf Leistungsverwaltung*
Einheitlich	uniform, united. See Creifelds under *Einheitlichkeit der Rechtsprechung* and Chapter XII, pp 95 and 113
Einigung	consensus, (real) agreement. See Creifelds under *Einigung* and see also: *Auflassung, Willensübereinstimmung*. See Chapter X, p 43
Einigungsmangel	failure to reach an *Einigung* (on *Nebenpunkt*). It can be *offen* or *versteckt*. See Creifelds under *Vertrag* I (§§ 154-155 BGB) and Chapter X, p 44
Einigungsstelle	arbitration body (dealing with problems in a *Betrieb*). See Chapter XVII, p 156
Einkommen	income
Einlassen	to engage (in an action); to respond to a writ (as defendant)
Einlassung	engagement (in an action); response to a writ (by a defendant). See Chapter XII (note 57)
Einlassungsfrist	period during which an *Einlassung* is possible. See Chapter XII, p 109
Einrede	objection. See also *Einwendung*, Chapter X, p 34; Chapter X *Exposé* and Creifelds under *Einrede*
Einreichung	lodging (of a writ). See Chapter XII, p 101
Einschränken	to limit, restrict. See Chapter VIII, p 24 *Einschränkung* restriction, limitation
Einschreiten	to intervene (normally a *Behörde*). See Chapter XVI, p 147
Einseitig	unilateral. See Chapter X, p 35
Einspruch	objection. See Creifelds under *Einspruch*. See also *Einwendung, Einrede, Widerspruch* and *Rüge*
Einspruchsgesetz	a proposed *Gesetz*, against which the *Bundesrat* can object under Article 77(iii) GG, but which does not have to be approved by it. *Cf Zustimmungsgesetz*

Einstellen	to recruit, take into employment. Also: to cease, drop (a matter, investigation, enforcement)
Einstellung	recruitment; cessation, suspension; attitude. See Chapters XII, p 116, XVI, p 150, XVII, p 157
Einstehenmüssen (für)	to take responsibility (be liable) (for). Also: *Haften (für)* and *Haftung*
Einstweilige Anordnung	temporary order. See: Creifelds under *Einstweilige Anordnung*
Einstweilige Verfügung	injunction. See Creifelds under *Einstweilige Verfügung*, §§ 916-945 ZPO and Chapter XII, p 118
Eintragung	entry (in a register); registration
Eintritt	entry
Einwendung	objection. See Creifelds under and *cf Einrede*. See also Chapter XII (note 57)
Einwilligung	(prior) consent. See *Rechtfertigungsgrund*
Einwohner	resident (of a local authority). See Chapter II, p 8
Einzelfall	(specific, particular) individual case
Einzelkaufmann	sole trader. See Chapter XI, p 81
Einzelrichter	single judge. See Creifelds under *Einzelrichter* and Chapter XII, p 107. See also *Strafrichter*
Einziehung	confiscation; forfeiture (of a *Gegenstand*). See Chapter XV, p 144
Elterliche Sorge	parental care. See Creifelds under *Elterliche Sorge* and Chapter X, p 79
Eltern	parents
Empfänger	recipient
Empfängerhorizont	the recipients point of view. See Chapter X, p 39 (Interpretation of a *Willenserklärung*)
Empfangsbedürftig	requiring receipt. See Chapter X, p 39 (Validity of a *Willenserklärung*)
Empfangsbekenntnis	acknowledgment of receipt. See Chapter XII, p 107
Endurteil	final judgment. See *Urteil*
Engste Verbindung	closest connection. See Chapter XVIII, p 163
Enteignung	expropriation, dispossession, compulsory acquisition. See Creifelds under *Enteignung*, Chapter VII (note 13); Article 14(iii) GG
Entfaltung	development, unfolding. See Chapter VIII, p 25.
Entgelt(lich)	remuneration; for money, reward

Entlassung	dismissal (of an employee). See *Kündigung*
Entschädigung	compensation (eg for *Enteignung*; for other examples see Creifelds under *Entschädigung*). *Cf Schadensersatz*
Entscheidung	decision. See Creifelds under *Entscheidung*, *Bescheid* and Chapter XII, p 95
(sich) Entschuldigen	to apologise, excuse
Entsprechende Anwendung	corresponding (analogous) application, application by analogy. See *Analogie*
Entziehung	withdrawal (of a right or licence to do something). See Chapter XV, p 144
Entziehungsanstalt	(drug) rejection institution. See Chapter XV, p 144
Enumerationsprinzip	enumeration principle. See Chapter VII (note 2)
Erbbaurecht	right to erect a building on another's land. See Creifelds under *Erbbaurecht* and Chapter X, p 77
Erbe	heir. See Creifelds under *Erbe* and Chapter X, p 80
Erbengemeinschaft	community between heirs. See Creifelds under *Erbengemeinschaft* and Chapter XI, p 82
Erbfolge	succession. See Creifelds under *Erbfolge* and Chapter X, p 80. See also *Rechtsnachfolge*
Erblasser	testator. See Creifelds under *Erblasser*
Erbrecht	law of succession; right of inheritance. See Creifelds under *Erbrecht*, Chapter X, p 80 and Article 14(i) GG
Erbschaft	estate. See *Nachlaß* and Creifelds under *Erbschaft*
Erbschaftskauf	purchase of an Erbschaft. See Chapter X, p 80
Erbschein	certificate of inheritance, probate. See Creifelds under *Erbschein* and Chapter X, p 80
Erbunwürdig(keit)	unworthy(iness) to inherit
Erbvertrag	contract of succession, estate contract. See Creifelds under *Erbvertrag* and Chapters X, p 80 and XIX, pp 167 and 179
Erbverzicht	disclaimer of inheritance. See Creifelds under *Erbverzicht*
Erfolg	success; result. See Chapter XV, p 136
Erfolgreich	successful
Erfolgsdelikt	crime requiring a particular result. See Chapter XV, p 136

Erfolgshaftung	liability for the result
Erforderlich	necessary. See Chapter VIII, p 25
Erforschen	to investigate, explore. See Chapter XVI, p 147
Erfüllung	performance, fulfilment. See Creifelds under *Erfüllung* and Chapter X, pp 50 and 56
Erfüllungsort	see *Leistungsort*
Erheblich	substantial, considerable. See Chapter XII (note 52)
Erhebung	making, raising (of a complaint); issue (of a writ); levying (eg of taxes). See Chapter XII, p 107
Erinnerung	legal remedy against decision of a *Rechtspfleger*. It goes initially back to the *Rechtspfleger* and then to the judge. See § 11 RPflG. *Cf Durchgriffserinnerung* and *Vollstreckungserinnerung*. See also Creifelds under *Erinnerung*
Erkennbar	recognisable. See Chapter X, p 39 (Interpretation of a *Willenserklärung*)
Erkenntnisverfahren	proceedings leading to a judgment, judgment proceedings. See Chapter XII, p 94 and *cf Vollstreckungsverfahren*
Erklären	to declare; explain
Erklärung	declaration; explanation. See Chapter X, p 38 (The term *Willenserklärung*)
Erklärung mit Nichtwissen	declaration of ignorance. See Chapter XII, p 104
Erklärungsbewußtsein	consciousness of (making) a declaration. See Chapter X (note 29)
Erlaß	remission (of debt); decree; issue (of a VA). See Chapter X, p 56 (Title 4) and Chapter XIV, p 124
Erlaubnis	permission. See Creifelds under *Erlaubnis* (*behördliche*), Chapter XIII, p 127 and see *Ermessen*
Erlaubnisvorbehalt	reservation of the right to grant an *Erlaubnis*
Erlöschen	to become extinct, discharged, end; extinction, discharge, end (of). See Chapter X, p 56
Ermächtigung	authorisation; authority (to exercise a particular right). See Creifelds under *Ermächtigung*, Chapter VIII (note 6) and Chapter X, (note 94). See also *Vollmacht* and *Zustimmung*
Ermächtigungsgesetz	Enablement Law. See Chapter II (note 2)

Ermächtigungsgrundlage	see *Gesetzesvorbehalt*
Ermessen	discretion. Can be *gebunden* or *frei*. See Creifelds under *Ermessen* (*Verwaltungsermessen*) and Chapter XIII, p 127. *Cf Unbestimmter Rechtsbegriff*
Ermessensfehler	faulty exercise of *Ermessen*. *Ermessensfehler* by the executive can be checked by the VG (§ 114 VwGO). See Chapter XIII, p 127
Ermessensmißbrauch	abuse of *Ermessen*. See Chapter XIII, p 127
Ermessensnichtgebrauch	non-use of *Ermessen*. See Chapter XIII, p 127
Ermessensreduzierung (*auf Null*)	reduction of *Ermessen* (to zero). See Chapter XIII, p 127
Ermessensüberschreitung	excess of *Ermessen*. See Chapter XIII, p 127
Ermessensunterschreitung	under-use of *Ermessen*; also called *Ermessensnichtgebrauch*
Ermittlung	investigation, inquiry. See Creifelds under *Ermittlungsverfahren in Strafsachen* and Chapter XVI, p 147
Ernennung	appointment (as a *Beamter* or to a public office). See Creifelds under *Ernennung* and Chapter XIX, p 166
Eröffnen	to open (proceedings)
Eröffnungsverfahren	(interim) proceedings dealing with the opening of main (criminal) proceedings. Also called *Zwischenverfahren*. See Chapter XVI (note 28)
Erörterungsgebühr	(lawyer's) fee for (merely) raising a matter
Errichten	to set up, form
Errichtung	formation
Error in obiecto	an error regarding the object of a criminal act; it has no effect on the *Schuld* of the *Täter*. *Cf Aberratio ictus*
Error in persona	an error regarding the person against whom a criminal act is committed; it has no effect on the *Schuld* of the *Täter*. *Cf Aberratio ictus*
Ersatzvornahme	substituted execution (of a measure by an authority). See Chapter XVII (note 39)
Ersatzzustellung	substituted service. See Creifelds under *Ersatzzustellung* and Chapter XII (note 45)
Erscheinen	to appear, appearance
Ersetzen	to replace
Erschöpfung des Rechtswegs	exhaustion of normal legal channels. See Chapter VII (note 9).

Ersitzung	acquisition of ownership to movables through the passage of time. See Creifelds under *Ersitzung* and Chapter X, p 75
Erstarken	to strengthen (into). See Chapter X, p 72
Erteilen	to grant (a licence or permission). See Chapter XIII, p 127
Erwachsener	adult, grown-up
Erweiterung	addition; extension
Erwerb	acquisition. See Chapter X, p 75
Erwerber	transferee; acquiror
Erwirkung	procurement; achievement, undertaking (of)
Erzeugnis	product
Essentialia negotii	see *Wesentliche Bestandteile*
Europäische Gemeinschaft(en)	European Community(ies). See Chapter XIII, p 121
Europäisches Übereinkommen über die gerichtliche Zuständigkeit und die Vollstreckung gerichtlicher Entscheidungen in Zivil- und Handelssachen (EuGVÜ)	European Convention on Jurisdiction and the Enforcement of Decisions in Civil and Commercial Matters (the Brussels Convention 1968, amended by conventions signed in San Sebastian and Lugano in 1988 and 1989). See Chapter XII (note 80)
Fabrikant	manufacturer
Fachkräfte für Arbeitssicherheit	qualified work safety personnel. See Creifelds under *Fachkräfte für Arbeitssicherheit* and Chapter XVII, p 159
Fahrerlaubnis	driving licence. See Creifelds under *Fahrerlaubnis* and Chapter XV, p 144
Fahrlässigkeit	negligence. See *Verschulden* and *Schuld*
Fahrverbot	driving ban. See Creifelds under *Fahrverbot* and Chapter XV (note 54)
Fall	case; matter
Fällig	due (for performance, payment)
Fälligkeit	time at which a *Leistung* (debt, payment) is due. See Chapter X (note 55) and *Leistungszeit*
Fallrecht	case law (system). See Creifelds under *Fallrecht* and *cf Präjudizien*
Falsa demonstratio (*non nocet*)	a false description of an item (does not harm). See Creifelds under *falsa demonstratio non nocet* and *cf* § 155 BGB

Familie	family. See Creifelds under *Familie* and Chapter VIII, p 26
Familiengericht	Family Court. See Creifelds under *Familiengericht* and Chapter XIX (note 54A)
Familienrecht	family law, right. See Chapter X, pp 34 and 79
Familiensache	family matter (dealt with by the *Familiengericht* (Family Court): § 23b GVG). See Creifelds under *Familiensachen* and Chapter XII, p 98
Fehler(haft)	fault(y), mistake. See §§ 459 BGB and Chapter XIII, p 124
Fehlerfrei	free of faults, perfect. See Chapter XIII, p 127
Fernmeldegeheimnis	telecommunication secrecy. See Article 10(i) GG and Creifelds under *Brief-, Post- und Fernmeldegeheimnis*
Festnahme	(physical) arrest; also : *Verhaftung. Cf Arrest.* See Chapter XVI, p 147
Feststellen	to ascertain, establish, declare
Feststellend	ascertaining, establishing, effecting a declaration (as to particular circumstances). See Chapter XIII, p 127
Feststellung	ascertainment, establishment, declaration (of)
Feststellungsklage	writ claiming the *Feststellung* of a legal relationship or particular rights. See Creifelds under *Feststellungsklage* and Chapters XII, p 108 (c) (ii) and XI, p 129
Finanzamt	tax office. It is a lower authority of a *Land.* See Creifelds under *Finanzamt* and Chapter IV
Finanzbehörde	tax authority
Finanzgerichtsbarkeit	finance jurisdiction. See Chapter XIX, p 170 and Creifelds under *Finanzgerichtsbarkeit*
Finanzgerichtsordnung (FGO)	Finance Courts Order. See Chapter XIX (note 38)
Finanzwesen	finance system. See Chapter VII, p 19 and Creifelds under *Finanzwesen*
Firma	(trade) firm (name); also called *Handelsfirma.* See Chapter XI, p 84 and Creifelds under *Firma*
Fiskalisch	fiscal(ly). See Chapter II, p 6 and *cf hoheitlich*
Fluchtgefahr	danger of flight (by the suspect). See Chapter XVI (note 23)
Folge	consequence
Folgesache	ancillary matter. See Chapter XII, p 115

Forderung	demand, (contractual) claim. See Chapter X, p 50
Formell	formal(ly)
Formelles Recht	formal law. See Chapter IX, p 30
Formkaufmann	businessman by reason of form. See Chapter XI, p 84
Formlos	informal(ly). See Chapter XIII, p 123
Fortsetzungsfeststellungsklage	type of *Feststellungsklage* to establish or declare that a past VA was illegal. See Chapter XIV, p 129
Fortsetzungsklausel	continuation clause (in company agreement). See Chapter XI, p 88
Fracht	freight. See Chapter XI, p 91
Frachtführer	freighter. See Creifelds under *Frachtführer* and Chapter X (note 109)
Fragen	to ask; questions
Fraktion	parliamentary grouping. See Chapter VII (note 14)
Freibeweis	(the principle of) free evidence. *Cf Strengbeweis* and see *Beweismittel*
Freibleibend	subject to availability, subject remaining unsold. See Chapter X, p 43
Freier Beruf	free profession; eg a Rechtsanwalt. See Chapter XIX, p 173 and Creifelds under *Freie Berufe*
Freiheit	freedom. See Creifelds under *Freiheit, persönliche* and Chapter VIII, p 25
Freiheit der Kunst, Wissenschaft, Forschung und Lehre	freedom of art, science, research and teaching. See: Creifelds under *Kunst, Freiheit der, Wissenschaft, Freiheit der* and *Lehrfreiheit*; Chapter VIII, p 26
Freiheitliche demokratische Grundordnung	basic order of freedom and democracy. See Creifelds under *Grundordnung, freiheitliche demokratische* and Chapter II, p 9
Freiheitsentziehung	deprivation of freedom, detention (in custody). See Creifelds under *Freiheitsentziehung*, Chapter VIII (note 15) and Chapter XVI, p 147
Freiheitsrecht(e)	freedom right(s). See Chapter VIII, p 23
Freiheitsstrafe	imprisonment; can be *zeitig* or *lebenslang*. See Chapter XV, pp 133 and 143
Freiwillige Gerichtsbarkeit	non-contentious (voluntary) civil jurisdiction. See Chapter XIX, p 168
Freizügigkeit	freedom of movement. See Creifelds under *Freizügigkeit* and Article 11(i) GG

Fremde Geschäfte	other person's business. See Chapter X, p 46
Friedenspflicht	duty of employer and *Betriebsrat* to maintain peace in the *Betrieb*. See Creifelds under *Friedenspflicht* and see Chapter XVII, pp 156 and 157
Frist	time-limit; notice period. See Creifelds under *Frist* and Chapters X, p 46 and XII, p 105
Fristlos	without notice. See *Kündigung*
Früher erster Termin	initial oral hearing. See Chapter XII, p 110
Führungsaufsicht	supervision of conduct. See Chapter XV (note 71)
Fund	finding of lost property. See Creifelds under *Fund* and Chapter X, p 76 (Statutory acquisition of ownership to movables)
Fürsorgepflicht	duty of care (towards someone). See Chapter XVII, p 159 (note 44)
Garantenpflicht	a special legal duty to act to prevent an *Unterlassungsdelikt*. See Chapter XV, p 138
Gastwirt(schaft)	inn (keeper). See Chapter X, p 59 (Title 13)
Gattungsschuld	generic debt. See Creifelds under *Gattungsschuld* and Chapter X, p 50 Title 1
Gebietskörperschaft	territorial corporation. See Chapter II (note 6)
Gebotsnorm	(criminal) norm requiring certain action to be carried out. See Chapter XV, p 138
Gebühr(en)	fee(s). See Creifelds under *Rechtsanwaltsgebühr* and see also *Gerichtskosten* and Chapter XIX, p 175
Gebührenstreitwert	*Streitwert* for the purpose of court fees. See Chapter XII, p 103
Geeignet	suitable. See Chapter VIII, p 25
Gefahr	danger, threat. Also: *Gefährdung*
Gefahrenabwehr	(the) warding-off of dangers. See Creifelds under *Gefahrenabwehr* and Chapter XVI (note 20)
Gefahr im Verzug	in a case of urgency; literally, danger in delay; See Chapter XIII (note 14)
Gefährden	to endanger, threaten
Gefährdungshaftung	strict liability. See Chapter X (note 74) and Chapter XV (note 14)
Gefälligkeit(sverhältnis)	(relationship of grace and) favour. See Chapter X (note 67)

Gegenbeweis	counter-evidence. See Chapter XII (note 3) and *cf Hauptbeweis*
Gegenleistung	counter-performance. See Chapter X, p 50
Gegennorm	counter-norm. See Chapter XII (note 33)
Gegenrecht	counter-right. See Chapter X, p 34
Gegenseitiger Vertrag	reciprocal (synallagmatic) contract. See Chapter X (notes 61 and 74). See also Creifelds under *Gegenseitiger Vertrag* and Chapter X, p 54 (Title 2)
Gegenstand	thing; matter. See Creifelds under *Gegenstand* and Chapter X, p 31
Gegenstandswert	value of the matter (for the fees of a *Rechtsanwalt*; can follow the *Streitwert* or *Geschäftswert*). See Creifelds under *Gegenstandswert* and Chapter XIX, p 175
Gegenvorstellung	counter-response. See Chapter XIV, p 129
Gegenwärtig	present(ly), current(ly). See Chapter VII, p 21
Geheimhaltung	(maintenance of) secrecy. See Chapter XIII, p 123
Gehemmt	prevented from running. See *Verjährung* and *Aufschiebende Wirkung*
Geldbuße	fine (punishment for *Ordnungswidrigkeit*). See Chapter XV (note 6)
Geldforderung	money claim. See Chapter XII, p 116
Geldschuld	money debt. See Creifelds under *Geldschuld*. See also *Leistungsort*
Geldstrafe	fine (punishment for *Straftat*). See Chapter XV, pp 133 and 143 and *cf Geldbuße*
Gemeinde	local authority (below a *Kreis*), commune. See Creifelds under *Gemeinde* and Chapter VI
Gemeindeordnung	local government law governing the *Gemeinden* in a *Land*. See Chapter VI
Gemeinderat	see *Gemeindevertretung*
Gemeindeverband	*Gemeinde* association. See Creifelds under *Gemeindeverbände* and Chapter VI (note 1)
Gemeindevertretung	legislative organ of a *Gemeinde*, assembly of *Gemeinde* representatives, council. See also: *Gemeinderat, Stadtverordnetenversammlung* and Chapter VI
Gemeindeverwaltung	administration, executive of a *Gemeinde*. See *Oberbürgermeister*

Gemeingefährliche Straftat	offence involving danger to the public (at large). See Chapter XV (note 11)
Gemeinsamer Ausschuß	(emergency) joint council. See Chapters III and VII, p 19
Gemeinsamer Senat der obersten Gerichtshöfe des Bundes	Joint Senate of the Supreme Federal Courts. See *Einheitlich*
Gemeinschaft nach Bruchteilen	community by shares (§ 741*ff* BGB). See Creifelds under *Gemeinschaft,* Chapter X, p 59 (Title 15) and Chapter XI, p 82. See also *Miteigentum nach Bruchteilen*
Gemeinschaft(lich)	community; jointly. Can be *zur gesamten Hand* (*Gesamthandsgemeinschaft*) or *nach Bruchteilen*
Gemeinschaftsaufgabe	joint matter, (community) task. The *Bund* can cooperate in the fulfilment of certain *Gemeinschaftsaufgaben*, where this is necessary to improve living conditions. See Creifelds under *Gemeinschaftsaufgaben* and Chapter VII (note 4)
Gemeinschaftswert	community value. See Chapter XV, p 134
Genehmigen	to approve, allow
Genehmigung	approval, permission. See Chapter X, p 36 and (note 25) and Chapter XIII (note 19)
Generalbundesanwalt	general federal prosecutor (at the BGH). See Chapter XVI, p 147
Generalklausel	general clause (eg § 40(i) VwGO). See Creifelds under *Generalklausel*
Generalstaatsanwalt	general state prosecutor (at the OLG). See Chapter XVI, p 147
Genossenschaft	co-operative (association/society). See Creifelds under *Genossenschaft* and Chapter XI (note 3). See also *Vorstand*
Gerecht(igkeit)	just(ice). See Creifelds under *Gerechtigkeit*. Cf *Recht*.
Gericht	court. See Creifelds under *Gericht* and Chapter XIX, p 168
Gerichtlich	judicial, by the court
Gerichtsbarkeit	particular (court) jurisdiction (according to branch (*Zweig*); also (functionally) the exercise (*Ausübung*) of the administration of justice (*Rechtspflege*). See Creifelds under *Gerichtsbarkeit* and Chapter XIX, p 168
Gerichtskosten	court fees. Part of the *Prozeßkosten*. See Creifelds under *Gerichtskosten* and Chapter XII, p 109

Gerichtskostengesetz (GKG)	Court Fees Law. See Chapter XII, p 109 and Chapter XIX, p 175
Gerichtsperson	member of court personnel. See Chapter XII, p 96
Gerichtsstand	local jurisdiction. See Chapter XII, p 96
Gerichtsverfassung	constitution of the court(s). See Creifelds under *Gerichtsverfassung*
Gerichtsverfassungsgesetz (GVG)	law relating to the constitution of the courts. See Chapter XII, pp 94 and 103 and Chapter XIX, p 168
Gerichtsvollzieher	(court) bailiff. See Chapter XII, p 118 and Creifelds under *Gerichtsvollzieher*
Geringfügig(keit)	insignificant; insignificance. See Chapter XVI (note 25)
Gesamthandseigentum	see *Gesamthandsvermögen*
Gesamthandsgemeinschaft	joint community. See Creifelds under *Gesamthandsgemeinschaft* and Chapter XI, p 81
Gesamthandsvermögen	joint property, assets. See also *Gesamthandsgemeinschaft*
Gesamtstaat	whole state. See Chapter II (note 1)
Geschäft	business; shop; transaction. See § 1(ii) HGB
Geschäftsbesorgungsvertrag	agreement of instruction for reward, contract to transact business for reward; cf *Auftrag*. See: Creifelds under *Geschäftsbesorgungsvertrag*; Chapters X, p 59 (Title 10) and XIX, p 172
Geschäftsfähig(keit)	capable of undertaking (capacity to undertake) a *Rechtsgeschäft* (legal transaction). See Creifelds under *Geschäftsfähigkeit* and Chapter X, pp 35 and 36
Geschäftsführung	(internal) management; direction (of a company). See Chapter XI, p 87 and cf *Vertretung*. See also Kallwass, Section 7, Chapter 2 (§ 112)
Geschäftsführung ohne Auftrag (GoA)	transaction (of a matter) without instruction. See Creifelds under *Geschäftsführung ohne Auftrag* and Chapter X, p 59 (Title 11)
Geschäftsführungsbefugnis	right of company member(s) to manage the company. See Chapter XI, p 87
Geschäftsgebühr	business fee. See Chapter XIX, p 178
Geschäftsgrundlage	basis of the transaction. See *Leistungsstörung*
Geschäftsherr	principal. See Chapter X, p 59 (Title 11)

Geschäftsordnung	standing orders (rules). See Creifelds under *Geschäftsordnung* and see also *Satzung*
Geschäftsstelle	business office (eg of a court). See Chapter XII, p 109
Geschäftswert	business value (for fees of the court and lawyers in non-contentious matters and for the fees of the *Notar*). See Creifelds under *Geschäftswert* and Chapter XIX, p 178
Geschäftswille	will to engage in a particular transaction. See Chapter X, p 38 (The term *Willenserklärung*)
Gesellschaft	company, society (G); as used in: GbR, BGB-G = civil law company, BGB company; OHG = open trading company; KG = limited partnership; GmbH = (private) company with limited liability; AG = public limited company; *Handels-G* = trading company (OHG or KG).
	See: Creifelds under the respective types; Chapters X, p 59 (Title 14) and XI, p 81. See also Chapter XIX (note 54)
Gesellschafter	member of a company, shareholder. Also: *Mitglied*
Gesellschaft mit beschränkter Haftung (GmbH)	(private) company with limited liability. See *Gesellschaft*
Gesellschaftsrecht	company law. See Chapter XI
Gesellschaftsvermögen	assets of a *Gesellschaft*. See Chapter XI, p 81
Gesellschaftsvertrag	company agreement, articles of association; sometimes called *Satzung*. See Creifelds under *Gesellschaftsvertrag* and Chapter XI, p 82
Gesetz	(statutory) law; statute.
	The *Grundgesetz* is a *Gesetz* subject to a more difficult procedure of amendment.
	If passed in accordance with the relevant constitutional procedure, a *Gesetz* is referred to as a(n) *(einfaches) Gesetz im formellen Sinne* (a (simple) law in the formal sense).
	The term can also be used in a wider, material sense to refer to any legal norm containing generally binding provisions (including *Rechtsverordnungen* (statutory instruments) and *Satzungen* (bye-laws).
	Cf Verwaltungsvorschriften ((internal) administrative regulations) and *Verwaltungsakte* (administrative acts).
	See Creifelds under *Gesetz*. See also Chapter XIII, p 121 and *Zustimmungsgesetz. Cf Recht*

Gesetz betreffend die Gesellschaften mit beschränkter Haftung (GmbHG)	Law relating to (private) companies with limited liability. See Chapter XI (note 3)
Gesetz über die Angelegenheiten der freiwilligen Gerichtsbarkeit (FGG)	Law Relating to Matters within the Non-contentious (Voluntary) Civil Jurisdiction. See Chapter XIX, p 168
Gesetz zur Regelung des Rechts der Allgemeinen Geschäftsbedingungen (AGBG)	Law to Regulate the Law of General Contract Terms. See Chapter X (note 52)
Gesetzesaufbau	construction of a law, statute. See Chapter X, p 48
Gesetzeskraft	force of law, statutory force. See Chapter VII, p 20
Gesetzesvorbehalt	the right to limit basic rights by means of a *Gesetz*; can also be used in the sense of *Vorbehalt des Gesetzes*, ie to refer to the need for the executive to act in accordance with law (*Gesetzmäßigkeit der Verwaltung*), to have a legal basis for their action (*Ermächtigungsgrundlage* or *Eingriffsbefugnis*). See Chapters VIII, p 23, II, p 9 and XIII, p 124
Gesetzgebende Gewalt	legislative power. Also: *Gesetzgebung*. See Creifelds under *Gesetzgebende Gewalt* and Chapter II, p 8
Gesetzgebung	legislature; legislation. See Creifelds under *Gesetzgebung* and Chapter I, p 8
Gesetzgebungskompetenz	competence to pass laws; legislative competence. See Chapter II, p 5
Gesetzliche Frist	*Frist* set by statute. See Chapter XII, p 105
Gesetzlicher Erwerb	statutory acquisition (of ownership). See Chapter X , p 75
Gesetzlicher Richter	the judge appointed by statute, ie it is a basic principle (*Grundsatz*) and basic right (*justizielles Grundrecht*) that everyone is entitled to a hearing before him (see Article 101(i) GG). See Chapter VIII (note 15) and Chapter XIX, p 166
Gesetzlicher Vertreter	legal (statutory) representative. See Chapters X, p 35 and XII, p 99
Gesetzliches Schuldverhältnis	obligation arising from statute. See Chapter X, p 48
Gesetzmäßigkeit der Verwaltung	duty of the executive to act in accordance with statute, law; also: *Rechtmäßigkeit der Verwaltung*. See Chapters II, p 9 and XIII, p 127
Gesichtspunkt	aspect

Gestaltungsklage	writ claiming the *Umgestaltung* (rearrangement) of a legal situation, position. See: Creifelds under *Gestaltungsklage*; Chapter XII, p 109 and Chapter XIV, p 129
Gestaltungsrecht	formulation right. See Creifelds under *Gestaltungsrecht* and Chapter X, p 34
Geständnis	confession; admission (of facts by a party). See Creifelds under *Geständnis* and Chapter XII (note 57)
Gesundheitsschutz	protection of health
Gewährleistung	guarantee. See §§ 442-444, §§ 459 BGB and Creifelds under *Gewährleistung*
Gewalt	power, force, violence
Gewaltenteilung	separation of power. See Creifelds under *Gewaltentrennung* and Chapter II, p 8
Gewerbe	business, trade. It does not include a *freier Beruf*. See Creifelds under *Gewerbe*. See also *Grundhandelsgewerbe* and *Unternehmen*
Gewerbeaufsichtsbehörde	business (trade) supervisory authority. See Creifelds under *Gewerbeaufsicht* and Chapter XVII, p 160
Gewerbeordnung (GewO)	Business (Trade) Order. See Creifelds under *Gewerbeordnung* and Chapter XVII, p 159
Gewerbeunternehmer	a person, who engages in a business (trade) enterprise; an entrepreneur
Gewerkschaft	trade union. See Creifelds under *Gewerkschaft, arbeitsrechtliche* and Chapter XVII, pp 157 and 158
Gewinn	profit, gain
Gewissen	conscience. See Creifelds under *Glaubens- u. Gewissensfreiheit* and Chapter VIII (Article 4(i) GG)
Gewissenhaft	conscientious(ly). See Chapter XIX, p 172
Gewohnheit	custom, habit. See Chapter IX, p 30
Gewohnheitsrecht	customary law. See Chapter I, p 4 and Chapter XIII, p 121
Gewöhnlich	usual(ly)
Glauben	to believe; belief
Glaubhaft	credible
Glaubhaftmachen	to substantiate
Glaubhaftmachung	substantiation. See Chapter XII (note 3)

Gläubiger	creditor. See Creifelds under *Gläubiger* and Chapter X, p 50
Gläubigerstreit	dispute between creditors. See Chapter XII, p 100
Gleichberechtigung	equal entitlement, right(s) (of). See Creifelds under *Gleichberechtigung* and Chapter VIII (Article 3(ii) GG)
Gleichheit (vor dem Gesetz)	equality (before the law). See Creifelds under *Gleichheit vor dem Gesetz* and Chapter VIII (Article 3(i) GG)
Gleichheitsrecht(e)	equality right(s). See Chapter VIII, p 23
Gleichordnung	equal level, basis. See Chapter IX, p 30
Gliedstaat	member state. See Chapter II, p 6
Grob	gross. See Chapter XV, p 140
Grund	ground, basis, reason
Grundbuch	land register. See Creifelds under *Grundbuch* and Chapter X, p 74
Grunddienstbarkeit	easement (over land). See Creifelds under *Grunddienstbarkeit* and Chapter X, p 77
Grundgesetz (GG)	Basic Law, federal constitution. See Creifelds under *Grundgesetz* and Chapter VII
Grundhandelsgewerbe	basic commercial trade, trading activity. See Chapter XI, p 83
Grundnorm	basic norm. See Chapter I (note 13)
Grundpfandrecht	security right (charge) over land. See Chapter X
Grundrecht(e)	basic right(s). See Creifelds under *Grundrechte* and Chapter VIII
Grundregel	basic rule
Grundschuld	land charge. See Chapter X, p 78
Grundstück(e)	piece(s) of land. See Chapter X, p 71
Grundverfügung	basic VA (administrative act (order)). See Chapter XVII (note 40)
Gutachten	written opinion, expertise. See Chapter XIX, p 178
Gütergemeinschaft	community of property between spouses. See Creifelds under *Gütergemeinschaft*, Chapter XI, p 81 and *Güterrecht* below

Güterrecht	(marital) property law.

By § 1363(i) BGB, the (statutory) property status (*Güterstand*) of spouses during their marriage is the so-called *Zugewinngemeinschaft*. During the marriage, the assets of each of the spouses remain under their respective, individual control. However, when the marriage ends (otherwise than by death), the amount of any *Zugewinn* (gain) is equalised between the former spouses. Thus, the spouse whose assets at the end of the marriage (*Endvermögen* (final assets)) exceed those owned by him or her at the beginning of the marriage (the *Anfangsvermögen* (initial assets)) must share the difference with his or her (former) partner, who has an *Ausgleichsforderung* (balancing claim); § 1378(i).

Other forms of *Güterstand* are *Gütertrennung* ((entire) separation of assets) and *Gütergemeinschaft* (community of property). These can be established by *Ehevertrag* (agreement between the spouses), which must be notarially documented and registered in the *Güterrechtsregister* at the *Amtsgericht*.

See: §§ 1363-1390, 1408-1415 and 1558-1563 BGB; Chapter X, p 78; Creifelds under *Ehevertrag, Gütergemeinschaft, Güterrecht, eheliches, Güterrechtsregister, Güterstände, Gütertrennung, Zugewinn, Zugewinnausgleich* and *Zugewinn-gemeinschaft*

Güterstand	property status (relationship) between spouses. See *Güterrecht*
Gutgläubiger Erwerb	*bona fide* acquisition (of ownership). See Creifelds under *Gutgläubiger Erwerb* and Chapter X, p 75
Haftbefehl	arrest warrant. See Chapter XVI, p 147 and Creifelds under *Haftbefehl*
Haften (für)	to be liable (for). It usually means the same as *schulden* (to owe) ie *wer schuldet, der haftet* (he who owes is liable). The term can also refer to the extent of liability. See *Haftung*. Also: *Einstehenmüssen (für)*
Haftgrund	ground (based on fact) for detaining a suspect in custody. See Chapter XVI (note 23)
Haftung	liability. See Chapter X (note 74); Creifelds under *Haftung*; Brox (AS), Chapter 2, § 2 III; Schwab (*Einführung*), Part III, Chapter 5 I (a)

Handakte	(lawyer's) file. See Chapter XIX, p 175 and also: *Akte*
Handelsbrauch	commercial (trade) custom, usage. See Chapter XI (note 28)
Handelsbücher	(trade) books. See Chapter XI
Handelsfirma	(trade) firm (name). Also: *Firma*
Handelsgeschäft	commercial transaction. It can mean a trading enterprise (*Unternehmen*). See Chapter XI, p 89
Handelsgesellschaft	see *Gesellschaft* and Chapter XI, p 81
Handelsgesetzbuch (HGB)	Commercial Code. See Chapter XI, p 81
Handelsgewerbe	trading activity. See Chapter XI, p 83
Handelskammer	see *Kammer für Handelssachen*
Handelskauf	trade purchase. See Chapter XI, p 90
Handelsmakler	(trade) broker. See Chapter XI, p 83 and *cf Makler*
Handelsrecht	commercial law. See Creifelds under *Handels-recht*
Handelsregister	commercial (trade) register. See Creifelds under *Handelsregister* and Chapter XI, p 83
Handelsrichter	(honorary) commercial judge. See Creifelds under *Handelsrichter* and Chapter XIX, p 165
Handelssache	commercial matter. See Creifelds under *Handels-sache*
Handelsstand	trade class(ification). See Chapter XI, p 83
Handelsvertreter	commercial agent. See Chapter XI, p 83
Handlung	act(ion). See Chapter XV, p 134
Handlungsfreiheit	freedom of action. See Chapter VIII (Article 2(i) GG)
Handlungsgehilfe	trading assistant; also referred to as *kaufmännische(r) Angestellte(r)*. See Creifelds under *Handlungsgehilfe* and Chapter XI, p 83
Handlungslehrling	see *Lehrling*
Handlungsvollmacht	authority to trade; trading power of attorney. See Creifelds under *Handlungsvollmacht* and Chapter XI, p 83. *Cf Prokura*
Handlungswille	will to act (at all). See Chapter X, p 38 (The term *Willenserklärung*)
Handwerker	manual worker
Hauptbeweis	main evidence. See Chapter XII (note 3) and *cf Gegenbeweis*

Hauptintervention	direct intervention. See Chapter XII, p 100
Hauptpartei	main party. See Chapter XII, p 100
Hauptstrafe	main punishment. See Chapter XV, p 143
Haupttermin	(main) hearing (in civil proceedings). See Chapter XII, p 111
Hauptverfahren	main (criminal) proceedings. See Chapter XVI, p 151 and Creifelds under *Hauptverfahren*
Hauptverhandlung	main (criminal) hearing. See Chapter XVI, p 151 and Creifelds under *Hauptverhandlung*
Hauptversammlung	main assembly, (annual) general meeting
Heiliges Römisches Reich (Deutscher Nation)	Holy Roman Empire (of the German Nation). See Chapter I (note 6)
Heranwachsender	youth (between 18 and 21). *Cf Jugendlicher*
Herausgabe(anspruch)	(right to claim) the return, release of a *Sache*. See *Vindikation*
Herrschaftsrecht	right of dominance. See Chapter X, p 34
Hersteller	manufacturer, producer. See Chapter X (§§ 631-651 BGB)
Herstellung	manufacture, production
Hilfsnorm	accessory norm. See Chapter X (note 13)
Hilfsperson	assistant. See Chapter XI, p 83
Hilfsweise Anwendung	subsidiary application. See Chapter XVII (note 1)
Hinauskündigungsklausel	clause in a company agreement enabling a member to be excluded by the others. See Chapter XI, p 88
Hinreichend	sufficient(ly). See Chapter XIII, p 124
Hinterlegung	deposit (of property). *Cf Anzahlung*. See Chapter X, p 56 (Title 2)
Historische Rechtsschule	historical school (of law). See Chapter I, p 4
Hochschule	high school. See Chapter II (note 6)
Hoheitlich	official(ly); based on public legal authority. See Chapter II, p 5 and *cf fiskalisch*
Holschuld	see *Leistungsort*
Homo homini lupus	man is the wolf of man. See Chapter I (note 9)
Honorar	(professional) fee. See Chapter XIX, p 178
Hypothek	mortgage; *cf Grundschuld*. See Chapter X, p 78

Im eigenen Namen	in (one's, his, her, its) own name. See *Kommissionär*
Im Falle (von)	in the event (of)
Immanent	implicit in. See Chapter VIII, p 23
Immaterialrechtsgut	intellectual property. See Chapter X, p 34
Im staatlichen Auftrag	on state instructions. See Chapter XV (note 3)
Indizienbeweis	circumstantial (or indirect) evidence (by means of *Hilfstatsachen* (auxiliary facts)). It can assist in establishing (concluding the truth of) a particular fact. Not to be confused with its subtype *Anscheinsbeweis*. See Chapter XII (note 3) and Baur/Grunsky, § 14 A 1 2
In dubio pro reo	in case of doubt: for the accused. See Chapter XII (note 3) and Creifelds under *In dubio pro reo*
Informationsfreiheit	freedom of information (access to public sources). See Creifelds under *Informationsfreiheit* and Chapter VIII, p 24
In fremdem Namen	in someone else's name. See Chapter XII, p 102
In gutem Glauben	in good faith. See Chapter X, p 75 (*Bona fide* acquisition of ownership to movables). See also Chapter XI (note 12)
Inhaber(schaft)	person entitled, owner; entitlement, ownership. See Chapter X, p 34
Inhaberpapier	bearer security (*Wertpapier*). Cf *Orderpapier*
Inhalt	content. See Chapter X, p 50
Innenverhältnis	internal relationship. See Chapter XII, p 102
Inquisitionsprinzip	inquisition principle (also referred to as the *Ermittlungsgrundsatz* or *Untersuchungsgrundsatz*). It applies in proceedings before criminal, administrative, finance and social courts and in FGG matters. Its opposite is the *Verhandlungsgrundsatz*. See Chapter XII, p 93, Chapter XII (note 3) and Creifelds under *Inquisitionsprinzip*
Interesse	interest (in). See Chapter I, p 4
Interessenjurisprudenz	jurisprudence based on (a balancing of) interests. Cf *Begriffsjurisprudenz* and see Chapter I, p 4
Internationales Privatrecht	private international law. See Chapter XVIII
Interventionswirkung	effect of *Nebenintervention*.
Inzidentkontrolle	incidental control (of a norm). See Chapter VII, p 20
Ipso iure	by operation of law

Iura novit curia	the court knows the law. See Chapter XII (note 53) and Creifelds under *iura novit curia*
Ius civile	civil law. See Chapter I (notes 2 and 5)
Ius cogens	compulsory law. See Chapter IX, p 30
Ius dispositivum	dispositive law. See Chapter IX, p 30
Ius gentium	public international law. See Chapter I (note 2) and *Völkerrecht*
Ius honorarium	honorary law (of the magistrate or *praetor*). See Chapter I (notes 2 and 5)
Ius privatum	private law. See Chapter I (note 2) and *Privatrecht*
Ius publicum	public law. See Chapter I (note 2) and *Öffentliches Recht*
Jugendgerichtsgesetz (JGG)	Juvenile Courts Law. See Chapter XV (note 34)
Jugendlicher	youth (between 14 and 18). See: Creifelds under *Jugendliche und Heranwachsende* and the JGG
Juristische Person	juristic person (of private or public law). It can be (and often is) a corporate body. See: Creifelds under *Juristische Person*, Chapter II (note 6), Chapter XI, p 81 and *Verein*
Juristische Person des öffentlichen Rechts	see *Körperschaft des öffentlichen Rechts*
Kammer	chamber (of a court; or of a professional or commercial body). See Creifelds under *Kammer*
Kammer für Handelssachen	chamber for commercial matters. See Chapter XI, p 103
Kapitalgesellschaft	capital(ised) company. See Creifelds under *Kapitalgesellschaft*, Chapter XI, p 83 and *cf Personengesellschaft*
Kauf	purchase. See Creifelds under *Kauf* and Chapter X, p 58 (Title 1) (§§ 433-514 BGB)
Käufer	purchaser. See also *Erwerber*
Kaufmann	businessman; trader. See Creifelds under *Kaufmann* and see *Formkaufmann*, *Mußkaufmann* and *Sollkaufmann*
Kaufmännische(r) Angestellte(r)	(trade) employee. See *Handlungsgehilfe*

Kaufmännisches Bestätigungsschreiben	commercial letter of confirmation. See Creifelds under *Bestätigungsschreiben* and Chapter X (note 50)
Kaufvertrag	purchase contract, contract of sale. See Chapter X, p 48 and *Kauf*
Kausalität	causation; also: *Ursächlichkeit*. See Creifelds under *Kausalität im Strafrecht* and Chapter XV, p 136
Kenntnis	knowledge
Kind	child
Kindschaftssache	(certain) matter concerning a child. See Chapter XII, p 115 and § 640(ii) ZPO
Kirchlich	ecclesiastical
Klage	writ. See Creifelds under *Klage* and Chapters XII, pp 95 and 107, XIV, p 129 and XVI, p 151
Klageänderung	amendment of a writ. See Chapter XII, p 110
Klageantrag	application (to the court) in a writ. See Chapter XII, p 110
Klageart	type of writ. See Chapter XII, p 108 and Chapter XIV, p 129
Klagebefugnis	(term of administrative procedure) authority to sue; used analogously in relation to the lodging of a *Widerspruch* (*Widerspruchsbefugnis*). See Chapter XIV, p 130
Klageerwiderung	defence to a writ. See Chapter XII, p 110
Klagegrund	factual basis for a writ (ie a fact). See Chapter XII, p 110
Klageschrift	statement of claim, writ. See Chapter XII, p 107
Klagevortrag	submission(s) in the *Klage* (of the *Kläger*). See Chapter XII (note 52)
Klar	clear(ly)
Klausel	clause (in an agreement). See Chapter XI, p 88
Koalition	coalition (ie trade union or employer association). See Chapter XVII, p 159
Koalitionsfreiheit	freedom to form coalitions. See Creifelds under *Koalitionsfreiheit* and Chapter VIII (Article 9(iii) GG)
Kommanditgesellschaft (KG)	limited partnership. See *Gesamthandsgemeinschaft, Gesellschaft, Personengesellschaft* and §§ 161-177a HGB. See also Creifelds under *Kommanditgesellschaft*

Kommanditgesellschaft auf Aktien (KGaA)	a KG by shares. See §§ 278-290 AktG, *Aufsichtsrat* and Creifelds under *Kommanditgesellschaft auf Aktien*
Kommanditist	member of a KG with limited liability. See Chapter XI, p 89
Kommissionär	commissioneer. See Chapter XI, p 84
Kommune	communal body, local authority (*Kreis* or *Gemeinde*). See Creifelds under *Kommunen* and Chapter VI
Komplementär	member of a KG with unlimited liability. See Chapter XI, p 83
Konkret	concrete (*adj*)
Konkrete Normkontrolle	see *Normkontrolle*
Konkurrierend	concurrent. See Chapter II, p 5
Konkursordnung (KO)	Bankruptcy Order (a statute). See Chapter X
Kontrollrecht	right of control
Konzentration	concentration. See Chapter XII, p 95
Körperschaft	corporation. See *Juristische Person*
Körperschaft des öffentlichen Rechts	public corporation. See Creifelds under *Körperschaft des öffentlichen Rechts* and *Juristische Person*
Kostenfestsetzung	fixing (taxation) of costs. See Creifelds under *Kostenfestsetzung, Kostenentscheidung* and Chapter XIX (note 20)
Kostenordnung (KostO)	Costs Order (for court and notary fees in non-contentious civil matters). See Chapter XIX, pp 178 and 179
Kostenstreitwert	see *Gebührenstreitwert*
Kostenvorschuß	(advance) payment on account of costs. See Chapter XII, p 108
Kreis	local authority (above a *Gemeinde*); also: *Landkreis*; literally, circle (of a *Land*). See: Chapter VI; *Kommune*; Creifelds under *Kreis*
Kreisangehörig	belonging to a *Kreis*. See Chapter VI
Kreisausschuß	(administrative) council of a *Kreis*. See Chapter VI
Kreisfrei	free, independent of a *Kreis*. See Chapter VI and Creifelds under *Kreisfreie Städte*
Kreisordnung	local government law governing the *Kreise* in a *Land*. See Chapter VI
Kreistag	parliament of a *Kreis*. See Chapter VI

Kriegsdienstverweigerung	objection to military service. See Chapter VIII, p 24 and Creifelds under *Kriegsdienstverweigerer*
Kriminalpolizei	criminal police. See Chapter XVI (note 19)
Kündigung	(notice of) termination; notice; dismissal. In respect of an employee, it can be *ordentlich* (*befristet* (with notice)) or *außerordentlich* (*fristlos* (without notice)). See Creifelds under *Kündigung* and *Entlassung des Arbeitnehmers*. See also *Auflösung*, *Gestaltungsrecht* and Chapter XVII, p 153
Kündigungsschutz	(employment) protection against *Kündigung*. See Chapter XVII, pp 153 and 154 and Creifelds under *Kündigungsschutz für Arbeitnehmer*
Kündigungsschutzgesetz (KSchG)	Employment Protection Law. See Chapter XVII, p 153
Ladung	summons, *subpoena* (of a person to a hearing, to attend court). See Creifelds under *Ladung* and Chapter XII, p 111
Lager	store. See Chapter XI, p 90
Land, Länder	(individual) state(s) (of Germany). See Chapter V
Länderverwaltung	(own) administration by the *Länder*. See *Landeseigene Verwaltung*, Chapter II, p 5 and V, p 15
Landesarbeitsgericht (LAG)	county employment court. See Creifelds under *Landesarbeitsgericht* and Chapter XIX, p 169
Landesbehörde	authority of a *Land*. See Chapter V, p 16
Landeseigene Verwaltung	(own) administration by a *Land*. See *Länderverwaltung* and Chapter II, p 5
Landesgesetz	statute of a *Land*, state statute. *Cf Bundesgesetz*. See Chapters II, p 5 and VII, pp 20–22
Landesoberbehörde	upper authority of a *Land*. See Chapter V, p 16
Landesregierung	government of a *Land*. See Chapter V, p 15
Landessozialgericht (LSG)	county social (security) court. See Creifelds under *Landessozialgericht* and Chapter XIX, p 169
Landesverfassung	constitution of a *Land*. See Chapter V, p 151
Landesverfassungsgericht	constitutional court of a *Land*. See Chapter VII, p 21
Landgericht (LG)	county court; literally, court of a *Land*. See Creifelds under *Landgericht* and Chapter XII, pp 103 and 107 and Chapter XIX, p 168
Landkreis	see *Kreis*

Landrat	chief executive of a *Kreis*; in Niedersachsen and Nordrhein-Westfalen: the *Oberkreisdirektor*. See Creifelds under *Landrat* and Chapter VI
Landtag	parliament of a *Land*. See Creifelds under *Landtag* and Chapter V, p 15
Leben	life. See Chapter VIII (Article 2(ii), first sentence GG)
Legalitätsgrundsatz	legality principle; obliges official intervention by a prosecuting authority. See Creifelds under *Legalitätsprinzip*, Chapter XVI, p 147 and *cf Opportunitätsgrundsatz*.
Lehrling	trainee, (trade) apprentice. See Creifelds under *Auszubildender* and *Handlungslehrling* and Chapter XI, p 83
Leibrente	annuity, pension for life. See Creifelds under *Leibrente* and Chapter X, p 59 (Title 16)
Leihe	gratuitous loan. See Creifelds under *Leihe* and Chapter X, p 58 (Title 4)
Leistung	performance (owed or carried out); achievement; accomplishment.
	In §§ 812ff BGB, the term *Leistung* is used to mean *eine Vermögenszuwendung* (a grant of a financial benefit or advantage) or, as is often said, *eine bewußte und zweckgerichtete Mehrung fremden Vermögens* (a conscious and purposeful increase in someone else's assets).
	For the purpose of § 326 BGB, the term *Leistung* means a *Hauptleistung* rather than a *Nebenleistung*.
	See Creifelds under *Leistung*, *Ungerechtfertigte Bereicherung* and *Gegenseitiger Vertrag* II 2. See also Chapter X, pp 50, 53 and 59
Leistungserfolg	(successful) performance. See Chapter X, p 50 and *Leistungsort*
Leistungshandlung	(act of) performance carried out. See Chapter X, p 50 and *Leistungsort*
Leistungsklage	writ claiming a *Leistung*. See Chapters XII, p 108 and XIV, p 129
Leistungskondiktion	ground of action (condiction) under § 812(i), first sentence, first alternative BGB to recover something (*etwas* = a financial advantage) from someone, who receives it without a legal basis (*ohne rechtlichen Grund*) due to the *Leistung* of the claimant. See Creifelds under *Ungerechtfertigte Bereicherung* and Chapter X, p 59 (Title 24)

Leistungsort	place of performance ie the place at which the *Leistungshandlung* must be carried out. It is sometimes referred to as the *Erfüllungsort*.
	Usually, the *Leistung* has to be collected by the creditor from the debtor (a *Holschuld*) and the place of the *Leistungshandlung* and *Leistungserfolg* coincide: they are both at the *Wohnsitz* ((place of) residence) of the debtor (§ 269(i) BGB).
	However, the *Leistungsort* and *Erfolgsort* can diverge – as where the *Schuldner* has to send his *Leistung* (a *Schickschuld*, eg a *Geldschuld*). In that case, the *Leistungsort* is at the *Schuldner's* address, but the *Leistungserfolg* occurs at the address of the creditor (as under § 270 and § 447 BGB).
	See: Creifelds under *Leistungsort*; Brox (AS), Chapter 4, § 11 IV; Fikentscher, Section 3 (§ 35); Klunzinger (*Einführung*), Part III, Chapter 2 (§ 26 II); Chapter X, p 51 (Title 1)
Leistungspflicht	duty of performance. See Chapter X, p 50
Leistungsrecht(e)	right(s) to a *Leistung*; rights(s) to a service (performance). See Chapter VIII, p 23
Leistungsstörung	disturbance in performance. See Chapter X, pp 35 and 36 (Titles 1 and 2) and (note 73)
Leistungsverpflichtung	see *Leistungspflicht*
Leistungsverwaltung	service administration. See Chapter II (note 7) and *cf Eingriffsverwaltung*
Leistungsverweigerungsrecht	right to decline performance. See Chapter X *Exposé*
Leistungszeit	time for performance. See Chapter X (note 52) and *Fälligkeit*
Leitender Angestellter	leading employee. See Creifelds under *Leitende Angestellte* and Chapter XVII, p 155
Lombardgeschäft	Lombard transaction, ie grant of a loan by a bank against creation of a *Pfandrecht* (lien). See Chapter X (note 109)
Luftfahrt-Bundesamt	Federal Office of Aviation. See Chapter XIII, p 121
Machtbereich (des Empfängers)	area of control (of the recipient). See Chapter X, p 39 (Validity of a *Willenserklärung*) (note 33)
Magistrat	(collective) magistrate; executive organ of a *Gemeinde*. See also *Oberbürgermeister* and Creifelds under *Magistratsverfassung*

Mahnbescheid	default notice. See Chapter XII, p 96 and *Mahnverfahren*
Mahnung	warning. See *Leistungsstörung* and *Verzug*
Mahnverfahren	default notice procedure. See Creifelds under *Mahnverfahren* and Chapter XII, p 115
Makler	(civil) agent. See Creifelds under *Makler* and *cf Handelsmakler*
Maklerlohn	broker's fee; also called *Courtage*
Mäklervertrag	(civil) agency contract. See Creifelds under *Mäklervertrag* and Chapter X, p 59 (Title 8)
Mandant	client (of a lawyer); also: *Auftraggeber*. See Chapter XIX, p 173
Mangel	fault; defect. See *Fehler(haft)*
Maßnahme	measure. See Chapter XIII, p 123 and Chapter XV, p 144
Maßregel der Besserung und Sicherung	measure of improvement and security. See Creifelds under *Maßregeln der Besserung und Sicherung* and Chapter XV, p 143
Materiell	material(ly)
Materielles Recht	material law. See Chapter IX, p 30
Mehrheit	majority; multitude. See Chapter X, p 58
Mehrparteiensystem	multi-party system. See Chapter II, p 9
Mehrseitig	multilateral. See Chapter X, p 35
Meinungsfreiheit	freedom of expression (opinion). See Creifelds under *Meinungsfreiheit* and Chapter VIII, p 24
Meinungsverschiedenheit	difference of opinion. See Chapter XVII
Menschenrecht(e)	human right(s)
Menschenwürde	human dignity. See Creifelds under *Menschenwürde* and Chapter VIII, p 24
Merkmal	element, characteristic (of)
Miete	rent; also called *Mietzins*. See *Mietvertrag* and Chapter X, p 58 (Title 3)
Mietvertrag	tenancy, lease. See Creifelds under *Miete*
Minderjährig	under the age of majority. *Cf Volljährig*
Minderjähriger	minor. See Chapter X, p 36
Minderkaufmann	lesser businessman. See Chapter XI, p 83, *Mußkaufmann* and Creifelds under *Minderkaufmann*
Ministerpräsident	prime minister; head of a *Landesregierung*. See Chapter V, p 15

Mitbestimmung(srecht)	(right of) co-decision, co-determination; stronger than *Mitspracherecht*. See Creifelds under *Mitbestimmung* and Chapter XVII, pp 155 and 159
Miteigentum nach Bruchteilen	joint ownership by shares (§ 1008ff BGB). It is a sub-category of the *Gemeinschaft nach Bruchteilen*. See Chapter X, p 77
Mitspracherecht	right of co-determination, consultation. See Chapter XVII, p 157 and *cf Mitbestimmungsrecht*
Mittäter	joint perpetrator(s). See *Täter* and Creifelds under *Mittäterschaft*
Mittelbar	indirect(ly). See Chapter II, p 5 and Chapter VIII, p 23
Mittelstufe	middle level. See Chapter V, p 16
Mitverschulden	contributory fault, contributory negligence. See Chapter X, p 51 (§ 254 BGB) and Creifelds under *Mitverschulden*
Mitwirken	to assist (by way of cooperation). See Chapter III
Mitwirkung	co-operation. Also: *Zusammenarbeit*. See Chapter III and Chapter XVII, p 157
Mündlichkeitsgrundsatz	oral principle. See Creifelds under *Mündlichkeitsgrundsatz* and Chapter XII, p 95
Mußkaufmann	compulsory businessman; two types: *Vollkaufmann* (full businessman) or *Minderkaufmann* (lesser businessman). See Chapter XI, p 83
Mutmaßlich	presumable, supposed(ly). Also: *Vermutlich*. See Chapter XV, p 138
Nach billigem Ermessen	in accordance with fair discretion. See Chapter XII, p 113
Nach Lage der Akten (Aktenlage)	on the basis of the file(s). See Chapter XII, p 105
Nachfolgeklausel	succession clause (in company agreement). See Chapter XI, p 88
Nachgiebig	yielding, indulgent. See *Dispositiv*
Nachlaß	see Chapter XIX, p 167 and *Erbschaft*
Nachlaßsache	matter relating to a *Nachlaß*, probate matter. See Chapter XIX, p 167
Nebenanspruch	accessory claim. See Chapter X (note 106)
Nebenbestimmung	collateral provision (to a VA). See Chapter XIII, p 123

Nebengesetz	secondary, accessory, collateral statute. See Chapter XV, p 133
Nebenintervenient	intervener. See *Nebenintervention*
Nebenintervention	assistance to a party in the dispute as intervener; also called *Streithilfe*. See Creifelds under *Nebenintervention*, Chapter XII, p 100 and *Interventionswirkung*
Nebenklage	collateral prosecution. See Creifelds under *Nebenklage* and Chapter XVI, p 151
Nebenpflicht	accessory duty. Breach can found a claim for positive *Vertragsverletzung* (PVV). See Chapter X, p 39 (Interpretation of a *Willenserklärung*) (note 35)
Nebenpunkt	accessory (collateral, subordinate) point. See Chapter X, p 44 (Failure to reach an *Einigung*)
Nebenstrafe	accessory punishment. See Creifelds under *Nebenstrafen* and Chapter XV, p 142
Ne bis in idem	not twice in the same matter. No punishment again for the same crime. See Creifelds under *Ne bis in idem* (*Strafklageverbrauch*) and Chapter VIII (note 14). *Cf* Chapter XII (note 5)
Nemo bonus iurista nisi bartolista	no-one is a good jurist, if he does not follow Bartolus. See Chapter I (note 4)
Nemo plus iuris ad alium transferre potest quam ipse habet	Nobody can transfer to another person a greater right than he himself has. See Chapter X, p 75 (The components of a transfer of ownership)
Neugliederung	new division. See Creifelds under *Neugliederung des Bundesgebietes* and Chapter II (note 11)
Nichtberechtigter	unauthorised (third) person. See Chapter X, pp 73 and 75 (*Bona fide* acquisition of ownership to movables)
Nichtbestehen	non-existence, not to exist. See Chapter XII, p 108
Nichtehelich	illegitimate (child). See Chapter X, p 79 and Creifelds under *Nichteheliche Kinder*
Nichterscheinen	non-appearance; a party's failure to attend a *Termin*. See Chapter XII, p 105 and *Versäumnis*

Nichtig(keit)	void; nullity. Can relate to a court decision, a *Gesetz*, a *Willenserklärung*, a *Rechtsgeschäft* or a VA.
	See, respectively, Chapters VII, p 21, X, pp 42 and 43 and XIII, p 124. See also Creifelds under *Nichtigkeit gerichtlicher Entscheidungen, Nichtigkeit von Gesetzen, Nichtigkeit von Rechtsgeschäften* and *Nichtigkeit von Verwaltungsakten*
Nichtigerklärung	declaration of nullity (of marriage). See Chapter XII, p 115
Nichtigkeitsklage	type of writ seeking *Wiederaufnahme*. See Chapter XII, p 114
Nichtleistungskondiktion	(subsidiary) ground of action (condiction) under § 812(i), first sentence, second alternative BGB to recover something (*etwas* = a financial advantage) from someone, who obtains it without a legal basis (*ohne rechtlichen Grund*), not due to the *Leistung* of the claimant, but in sonstiger *Weise* (in another way). There are three types of *Nichtleistungskondiktion*: *Eingriffskondiktion, Verwendungskondiktion* and *Rückgriffskondiktion. Cf Leistungskondiktion* and see Chapter X, p 59 (Title 24)
Nichtrechtsfähig	incapable of carrying rights and obligations (not possessing legal capacity). See Chapter II (note 6). *Cf Rechtsfähig(keit)*
Nichtstun	inaction, idleness. See Chapter X, p 44
Nichtverhandeln	a party's failure to make submissions at a *Termin*; equivalent to *Nichterscheinen* (§ 333 ZPO). See Chapter XII, p 105
Nichtvermögensrechtlich	non-monetary. See Chapter XII, p 114
Niederlassungsfreiheit	freedom of establishment. See Chapter VIII, p 26
Niedersachsen	Lower Saxony. See Chapter V, p 15
Niederschrift	written record. See Chapter XIX, p 179
Nießbrauch	*usufruct*. See Creifelds under *Nießbrauch* and Chapter X, p 76
Non liquet	(the matter is) not clear. See Chapter XII (note 3)
Norddeutscher Bund	North German Confederation. See Chapter I (note 6)
Nordrhein-Westfalen	North Rhine-Westphalia. See Chapter V, p 15
Norm	norm, legal provision. Also: *Rechtssatz*

Normkontrolle	norm-control (by a court); a norm-control reference to the BVerfG can be *konkret* (concrete: within particular proceedings) or *abstrakt* (abstract: on application). See Creifelds under *Normenkontrolle* and Chapters VII, p 20 and XIV, p 129
Normkontrollverfahren	norm-control procedure (particularly under § 47 VwGO). See *Normkontrolle*
Notar	notary. See Creifelds under *Notar* and Chapter XIX, p 177
Notarkammer	Notaries' Chamber. See Chapter XIX, p 179
Notfrist	a *Frist* described as such in a statute and which cannot be extended or shortened. See Creifelds under *Notfrist* and Chapter XII, p 105
Notstand	(state of) emergency; can be a *Rechtfertigungsgrund* (§ 34 StGB) or a *Schuldausschließungsgrund*.
	An illegal act can be excused if it is carried out in an emergency (*entschuldigender Notstand*), although not if this was on the basis of an (avoidable) mistake (*Putativnotstand*) (§ 35 StGB). See Creifelds under *Notstand* I and Chapter XV, pp 138 and 141
Notwehr	self-defence; a person acting in *Notwehr* has a *Rechtfertigungsgrund* (§ 32 StGB). If the appropriate *Notwehr* is exceeded (*Notwehrexzeß*), *Schuld* can be excluded. See Creifelds under *Notwehr* I and Chapter XV (note 24) and (note 41)
Notwendig	necessary
Nulla poena sine culpa	no punishment without blame. See Chapter XV (note 14)
Nulla poena sine lege	no punishment without law. See Chapter VIII (note 14) and Chapter XV, p 133
Nullum crimen sine lege	no crime without law. See Creifelds under *Nullum crimen (nulla poena) sine lege* and Chapter XV (note 3)
Numerus clausus	closed (fixed) number. See Creifelds under *numerus clausus*; Chapter VII (note 13); Chapter X, p 71
Nutzungsherausgabe	replacement of benefit(s). See Chapter X (note 106). See also § 100 BGB and Creifelds under *Früchte*
Nutzungsrecht	right of user; (copyright) licence. See Creifelds under *Nutzungsrecht* and Chapter X, p 71

Oberbürgermeister	senior mayor; executive organ of a larger *Gemeinde*. See also: *Bürgermeister*; *Magistrat*; *Gemeindeverwaltung*; Chapter VI; Creifelds under *Oberbürgermeister*
Oberfinanzdirektion	Upper Finance Directorate. It is both a *Bundesbehörde* and a *Landesbehörde*. See Chapter IV
Oberkreisdirektor	see *Landrat*, Chapter VI and Creifelds under *Oberkreisdirektor*
Oberlandesgericht (OLG)	county court of appeal; superior (county) court (of a *Land*). See Creifelds under *Oberlandesgericht* and Chapters XII, p 113 and XIX, p 168
Oberpostdirektion	Upper Post Directorate. It is a *Bundesbehörde*. See Chapter IV
Oberstaatsanwalt	senior state prosecutor (at the LG). See Chapter XVI, p 147
Oberste Bundesbehörde	supreme federal authority. See Chapter IV and Creifelds under *Oberste Bundesbehörden*
Oberste Bundesorgan(e)	supreme organ(s) of the *Bund*. See Chapter III
Oberste Landesbehörde	supreme authority of a *Land*. See Chapter V, p 16
Oberstes Landesgericht	supreme county court (in Bavaria). See Chapter XIX, p 169
Oberstufe	upper level. See Chapter V, p 16
Oberverwaltungsgericht (OVG)	administrative court of appeal; sometimes called *Verwaltungsgerichtshof* (VGH). See Creifelds under *Oberverwaltungsgericht* and Chapters XIV, p 129 and XIX, p 168
Objektive Bedingungen der Strafbarkeit	objective conditions of punishability. See Chapter XV (note 14)
Objektives Recht	objective law. See Chapter X, p 34
Offene Handelsgesellschaft (OHG)	open trading company. See Creifelds under *Offene Handelsgesellschaft*, Chapter XI, p 81 and *Gesamthandsgemeinschaft*, *Gesellschaft* and *Personengesellschaft*
Offenkundig	(patently) obvious(ly). See Chapter XII (note 52 2)
Öffentlich	(in) public
Öffentliche Einrichtung	public facility. See Chapter II, p 7
Öffentliche Gewalt	(the) public power. See Chapter VII, p 20

Öffentlich-rechtlicher Vertrag	contract governed by public law, public contract. See Creifelds under *Öffentlich-rechtliche Verträge* and Chapter XIII, p 123
Öffentliches Recht	public law. See Chapter IX and Creifelds under *Recht* II. See also *ius publicum*
Öffentlichkeit	(the) public
Öffentlichkeitsgrundsatz	the principle that a hearing (usually) takes place in public. See Creifelds under *Öffentlichkeitsgrundsatz* and Chapter XII, p 95
Ohne Obligo	without obligation. See Chapter X, p 43
Ohne rechtlichen Grund	without (a) legal basis. See: Chapter X, p 38; Chapter X, p 59 (Title 24); Chapter X (note 96); *Leistungskondiktion*
Ohne sachlichen Grund	without (a) substantial reason. See Chapter XIII (note 23)
Opportunitätsgrundsatz	opportunity principle; gives a *Behörde* discretion as to whether to intervene. See Creifelds under *Opportunitätsprinzip*, Chapter XVI, p 146 and *cf Legalitätsgrundsatz*
Ordentlich	ordinary, (in) proper (form). See *Kündigung*
Ordentliche Gerichtsbarkeit	ordinary jurisdiction; deals with civil, criminal and FGG matters. See Creifelds under *Ordentliche Gerichtsbarkeit* and Chapter XIX, p 168
Orderpapier	security (*Wertpapier*) in the name of a particular person or order. See Creifelds under *Orderpapier* and *cf Inhaberpapier*
Ordnung	order. See Chapter XVI (note 19)
Ordnungsbehörde	order authority. See *Verwaltungspolizei*
Ordnungsmäßig	correct(ly), proper(ly). See Chapter XII, p 99
Ordnungswidrigkeit	minor offence punishable by a fine (*Geldbuße*). See Creifelds under *Ordnungswidrigkeiten* and Chapter XV, p 101
Ordnungswidrigkeitengesetz (OWiG)	Minor Offences Law. See Chapter XV (note 6)
Organ	organ (of a corporate body); eg of the *Bund* or a *Land*: see Creifelds under *Organe der BRep* and Chapters II, p 5, III and V, p 15. See also Chapter XI, p 81
Organisationsverschulden	organisational fault. See Chapter X (note 89)
Organstreit(igkeit)	dispute between (supreme) constitutional organs. See Creifelds under *Organstreitigkeiten* and Chapter VII, p 20
Örtlich	local. See *Zuständigkeit*

Pacht	(commercial) lease. See Creifelds under *Pacht* and Chapter X, p 58 (Title 3)
Pacta sunt servanda	contracts are to (must) be observed (performed). See Creifelds under *pacta sunt servanda* and Chapter I, p 4
Pandektenwissenschaft	science of the pandects. See Chapter I, p 4
Parlamentarische Demokratie	parliamentary democracy. See Chapter III (note 2) and *cf Präsidialdemokratie*
Partei	party (to civil proceedings). See Chapter XII, p 99
Parteifähig(keit)	capable of being (capacity to be) a party. See Creifelds under *Parteifähigkeit* and Chapter XII, p 99
Parteiöffentlichkeit	party openess (principle). See Chapter XII note 54)
Parteiprozeß	party action. See Creifelds under *Parteiprozeß*, Chapter XII, p 102 and *cf Anwaltsprozeß*
Parteivernehmung	examination of a party (in a civil court). See Creifelds under *Parteivernehmung*
Parteivortrag	submission(s) of a party. See Chapter XII (note 52 4)
Partnerschaftsgesellschaft	partnership (company). See Chapter XIX (note 54 B)
Partnerschaftsvertrag	partnership agreement. See Chapter XIX (note 54 B)
Personal	staff
Personalkörperschaft	personal corporation. See Chapter II (note 6) and *cf Gebietskörperschaft*
Personalrat	personnel council (in public sector). See Creifelds under *Personalvertretung* (representation of personnel), Chapter XVII, p 154 and *cf Betriebsrat*
Personengesellschaft	a personal company; as opposed to a *Kapitalgesellschaft*. See Creifelds under *Personengesellschaft*. Examples: BGB-*Gesellschaft*, OHG and KG. See also Chapter XIX (note 54)
Personenkreis	group of persons. See Chapter XIII, p 124
Personenschaden	personal injury
Personenzusammenschluß	alliance (group, union) of persons. See Chapter XI (note 2)
Persönlich	personal
Persönlichkeit	personality

Persönlichkeitsrecht	personality right. See Creifelds under *Persönlichkeitsrecht* and Chapter VIII, p 24
Petitionsrecht	right of petition. See Chapter XIV (note 1)
Pfandleihe	pawnbroking. See Chapter X (note 109)
Pfandrecht	pledge, lien. See Chapter X (note 109)
Pfändung	distraint, seizure. See Creifelds under *Pfändung* and Chapter XII, p 118
Pfändungspfandrecht	distraint lien. See Chapter X (note 99)
Pfleger(in)	attendant, administrator, executive; nurse. See Chapter X, p 80 and also *Rechtspfleger*
Pflegschaft	administration (over a person unable to deal with his or her affairs in the cases specified in §§ 1909-1921 BGB). See Creifelds under *Pflegschaft* and Chapter X, p 80
Pflicht	duty. See Chapter X, pp 35 and 50
Pflichtgemäß	in accordance with legal obligation, dutifully. See Chapter XIII, p 128
Pflichtteil	compulsory portion (of an estate). See Creifelds under *Pflichtteil* and Chapter X, p 80
Pflichtverteidiger	compulsory defence lawyer. See Creifelds under *Pflichtverteidiger* and Chapter XIX, p 174 (note 59)
Polizei	police. See Chapter XIII (note 14) and Chapter XVI, p 146
Polizeibehörde	police authority. See *Verwaltungspolizei*
Polizeivollzugsbeamter	(executive) police officer
Polizeivollzugsdienst	executive police service. See Chapter XVI (note 19)
Popularklage	popular action. See Chapter XIV, p 130 and Creifelds under *Popularklage*
Positive Vertragsverletzung (PVV)	positive breach of contract. See Chapter X (note 13), Chapter X (note 36), Chapter X (note 74) and Chapter XVII, p 160
Postamt	post office; is a *Bundesunterbehörde*. See Chapter IV
Postulationsfähig(keit)	capable of appearing (capacity to appear) (before a particular court), right of audience. See Creifelds under *Postulationsfähigkeit* and Chapter XII, p 103
Präjudiz	(case) precedent. See Chapter XII, p 95. *Cf Fallrecht*

Präsidialdemokratie	presidential democracy. See Chapter III (note 2) and *cf parlamentarische Demokratie*
Presse- und Informationsamt der Bundesregierung	press and information office of the federal government. See Chapter IV
Prinzip	principle
Privatautonomie	private autonomy (principle). See Chapter X, p 35
Privatklage	private prosecution. See Creifelds under *Privatklage* and Chapter XVI, p 146
Privatrecht	private law. See Creifelds under *Privatrecht* and Chapter IX. See also *ius privatum*
Produkthaftung	product liability. See Chapter XII (note 3)
Prokura	*procura*. See Creifelds under *Prokura* and Chapter XI, p 83
Protestatio (facto contraria) non valet	a reservation (which does not accord with the external circumstances) is ineffective. Also: *Vorbehalt*. See Chapter X (note 39)
Provision	commission, fee. See Chapter XI, p 84
Prozeß	case, action, proceedings
Prozeßbevollmächtigter	person possessing a *Prozeßvollmacht*
Prozeßfähig(keit)	capable of taking (capacity to take) steps in the proceedings. See Creifelds under *Prozeßfähigkeit* and Chapter XII, p 99
Prozeßförderungspflicht	duty of the parties to further the proceedings. See Chapter XII, p 111
Prozeßführungsbefugnis	right to conduct an action. See Creifelds under *Prozeßführungsbefugnis* and see Chapter XII, p 103
Prozeßführungsrecht	right to conduct an action. Also called *Prozeßführungsbefugnis*
Prozeßgebühr	procedure fee. See Chapter XIX, p 176
Prozeßgericht	court hearing the case, action. See Creifelds under *Prozeßgericht* and *cf Vollstreckungsgericht*
Prozeßhandlung	step in the proceedings. See Chapter XII, p 100 and Creifelds under *Prozeßhandlung*
Prozeßhandlungsvoraussetzung	pre-condition for a *Prozeßhandlung* (eg *Parteifähigkeit*, *Prozeßfähigkeit*, *Prozeßvollmacht* and *Postulationsfähigkeit*)
Prozeßkosten	costs (in (of) the proceedings). They comprise the *Gerichtskosten* and *außergerichtliche Kosten*. See Chapter XII, pp 98 and 103. See also Creifelds under *Prozeßkosten*

Prozeßkostenhilfe	legal aid. See: Chapter XIX (note 90); Creifelds under *Prozeßkostenhilfe*; §§ 114-127a ZPO
Prozeßkostenvorschuß	payment on account of costs. See Creifelds under *Prozeßkostenvorschuß* and Chapter XII, p 109
Prozeßleitende Verfügung	(interlocutory) direction from the court in the course of proceedings. See Chapters X, p 72 and XII, p 111
Prozeßrecht	procedural law. See Chapter IX, p 30
Prozeßstandschaft	transfer of *Prozeßführungsrecht* to someone who has no *Sachlegitimation*. See Creifelds under *Prozeßstandschaft* and *Ermächtigung*; Chapter XII, p 103
Prozeßunfähig	not *prozeßfähig*
Prozeßvollmacht	authority to act, power of attorney in proceedings. See Creifelds under *Prozeßvollmacht* and Chapter XII, p 100
Prozeßvoraussetzung	see Creifelds under *Prozeßvoraussetzungen* and Chapter XII, p 99. See also *Sachurteilsvoraussetzung*
Prüfen	to examine, test, check. See Chapter X (note 13)
Prüfung	examination, test, check. See Chapter XIX, pp 165 and 173
Prüfungsmaßstab	standard against which an examination is (to be) made (measured). See Chapter VIII (note 13).
Publicum ius est, quod ad statum rei Romanae spectat, privatum quod ad singulorum utilitatem	public law looks to the situation of the Roman state, private (law) to the advantage of single persons (ie public law serves the interests of the state, private law the interests of the individual) (Ulpian). See Chapter IX (note 1)
Putativnotstand	see *Notstand*
Putativnotwehr	where a person mistakenly believes he is acting in self-defence. See Chapter XV (note 45)
Quelle	source. See *Rechtsquelle*
Quidquid non agnoscit glossa, non agnoscit curia	what is not acknowledged by the gloss is not acknowledged by the court. See Chapter I (note 3)
Quota litis	proportion of (the amount recovered in) an action. It is forbidden for a *Rechtsanwalt* to agree in advance that he should receive it as his fee. See Chapter XIX, p 179 and § 52 BRAK *Richtlinien*

Rahmen	frame(work). See Chapter II, p 5 and Chapter XIX, p 179
Rat	advice; council
Realakt	pure factual act. See Chapter X, p 35 and Chapter XIV, p 132
Reallast	successive duty of supply from a property. See Chapter X, p 77 and Creifelds under *Reallast*
Rechnungshof	accounts court. See Chapter IV
Recht	law; right. Can be understood in an objective or subjective sense: see Chapter X, p 34 and also Creifelds under *Recht*. *Cf Gesetz* and *Gerecht(igkeit)*
Recht der Selbstverwaltung	right of self-administration; autonomy. See Chapter VI
Recht zum Besitz	right to possession. See Chapter X, p 76 and *cf Besitz*
Rechtfertigen	to justify
Rechtfertigung	justification
Rechtfertigungsgrund	justifying reason. See Chapter XV, p 138 and *Einwilligung, Notwehr, Notstand*
Rechtliches Gehör	see *Anspruch auf rechtliches Gehör*
Rechtlich geschütztes Interesse	legally protected interest. See Chapter X, p 34
Rechtmäßig(keit)	legal(ity). See Chapter XIII, p 123 and *Gesetzmäßigkeit der Verwaltung*
Rechtmäßiger Eingriff	legitimate infringement (of a basic right). See Chapter VIII, p 24
Rechtsanwalt	lawyer. See Creifelds under *Rechtsanwalt* and Chapter XIX, p 172
Rechtsanwaltskammer (RAK)	lawyer's chamber. See Chapter XIX
Rechtsbegriff	legal term. See *Unbestimmt*
Rechtsbehelf	(every form of) legal remedy, formal or informal; includes *Rechtsmittel*. See Creifelds under *Rechtsbehelf* and Chapter XIV, p 129
Rechtsbeziehung	legal relationship. See *Rechtsverhältnis*
Rechtsbindungswille	will to be legally bound by one's act. See Chapter X, p 37 (The term *Willenserklärung*)
Rechtsfähig(keit)	capable of carrying (capacity to be a carrier of) rights and obligations; legally capable (legal capacity). See Chapter X, p 33 and Creifelds under *Rechtsfähigkeit*. *Cf Nichtrechtsfähig*
Rechtsfolge	legal consequence. See Chapter X, pp 36 and 48

Rechtsfolgeirrtum	mistake as to the legal consequence. See Chapter XV (note 44)
Rechtsfrage	legal question; question of law. See Chapter XVII (note 22)
Rechtsgeschäft	legal transaction; juristic act. See Creifelds under *Rechtsgeschäft* and Chapter X, p 36
Rechtsgeschäftliches Schuldverhältnis	obligation arising from a *Rechtsgeschäft*. See Chapter X, p 48
Rechtsgeschäftsähnlich	similar to a *Rechtsgeschäft*. See Chapter X, p 36
Rechtsgestaltend	creating or amending a legal relationship or situation. See Chapter XIII, p 127
Rechtsgut	asset of legal (social) importance. See Chapter XV, p 134
Rechtshandlung	legal action; legal act. See Chapter X, p 36
Rechtshängig(keit)	(the fact that a matter is) *sub judice*. See Creifelds under *Rechtshängigkeit* and Chapter XII, pp 107 and 109. *Cf Anhängig*
Rechtskraft	legal force, legally binding nature (of a court decision); a decision has *formelle Rechtskraft* (formal legal force) when it can no longer be challenged. This is a condition for the decision having *materielle Rechtskraft* (material legal force), ie being final for the court and parties: *Bis de eadem re ne sit actio*. See Creifelds under *Rechtskraft* and Chapter XII, p 95
Rechtskräftig	possessing *Rechtskraft*
Rechtsmacht	legal power. See *Subjektives Recht*
Rechtsmittel	(devolutive) legal remedy, appeal. See Creifelds under *Rechtsmittel*, Chapter XII, p 113 and *cf Rechtsbehelf*
Rechtsnachfolge	succession (to the right/interest/title of another person). Also: *Sukzession*. It can be based on a *Rechtsgeschäft* (eg transfer of ownership) or arise from statute (eg *gesetzliche Erbfolge*). See Chapter X, note 134
Rechtsnorm	legal norm. See Chapters VII, p 20 and IX, pp 29-30
Rechtsobjekt	legal object. See Chapter X, p 32
Rechtsordnung	legal system. See Chapter X, p 34
Rechtspflege	administration of justice. See Creifelds under *Rechtspflege* and Chapter XIX (note 39)

Rechtspfleger	legal executive, ie a civil servant who can conduct various judicial matters which are not entrusted to a judge. See Chapter XIX, p 166 and Creifelds under *Rechtspfleger*
Rechtspflegergesetz (RPflG)	Law Relating to the *Rechtspfleger*. See Chapter XIX, p 166
Rechtsprechende Gewalt	judicative power. Also: *Rechtsprechung*. See Creifelds under *Rechtsprechende Gewalt* and Chapter II, p 8
Rechtsprechung	judicature; case-law. See Creifelds under *Rechtsprechung* and Chapter II, p 8
Rechtsquelle	legal source. See Chapters X, p 32 and XIII, p 60
Rechtsreflex	legal reflex. *Cf Subjektives Recht*
Rechtssatz	legal provision. Also: *Norm*. See: Chapter X (note 17) and (note 60)
Rechtsschutzbedürfnis	need for legal protection; also called *Rechtsschutzinteresse*. See Chapter XI, p 99. See also: Creifelds under *Rechtsschutzbedürfnis*; Stern, Part I, § 12
Rechtsschutzgarantie	right of everyone to protection of the courts (Article 19(iv) GG). See Creifelds under *Rechtsweggarantie* and Chapter VIII, p 25
Rechtsschutzinteresse	see *Rechtsschutzbedürfnis*
Rechtssphäre	legal sphere. See Chapter VII (note 11)
Rechtsstaat	state in which the (rule of) law prevails. See Creifelds under *Rechtsstaat* and Chapter II, p 8
Rechtsstreit	legal dispute. Also: *Streit; Streitigkeit*
Rechtssubjekt	legal subject, person. See Creifelds under *Rechtssubjekt* and Chapter X, p 32
Rechtsunwirksam	legally ineffective, of no legal effect. Also: *Unwirksam*
Rechtsverhältnis	legal relationship. See Chapter X, p 34
Rechtsverordnung	statutory instrument, regulation (issued by the executive). See Chapters VII, p 20, VIII (note 10) and XIII, p 121. See also *Gesetz* and *Zustimmungs gesetz*
Rechtsweg	legal route (to a particular court). See Creifelds under *Rechtsweg* and Chapters XII, p 99 and XIV, p 132
Rechtswidrig(keit)	illegal(ity). Also: *Widerrechtlich*
Rechtszug	(court) instance. See Chapter XII, pp 94 and 105
Rechtzeitig	in (good) time. See Chapter XII, p 112

Referendar	a prospective *Rechtsanwalt* between the first and second *Staatsprüfung*; after the second: *Assessor*. See Chapter XIX, pp 165 and 172. See also Creifelds under *Referendar*
Reformatio in peius	it is not permitted, on appeal, to amend a decision to the detriment of the appellant. See Creifelds under *reformatio in peius*; Chapter XV (note 11)
Regelunterhalt	type of maintenance for an illegitimate child. See Chapter XII, p 114 and Creifelds under *Unterhaltsprozeß*
Regelungsfrage	regulatory question; question of regulation. See Chapter XVII (note 22)
Regierung	government. See Creifelds under *Regierung*
Regierungsbezirk	governmental area, district. See Creifelds under *Regierungsbezirk* and Chapter V, p 16
Regierungspräsident	president of the government (of a *Regierungsbezirk*). See Chapter V, p 16
Regreß	regress. Also: *Rückgriff*
Reichskammergericht	Imperial Chamber (Court). See Chapter I, p 2
Reichsversicherungsordnung(RVO)	Imperial Insurance Order. See Chapter XVII, p 160
Reisevertrag	travel contract. See Creifelds under *Reisevertrag* and Chapter X, p 58 (Title 7)
Relatives Recht	relative right. *Cf Absolutes Recht* and see Chapter X, p 33
Religionsunterricht	religious instruction. See Chapter VIII (Article 7 GG) and Creifelds under *Religions-unterricht*
Rentenschuld	regular land charge, ie a property is charged not for a fixed amount, but as security for regular, successive payments. See Chapter X and Creifelds under *Rentenschuld*
Replik	the plaintiff's reply to a *Klageerwiderung*. See Chapter XII, p 111
Restitutionsklage	type of writ seeking *Wiederaufnahme*. See also *Nichtigkeitsklage*
Revisio	appeal (on point of law). See Creifelds under *Revision, Einheitlichkeit der Rechtsprechung* and Chapter XII, p 112
Rezeption des römischen Rechts	reception of Roman law (in Germany in the Middle Ages). See Chapter I (note 5)
Rheinbund	Confederation of the Rhine. See Chapter I (note 6)

Rheinland-Pfalz	Rhineland-Palatinate. See Chapter V, p 15
Richter	judge. See Creifelds under *Richter* and *Richtergesetze* and Chapter XIX, p 165
Richterliche Frist	*Frist* set by a judge. See Chapter XII, p 105
Richterliche Rechtsfortbildung	development of the law by the judiciary. Also: *Richterrecht*
Richterliches Prüfungsrecht	the judiciary's (inherent) right to check the validity and constitutionality of a *Rechtsnorm*. See Creifelds under *Richterliches Prüfungsrecht* and Chapter VII, pp 19 and 20
Richterrecht	judge-made law. See Chapter XIII (note 1). Also: *Richterliche Rechtsfortbildung*
Richterwahlausschuß	judicial selection council. See Chapter XIX, p 165
Richtlinie	directive. See: Chapter XIX, p 173; Creifelds under *Richtlinien*; *Verwaltungsvorschrift*
Rückgriff	regress. See Creifelds under *Regreß*
Rückgriffskondiktion	type of *Nichtleistungskondiktion*, where the claimant takes regress against a person, who has obtained a benefit at the former's expense
Rücknahme	withdrawal, taking back. Can refer to a *Klage*, *Rechtsmittel* or VA. See Chapter XIII, p 127 and *cf Rücktritt*
Rücksicht(nehmen)	(to take into) consideration, account
Rücktritt	withdrawal, rescission. See Creifelds under *Rücktritt vom Vertrag* and Chapter X, p 53 (Title 5)
Rückwirkung	retrospective effect, application. See Creifelds under *Rückwirkung von Gesetzen* and Chapter XV, p 133
Rüge	objection. See also: *Einspruch*, *Einwendung* and *Einrede*
Ruhen	to rest; the resting of. See Chapter XII, p 105
Rundfunk- und Fernsehanstalt	radio and television station; broadcasting institution. See Chapter II (note 6)
Sach- und Streitstand	(the) non-contentious and contentious subject-matter, position (in the case). See Chapter XII, p 112
Sachdienlich	appropriate, helpful (to the matter). See Chapter XII, p 104

Sache	(corporeal) thing; matter. See Creifelds under *Sache* and Chapter X, pp 32 and 71. See also *Bestandteil* and *Zubehör*
Sachenrecht	law of property. See Chapter X, p 71
Sachgebiet	subject area. See Chapter X (note 3)
Sachgesamtheit	collection of *Sachen*. See Chapter X, p 71
Sachherrschaft	dominance over a *Sache*. See Chapter X, p 71
Sachlegitimation	legitimation (in proceedings); can be active or passive. See Chapter XII, p 103
Sachlich	factual; pertinent; to the point; substantive
Sachurteil	judgment on the substantive matter, point
Sachurteilsvoraussetzung	(pre)condition for a (substantive) judgment in the proceedings. Also called *Prozeßvoraussetzung* and *Zulässigkeitsvoraus-setzung*. See Chapter XII, p 99
Sachverhalt	set of facts, position (in a particular case)
Sachverständiger	expert. See *Beweismittel*
Satzung	bye-law; company agreement of a *Verein* or *Juristische Person*. See Chapters VI, XI, p 83 and XIII, p 121. See also *Gesetz*. The *Geschäftsordnung* of federal, state and local parliaments can be issued in this form.
Schadensersatz	damages, compensation. See Creifelds under *Schadensersatz* and *cf Entschädigung*. See also Chapter X, p 51 (Title 1)
Schadloshalten	to indemnify. See Chapter XII, p 98
Scheidung	divorce. See Creifelds under *Ehescheidung* and Chapter X, p 78
Schenkung	gift. See Chapter X, p 58 (Title 2)
Schickschuld	see *Leistungsort*
Schiedsgericht	court of arbitration. See Chapter XII, p 119
Schiedsrichterliches Verfahren	arbitration procedure. See Chapter XII, pp 94 and 119
Schiedsvertrag	arbitration agreement. See Chapter XII, p 119
Schlechtleistung	bad performance. Can found a claim for positive *Vertragsverletzung* (PVV)
Schlichte Tätigkeitsdelikt	crime merely requiring a particular activity. *Cf Erfolgsdelikt* and see Chapter XV, p 134
Schlichtes Verwaltungshandeln	pure administrative action, rather than *Hoheitliches Verwaltungshandeln*. See Chapter XIV, p 131

Schlüssig(keit)	apparent(ly) well-founded(ness) (of a *Klage*). See Chapter XII, p 110 and Creifelds under *Schlüssigkeit*
Schlüssiges Verhalten	conduct amounting to, by implication to (a *Willenserklärung*). See Chapter X, p 39 (The term *Willenserklärung*)
Schlüssigkeitsprüfung	test of apparent well-foundedness. See Chapter XII (note 52)
Schmerzensgeld	damages for pain and suffering. See Creifelds under *Schmerzensgeld*. *Cf Schadensersatz*
Schöffe	lay criminal judge, magistrate. See Creifelds under *Schöffen* and Chapter XIX, p 166 (note 4)
Schranke(n)	limit(s) of (a) basic right(s); can in turn be subject to a *Schranke-Schranke*. See Creifelds under *Grundrechte* 4 and Chapter VIII, p 24
Schranke-Schranke	see *Schranke*
Schreiben	to write; letter. See Chapter XIX, p 177 (note 85)
Schriftliches Vorverfahren	preliminary written procedure. See Creifelds under *Mündliche Verhandlung* and Chapter XII, p 110
Schriftsatz	pleading. See Chapter XII, p 104 and Creifelds under *Schriftsätze*
Schuld	blame, guilt (in criminal law); debt. See Chapter XV, p 138 and *cf Verschulden*
Schuldanerkenntnis	acknowledgement of debt. See Creifelds under *Schuldanerkenntnis* and Chapter X, p 59 (Title 20). *Cf Schuldversprechen*
Schuldangemessen	appropriate to (the) *Schuld*. See Chapter XV (note 63)
Schuldausschließungsgrund	reason excluding (justifying the exclusion of) *Schuld*. See Chapter XV, p 140. See also *Tatbestandsirrtum*, *Verbotsirrtum* and *Notstand*
Schuldbeitritt	accession of a debtor in addition to the existing one(s). *Cf Schuldübernahme*
Schuldfähig	capable of blame. See Chapter XV, p 138. *Cf Schuldunfähig*
Schuldner	debtor. See Chapter X, p 50
Schuldrecht	law of obligations. Also: *Recht der Schuldverhältnisse*. See Creifelds under *Schuldrecht* and Chapter X, p 47

Schuldübernahme	substitution (of one debtor for another). See Creifelds under *Schuldübernahme*. Cf *Schuldbeitritt* and *Abtretung*. See also Chapter X, p 58
Schuldunfähig(keit)	incapable of (incapacity for) blame. See Chapter XV (note 42)
Schuldverhältnis	obligation. See: Chapter X, p 59; Creifelds under *Schuldverhältnis* and *Schuldrecht*
Schuldverschreibung auf den Inhaber	promissory note, debenture. See Creifelds under *Inhaberschuldverschreibung* and *Inhaberpapier*. See also Chapter X (Title 22)
Schuldversprechen	(binding) promise. See Chapter X, p 59 (Title 20). Cf *Schuldanerkenntnis*
Schulwesen	school system. See Chapter VIII (Article 7 GG)
Schutz	protection
Schutzbereich	protected area. See Chapter VIII, p 24
Schutzgesetz	protective statute. See Chapter X (note 87)
Schutzpflicht	duty of protection. See Chapter XVII, p 161
Schweben(d)	(to be) pending, remain(ing) in suspense, abeyance. See Chapter X, p 36 and (note 25)
Schweigen	to be silent; silence. Also: *Stillschweigen*. See Chapter X, pp 39 and 44
Schwierig(keit)	difficult(y)
Seehandel	sea trade. See Chapter XI, p 82
Selbstbestimmungsrecht	right of self-determination. See Chapter II, p 9
Selbsthilfe	self-help. See Creifelds under *Selbsthilfe* and Chapter X, p 46
Selbstorganschaft	(principle of the) personal direction of a company by its members. See Chapter XI, p 62
Selbstverteidigung	self-defence. Also: *Notwehr*. See Chapter X, p 46
Selbstverwaltungsangelegenheiten	autonomous matters; also known as *eigene Aufgaben*. See Chapter VI
Sicherheit	security
Sicherheitsbeauftragter	safety officer. See Chapter XVII, p 160
Sicherheitsleistung	(provision of) security (for costs). See Creifelds under *Sicherheitsleistung*; Chapter X, p 46; Chapter XII, p 97
Sichern	to secure
Sicherung	the securing of

Sicherungshypothek	security mortgage. It is a means of enforcement regarding a money claim. See Chapter XII (note 82)
Sicherungsrecht	security right. See Chapter X, p 71
Sicherungsübereignung	transfer of ownership (of a movable) as security, chattel mortgage. See Creifelds under *Sicherungsübereignung*, Chapter X, p 75 and (note 109). See also *Besitzkonstitut*
Sicherungsverfahren	security proceedings. See Creifelds under *Sicherungsverfahren* and Chapter XVI, p 149
Sicherungsverwahrung	placement in secure custody. See Chapter XV, p 144
Singularzulassung	(principle of) simultaneous admission (of *Rechtsanwälte*). See Chapter XIX, p 173
Sittenwidrig(keit)	(in) breach of good morals. See Creifelds under *Sittenwidrigkeit* and Chapter X (note 43)
Sitz	seat, registered address (of a company). A *Wohnsitz* is the residence of a person
Sofortige Vollziehung	immediate enforcement (of a VA). See Creifelds under *Vollziehung, sofortige*, Chapter XIII (note 14) and Chapter XVII (note 39)
Sofortiger Vollzug	see *Sofortige Vollziehung*
Sollkaufmann	a person who, due to the type and extent of his or her activities, should be a *Kaufmann*. See Chapter XI, p 84
Sondergesetz	special law. See Chapter IX, p 29
Sonderrecht	special law, right. See Chapter XI, p 81
Sorgfalt	care. See Chapter XV, p 141
Sorgfaltspflicht	duty of care. See Chapter XI, p 90. See also *Verkehrs(sicherungs)pflicht*
Sozialgericht (SG)	Social (Security) Court. See Chapter XIX, p 171
Sozialgerichtsbarkeit	social jurisdiction. See Creifelds under *Sozialgerichtsbarkeit* and Chapter XIX, p 171
Sozialgerichtsgesetz (SGG)	Law Relating to the Social (Security) Courts. See Chapter XIX, p 171
Sozialtypisches Verhalten	socio-typical behaviour. See Chapter X (note 49)
Spediteur	carrier, forwarder, haulier. See Creifelds under *Spediteur* and Chapter X (note 109)
Spedition	forwarding agency. See Chapter XI, p 71
Spezial	special. See Chapter X, p 71

Spezialität	speciality. See Chapter X, p 71
Spiel	game. See Chapter X, p 59 (Title 17)
Staatenbund	confederation (of states). See Creifelds under *Staatenbund*, Chapter I (note 12) and Chapter II, p 5
Staatsangehörigkeit	citizenship. See Creifelds under *Staatsangehörigkeit*. See also *Ausbürgerung*
Staatsanwalt(schaft)	public prosecutor(s office). See Creifelds under *Staatsanwaltschaft* and Chapter XVI, p 146
Staatsgerichtshof	constitutional court (in Baden-Württemberg, Bremen, Hessen and Niedersachsen). See Creifelds under *Staatsgerichtshof* and Chapter VII (note 6)
Staatsgewalt	state power. See Creifelds under *Staatsgewalt* and Chapter II, pp 5 and 7
Staatskanzlei	state chancellery (of a *Land*). See Chapter V, p 16
Staatsprüfung	State Examination (eg to become a *Rechtsanwalt*). See Chapter XIX, p 165
Staatsrecht	state law. See Chapter IX, p 29 and Creifelds under *Staatsrecht*
Staatsverwaltung	state administration, executive. See Chapters II, p 5, IV and V, p 15
Stadt	town, city. See Chapter VI
Stadtstaat	city state. See Chapter V, p 15
Stadtverordnetenversammlung	see *Gemeindevertretung*
Standesrecht	(legal) principles of professional conduct. See Chapter XIX, p 175
Ständig	continuous(ly), constantly. See *Handelsvertreter*
Steckbrief	warrant of apprehension. See Chapter XVI (note 23) and *cf Haftbefehl*
Stelle	point, place, office. See Chapter XII, p 107 and Chapter XIII, p 61
Stellvertreter	see *Vertreter*
Steuer(recht)	tax (law). See the terminology in Creifelds after *Steuer*
Stiftung	foundation; it can be one of private or public law. See Creifelds under *Stiftung des Privatrechts* and *Stiftung öffentlichen Rechts*. See also Chapter II, p 5
Stille Gesellschaft	silent partnership. See Chapter XI, pp 85 and 89

Stillschweigen	silence. See *Schweigen*
Strafantrag	application for prosecution. See Creifelds under *Strafantrag* and Chapter XVI, p 145
Strafanzeige	notice of an offence, complaint. See Creifelds under *Strafanzeige* and Chapter XVI, p 145
Strafaufhebungsgrund	reason to lift a *Strafe*. See *Strafausschließungs-grund*
Strafausschließungsgrund	reason to exclude a *Strafe*. See Creifelds under *Strafausschließungsgründe*, Chapter XV, p 142 and also: *Strafaufhebungsgrund*
Strafaussetzung zur Bewährung	suspension of sentence on probation. See Creifelds under *Probation*, *Strafaussetzung* and Chapter XV, p 142
Strafbarkeit	punishability. See Chapter XV, p 133
Strafbefehl	punishment order. See Creifelds under *Straf-befehl* and Chapter XVI, p 150
Strafe	punishment. See Chapter XV, p 142
Strafgesetzbuch (StGB)	Criminal Code; Penal Code. See Creifelds under *Strafgesetzbuch* and Chapter XV, p 133
Strafprozeßordnung (StPO)	Criminal Procedure Order. See Creifelds under *Strafprozeß(recht)* III and Chapter XVI, p 145
Strafrecht	criminal law. See Creifelds under *Strafrecht* and Chapter XV
Strafrichter	single criminal judge. See Chapter XVI (note 2) and *Einzelrichter*
Straftat	(criminal) offence, crime. It can be a *Verbrechen* or a *Vergehen*: see Chapter XV, p 133
Strafverfahren	criminal (punishment) proceedings. See Chapter XVI
Strafverfolgung	pursuit of crime. See Chapter XVI (note 20)
Strafvollstreckung	enforcement of punishment. See Chapter XVI, pp 145 and 152
Strafvorbehalt	reservation of punishment. See Chapter XV (note 62) and *Verwarnung*
Straßenverkehrsgesetz	Road Traffic Law. See Chapter XV (note 6) and Creifelds under *Straßenverkehrsrecht*
Streik	strike. It is a means of *Arbeitskampf*. See Chapter XVII (note 36) and Creifelds under *Streik*.
Streit	dispute. Also: *Rechtsstreit*
Streitgegenstand	object of the action, matter in dispute. Also: *Streitsache*. See Chapter XII, p 107

Streitgenossen	joint parties. See Chapter XII, p 96 and *Streitgenossenschaft*
Streitgenossenschaft	joinder of parties. See Creifelds under *Streitgenossenschaft*
Streithilfe	see *Nebenintervention*
Streitig(keit)	in dispute, disputed, contentious; dispute
Streitsache	see *Streitgegenstand*
Streitverkündung	notification of dispute, third party notice. See Creifelds under *Streitverkündung* and Chapter XII, p 98
Streitwert	value of the (matter in) dispute. See Creifelds under *Streitwert* and Chapter XIX, p 174 (note 70)
Strengbeweis	(the principle of) strict evidence. *Cf Freibeweis* and see *Beweismittel*
Stückschuld	specific (individual) debt
Stundung	respite. It postpones the *Fälligkeit* of a *Leistung*. See Chapter X (note 55)
Sub judice	see *Rechtshängig*
Subjektives öffentliches Recht	public subjective right. See Chapter X (note 16) and Creifelds under *Subjektives öffentliches Recht*
Subjektives Recht	subjective legal right. See Creifelds under *Subjektives Recht* and Chapter X, p 33. *Cf Rechtsreflex*
Subsidiaritätsprinzip	subsidiarity principle. See Creifelds under *Subsidiarität* and Chapter VII (note 11)
Subsumtion	subsumption (of facts under a legal norm). See Chapter X (note 60)
Syndikus(anwalt)	in-house lawyer. He cannot represent his employer in his capacity of *Rechtsanwalt* before a court. See Chapter XIX (note 58); § 46 BRAO and § 40 BRAK *Richtlinien*
Tagessatz	daily rate. See Chapter XV, p 142
Tarifvertrag	tariff agreement. See Chapter XVII
Tarifvertragsgesetz (TVG)	Law Relating to Tariff Agreements. See Chapter XVII (note 37)
Tat(be/um)standsirrtum	mistaken belief that an element of a (criminal) *Tatbestand* does not exist. It is a *Schuldausschließungsgrund* (§ 16 StGB). See Chapter XV, p 140

Tatbestand	substantive part of a legal norm, its content; to be distinguished from its *Rechtsfolge*. See Chapter X (note 17); Chapter XIII, p 128 and Chapter XV, p 135. See also *Urteil*
Tatbestandsmäßig(keit)	(in) accordance with a *Tatbestand*
Tatbestandsmerkmal	element of a *Tatbestand*. Also called a *Tatumstand*
Täter	perpetrator (of a crime). See Creifelds under *Täter*, Chapter XV, pp 137 and 138. See also *Mittäter*
Tätig(keit)	active(ity)
Tatsache	fact. See Chapter XII, p 104
Tatsächlich	actual; really. See Chapter X, p 71
Tatsächliche Vermutung	actual presumption. See *Vermutung*
Tatsachenvermutung	presumption of fact. *Cf Tatsächliche Vermutung* and see Chapter XII (note 3)
Tausch	exchange, barter. See Chapter X, p 61 and Creifelds under *Tausch*
Teilhaber	shareholder, participant. See *Gemeinschaft nach Bruchteilen* and Chapter XI, p 82
Teilnahme am allgemeinen Verkehr	participation in general traffic. See Chapter XVII, p 160
Teilurteil	partial judgment. See *Urteil*
Tendenzbetrieb	*Betrieb* with a particular social purpose
Termin	hearing (date), appointment, date. See Chapter XII, p 105
Testament	will. See: Creifelds under *Testament* and *Verfügung von Todes wegen*; Chapter X, pp 72 and 80 and Chapter XIX, p 178
Titel	title; can include a court judgment. See Chapter XII, p 116
Tod	death. See Chapter X, p 80 (§ 1922(i) BGB)
Todeserklärung	declaration of death. See Creifelds under *Todeserklärung* and see Chapter X, p 79
Träger	carrier(s). See *Rechtsfähigkeit* and *Verwaltungsträger*
Tragweite	range, implication, effect. See Chapter XIX, p 178
Treuepflicht	(employee's) duty of loyalty. See Chapter XVII (note 44)

Treu und Glauben	(principle of) trust and good faith. It applies throughout German private, public and procedural law. See Creifelds under *Treu und Glauben*, Chapter X (note 36) and p 45 and see also §§ 157, 162 and 242 BGB.
Tun	to do; can also mean act (noun). See Chapter XV, p 137
Typenfreiheit	free choice of type. See Chapter X, p 71 and *cf* *Typenzwang*
Typenzwang	compulsory choice of type. *Cf Typenfreiheit*
Übereignung	transfer of ownership. See Chapter X, p 75
Übergabe	transfer of physical possession, handing over, delivery (of). See Chapter X, p 75
Übermaßverbot	prohibition of excess. See Creifelds under *Übermaßverbot* and Chapter, p 25
Überordnung	dominance. See Chapter IX, p 29
Überörtliche Angelegenheiten	local matters extending beyond the capacity of a *Gemeinde*. See Chapter VI
Überschreiten	to transgress, exceed. See Chapter XIII, p 127 and Chapter XV (note 43)
Übertragen	to transfer, allocate, transmit
Übertragene Aufgaben	transferred or allocated tasks, matters. Also: *Auftragsangelegenheiten*. See Chapter VI
Übertragene Geschäfte	transferred business, matters. See Chapter XIX, p 167
Übertragung	transfer; allocation; transmission. See *Übereignung*
Überwiegend	predominantly, mainly
Überzeugen	to convince
Überzeugung	conviction, firm belief. See *Beweiswürdigung*
Ultima ratio	final measure, step; last resort. See Chapter XV, p 142
Umfang	extent. See *Vollmacht*
Umgestalten	to rearrange, reshape
Umgestaltung	rearrangement, reshaping. See Chapter XII, p 107
Umkehr der Beweislast	reversal of the burden of proof. See Chapter XII (note 3)
Umweltrecht	environmental law. See Chapter XIV (note 11)

Unabhängig(keit)	independent(ce). See Chapters II, p 9, XIX, pp 166 and 172
Unanfechtbar(keit)	non-(un-)challengeable(ility). See Chapter XVII (note 39)
Unaufschiebbar	incapable of postponement. See Chapter XIII (note 14)
Unbegründet	unfounded. *Cf Begründet*
Unbeschränkt	unlimited
Unbestimmt	indefinite.
Unbestimmter Rechtsbegriff	indefinite legal term. See Creifelds under *Unbestimmte Rechtsbegriffe* and Chapter XIII, p 127. *Cf Ermessen*
Unbeweglich	immovable (*adj*). *Cf Beweglich*
Unbewußt	unconscious (non-medical sense). See Chapter XV, p 140
Unbrauchbarmachung	rendering (something) useless; neutralisation (of). See Creifelds under *Unbrauchbarmachung* and Chapter XV, p 144
Unecht	not genuine, false, artificial. See Chapter XV, p 137
Unehelich	illegitimate (child). Also *Nichtehelich*
Unerläßlich	essential. See Chapter XV, p 142
Unerlaubte Handlung	tort, tortious act. See Creifelds under *Unerlaubte Handlung, Delikt* and Chapter X, p 59 (Title 25)
Unfallschutz	protection against accident. See Creifelds under *Unfallschutz* and Chapter XVII, p 161
Unfallverhütungsvorschriften	regulations for the prevention of accidents. See Chapter XVII, p 161
Ungerechtfertigte Bereicherung	unjust enrichment. See Creifelds under *Ungerechtfertigte Bereicherung*, Chapter X, p 59 (Title 24), *Leistungskondiktion* and *Nichtleistungskondiktion*
Unkenntnis	ignorance
Unmittelbar	direct(ly)
Unmittelbar betroffen	directly affected. See Chapter VII, p 20
Unmittelbar drohende Gefahr	immediate threat of danger. See Chapter XVII (note 39)
Unmittelbarer Zwang	direct force. See Chapter XVII (note 39)
Unmittelbar geltendes Recht	directly applicable law. See Chapter VIII, p 23

Unmittelbarkeitsgrundsatz	directness principle, ie hearing and evidence must take place/be presented directly before the court considering the case. See Creifelds under *Unmittelbarkeitsgrundsatz* and Chapter XII, p 95
Unmöglichkeit	impossibility. See Chapter X (note 74) and Chapter X, p 54
Unparteiisch	impartial. See Chapter XIX, p 179
Unrechtmäßiger Besitzer	person in illegal possession. See Chapter X note 106
Unrechtsbewußtsein	consciousness of illegality. See Creifelds under *Bewußtsein der Rechtswidrigkeit* and Chapter XV, p 141
Unterbrechung	interruption. See Chapters X, p 47 and XII, p 105
Untere Landesbehörde	lower authority of a *Land*. See Chapter V, p 16
Untere Verwaltungsbehörde	lower administrative authority. See Chapters IV and V, p 16
Untereinander	amongst each other. See Chapter XI, p 86
Unterhalt	maintenance (payment). See Creifelds under *Unterhaltspflicht* and Chapter X, p 79
Unterlassen	to omit (stop) to do. It can also mean omission (noun)
Unterlassung	omission. It can mean stoppage/restraint (of a disturbance (*Störung*). See Creifelds under *Unterlassungsanspruch*, Chapter X, p 77 and Chapter XI, p 131
Unterlassungsdelikt	crime by omission. See Chapter XV, p 137
Unternehmen	(whole) enterprise, business. See Creifelds under *Unternehmen*. Cf *Betrieb* and *Gewerbe*
Unternehmer	businessman, *entrepreneur*. See Chapter XI, p 84 and also *Kaufmann*
Unterordnung	subordination. See Chapter IX, p 29
Unterstufe	lower level. See Chapter V, p 16
Untersuchung	examination, investigation. See Chapter XVI, pp 145 and 146 and see also *Ermittlung, Durchsuchung, Prüfung*
Untersuchungsgrundsatz	inquisition maxim; applies in criminal and administrative law and in FGG matters. See Creifelds under *Untersuchungsgrundsatz* and Chapter XII, p 93

Untersuchungshaft	remand in custody (for investigation). See Creifelds under *Untersuchungshaft* and Chapter XVI, p 146
Unvereinbar	incompatible. See Chapter VII (note 13)
Unverhältnismäßig	disproportionate; unreasonable
Unverjährbar	not subject to *Verjährung*
Unverletzlich(keit)	inviolable(ility). See Chapter VIII, p 26
Unversehrtheit	intactness, integrity. See Chapter VIII, p 24
Unverzüglich	without delay, forthwith. See Creifelds under *Unverzüglich* and Chapter X, pp 42 and 44
Unwirksam	ineffective. See Chapter X (note 26) and Chapter XIII, p 124 (note 12)
Unzulässig	inadmissible; not allowed. See Creifelds under *Unzulässigkeit* and Chapters XI, p 99 and XIV, p 131
Unzweideutig	in no uncertain terms, unequivocal(ly). See Chapter XIX, p 178
Urheber	author, creator. See Chapter XII, p 100
Urheberrecht	copyright (law). See Creifelds under *Urheberrecht*
Urkunde	a document. Formal definition: *eine in Schriftzeichen verkörperte Gedankenäusserung* (a declaration of thoughts incorporated in script). See Creifelds under *Urkunde* and Chapter XIX, p 178
Urkundenprozeß	(particular form of) action on the basis of (an) *Urkunde(n)*. See Creifelds under *Urkundenprozeß* and Chapter XII, p 114
Urkundenrolle	(annual) roll of *Urkunden* (maintained by a *Notar*). See Chapter XIX, p 178
Ursächlich(keit)	causal, causation; also: *Kausal(ität)*. See Chapter XV, p 135
Urteil	judgment; can be final (*Endurteil*) or interim (*Zwischenurteil*). A final judgment can be full (*Vollurteil*) or partial (*Teilurteil*). An *Urteil* consists of a heading (*Urteilskopf* or *Rubrum*), a tenor (*Urteilsformel*) and (usually separately) a *Tatbestand* (substantive part) and *Entscheidungsgründe* (reasons); § 313(i) ZPO. See Creifelds under *Urteil* and *Urteilsverfahren* and see Chapter XII, p 95

Valutaverhältnis	value relationship, relationship in which value (is to) pass(es). *Cf Deckungsverhältnis.* See Chapter X, p 59 (Title 21)
Verantworten	to answer (take responsibility) for
Verantwortung	responsibility
Verarbeitung	processing. See Creifelds under *Verarbeitung* and Chapter X, p 75
Veräußerer	transferor (vendor). See Chapter X, p 75 (*Bona fide* acquisition of ownership to movables)
Veräußerungsverbot	provision restricting disposal (sale). See Creifelds under *Veräußerungsverbot* and Chapter X, p 72
Verband	federation. See Creifelds under *Verbände*
Verbandsklage	action by a federation. See Creifelds under *Verbandsklage* and Chapter XIV (note 11)
Verbindung	connection. See Creifelds under *Verbindung von Sachen* and Chapter X, p 75
Verbot	prohibition. See Chapter XIII, p 126
Verbotsirrtum	mistaken belief that an act is not illegal. It can be a *Schuldausschließungsgrund*, if the mistake was unavoidable (§ 17 StGB). See Creifelds under *Verbotsirrtum* and Chapter XV, p 140
Verbotsnorm	(criminal) norm forbidding certain action or injury to a *Rechtsgut.* See Chapter XV, p 137
Verbraucher	consumer. See Chapter XVIII, p 163
Verbraucherkreditgesetz	Consumer Credit Law. See *Abzahlungskauf*
Verbrechen	category of *Straftat.* See Chapter XV, p 133
Verdacht	suspicion. See Chapter XVI, p 150
Verdächtigter	suspect (person). See Chapter XVI, p 150
Verdunkeln	to obscure. See Chapter XVI (note 23)
Verdunkelungsgefahr	danger of justice being obstructed (obscured). See Chapter XVI (note 23)
Verein	club, association; eV = *eingetragener* (registered) *Verein.* Prototype of *Juristische Person, Körperschaft.* See Creifelds under *Verein* and Chapter XI, p 82. See also *Vorstand*
Vereinbar	compatible. See Chapter VII (note 13)
Vereinfacht	simplified; simply
Vereinigung	association; union. See Chapter V, p 15 and Chapter VIII, p 26. *Cf Gewerkschaft*

Vereinigungsfreiheit	freedom of (private) association, also called *Vereinsautonomie*. See Creifelds under *Vereins(Vereinigungs)freiheit* and Chapter VIII (Article 9 GG). *Cf Koalitionsfreiheit*
Verfahren	procedure; proceedings
Verfahrensrecht	procedural law. Also *Prozeßrecht*
Verfall	forfeiture, expiration. See Chapter XV, p 144
Verfassung	constitution; (physical) condition. See Creifelds under *Verfassung* and Chapters V, p 15 and VII
Verfassungsbeschwerde	constitutional complaint. See Creifelds under *Verfassungsbeschwerde* and Chapter VII, p 20
Verfassungsgemäß	in accordance with the constitution, constitutional
Verfassungsgericht	constitutional court. See Creifelds under *Verfassungsgerichtsbarkeit* and Chapter VII, p 20
Verfassungskonforme Auslegung	interpretation of *Rechtsnormen* so as to conform with the constitution (GG). See Creifelds under *Auslegung I 5* and *Verfassungswidrigkeit von Gesetzen* and see Chapter VII, p 20
Verfassungsmäßige Ordnung	constitutional order. See Chapter II, p 9
Verfassungsmäßigkeit	accordance with the constitution, constitutionality. *Cf Verfassungswidrig*
Verfassungsorgan	supreme federal (constitutional) organ (ie mentioned in the constitution). See Chapter III
Verfassungsrecht	constitutional law (ie law of the constitution only). *Cf Staatsrecht*
Verfassungsschutz	protection of the constitution, constitutional protection. See Chapter XVI (note 19)
Verfassungsstreit(igkeit)	constitutional dispute. See Chapter VII (note 5) and *Enumerationsprinzip*
Verfassungswidrig(keit)	unconstitutional(ity). See Creifelds under *Verfassungswidrigkeit von Gesetzen*; Chapter II, p 9; and Chapter VII, pp 20 and 21
Verfügung	the transfer, release, burdening or variation of a (subjective) right; legal act or legal transaction in that sense.
	Different senses in which the word can be used: a decision or direction of the presiding judge (*Verfügung des Vorsitzenden*); an injunction (*einstweilige Verfügung*); a police order (*polizeiliche Verfügung*); an official order or direction (*ordnungsbehördliche Verfügung*). See Creifelds under *Verfügung* (*rechtsgeschäftliche*, *gerichtliche* and *behördliche*) and Chapter X, p 72

Verfügungsbefugnis	entitlement to undertake a *Verfügung*. See Creifelds under *Verfügungsbefugnis* and Chapter X, p 72.
	Regarding the effect of a *Verfügung* purported to be undertaken by a third party without *Verfügungsbefugnis* see Creifelds under *Verfügung eines Nichtberechtigten* and *Gutglaubensschutz*
Verfügungsbeschränkung	provision limiting a person's *Verfügungsbefugnis*. See Chapter X, p 72
Verfügungsgrundsatz	see *Dispositionsgrundsatz*
Vergehen	category of *Straftat*. See Chapter XV, p 133
Vergleich	settlement (of dispute by way of agreement); comparison. See Creifelds under *Vergleich* and Chapter X, p 59 (Title 19)
Vergleichsgebühr	settlement fee. See Chapter XIX (note 75)
Vergütung	reimbursement, reward, payment
Verhaftung	see *Festnahme*
Verhalten	behaviour; conduct. See Chapter X, p 39. (The term *Willenserklärung*); Chapter X (note 49) and Chapter XV, p 135
Verhältnismäßig	proportional, fair. See Chapter VIII, p 24
Verhältnismäßigkeitsgrundsatz	principle of proportionality, relative fairness. See Creifelds under *Verhältnismäßigkeit(sgrundsatz)* and Chapters VIII (note 9), XIII (note 20), XV (note 66) and XVI (note 18)
Verhandlung	hearing
Verhandlung zur Hauptsache	hearing on the substantive issue. See Chapter XII (note 62). *Cf Hauptverhandlung*
Verhandlungsgebühr	hearing fee. See Chapter XIX, p 175
Verhandlungsgrundsatz	principle that an action proceeds on the basis of facts and applications made by the parties; also: *Beibringungsgrundsatz*. See: Creifelds under *Verhandlungsgrundsatz* and *Da mihi factum, dabo tibi ius*; Chapter XII, p 93
Verhandlungsprotokoll	record, protocol of the hearing. See Chapter XII, p 104
Verhüten	to prevent. See Chapter XVI, p 146
Verjährung	limitation (of action), prescription. See Creifelds under *Verjährung* I and Chapter X *Exposé*

Verkehrs(sicherungs)pflicht	duty of care (safety). An *unerlaubte Handlung* (tort) can be committed through an omission to observe it. See Creifelds under *Verkehrs-sicherungspflicht*; Chapter X (note 89). See also *Sorgfaltspflicht*
Verkünden	to proclaim, pronounce
Verkündung	proclamation (of a law or legal provision); pronouncement (of court's decision). See Chapter XII, p 113; Creifelds under *Ver-kündung von Rechtsvorschriften* and *Urteil* and see also *Bekanntmachung* and *Veröffentlichung*
Verletzen	to injure, infringe, breach
Verletzung	injury, infringement, breach. See Chapter VIII, p 24
Verlöbnis	engagement (before marriage). See Creifelds under *Verlöbnis* and Chapter X, p 79
Verlust	loss. See Chapter X, p 75
Vermächtnis	legacy, bequest (§§ 1939, 2147-2191 BGB). See Creifelds under *Vermächtnis* and Chapter X, p 80
Vermeidbar	avoidable. See Chapter XV, p 140
Vermeiden	to avoid
Vermerk	note (under seal). See Chapter XIX, p 179
Vermischung	mixture. See Creifelds under *Vermischung* and Chapter X, p 75
Vermitteln	to mediate, procure, arrange, obtain (for)
Vermittlung	mediation, arrangement, intercession (good offices)
Vermittlungsausschuß	mediation board/council. It is often convened (einberufen) under Article 77(ii) GG to resolve differences of opinion (*Meinungsverschieden-heiten*) between the *Bundestag* and *Bundesrat* regarding proposed legislation. See Chapter VII (note 2) and Creifelds under *Vermitt-lungsausschuß*. See also *Zustimmungsgesetz* and *Einspruchsgesetz*
Vermögen	assets, property, fortune, wealth. See Creifelds under *Vermögen*; Chapter X (note 8) and (note 99); Chapter XV (note 11)
Vermögensrechtlich	monetary. See Chapter XII, p 114
Vermuten	to presume, suppose
Vermutlich	presumably. See also *Mutmaßlich*

Vermutung	presumption. It can be *tatsächlich* (actual) or *gesetzlich* (emanating from statute; statutory). See Chapter XII (note 3) and see Creifelds under *Vermutung*
Vernehmung	questioning, interrogation (in criminal proceedings). See Chapter XVI (note 13)
Vernunft	reason; (good) sense. See Chapter I, p 4
Vernünftig	sensible, reasonable. See Chapter XII, p 95
Veröffentlichung	publication. See also *Verkündung*
Verordnung	see *Rechtsverordnung*
Verpflichtung	obligation. See Chapter X, pp 48 and 72
Verpflichtungsklage	writ issued at the VG claiming (obligation to) issue (of) a VA. See Creifelds under *Verwaltungsstreitverfahren* I (a) and Chapter XIV, p 130
Verrat	treason. See Chapter II, p 9
Verrichtungsgehilfe	person entrusted with a particular task; see Creifelds under *unerlaubte Handlung* V and Chapter X, p 59 (Title 25)
Versammlungsfreiheit	freedom of assembly. See Creifelds under *Versammlungsfreiheit* and Chapter VIII, p 26
Versäumnis	a *Nichterscheinen* or *Nichtverhandeln* by a party. Can lead to a *Versäumnisurteil*
Versäumnisurteil	judgment in default (on the basis of a *Versäumnis*; otherwise referred to as being *unecht* (not genuine)). See Creifelds under *Versäumnisurteil* and Chapter XII, p 105
Versäumung	failure to observe time-limit. See Chapter XII, p 105
Verschaffung	procurement, provision (of)
Verschulden	fault, blame (in civil law; § 276 BGB). There are two forms: *Vorsatz* (intent) and *Fahrlässigkeit* (negligence). See Creifelds under *Verschulden* and *cf* the term *Schuld*. See also: *Vertretenmüssen* and *Mitverschulden*; Chapter X (note 74) and Chapter XV, p 139
Verschulden bei Vertragsschluß	see *Culpa in contrahendo*
Versetzen	to transfer, remove (a person), transplant; put into (a position, state). See Chapters XVII and XIX, p 167 (note 17)
Versetzung	transfer, removal, transplanting; putting (into). See Chapter XVII, p 157 and Chapter XIX, p 167 (note 17)

Verspätet	too late, out of time, delayed. See Chapter XII, p 111
Verspätung	delay
Versprechen	promise. See Chapter X, p 53 (Title 3)
Vertagung	postponement, adjournment (of a hearing). See Chapter XII, p 105
Verteidigung	defence
Verteidigungsabsicht	intention to defend. See Chapter XII, p 110
Verteidigungsfall	defence situation. It can arise in the event of a military attack (or threat thereof) on Germany. See Creifelds under *Verteidigungsfall* and Chapter VII (note 4)
Verteidigungsvortrag	submission(s) in the defence (of the *Beklagter*)
Verteilungsverfahren	distribution procedure. See Chapter XII, p 118
Vertrag	contract, agreement. See: Creifelds under *Vertrag*; Chapter X, pp 43 and 48
Vertrag mit Schutzwirkung zugunsten Dritter	contract with protective effect in favour of a third party. See Chapter X (note 77)
Vertragsbedingungen	see *Allgemeine Geschäftsbedingungen*
Vertragsfreiheit	freedom of contract (principle). It is part of the principle of *Privatautonomie*
Vertragsstrafe	contractual penalty. See Chapter X, p 53 (Title 4) and Chapter XI, p 90
Vertrag zugunsten Dritter	contract for the benefit of a third party. See Chapter X, p 53 (Title 3)
Vertretenmüssen	see *Verschulden*
Vertreter	representative, agent. See Chapter XII, p 101
Vertreter ohne Vertretungsmacht	unauthorised representative. See Chapter XII, p 102
Vertretung	representation, representative body, agency. *Cf Geschäftsführung*
Vertretungsbefugnis	right of representation. See Chapter XIX (note 54 B) and also *Vertretungsmacht*
Vertretungsmacht	power to represent, authority. See Chapter XI, p 84 and *Vollmacht*
Verursachen	to cause
Verwahrung	deposit in custody, safe-keeping. See Creifelds under *Verwahrung* and Chapter X, p 59 (Title 12)

Verwaltung	administration, executive. See: Creifelds under *Verwaltung, öffentliche* and *Vollziehende Gewalt*; Chapter II, p 5
Verwaltungsakt	administrative act. See: Creifelds under *Verwaltungsakt*; Chapter XIII, p 123
Verwaltungsaufgabe	administrative function, task. See Chapter II, p 5
Verwaltungsgericht (VG)	administrative court. See Chapters II, p 7, XIV, p 129 and XIX, p 170
Verwaltungsgerichtshof (VGH)	see *Oberverwaltungsgericht*
Verwaltungsgerichtsordnung (VwGO)	Administrative Courts Order. See: Creifelds under *Verwaltungsgerichtsbarkeit*; Chapter XIV, p 129
Verwaltungspolizei	(so-called) administrative police. Incorporated in this term are the terms *Polizeibehörde* and *Ordnungsbehörde. Cf Vollzugspolizei* and see Chapter XVI (note 19)
Verwaltungsprivatrecht	administration in private law form. See: Creifelds under *Verwaltungsprivatrecht*; Chapter II, p 5
Verwaltungsrecht	administrative law. See: Creifelds under *Verwaltungsrecht*; Chapter XIII
Verwaltungsrechtsweg	legal route (access) to the administrative courts. See Chapter XIV, p 130
Verwaltungstätigkeit	administrative activity. See Chapter II, p 5
Verwaltungsträger	carrier of administration. See Chapter II, p 5
Verwaltungsunterbau	administrative sub-construction (structure). See Chapter XIII, p 122
Verwaltungsverfahrensgesetz (VwVfG)	Administrative Procedure Law. See: Creifelds under *Verwaltungsverfahren(sgesetz)*; Chapter XIII, p 122
Verwaltungsvollstreckungsgesetz (VwVG)	Administrative Enforcement Law. See: Creifelds under *Verwaltungsvollstreckungsgesetz*; Chapter XVII (note 39)
Verwaltungsvorschrift	(internal) administrative regulation. See Chapter XIII, p 122, Maurer, Part 6, § 24 and Creifelds under *Verwaltungsvorschriften* and *Weisungsrecht*. See also *Richtlinie*
Verwaltungszwang	administrative force. See: Creifelds under *Verwaltungszwang*; Chapter XVII (note 39)
Verwandlung	transformation. See Chapter X (note 19)
Verwandt(er/schaft)	related, relative, kinship. See Creifelds under *Verwandtschaft* and Chapter X, p 79

Verwarnung	warning, caution. See: Creifelds under *Verwarnung bei Ordnungswidrigkeiten, Verwarnung mit Strafvorbehalt* and *Probation*; Chapter XV (note 6) and (note 62)
Verwarnungsgeld	(money) penalty. *Cf Geldbuße*
Verweisung	(statutory) reference; (procedural) transfer (to another court). See Creifelds under *Verweisung*, Chapter XVIII, p 163 and Chapter XIX (note 54 B)
Verwendung	expenditure (on a *Sache*, whereby it is repaired, maintained or improved, but not fundamentally changed). A *Verwendung* can be *notwendig* (necessary) or *nützlich* (useful). See Chapter X (note 106) and Creifelds under *Verwendungen*. *Cf Aufwendung*
Verwendungskondiktion	type of *Nichtleistungskondiktion*, where the recipient obtains a benefit due to a *Verwendung* by the claimant on something belonging to the recipient
Verwertungsrecht	disposal right. See Chapter X
Verwirkung	forfeiture. See Chapter II, p 9 and Chapter X (Interpretation of a *Willenserklärung*) (note 36)
Verzicht (auf)	renunciation, waiver (of)
Verzug	delay. See Chapter X (note 74)
Vindikation	vindication; return of a *Sache* from someone without a *Recht zum Besitz*. See Creifelds under *Eigentumsherausgabeanspruch* and Chapter X, p 77
Volenti non fit iniuria	no wrong is done to him who consents. See *Einwilligung*
Volk	people. See Chapter II, p 8
Volksabstimmung (Volksentscheid)	plebiscite. See Chapter II (note 11)
Volksgeist	spirit of the people. See Chapter I, p 4
Volkssouveranität	sovereignty of the people. See Chapter II, p 8
Volkszählung	public census. See Chapter VII (note 11)
Völkerrecht	public international law. See Chapter XIII, p 122 and *ius gentium*. See also Creifelds under *Völkerrecht* and *Primat des Völkerrechts*
Volljährig(er)	over the age of majority, adult. Also: *Erwachsen(er)*. *Cf Minderjährig*
Volljährigkeit	age of majority. See Chapter X, p 37

Vollmacht	power of representation, power of attorney, authority (granted by *Rechtsgeschäft* cf statutory authority). See Chapter XII, p 101
Vollmachtgeber	grantor of a *Vollmacht*
Vollmachtlos	without a *Vollmacht*
Vollrecht	full right. See Chapter X, p 72
Vollständig	complete; full(y). See Chapter XII, p 111
Vollstreckbarerklarung	declaration of enforceability. See Chapter XII (note 80)
Vollstreckbar(keit)	enforceable(ility). See Creifelds under *Vollstreckbarkeit*. See also Chapter XII, p 116 and Chapter XVII (note 39)
Vollstreckbare Ausfertigung	enforcement duplicate, copy. See Chapter XII, p 116
Vollstreckung	enforcement. Also: *Zwangsvollstreckung*
Vollstreckungsbescheid	enforcement notice. See Chapter XII, p 96 and *Mahnverfahren*
Vollstreckungserinnerung	legal remedy (to the judge) against a measure taken by a *Rechtspfleger* or judge in enforcement proceedings. See § 766 ZPO. *Cf Erinnerung*
Vollstreckungsgericht	enforcement court. Always the *Amtsgericht*. See Creifelds under *Vollstreckungsgericht*, Chapter XII, p 116 and *cf Prozeßgericht*
Vollstreckungshandlung	act of enforcement
Vollstreckungstitel	title capable of enforcement (*vollstreckbar*). See Creifelds under *Vollstreckungstitel*
Vollstreckungsverfahren	enforcement proceedings. *Cf Erkenntnisverfahren*. See Chapter XII, pp 94 and 116
Vollurteil	full judgment. See *Urteil*
Vollziehbar	enforceable. Also: *Vollstreckbar*
Vollziehbare Anordnung	enforceable order
Vollziehende Gewalt	executive power, executive; also: *Verwaltung*. See Creifelds under *Vollziehende Gewalt* and Chapter II, p 8
Vollziehung	enforcement, execution. See also: *Vollstreckung*, *Vollzug* and *sofortige Vollziehung*
Vollzug	enforcement. See *Vollziehung*
Vollzugsakt	act of implementation, enforcement; implementing measure. See Chapter VII (note 11)
Vollzugspolizei	(so-called) executive police. *Cf Verwaltungspolizei* and see Chapter XVI (note 19)

Von Amts wegen	officially; by the court or authority. See Creifelds under *Amtsgrundsatz*
Von neuem	anew, afresh. See Chapter XII, p 105
Vor die Klammer gezogen	drawn before the clasp, to the front. See Chapter X, p 48
Voraussetzung	(pre-)condition (for)
Vorauszahlung	prepayment
Vorbehalt	reservation. See also *Protestatio*
Vorbehalt des Gesetzes	see *Gesetzesvorbehalt*
Vorbereiten	to prepare
Vorbereitende Maßnahme	preparatory measure. See Chapter XII, p 111
Vorbereitung	preparation (for)
Vorbereitungsdienst	preparatory period of service. See Chapter XIX, p 165
Vorkaufsrecht	right of pre-emption. See Chapter X, p 77
Vorlage(verfahren)	reference (procedure). See *konkrete Normkontrolle*
Vorläufig	provisional(ly), temporary(ily). See *Vollstreckbar(keit)* and *Vorläufiger Rechtsschutz*
Vorläufiger Rechtsschutz	provisional legal protection. See Chapter XIII (note 14)
Vorlegung	presentation. See Chapter X, p 59 (Title 23)
Vormerkung	priority notice (reservation). See Creifelds under *Vormerkung* and Chapter X, p 74
Vormund(schaft)	guardian(ship). See Chapter X, p 78
Vorrang	priority
Vorrang des Gesetzes	(the) priority of statute (and, in a wider sense, of higher ranking norms). See Creifelds under *Vorrang des Gesetzes* and Chapters II, p 9 and VII, p 20
Vorsatz	intent; a form of *Verschulden* in civil law and of *Schuld* in criminal law. Cf *Absicht*
Vorsätzlich	intentionally. Cf *Absichtlich*
Vorschlag(en)	suggestion, to suggest
Vorschrift	provision, rule, regulation. Cf *Abschnitt*
Vorsitzender	presiding person (judge), chairman
Vorsorgende Rechtspflege	precautionary administration of justice. See Chapter XIX, p 178 (note 92)
Vorsorglich	by way of (as a) precaution(ary measure)

Vorstand	board (of directors). It is a compulsory organ of: – a *Verein* (§§ 26-31 BGB); – an *Aktiengesellschaft* (§§ 76-94 AktG); and – a *Genossenschaft* (§§ 24-35 GenG). See Chapter XI, p 82 and Creifelds under *Vorstand*
Vorwerfbar	reproachable, blameworthy. See Chapter XV, p 139
Vorwerfen	to reproach, blame, accuse (of); *cf Anklagen, Beschuldigen*
Vorwurf	reproach, accusation
Wahl	election, choice
Wahlfreiheit	freedom of choice
Wahlschuld	selectable (alternative) debt. See Chapter X, p 48 (Title 1)
Wählbar	capable of election. See Chapter XVII, p 154 (note 12)
Wahndelikt	an offence of madness (ie one that does not exist). See Chapter XV, p 140
Wahrheitsgemäß	truthful
Wahrheitspflicht	duty to be truthful. See Chapter XII, pp 93 and 105
Wahrnehmung	perception; safeguarding, pursuit (of ones interests)
Wahrscheinlich(keit)	probable, probability. See Chapter XII, p 94 and *Beweis*
Ware(n)	product, goods. See Chapter XI, p 91
Wechsel	bill of exchange. See Creifelds under *Wechsel*
Wechselprozeß	(particular form of) action on the basis of a *Wechsel*. See Chapter XII, p 114
Wechselwirkungstheorie	theory of reciprocal effect. See Chapter VIII, p 24
Wegfall der Geschäftsgrundlage	falling-away (collapse) of the basis of the transaction; frustration. See *Geschäftsgrundlage*
Weimare Reichsverfassung	(Imperial) Constitution of (the) Weimar (Republic). See Chapter II (note 2)
Weiterbeschäftigung	continued employment. See Chapter XVII, p 157
Werkvertrag	contract of service. *Cf Dienstvertrag.* See Creifelds under *Werkvertrag and* Chapter X, p 58 (Title 7)

Wert	value
Wertordnung	value-order. See Chapter VIII, p 24
Wertpapier	valuable paper documenting a particular right, security (eg *Wechsel*). See Creifelds under *Wertpapier, Inhaberpapier* and *Orderpapier*
Wesensgehalt	essence. See Chapter VIII, p 24
Wesensgleich	essentially similar (to). See Chapter X, p 71
Wesentlich(keit)	essential; importance. See Chapter VIII, p 24
Wesentliche Bestandteile	essential components. See Chapter X, p 39 (Failure to reach an *Einigung*)
Wettbewerbsverbot	restraint of competition. See Creifelds under *Wettbewerbsverbot*
Wette	bet. See Chapter X, p 59 (Title 17)
Widerklage	counterclaim. See Chapter XII, p 98 and (note 57)
Widerrechtlich	illegal. Also: *Rechtswidrig*. See § 823(i) BGB
Widerruf	revocation. See Chapter XIII, p 127 and *cf Rücknahme*
Widersprechen	to contradict, object to
Widerspruch	(formal) objection; can be raised in connection with a VA, an entry in the land register (*Grundbuch*) or certain decisions in civil matters.
	See: Chapter XIII, p 123; Chapter XIV, p 129; Creifelds under *Widerspruchsverfahren, Widerspruch im Grundbuch* and *Widerspruch im Zivilprozeß*. See also *Einwendung, Einrede* and *Einspruch*
Widerspruchsbehörde	objection authority ie the *Behörde* responsible for handling a *Widerspruch* and issuing a *Widerspruchsbescheid*
Widerspruchsbescheid	notice giving decision after a *Widerspruch* in connection with a VA
Widerspruchsverfahren	objection proceedings (in connection with a VA). See *Widerspruch*
Widerstandsrecht	right of resistance. See Creifelds under *Widerstandsrecht* and Chapter VIII (note 15)
Wiederheirat	see *Wiederverheiratung*
Wiederaufgreifen	to reconsider, reconsideration. See Chapter XIII, p 127

Wiederaufnahme (des Verfahrens)	resumption, reopening (of proceedings) after *Rechtskraft*. See Chapter XII, pp 93 and 114, *Nichtigkeitsklage* and *Restitutionsklage*. See also Chapter XVI, p 145
Wiedereinsetzung in den vorigen Stand	reinstitution (of proceedings) into the previous position. See Chapter XII (note 5)
Wiederherstellung	restoration. See Chapter XIII (note 4) and *aufschiebende Wirkung*
Wiederholungsgefahr	danger of repetition. See Chapter XVI (note 23)
Wiedervereinigung	reunification. See Creifelds under *Wiedervereinigung* and Chapter V, p 15
Wiederverheiratung	re-marriage. See Creifelds under *Wiederverheiratung im Falle der Todeserklärung* and Chapter X, p 79
Willenserklärung	declaration of will; made up of *Handlungswille*, *Rechtsbindungswille* and *Geschäftswille*. See Creifelds under *Willenserklärung* and Chapter X, pp 34 and 38
Willensübereinstimmung	see *Einigung*
Willkür	arbitrariness. See Chapter I, p 4
Wirksam(keit)	effective(ness)
Wirkung	effect
Wirkung nach außen	see Chapter XIII, p 124 and *Außenwirkung*
Wirtschaft	economy, industry
Wohnsitz	(place of) residence. See Creifelds under *Wohnsitz*. See also *Leistungsort*
Wohnung	flat, home. See Creifelds under *Wohnung, Unverletzlichkeit der* and Chapter VIII (Article 13 GG)
Würde	dignity. See Chapter VIII (Article 1(i) GG)
Würdig	worthy. See Chapter X, p 80
Zeitablauf	effluxion of time. See Chapters X, p 56 and XVII, p 153
Zeitbestimmung	time provision. See Chapter X, p 46
Zeugenbeweis	witness evidence. See Chapter XII, p 107
Zinsen	interest. See Creifelds under *Zinsschuld* and Chapter X, p 50 (§§ 246-248 BGB)
Zitiergebot	citation requirement. See Chapter VIII, p 23
Zivilkammer	civil chamber (of a LG). See Chapter XII, p 98

Zivilprozeß	civil procedure, civil proceedings. See Chapter XII
Zivilprozeßordnung (ZPO)	Civil Procedure Order. See Chapter XII, p 93
Zubehör	accessories. See: Chapter X, p 53 (Title 1); §§ 97 and 314 BGB; Creifelds under *Zubehör*
Zugang	receipt (eg of a *Willenserklärung*). See Chapter X, p 39 (Validity of a *Willenserklärung*)
Zugehen	to be received (by), reach
Zugewinn(gemeinschaft)	(community based on) gain. See *Güterrecht*
Zulässig(keit)	admissible, admissibility. *Cf Begründet(heit)*
Zulässigkeitsvoraussetzung	see *Sachurteilsvoraussetzung*
Zulassung	admission, leave (of a court). See Chapter XII, p 113
Zunächst	in the first instance, first of all. See Chapter XI, p 87
Zurückbehaltungsrecht	(debtor's) right of retention, withholding (of performance). See: Creifelds under *Zurück-behaltungsrecht*; Chapter X, pp 51 and 53 (§§ 273, 274 and 320 BGB) and Chapter X (note 106)
Zurücknahme	withdrawal. See Chapter XIII, p 126
Zusammenarbeit	cooperation. See also *Mitwirkung*
Zuständig	competent
Zuständigkeit	competence, jurisdiction; can be *sachlich*, *örtlich* or *funktionell* (*instanziell*). See Creifelds under *Zuständigkeit von Verwaltungsbehör den*, *Gerichtliche Zuständigkeit* and *Örtliche Zuständigkeit des Gerichts*. See also: Chapter XII, p 98 and Chapter XVI (note 2)
Zuständigkeitsstreitwert	*Streitwert* for the purpose of *Zuständigkeit* (of a court). See Chapter XII, p 98
Zustellung	service (of document). See Creifelds under *Zustellung* and Chapter XII, p 107
Zustellungsurkunde	certificate of service. See Chapter XII, p 107
Zustimmung	approval, agreement. It can be prior (*Einwilligung*) or subsequent (*Genehmigung*). See Creifelds under *Zustimmung* and Chapter X, p 37

Zustimmungsgesetz	a proposed *Gesetz* requiring the *Zustimmung* (approval) of the *Bundesrat* ie one that alters the constitution (*verfassungsändernd*) or affects the federal structure of the *Bund* (*föderativ*).
	Federal *Rechtsverordnungen* (statutory instruments) often require *Zustimmung* or are based on a *Zustimmungsgesetz* (Article 80(ii) GG).
	See Model/Creifelds/Lichtenberger, Part I D III (60 IV) and D IV (64 III) and Creifelds under *Zustimmungsgesetz*. See also *Vermittlungsausschuß* and Chapter VIII (note 10). *Cf Einspruchsgesetz*
Zwangsgeld	(compulsory) fine. See Chapter XVII (note 39)
Zwangshypothek	compulsory mortgage. See *Sicherungshypothek*
Zwangsmittel	compulsory measure(s). See Chapter XVII (note 39)
Zwangsversteigerung	compulsory sale by auction. See Chapter XII (note 86)
Zwangsverwaltung	compulsory administration. See Chapter XII (note 86)
Zwangsvollstreckung	enforcement. Also: *Vollstreckung*. See Chapter XII, p 116
Zweck	purpose; aim. See Chapter I, p 3 and Chapter XI, p 86
Zweckmäßig(keit)	appropriate(ness), expediency, expedient(ly). See Chapter XIII (note 20)
Zweifel	doubt. See Chapter XII (note 3)
Zweig	branch. See Chapter XIX, p 168
Zweispurig	two-tracked. See Chapter XV, p 143
Zweistufentheorie	two-tier theory. See Chapter II, p 8
Zwingend	compulsory. See Chapter IX, p 30
Zwischenurteil	interim judgment. See *Urteil* and Creifelds under *Zwischenurteil* and *Grundurteil*. See also *Dem Grunde nach*
Zwischenverfahren	see *Eröffnungsverfahren*

ABBREVIATIONS

referred to in the text (for English meanings see Appendix A)

ABGB	*Allgemeines Bürgerliches Gesetzbuch*
adj	adjective
AG	*Aktiengesellschaft*
AG	*Amtsgericht*
AGBG	*Gesetz zur Regelung des Rechts der Allgemeinen Geschäftsbedingungen*
AktG	*Aktiengesetz*
ALR	*Allgemeines Landrecht für die Preußischen Staaten*
AO	*Abgabenordnung*
ArbG	*Arbeitsgericht*
ArbGG	*Arbeitsgerichtsgesetz*
ArbStättVO	*Verordnung über Arbeitsstätten*
ASiG	*Arbeitssicherheitsgesetz*
AT	*Allgemeiner Teil*
BAG	*Bundesarbeitsgericht*
BerHG	*Beratungshilfegesetz*
BetrVG	*Betriebsverfassungsgesetz*
BeurkG	*Beurkundungsgesetz*
BFH	*Bundesfinanzhof*
BGB	*Bürgerliches Gesetzbuch*
BGH	*Bundesgerichtshof*
BGS	*Bundesgrenzschutz*
BKA	*Bundeskriminalamt*
BNotO	*Bundesnotarordnung*
BRAGO	*Bundesgebührenordnung für Rechtsanwälte*
BRAK	*Bundesrechtsanwaltskammer*
BRAO	*Bundesrechtsanwaltsordnung*
BSG	*Bundessozialgericht*
BT	*Besonderer Teil*
BVerfG	*Bundesverfassungsgericht*
BVerfGG	*Bundesverfassungsgerichtsgesetz*
BVerwG	*Bundesverwaltungsgericht*

cf	compare
DRiG	*Deutsches Richtergesetz*
EGBGB	*Einführungsgesetz zum BGB*
EGGVG	*Einführungsgesetz zum GVG*
EuGVU	*Europäisches Übereinkommen über die gerichtliche Zuständigkeit und die Vollstreckung gerichtlicher Entscheidungen in Zivil- und Handelssachen*
eg	for example (*exempli gratia*)
eG	*eingetragene Genossenschaft*
eV	*eingetragener Verein*
FGG	*Gesetz über die Angelegenheiten der freiwilligen Gerichtsbarkeit*
FGO	*Finanzgerichtsordnung*
GBO	*Grundbuchordnung*
GbR	*Gesellschaft des bürgerlichen Rechts*
GenG	*Gesetz betreffend die Erwerbs- und Wirtschaftsgenossenschaften*
GewO	*Gewerbeordnung*
GG	*Grundgesetz*
GKG	*Gerichtskostengesetz*
GmbH	*Gesellschaft mit beschränkter Haftung*
GmbHG	*Gesetz betreffend die Gesellschaften mit beschränkter Haftung*
GVG	*Gerichtsverfassungsgesetz*
HGB	*Handelsgesetzbuch*
ie	that is (*id est*)
JGG	*Jugendgerichtsgesetz*
KG	*Kommanditgesellschaft*
KO	*Konkursordnung*
KostO	*Kostenordnung*
KSchG	*Kündigungsschutzgesetz*

LAG	*Landesarbeitsgericht*
LG	*Landgericht*
lit	literally
LSG	*Landessozialgericht*
OHG	*Offene Handelsgesellschaft*
OLG	*Oberlandesgericht*
OVG	*Oberverwaltungsgericht*
OWiG	*Ordnungswidrigkeitengesetz*
PartGG	*Partnerschaftsgesellschaftsgesetz*
RAK	*Rechtsanwaltskammer*
RPflG	*Rechtspflegergesetz*
RVO	*Reichsversicherungsordnung*
SG	*Sozialgericht*
SGG	*Sozialgerichtsgesetz*
StGB	*Strafgesetzbuch*
StPO	*Strafprozeßordnung*
TVG	*Tarifvertragsgesetz*
VA	*Verwaltungsakt*
VG	*Verwaltungsgericht*
VGH	*Verwaltungsgerichtshof*
VwGO	*Verwaltungsgerichtsordnung*
VwVfG	*Verwaltungsverfahrensgesetz*
ZPO	*Zivilprozeßordnung*
ZVG	*Gesetz über die Zwangsversteigerung und die Zwangsverwaltung*

APPENDIX C

PARAGRAPH REGISTER

BNotO

BRAK *Richtlinien*: see *Grundsätze des anwaltlichen Standesrechts*

BRAO

BVerfGG

DRiG

EGBGB

Article(s)

EGGVG

EuGVU
Article(s)

GenG

GewO

GG
Article(s)

VwGO

WStG

ZPO

APPENDIX D

TABLE OF CASES

Chapter(s) and Note(s) in which referred to	Name of case (Head-word or parties)	Court	Date of decision	Example of
Chapter II; Chapter X Note 7; Notes 39 and 49	The *Bus Station Case*	BGH	16 December 1964	*Daseinsvorsorge*; the 'factual contract' doctrine; payment for a *Sondernutzungsrecht*; *protestatio facto contraria*
Chapter II Note 15	The *All Germany Election Case*	BVerfG	29 September 1990	a V*erfassungsbeschwerde* against provisions in the *Bundes wahlgesetz*; *Organstreit*; validity of the *Sperrklausel* (barrier clause) in the first election after reunification
Chapter VII; Chapter X Note 9; Note 99	The *Investment Aid Act Case*	BVerfG	20 July 1954	a *Verfassungsbeschwerde* against a statute (the *Investitionshilfegesetz*) before exhaustion of normal legal channels; complainants commercial firms; the *wirtschaftspolitis che Neutralität* of the Basic Law
Chapter VII Note 11	*Volkszählung* (public census)	BVerfG	15 December 1983	a *Verfassungsbeschwerde* against a statute (the *Volkszählungsgesetz*)

Chapter VII; **Chapter VIII** Note 12; Notes 5 and 8	*Lüth/Harlan =* The *Film Director Case*	BVerfG	15 January 1958	a *Verfassungsbeschwerde against* a court decision; the *Drittwirkung* of basic rights; the *Wechselwirkungstheorie; allgemeine Gesetze* (Article 5(ii)GG); § 826 BGB
Chapter VII Note 13	*Apotheken* (chemists)	BVerfG	11 June 1958	a *Verfassungsbeschwerde* against an act of the executive (a *Verwaltungsakt*); declaration of nullity of a statutory provision
Chapter VII; **Chapter VIII** Note 13; Note 13	The *Housework Day Case*	BVerfG	13 November 1979	incompatibility of a statutory provision with the Basic Law
Chapter VII Note 13	*Naßauskiesung* (wet gravelling)	BVerfG	15 July 1981	compatibility of a statutory provision with the Basic Law
Chapter VII Note 13	*Numerus clausus* (fixed number)	BVerfG	18 July 1972	incompatibility of a statutory provision with the Basic Law

Chapter VII; **Chapter VIII** Note 14; Note 7	The *Bosnia Flight Exclusion Zone Case*	BVerfG	8 April 1993	an application for issue of a temporary order concerning a government decision pending hearing of an *Organstreit* initiated by a political party *Abwägung* (balancing) of the consequences of a temporary order
Chapters VIII; **Chapter X** Note 4; Note 16	*Fürsorge- unterstützung* (welfare support)	BVerwG	1954	basic rights as *Leistungs- rechte*
Chapter VIII; **Chapter X** Note 5; Note 87	The *Publication of a Letter Case*	BGH	25 May 1954	*Drittwirkung* of basic rights; general right of personality as a *sonstiges Recht* (§ 823(i) BGB)
Chapter VIII Note 7	*Mephisto* (*Gründgens/ Mann*)	BVerfG	24 February 1971	balancing between conflicting basic rights
Chapter VIII Note 7	The *East German Politicians Trial Publicity Cases*	BVerfG	11 November 1992	an application for issue of a temporary order concerning a judge's order pending hearing of a *Verfassungs- beschwerde*; balancing of conflicting basic rights and of the consequences of a temporary order

Chapter VIII; Chapter XVI Note 9; Note 18	The *Arrested* *Admiral Case*	BVerfG	15 December 1965	a *Verfassungs-* *beschwerde* against a court decision; applica- tion of the *Ver-* *hältnismäßig-* *keitsgrundsatz* (principle of proportionality); *Untersuchungshaft*
Chapter VIII; Chapter XV Note 9; Notes 3, 10, 28 and 49	The *Shootings* *at the Berlin* *Wall Case*	BGH	3 November 1992	application of the *Verhältnismäßig-* *keitsgrundsatz* in the interpretation of the law of the former GDR; *Rechtfertigung* under that law to be disregarded; *Verbotsirrtum*
Chapter X Notes 5 and 6	The *Injured* *Foetus Case*	BGH	11 January 1972	tort committed before birth; damage to health of child (§ 823 BGB); causation; proof required (§§ 286, 287 ZPO)
Chapter X Note 30	The *Unintended* *Declaration of* *Will Case*	BGH	7 June 1984	*Erklärungs-* *bewusstsein* not necessary for a *Willenserklärung*; it can be attri- buted to the person making it on other grounds; *Anfechtung*
Chapter X Note 34	The *Misdirected* *Withdrawal* *Declaration Case*	BGH	11 May 1979	when a *Willens-* *erklärung*, which requires to be received by another person becomes effective

Chapter X; **Chapter XII** Note 36; Note 3 No 6	The *Allergy to* *Hair Tonic Case*	BGH	19 February 1975	breach of a *Nebenpflicht*, ie a *Hinweispflicht* (duty to warn); reversal of the burden of proof
Chapter X Note 49	The *Hamburg* *Parking Case*	BGH	14 July 1956	*Sondernutzungs-* *recht* (special right of use); the factual contract doctrine
Chapter X Note 77	The *Fall in the* *Supermarket* *Case*	BGH	28 January 1976	*Vertrag mit* *Schutzwirkung* *zugunsten* *Dritter; culpa in* *contrahendo*
Chapter X Note 77	The *Termination* *of Negotiations* *Case*	BGH	12 June 1975	*culpa in* *contrahendo*
Chapter X; **Chapter XII** Note 87; Note 3 No. 6	The *Fowl Pest* *Case*	BGH	26 November 1968	reversal of the burden of proof
Chapter X Note 87	The *Newspaper* *Delivery* *Obstruction Case*	BGH	30 May 1972	*Drittwirkung* of basic rights; carrying on of business as a *sonstiges Recht* (§ 823(i) BGB)
Chapter X Notes 87 and 90	The *Air Traffic* *Controllers* *Strike Case*	BGH	16 June 1977	carrying on of a business as a *sonstiges Recht* (§ 823(i) BGB); breach of *Amtspflichten* (official duties) (§ 839 BGB and Article 34 GG)
Chapter X Note 89	The *Fallen* *Telegraph Pole* *Case*	BGH	14 January 1954	exclusion of liability under § 831 BGB

Chapter XV Note 10	The *Insult of Soldiers Case*	BGH	19 January 1989	*Ehre* as a *Rechtsgut*; insult of a group collectively (*kollektive Beleidigung*)
Chapter XV Note 10	The *Base Motive Case*	BGH	25 July 1952	*Leben* as a *Rechtsgut*; meaning of *niedriger Beweggrund*
Chapter XV Note 10	The *Rough Ill-Treatment Case*	BGH	23 January 1974	meaning of *rohe Mißhandlung*
Chapter XV Notes 11 and 18	The *Neglected Assistance Case*	BGH	6 May 1960	duty to assist; rank of § 323c StGB

INDEX